ISBN 978-0-365-40426-2
PIBN 10003822

This book is a reproduction of an important historical work. Forgotten Books uses
state-of-the-art technology to digitally reconstruct the work, preserving the original format
whilst repairing imperfections present in the aged copy. In rare cases, an imperfection in
the original, such as a blemish or missing page, may be replicated in our edition. We do,
however, repair the vast majority of imperfections successfully; any imperfections that
remain are intentionally left to preserve the state of such historical works.

MODERN BUSINESS

THE PRINCIPLES AND PRACTICE OF COMMERCE, ACCOUNTS AND FINANCE

PREPARED AND EDITED UNDER THE DIRECT SUPERVISION
OF

JOSEPH FRENCH JOHNSON, A.B., D.C.S.

DEAN NEW YORK UNIVERSITY SCHOOL OF COMMERCE, ACCOUNTS AND FINANCE
AUTHOR "MONEY AND CURRENCY," "SYLLABUS OF MONEY AND BANKING," ETC.

ACCOUNTING
THEORY AND PRACTICE

A COMPREHENSIVE STATEMENT OF ACCOUNTING PRINCIPLES AND METHODS, ILLUSTRATED BY MODERN FORMS AND PROBLEMS

BY

LEO GREENDLINGER

STAFF LECTURER ON ACCOUNTING IN THE NEW YORK UNIVERSITY SCHOOL OF
COMMERCE; EDITOR OF THE C. P. A. QUESTION DEPARTMENT OF
"THE JOURNAL OF ACCOUNTANCY"

MODERN BUSINESS
VOLUME III

ALEXANDER HAMILTON INSTITUTE
NEW YORK CITY

Copyright, 1910
BY
ALEXANDER HAMILTON INSTITUTE

Copyright, 1911
BY
ALEXANDER HAMILTON INSTITUTE

TABLE OF CONTENTS

PART I: PRINCIPLES OF ACCOUNTING.

CHAPTER I.
MECHANISM OF BOOKKEEPING.

SECTION   PAGE
1. Definition of Bookkeeping 1
2. Single Entry and Double Entry 3
3. Definition of Terms 4
4. Classification of Accounts 7
5. Universal Principles of Debit or Credit 8

CHAPTER II.
BOOKS OF A MERCANTILE TRADING CONCERN.

6. General Explanation of Mercantile Books 12
7. Uses of Various Books of Account 14
8. Explanation of the Ledger 16
9. Memorandum Books 19

CHAPTER III.
APPLICATION OF BOOKS OF ACCOUNT ILLUSTRATED.

10. Commencement of a Wholesale and Retail Business . 20
11. Illustrations of the Various Books Used by Roberts . 25
12. Analysis of Transactions in January 32
13. Posting the Entries 38
14. Preparation of the Trial Balance 49
15. Illustration of Entries for February 54
16. Analysis of Transactions in February 54

774279

CHAPTER IV.

TRIAL BALANCE, PROFIT AND LOSS STATEMENTS AND. BALANCE SHEETS.

SECTION   PAGE
17. Definition of the Trial Balance 89
18. Explanation of the Trial Balance Book 90
19. Relation of the Trial Balance to the Business State-
    ments 91
20. Preparation of Profit and Loss Account 92
21. Definition of the Balance Sheet 94
22. Arrangement of the Balance Sheet 94
23. Illustration of the Trial Balance, Profit and Loss Ac-
    count, etc. 96
24. Explanation of Profit and Loss Account 97
25. Preparation of the Balance Sheet 102
26. " Closing " Entries 103
27. Illustration of the Closing Entries 104
28. Illustration of the Statement of Profit and Loss . . 107
29. Illustration of the Balance Sheet 113

CHAPTER V.

SINGLE ENTRY METHOD.

30. Distinction Between Single Entry and Double Entry . 114
31. Definition of Proprietorship 116
32. The Ascertainment of Profits Under Single Entry . . 116
33. Procedure in Connection with a Change from Single
    Entry to Double Entry Bookkeeping 120
34. Illustration of Change from Single to Double Entry . 122

CHAPTER VI.

MANUFACTURING ACCOUNTS.

35. Definition of Manufacturing Accounts 125
36. Purposes of a Manufacturing Concern 126
37. Treatment of Manufacturing Accounts 127
38. Illustration of the Working of Manufacturing Accounts 129
39. Analysis of Transactions in Manufacturing Accounts . 130
40. Further Illustrations of Manufacturing Accounts . . 136

PART II: PARTNERSHIP AFFAIRS.

CHAPTER VII.

FORMATION AND MANAGEMENT OF PARTNERSHIPS.

SECTION   PAGE
41. The Importance of Partnership Agreements 147
42. Qualifications of Partners 149
43. Certain Essential Legal Provisions of Partnership Agree-
      ments 150
44. Adjustment of Partnership Accounts 154
45. Various Classes of Partnerships 155
46. Kinds of Partners 156
47. Distinctive Characteristics of Partnerships 157
48. Provisions of English Partnership Acts 160
49. Business Men's Ideas of Partnership 161
50. Legal View of Partnership 162
51. Usual Clauses in Co-Partnership Articles 162
52. Explanation of "Goodwill" 166
53. Definition of Partnership Settlement 168
54. General Miscomprehension of Financial Statements . . 170
55. Advantages of a Fixed Rate of Interest on Capital . . 171
56. Treatment of Partnership Accounts 172
57. Illustration of Division of Profits in Proportion to the
      Capital Invested and the Time Such Capital has been
      Employed 173
58. Preparation of Partnership Accounts 176
59. Analysis of Transactions 182

CHAPTER VIII.

PARTNERSHIP DISSOLUTION.

60. Reasons for Dissolution of a Partnership 185
61. Application of Partnership Assets After a Dissolution . 186
62. Illustration of the Adjustment of Partnership Accounts 186
63. Adjustment of Partnership Affairs, on the Retirement of
      a Partner 195
64. Preparation of Necessary Statements for Adjustments . 196
65. Analysis of Transactions 212
66. Another Illustration of a Partnership Dissolution with
      Certain Special Provisions 214

CHAPTER IX.

PROBLEMS IN PARTNERSHIP ACCOUNTS. . . 226

PART III: CORPORATION ACCOUNTING.

CHAPTER X

CLASSIFICATION OF CORPORATIONS.

SECTION   PAGE
67. Limited Partnerships 253
68. Classification of Corporations 254
69. Books Incidental to Corporations 256

CHAPTER XI.

DEFINITIONS OF CORPORATE TERMS.

70. Use of Word " Capital " 266
71. Increase or Decrease of Capital Stock 267
72. Surplus and Deficiency Accounts 268
73. Reserve Account and Reserve Fund Distinguished . . 269
74. What the Sinking Fund Denotes 270
75. Redemption and Contingent Funds 271

CHAPTER XII.

PROCEDURE IN CHANGING A SET OF BOOKS FROM PARTNER-SHIP TO CORPORATE FORM.

76. Procedure in the Case of a New Corporation . . . 274
77. Procedure when a Partnership is Converted into a Cor-
    poration 277
78. Special Features of Entries in Corporation Books . . 295

CHAPTER XIII.

PREMIUMS AND DISCOUNTS ON THE SALE OR PURCHASE OF STOCKS OR BONDS.

79. Complications Due to Premiums and Discounts . . . 298
80. Bonds at a Discount 299
81. Bonds Sold at a Premium 301
82. Treatment of Securities Purchased 301

CHAPTER XIV.

VARIOUS PROBLEMS IN CORPORATE ACCOUNTING. 303

CHAPTER XV.

CORPORATION FORMS.

SECTION   PAGE
83. Waiver of Notice 342
84. Proxy 343
85. Waivers and Proxies for Subsequent Meetings . . . 344
86. Annual Meeting 345
87. Certificate as to Paid-up Stock 347
88. Treasurer's Report 348

PART IV: SPECIAL TOPICS.

CHAPTER XVI.

DISTINCTION BETWEEN CAPITAL AND REVENUE.

89. Capital Receipts and Expenditures and Revenue Re-
       ceipts 352
90. Revenue Receipts more than Cash Receipts 352
91. Intentional Confusion of Capital and Revenue Expen-
       ditures 353
92. Surplus Produced by Wrong Classification 354
93. Capital Expenditures are Extended or Acquired Assets 354
94. How to Charge Replacements 355
95. Acquisitions and not Renewals Capitalized 355
96. No Accounting of Shrinkage 356

CHAPTER XVII.

DEPRECIATION AND OTHER RESERVES.

97. Depreciation 357
98. Wear and Tear a Cost of Production 357
99. Depreciations not Offset by Appreciations 358
100. Argument Against Opposite Opinion 358

SECTION		PAGE
101.	Depreciation of Current Assets	359
102.	How to Provide for Depreciation	359
103.	Four Ways of Charging Depreciation	360
104.	Different Rates for Depreciation	362
105.	Out-of-Date Machinery	362
106.	Tools, Moulds and Patterns, Patents and Copyrights	363
107.	Depreciation of Good Will	363
108.	Reserves	363
109.	When the Reserve Applies to General or to Special Assets	364
110.	Secret Reserves	364
111.	Authorities Dispute the Propriety of Secret Reserves	365
112.	Sinking Funds or Debt Extinguishment Funds	366
113.	Theory and Practice of Charging Sinking Fund at Variance	367
114.	Place of a Sinking Fund in a Company's Books	367

CHAPTER XVIII.

CONSIGNMENTS AND VENTURES.

115.	Consignments Inward and Outward	371
116.	Treatment of Consignments	371
117.	How to Enter Joint Transactions	372

CHAPTER XIX.

REALIZATION, LIQUIDATION AND INSOLVENCY ACCOUNTS.

118.	Realization and Liquidation Accounts	379
119.	Other Uses of a Realization and Liquidation Account	382
120.	Insolvency Accounts	405
121.	Preferential Claims	406

PART V: ACCOUNTANCY PROBLEMS AND SOLUTIONS.

CHAPTER XX.

QUESTIONS AND ANSWERS IN THEORY OF ACCOUNTS. . 421

CHAPTER XXI.

PROBLEMS AND SOLUTIONS IN PRACTICAL ACCOUNTING. 457

INTRODUCTION

Although history is silent regarding the origin of accountancy, we are, nevertheless, safe in assuming that, at least in its rudest form, it must have come into existence at a very early period. In all probability, the human instinct to exchange something in one's possession for something belonging to another, is responsible for the invention of some system of account-keeping. Wherever such exchange or barter required more than the mere handing over of one article in exchange for another, e.g., when it required an adjustment of valuations, a calculation was necessary to enable the carrying out of the exchange to the satisfaction of both parties.

That the accountancy profession can claim antiquity is made evident in the relics of the earliest civilizations. Research among the ruins of ancient Babylon has brought to light a large number of tablets, many of which are as old as 2500 B. C., containing complete records of commercial transactions.[1]

It is even suggested that the Phœnicians evolved the alphabet for the purpose of bookkeeping, in order that they might be able to express the debits and credits and so avoid being cheated.

[1] Thus we find in Jobn's translations of some of the early Babylonian codes the following extract, with regard to commerce: "(104) If the merchant has given to the agent corn, wool, oil or any sort of goods to traffic with, the agent shall write down the price and hand over to the merchant; the agent shall take a sealed memorandum of the price which he shall give to the merchant." "(105) If an agent has forgotten and has not taken a sealed memorandum of the money he has given to the merchant, money that is not sealed for, he shall not put in his accounts."

The Athenians had a highly-developed system of accounting. The public accounts were kept by clerks, among whom was a checking-clerk of the senate for money received, another one for money disbursed, with a number of subordinate checking-clerks. All the accounts were carefully scrutinized, and every person who had had any share in the administration was subject to investigation.

The system of state accounting in Rome was based on the system prevalent in private life. The head of the Roman family entered in a sort of day-book (*adversaria*) all receipts and expenditures of the household, and posted these items monthly to a register (*codex accepti et depensi*). According to Roman jurisprudence, an entry, made with the consent of the debtor, was considered good evidence of civil obligation.

In Great Britain we find a system of accounting as early as the twelfth century. The exchequer kept the accounts for the Crown and each sheriff was required to appear twice a year and render an account as well as to make payment of revenues. In receipt the sheriff received a "tally," consisting of a piece of wood on which was a complete statement, notches being cut on it to represent the payment of pounds, shillings and pence. This "tally" was then split into two parts, each part showing the same amount, one-half remaining with the exchequer, the other half being given to the sheriff. The presentation of the half "tally" matching the other half in the possession of the exchequer, was evidence of payment; and the turning over of the balance on hand by the sheriff closed the account.

In all these primitive methods there was no thought of making the records permanent. All the records were of a temporary nature, as they were never referred to for any purpose whatever. When a settlement was made, the transaction was completed, and in many cases the records were then destroyed. Yet these crude records, these "tallies," were accounts, and were probably the first expression of double-entry bookkeeping and the first evidence of precaution in account-keeping.

During the latter part of the fifteenth century the Venetian traders evolved and gave to the business world the double-entry system of bookkeeping. By this method there is a debit and a credit of equal amount for each transaction, thus necessitating two postings for each transaction, giving the system its name, double entry.

With the sixteenth century, accountancy, so far as it relates to keeping permanent records of monetary transactions, was established as indispensable to the adjustment of business.

With each successive century new ideas were introduced, resulting in certain changes in the systems of account-keeping. Modern inventions—mechanical devices and labor-saving appliances—have made manifold changes in the practice of the science, but the underlying idea, of maintaining debits and credits in equilibrium, remains the same.

Briefly described, accountancy is the science which treats of the methods of recording monetary transactions of every description. There are two classes of individuals that are mainly concerned with the practice of accountancy, namely, the bookkeepers, and the professional accountants, known as public accountants, or certified public accountants. Their interests are in entirely different directions and the relation of the bookkeeper to the accountant is about the same as that of the bricklayer to the builder. In the first number of *The*

Journal of Accountancy a public accountant is defined and his functions given as follows:

A public accountant is one, who by training and by experience, is fitted to perform, and who holds himself ready to render services of the following kind: (1) To devise systems of accounting control adapted to the administrative needs of undertakings, public or private; to improve systems of control which are already installed. (2) To audit or critically examine systems of account as a means of detecting irregularities of any kind, whether of ignorance, fraud or mistake, and of determining and certifying to the accuracy of accounting results; to report to managers and to others interested the financial condition, the operative results, the gains and losses, the distribution in dividends of net profits or surplus of a going concern, or the distribution of the estate of a concern on winding up. (3) To make examinations and special reports pertaining to any matter or aspect of a business or undertaking, public or private, involving financial analysis.

Although the practice of double-entry bookkeeping was known and used in Italy as early as 1340, there is no trace of any literature on the subject until 1494. In that year bookkeeping, as distinguished from the mere memorandum form of entry belonging to the old notation, was described in the first printed treatise on arithmetic, published at Venice in 1494 by Luca Paciolio, who is also known as Lucas di Borgo. This book, entitled "Suma de Arithmetica Geometria proportioni et proportionalita," laid a foundation for the scientific study of the art of keeping accounts which soon became the recording system of the nations.

In 1523 Heinrich Schreiber's first German work on bookkeeping was published at Erfurt, but was of little importance. In 1531 Johann Gotlieb's work on the subject was published at Nuremberg. This treatise may be said to have been the first real work on book-keeping in the German language.

The first English treatise on the subject of bookkeep-ing was a translation of Borgo's work by Hugh Old-castle, and was published in 1543.

In 1602, Simon Stevin published in French a book on the application of bookkeeping to finance.

In 1796, E. T. Jones of Bristol, England, published a treatise in which he introduced into the journal two money columns, one for debits and one for credits. By this means one was enabled to have some proof, though not positive, of the correctness of the ledger accounts. Each column could be added and the footing checked or tallied with the total footings of the ledger, as all transactions were then passed through the journal.

This work was revised and republished in 1821 and again in 1831. The methods advocated in Mr. Jones's works have now become almost obsolete. Modern ac-countants do not carry everything through the journal, although we do find occasionally some of the old-timers adhering to this method and thus wasting time and labor. At present the journal is used only for such transac-tions as can not conveniently be recorded in any of the other books of original entry.

Coming to our own times we find that Great Britain has been flooded with works on the various subjects of the science of accountancy. Many of these publications are of inestimable value to both practitioners and stu-dents, while others are worthless. In our own country we find a mass of literature on bookkeeping, but hardly one work treats the subject from an accountant's point of view. The majority of the authors of bookkeeping text-books fail to use proper terminology; they show a lack of correct form and style in their solutions, and in many cases reveal a meager knowledge of the subject they are treating. With all these defects, however, they have all served a good purpose in the evolution of the science. Within the last few years accountancy literature has been enriched with a number of works by eminent men of the profession. It is now only a question of time until we shall have a number of scientific books on bookkeeping and accountancy.

At present further development is confined to the perfection of practical forms of books and to methods of detail. With regard to the first—the practical forms of books—the forward strides have been marvelous.

If we contrast the standard ruling of a cashbook or journal of the early Nineteenth Century type with that of a Twentieth Century type, we shall perceive the immense change in that direction.

It is in this field, which is almost boundless, that the accountant of the present and of the future must work.

Taking into consideration the manifold mechanical devices, modern contrivances and inventions it is but reasonable to assume that the manual labor accompanying the art of bookkeeping will be reduced to a minimum.

STANDARD CASH BOOK OF THE EARLY 19TH CENTURY

Dr.					Cr.
Date	Name and Explanation	Amount	Date	Name and Explanation	Amount

STANDARD CASH BOOK OF THE 20TH CENTURY

Dr.													Cr.
Date	Ledger Folio	Name of Account to be Credited	Explanation	Net Cash	Disc't	Total	Date	Ledger Folio	Name of Account to be Debited	Explanation	Net Cash	Disc't	Total

ACCOUNTING IN THEORY AND PRACTICE

PART I: PRINCIPLES OF ACCOUNTING

CHAPTER I

MECHANISM OF BOOKKEEPING

1. *Definition of bookkeeping.*—The Standard Dictionary defines "bookkeeping" as follows:

The art, method or practice of recording business transactions distinctly and systematically in blank books provided for the purpose, so as to show the goods and moneys received, disposed of, and on hand, the credits given, and the assets. liabilities, and general status of the business, person, or house.

This is a fair definition of the term, but it is general and untechnical. As the best way to approach the subject matter is to regard every business transaction as an exchange, we may deduce the following technical definition:

Bookkeeping is the art of recording exchanges of the pecuniary rights and obligations of a firm, in such a way as to exhibit the exact facts and their results in a complete, systematic and convenient form, and to prove the accuracy of the records.

Notice that in recording transactions we must bear in mind three important points, viz.:

(a) The record should be so explicit and minute in detail that, at any subsequent time, the nature and character of the exchange may be readily perceived, without any oral explanations, even if such were possible.

(b) As the leading principle of bookkeeping is classification, the exchanges should be so classified that at any time the total result of such exchanges, or of any particular class thereof, during any given period, may be readily ascertained.

(c) The system of account-keeping should be so devised that the maximum amount of information may be obtained through the minimum of clerical labor.

The exchanges or business transactions differ in character and may be classified as follows:

1. An exchange of merchandise for cash.
2. An exchange of merchandise for debts.
3. An exchange of services for cash.
4. An exchange of services for merchandise.
5. An exchange of services for debts.

They may be also reversed, e.g., An exchange of cash for merchandise, etc., etc.

It must be borne in mind that many of these exchanges are of a compound nature, involving the exchange of two or more items for a single one; merchandise and services may be exchanged for cash, or merchandise may be exchanged for cash and debts, etc.; together they embrace all the facts of which bookkeeping takes cognizance.

It is evident that not all keeping of books is "bookkeeping." If bookkeeping is to accomplish anything, it must show every exchange as a concrete fact. If it fails in this, it does not deserve the name it bears.

Faulty and incomplete records are useless and a waste of time, energy and labor.

Exchanges are recorded in the books of a firm in two ways, namely: First, we maintain a chronological record; and second, a classified record. The former is kept for convenience of entries; the latter, compiled from the records of the former, for reference purposes.

Business men and bookkeepers often procure from a stationer a ready-made set of books, bearing the titles of books of account, and adapt the business records accordingly. A little reflection ought to convince any one that the books are made for the business, and not the business for the books. The additional expense of a set of books that will meet the demands of a business, is so small when compared with the results obtained that one wonders why the practice of having the books made to order is not universal.

2. *Single entry and double entry.*—One of our great philosophers, Locke, stated that half the disputes which separate mankind have arisen from a neglect to define terms and premises. A definition is a prerequisite to a proper discussion of any subject; without one men can never get together in an argument and agree as to the issue and points involved. Like other artisans the bookkeeper uses certain tools for his labor. His tools are the terms with which he shapes and welds together the occurrences of a business into one definite result.

There are two fundamental methods for recording exchanges, viz., single entry and double entry. Where the books are kept upon a partial or incomplete system of bookkeeping they are said to be kept by single entry. Theoretically, single entry deals with personal accounts only. If, as is often the case, a single entry system contains other accounts, these are used for statistical purposes only. Thus, a merchant may desire to keep a commission account for the definite purpose of knowing the amount paid in commissions. Under single entry we may find the books in all stages of incompleteness; for every exchange, however, only one entry is made and hence its name "single entry." There are no complementary accounts relating to purchases or sales of merchandise, or to the income and expenditures of the business.

Double-entry bookkeeping is that method of bookkeeping by which accounts are kept, not only with customers and creditors, but with all kinds of values received or disbursed. It is assumed that each individual exchange has a twofold effect. Thus, if a merchant buys five dollars worth of merchandise and pays cash, it is evident that his stock of merchandise has increased, while his cash has decreased. When the bookkeeper records this twofold effect he does it by double entry.

3. *Definition of terms.*—Two words of Latin origin play the most important part in the bookkeeper's lexicon, viz., "debit" (he owes), "credit" (he intrusts). It is quite often wrongly assumed that double entry is based on the theory that for every debit there must be a credit, and vice versa. This assumption is erroneous. The existence of a credit for each debit is the result of the system. Double entry takes advantage of the fact that every exchange that can be recorded in terms of account has two aspects; one involves the receiving of benefit by one account or accounts, and the other the yielding of that benefit by another account or accounts. The account that receives the benefit is debited, the account that yields the benefit is credited. The result is thus a debit for every credit. The yielding and receiving refer to accounts and not to persons. For example,

if a merchant sells five dollars worth of merchandise to X, without receiving payment for it, but on his promise to pay within 10 days, X's account is debited, because he received the benefit of the exchange, and merchandise sales account is credited, because that account yields the benefit.

An "account" is a systematic statement of financial facts of the same or opposite tendency leading to a conclusion.

By convention the following standard form of account is commonly used:

Debit									Credit
Date	Explanation	Folio	$	¢	Date	Explanation	Folio	$	¢

To debit an account is to make an entry on the debit side; to credit an account is to make an entry on the credit side. There is no principle or law to tell us which side of an account is to be used for debit and which side for credit. By custom or convention we use the right-hand side of an account for recording credits, or the yielding of benefits; and the left-hand side for recording debits, or the receiving of benefits.

Any part of a man's property in business that may be used for the extinction of his debts is called assets.

Obligations to pay money due to others are called liabilities.

Assets are usually divided into the following classes, viz.:

(a) *Current* or *floating assets,* by which we mean

assets which may be sold or realized upon without, in any way, interfering with the plant of the business or its operations; as, cash, investments or securities, stock of merchandise, debts due to us, notes given to us by others, etc.

(b) *Fixed assets,* representing assets of a permanent nature, and which can not be sold without crippling the business; assets held for the purpose of earning income, and not for the purpose of sale; as, buildings, plant and machinery, leasehold property, goodwill, etc.

(c) *Deferred assets,* representing an expenditure of a deferred revenue nature the benefit of which is assumed to extend over another period or periods; as, unconsumed advertising, unexpired insurance premium, etc.

Liabilities are also divided into *current* or *floating, fixed* and *deferred.*

By current or floating liabilities we mean those obligations which we will have to meet within a short period, such as our notes given to creditors or amounts due to creditors.

By fixed liabilities we mean the permanent obligations of a business which extend usually over long periods, such as mortgages given on real estate and buildings, etc.

By deferred liabilities we mean expenditures incurred but not paid for as yet, such as accrued wages or salaries, accrued interest, etc.

There is another class of liabilities known as contingent liabilities, by which is meant a possible claim which, although it has not arisen as yet, may arise in the future, such as notes indorsed by us for accommodation.

Notes or *bills receivable* include all notes received by

us from others (made and signed by others), while *notes* or *bills payable* mean our own notes (made and signed by us). We term these notes "receivable" and "payable," respectively, regardless whether received or parted with. Thus if we receive from John Smith a note, we class it among "notes receivable"; if we part with it, we still call it "note receivable." If we issue our note to John Smith we call it "note payable"; if we redeem it, we still call it "note payable."

Accounts receivable is a term given to customers' accounts and represents the amount outstanding and due to us from all our customers.

Accounts payable is a term given to creditors' accounts and represents the amount we owe to all our creditors.

By "journalizing" we determine which account, in a given exchange, is to be debited, and which credited, and then arrange it in a form convenient for transfer to the classified records.

By "posting" is meant the transfer of the respective debits and credits from the books of original entry, the chronological record, to the book wherein the classified record is kept, known as "ledger."

The term "value" in reference to exchange means purchasing power. By the expression "an entry" is meant a record of an exchange or business transaction.

4. *Classification of accounts.*—All the accounts which appear in a firm's books may be divided into two main divisions:

1. Personal.
2. Impersonal.

Personal accounts record all our dealings with persons.

Impersonal accounts record the aspect of exchanges as they relate to and affect the business, and not as they affect persons.

The impersonal accounts are further subdivided into:

(1) Nominal or economic.

(2) Real or specific.

The nominal or economic accounts relate to the economic condition of a business. They show whether we are progressing or retrogressing, but do not represent tangible things. Salaries, rent, interest, discount and commission, are representative accounts of this class.

The real or specific accounts represent tangible things and relate to property of all kind, such as cash, machinery, bills or notes receivable, etc.

5. *Universal principles of debit or credit.*—The following are the universal principles in the science of accounts which govern all business transactions to which debits and credits apply:

ACTIVE OR DEBIT SIDE.

(a) Debit whoever owes the business or firm.

(b) Debit whatever is bought at cost value.

(c) Debit cash received.

(d) Debit notes receivable account, for others' notes received.

(e) Debit notes payable account, for our own notes redeemed.

(f) Debit profit and loss account for all losses.

(g) Debit proprietorship account or accounts for withdrawals as well as for debit balances carried forward from the profit and loss account.

REASONS.

(a) All parties who owe the firm should be debited, in order that the firm may know how much other persons owe it.

(b) All property bought should be debited, under appropriate titles, that the firm may know how much it cost.

(c) Cash received is debited, in order to show how much cash has been received.

(d) Bills or notes receivable account should be debited for all notes received by us, in order to show the amount received.

(e) Bills or notes payable account should be debited for all notes previously issued by us and now redeemed, in order to show the amount of our notes redeemed.

(f) All losses should be charged to the profit and loss account, in order to show the amount lost.

(g) Proprietorship account or accounts should be debited in order to adjust losses and withdrawals against capital contributed.

Another and potent reason why all these accounts should be debited is, as explained before, because they receive the benefit of the exchange.

PASSIVE OR CREDIT SIDE.

(a) Credit whomever the business owes.

(b) Credit whatever is sold and produces value.

(c) Credit cash paid out.

(d) Credit notes receivable account for others' notes, redeemed by makers thereof.

(e) Credit notes receivable discounted account for others' notes, discounted by the firm.

(f) Credit notes payable account for our notes issued.

(g) Credit profit and loss account for all gains.

(h) Credit the proprietorship account or accounts for capital invested, for interest on capital invested, and also for credit balances carried forward from the profit and loss account.

REASONS.

(a) All parties whom the firm owes should be credited, in order that the firm may know how much it owes to other parties.

(b) All property sold should be credited under appropriate titles, that the firm may know how much was sold.

(c) Cash disbursed is credited, in order to show how much has been paid out.

(d) Bills or notes receivable account is credited for all notes paid by the respective makers or indorsers thereof, in order to show the amount of notes redeemed by others.

(e) Notes receivable discounted account is credited for others' notes discounted by us, in order to show the contingent or doubtful liabilities created by us.

(f) Bills or notes payable account is credited for all notes issued by us, in order to show amount of our notes issued and outstanding.

(g) All gains should be credited to profit and loss account, in order to show amount gained.

(h) Proprietorship accounts should be credited, in

order to adjust profits against withdrawals and thus show present worth.

All these accounts are credited because they yield the benefit of an exchange.

CHAPTER II

BOOKS OF A MERCANTILE TRADING CONCERN

6. *General explanation of mercantile books.*—Three books were used in the early days of double-entry bookkeeping; viz., daybook, journal and ledger. The first of these books narrated the occurrence of the exchange in untechnical words and in chronological form. The second contained the same material as the first, but in technical form; it was "journalized." The third contained the posting of the entries of the second book, properly classified, in ledger accounts.

For a long time it was considered that there could not be double-entry bookkeeping without these three books. At present, however, the daybook, as a book of narration, is practically abolished, while the journal contains only the records that cannot conveniently be entered in any of the other books into which the journal has been subdivided.

The form of making an entry in the journal has also been modified, the modern tendency being to save as much time and labor as possible. The old form of journal entry,

Merchandise Dr.	$...........
To Sundries Cr.	$...
Bills Payable	$...
John Smith	$...

gave way to the modern form of

Merchandise $...........
   To Bills Payable $...
     John Smith $...

In modern days the books used in any mercantile concern may be subdivided into:

1. Books of account or financial books.
2. Memorandum or statistical books.

To the first group belong such books as, journal, purchase book, sales book, cashbook, ledger, etc.

To the second group belong such books as, order book, draft book, notebook, etc.

The books of account or financial books may be further subdivided into:

(a) Books of original entry.
(b) Books of subsequent entry.

By books of original entry are meant those books in which the business transactions are recorded as they occur, and from which they are transferred or posted to the ledger, such as: cashbook, sales book, etc. By books of subsequent entry are meant those books into which the records in the books of original entry are afterwards transferred, such as the ledger.

Auxiliary books, such as order books, receipt books, etc., represent the memorandum or statistical books. They show a record of details not disclosed in full in the financial books.

The general requisites of books of original entry are as follows:

1. The respective dates of the entries are given.
2. The entries are made at or about the time when the exchange takes place.

8. The entries are complete, giving all details in connection with the transactions.

The following are the ordinary books of account commonly used by trading concerns:

1. Journal.
2. Cashbook.
3. Purchase book.
4. Sales book.
5. Petty cashbook.
6. Ledger.

The following are the ordinary memorandum books commonly used by trading concerns:

(a) Order book.
(b) Receipt book.
(c) Notebook.
(d) Draft book.
(e) Check book.

7. *Uses of various books of account.*—The journal records exchanges not otherwise provided for in the classified books of original entry, and shows the arrangement of debits and credits in a convenient form for posting to the ledger. The journal is further used as follows:

1. For opening entries for the formation of partnership or incorporation.
2. For adjustment entries for values wrongly classified.
3. For closing entries at the end of a fiscal period.
4. For transfers from one account to another.

The ruling of this book is rather simple, viz.,

Date	Account and explanation	Ledger folio	Debit	Credit

The cashbook records all moneys received, all moneys paid out and the balance on hand. The entries in this book are made as the transactions occur and contain such explanations as are necessary for an intelligent record.

In the average cashbook two pages are used; the left-hand page to record cash receipts, the right-hand for cash payments. The ruling may vary as shown in the introduction. The entries made in this book are also classified with regard to debit and credit. An entry in the left-hand or debit side means a debit to cash, while the account that appears on this debit side, showing the yielding of a benefit, represents the corresponding credit. An entry on the right-hand side or credit side of this book indicates a credit to cash and a debit to the account appearing there, as the account is the recipient of the benefit yielded by the cash.

The purchase book shows all purchases of merchandise at cost, the record being usually made directly from the invoice. It is advisable that this book should be so columnarized as to distribute the various purchases to their respective accounts. By this means a good deal of posting may be saved, as at the end of each month the totals of the columns, instead of the itemized entries, would be entered. An illustration is given on page 17.

The sales book shows all sales of merchandise, the record being made about the same time when the bill for the sale is forwarded to the buyer. What has been said, in the previous case, with regard to columnar ruling applies here as well. Return purchases and return sales may either be passed through the journal, or recorded in a separate book kept for that purpose. An illustration is given on page 17.

The petty cashbook shows the amount received for petty cash expenses, the amount actually expended, and the balance on hand with the petty cashier. As in the previous cases the best form to adopt is the columnar as shown in the illustration on page 17.

The receipts from the general cashier are entered in the receipts column; the payments are entered first in the total column, and then distributed into the subsidiary column, under convenient headings. At the end of the month the totals of the distribution columns are posted to the debit of the respective accounts. The expenditures are then balanced against the receipts and the balance of cash on hand with the petty cashier is shown.

Where the petty cashier is a separate individual from the cashier, it is advisable that the "imprest" system be adopted. By this method the petty cashier is started with a fixed sum, and at each balancing period he receives a check for his actual disbursements, bringing back his balance to the original sum. The cashier, to whom the petty cashier is responsible, is thus enabled to notice all periodical disbursements.

Usually the petty cashier must produce evidence for his expenditures in the form of vouchers.

8. *Explanation of the ledger.*—The ledger is the final book of record; it is the principal book of all the books

Date	Folio Ledger	Name	Address	Remarks	Terms	Amount Dr.	Sales	Departmental Columns

PURCHASE BOOK............190

Date	Ledger Folio	Name	Address	Terms	Amount Cr.	Raw Material	Labor	Heat and Power	Sundries

PETTY CASH BOOK............190

Receipts					Payments					
Date	$	c.	Date	Cash Book Folio	Particulars	Total	Stationery	Postage	Sundries	Etc, Etc.

of record. In the German language it is known by
the name *Hauptbuch* (main book), as it contains a
summary of all the exchanges, in classified form, arranged under appropriate headings called accounts.
The standard form for ledger ruling is as follows:

HEADING OF THE ACCOUNT.

Date	Explanation (if desired)	Folio	$	¢	Date	Explanation (if desired)	Folio	$	¢

The first two columns in the left hand or debit side
are used for the date; the third may be used for explanations; thus if the account debited is interest and
its complement, credit, is cash, the name of the latter
may be entered in this explanatory column. Although
this method of posting (adding the explanation) is becoming rapidly obsolete, it has an advantage in an analysis of the ledger. The next column is for the page of
the book of original entry from which we post; the final
is the money column for the debit amount.

The right-hand or credit side contains the same columns and serves the same purpose except that the
record is the reverse of that of the debit side.

There is another form of ledger ruling, especially
adapted for customers' and creditors' ledgers when such
are kept separately from the general ledger, viz.,

Date	Explanation (if desired)	Folio	Folio	Folio	$	¢	$	¢	$	¢

In this form of ruling there are separate folio columns for each of the books of original entry from which postings are made into this ledger, namely: purchase book, cashbook and journal in the case of the creditors' ledger, and sales book, cashbook and journal in the case of the customers' ledger. The third money column is for resultants or balances of the two other columns.

9. *Memorandum books.*—The memorandum books do not need much explanation. The order book does not need to be in accordance with any form. The receipt book is known to everybody and so are the note, draft and check books. Illustrations of some of these are given below:

FORM OF DRAFT BOOK.

$........	Perforated and cut here	$........ NEW YORK, N. Y. ....190..
Drawn on		.... days (months) after sight (date)
In favor of		
Time		pay to the order of ....
Payable at		the sum of .... Dollars,
On account		Value received and charge to the account of,
....		To M............ ....
#........		....

FORM OF NOTEBOOK.

Given to	Perforated and cut here	$........ NEW YORK, N. Y. ....190..
Date of paper		.... days (months) after date ......
Time		
When due		promise to pay to the order of ....
Where payable		.... the sum of ....
Payment on account....		Dollars at ....
....		for value received.
....		....
#........ $........		No. ....

CHAPTER III

APPLICATION OF BOOKS OF ACCOUNT ILLUSTRATED

10. *Commencement of a wholesale and retail business.*—Following is a complete set of transactions worked out, showing the practical use of books of account:

January 2, 1908.

A man named A. Roberts begins in New York city a wholesale and retail carpet business and invests cash $5,000.00, which he deposits at the Central Bank:

He rented a store and basement at ...., on a five (5) years' lease at a yearly rental of $1,800.00, payable monthly in advance. He paid by check his rent for the month of January. He engaged a bookkeeper at a weekly salary of $20.00; a stenographer at $15.00; and a clerk at $10.00.

3.

He bought of King & Company, City, the following:

6 pieces Ingrain, 1,109 yds. a piece @ $ .55½ per yd.
3 pieces Moquette, 887 yds. a piece @ 1.25 per yd.
2 pieces Brussels, 915 yds. a piece @ .92¼ per yd.
2,000 yds. assorted Oilcloth @ .19⅛ per yd.
3,000 yds. assorted Oilcloth @ .16¾ per yd.
2,000 yds. assorted Linoleum @ .48½ per yd.

4.

He pays King & Company on account $2,000.00 and gives his three months' note, bearing 4% interest, for the balance.

He insures store and contents with the Hanover Fire Insurance Co., for $15,000.00 and pays premium @ 1 1-16%, by check.

He withdraws from the bank for petty cash expenses $100.00.

5.

He pays by check to J. Walters $250.00, viz.—for sundry shelving, $75.00, furniture and fixtures $175.00.

Cash sales to-day were as follows:

26 yds. Moquette	@ $1.87	per yd.
12 yds. Linoleum	@ .60	per yd.
16 yds. Oilcloth	@ .20¼	per yd.

6.

Sold to Girard & Company, Buffalo, N. Y., the following:

150 yds. Ingrain	@ $ .69½	per yd.
300 yds. Oilcloth	@ .22⅛	per yd.

Terms $2/_{10}$, $^n/_{30}$.

7.

Sold to B. Eckert & Son, City, the following:

200 yds. Brussels	@ $1.22	per yd.
500 yds. Oilcloth	@ .22⅛	per yd.
300 yds. Linoleum	@ .56½	per yd.

Received in part payment check for $200.00, balance due in 10 days.

Cash sales to-day were:

56 yds. Linoleum	@ $ .64	per yd.
39 yds. Oilcloth	@ .25	per yd.

Paid salaries in cash and deposited all cash on hand in the bank.

9.

Bought at auction 1,000 yds. oilcloth @ 14¢ per yd.; 1,000 yds. linoleum @ 40¢ per yd., for which I gave my check.

Withdrew check for private use $50.00.

10.

Girard & Company remit for bill of the 6th inst., by check.

Sold to the Eastern Rug & Carpet Company the oilcloth and linoleum bought at the auction @ 10% profit.

11.

Received check from the Eastern Rug & Carpet Company for bill of the 10th inst.

Cash sales to-day are as follows:

26 yds. Ingrain	@ $ .80	per yd.
40 yds. Moquette	@ 1.75	per yd.
18 yds. Brussels	@ 1.40	per yd.
48 yds. Linoleum	@ .54	per yd.

12.

Bought of Hooker & Sons, City, the following:

1,500 yds. Wilton @ $2.25 per yd.
Terms $^5/_{10}$, $^2/_{30}$.

Sold M. Philips, Buffalo, N. Y., the following:

350 yds. Wilton	@ $2.85	per yd.
250 yds. Brussels	@ 1.05	per yd.
500 yds. Oilcloth	@ .19$\frac{1}{8}$	per yd.

Terms $^2/_{10}$.

13.

Eckert & Son remit balance due us by check.

Cash sales to-day are as follows:

22 yds. Brussels	@ $1.40	per yd.
52 yds. Linoleum	@ .54	per yd.

Paid for sundry advertising by check $28.50; paid in cash for sundry petty expenses $12.39.

14.

Sold to William Johnson & Bro., Troy, N. Y., the following:

1,000 yds. Ingrain	@ $ .64$\frac{3}{4}$	per yd.
500 yds. Wilton	@ 2.85	per yd.
600 yds. Moquette	@ 1.50	per yd.

Received in payment check for $500.00, their 30ds. note for $1,000.00, balance due in 20 days.

Paid salaries in cash; paid also for freight and deliveries on sales, $22.16 in cash.

Deposited all cash on hand in the bank.

16.

Have discounted Johnson & Bro.'s note at the bank and had proceeds, less 6% discount per annum for unexpired time, placed to my credit.

Paid Hooker & Sons' invoice of the 12th inst.

Cash sales to-day were 89 yds. oilcloth at $ .21 per yd.

18.

Sold Eckert & Son the following:

250 yds. Wilton	@ $2.85 per yd.
250 yds. Brussels	@ 1.05 per yd.

Terms $^2/_{10}$, $^n/_{30}$.

Sold Foster Bros., City, the following:

350 yds. Ingrain	@ $ .65$\frac{1}{2}$ per yd.
300 yds. Moquette	@ 1.50 per yd.
500 yds. Oilcloth	@ .19$\frac{1}{8}$ per yd.

Received in payment check for $300.00, balance due in 30 ds.

19.

Bought of P. Jacobs & Sons, City, the following:

1,000 yds. Wilton	@ 2.22\frac{1}{2}$ per yd.
1,000 yds. Oilcloth	@ .16$\frac{1}{2}$ per yd.
1,000 yds. Linoleum	@ .47$\frac{1}{2}$ per yd.

Terms $^2/_{30}$, $^n/_{60}$.

Cash sales to-day were as follows:

112 yds. Ingrain	@ $ .80 per yd.
38 yds. Brussels	@ 1.45 per yd.
62 yds. Oilcloth	@ .21 per yd.

20.

Have this day discounted at the bank our 60 days' note for $2,000.00 and had proceeds, less 6% discount per annum, placed to my credit.

By special arrangement Jacobs & Son allowed us 5% instead of 3% discount for prepaying, to-day, invoice of the 19th inst.

Paid by check for sundry printing matter, $21.30; for advertising, $28.50.

Paid sundry petty expenses, $11.85.

21.

Cash sales to-day are as follows:

63 yds. Ingrain	@ $ .80 per yd.

42 yds. Brussels	@	1.40 per yd.
86 yds. Oilcloth	@	.21 per yd.
52 yds. Linoleum	@	.64 per yd.

Withdrew for private use, $100.00; paid salaries in cash, $55.00; for sundry postage, $2.85; sundry petty expenses, $1.87.

23.

Sold to R. Roberts, City:

500 yds. Wilton	@	$2.80 per yd.
500 yds. Linoleum	@	.60 per yd.

Received in payment check for $500.00, balance due in 10 days.

Paid to A. Simpson 5% commission on sale to Roberts, by check.

25.

Sold to James Farott & Co., Troy, N. Y., the following:

500 yds. Wilton	@	$2.80 per yd.
500 yds. Linoleum	@	.60 per yd.
500 yds. Oilcloth	@	.19 per yd.

Terms $2/10$, $n/30$. Paid freight on same, $18.65 in cash.

26.

Paid to A. Simpson 5% commission on sale to Farott & Co. Cash sales to-day were as follows:

125 yds. Oilcloth	@	$ .21 per yd.
42 yds. Brussels	@	1.45 per yd.

Paid in cash sundry petty expenses, $1.65.

27.

Bought of King & Co. the following:

2,000 yds. Linoleum	@	$ .48 per yd.
1,000 yds. Brussels	@	.92 per yd.
2,000 yds. Oilcloth	@	.19 per yd.

Gave in payment our check for $1,000.00, our 30 days' note for the balance.

28.

Paid in cash salaries, $60.00; sundry office expenses, $2.96. Deposited all cash on hand.

30.

Sold to Brolt & Co., Albany, N. Y., the following:

300 yds. Brussels	@ $1.15 per yd.
500 yds. Linoleum	@ .60 per yd.
500 yds. Oilcloth	@ .19 per yd.

Received in payment check for $300.00, their 30 days' note, with 6% interest for balance.

Cash sales to-day were 25 yds. Brussels @ $1.45 per yd.

31.

James Farrott & Co. remitted for bill of the 25th inst., by check.

Sold F. Peters & Bro., City, the following:

300 yds. Oilcloth	@ $ .22$\frac{1}{2}$ per yd.
200 yds. Linoleum	@ .65 per yd.

Terms $2/10$, $n/30$.

Cash sales to-day were as follows:

92 yds. Linoleum	@ $ .63 per yd.
57 yds. Moquette	@ 1.85 per yd.
86 yds. Oilcloth	@ .21$\frac{1}{2}$ per yd.

11. *Illustrations of the various books used by Roberts.*—Roberts had an expert accountant install for him a system for the account-keeping of his transactions. In this system the following books are used:

1. Journal.
2. Purchase book.
3. Sales book.
4. Cashbook.
5. Petty cashbook.
6. Ledger.

All of these books, excepting the ledger, have been especially designed by this accountant and a columnar system provided. Each column in the respective books is properly headed and therefore self-explanatory.

At Roberts' suggestion separate accounts are kept

for each class of goods bought or sold, so that he may be able to tell the profits made, or losses sustained, on each class of goods separately.

In making the proper entries for each transaction we must bear in mind the rules with regard to correct journalizing that *the account that receives the benefit of the exchange is to be debited; while the account that yields the benefit is to be credited.*

JOURNAL.

January 1908.	Ledger folio	Dr. column	Cr. column
2.			
Have this day rented the store and basement at .... on a five years' lease, at a yearly rental of $1,800, payable monthly, in advance.			
4.			
King & Co., Dr.	41	$8,562.39	
To Notes Payable Cr.	41		$8,562.39
my (3) three months note with interest @ 4%, for balance due them.			
14.			
Note Receivable Dr.	41	1,000.00	
To Wm. Johnson & Bro., Cr................	41		1,000.00
for their 30 ds. note, given me.			
27.			
King & Co., Dr.	41	1,260.00	
To Notes Payable Cr.	41		1,260.00
for my 30 ds. note, for balance due on invoice of this date.			
30.			
Notes Receivable Dr.	41	440.00	
To Brolt & Co., Cr.	41		440.00
for their 30 ds. note, with interest @ 6%, in settlement of bill of the 30th inst.			

PURCHASE BOOK—JANUARY, 1908

Date	Ledger Folio	Name and Address	Explanation	Terms	Amount Cr.	Ingrain	Moquette	Brussels	Wilton	Linoleum	Oilcloth
3	41	King & Co., City.....	Invoice dated...	On %......	10,562 39	3,692 97	3,326 25	1,688 17		970 00	885 00
9		Auction house.......	1,000 yds. oil-cloth @ 14c.. 1000 yds. lino-leum @ 40c..		540 00					400 00	140 00
12	42	Hooker & Sons, City..	Invoice dated...	5/10, 2/30..	3,375 00				3,375 00		
19	42	P. Jacobs & Sons, City	Invoice dated...	2/30, n/60	2,865 00				2,225 00	475 00	165 00
27	41	King & Co., City.....	Invoice dated...	check $1,000 bal.30ds.note	2,260 00			920 00		960 00	380 00
					19,602 39	3,692 97	3,326 25	2,608 17	5,600 00	2,805 00	1,570 00
						42	42	42	43	43	43

Date	Ledger Folio	Name and address	Explanation	Terms	Amount Dr.	Ingrain	Moquette	Brussels	Wilton	Linoleum	Oilcloth
5		Cash sales.....	For the day.....		59.06						3.24
6	43	Card & Co., Buffal o N.Y.	150 yds. Wgn @$0 69¼		170.62		48.62			7.20	66.37
			300 yds. 1 loth .22½								
7	43	B. Eckert & Son, City....	300 yds. Brussels @ 1.22	2/10, n/30......	524.13	104.25		244.00		169.50	110.63
			500 yds. loth .22½	Check for $200,	45.59					35.84	9.75
			300 yds. Burn .56¼	Balance in 10 days...							
7		Cash sales.	For the day.....		594.00					440.00	154.00
10	44	Eastern Rug and Mat Co.	Goods bought at auction at	On account.......	141.92	20.80	70.00	25.20		25.92	
			10% advance......								
11		Cash sales......	For the day.......		1,451.25				997.50		191.25
12	44	M. Phillips, Buffalo, N.Y.	350 yds Wilton @$2.85	2/10.............	58.88			262.50		28.08	
			250 yds. Brussels @ 1.05					30.80			
			1000 yds. loth .19¾								
13		Cash sales......	For the day.......	Check $500,	2,972.50	647.50	900.00		1,425.00		18.69
14	41	W. Johnson & Son, Troy, N.Y.	1000 yds. Ingrain @ 64¾	30 ds. note $1,000,	18.69						
			500 yds. Wilton @$2.85	Balance due in 20							
			600 yds. uWe @ 1.50	days......							
16		Cash sales......	For the day......	2/ 10 n/30......	975.00			262.50	712.50		
18	43	Eckert & Son, City......	250 yds. Wilton @$2.85								
			250 yds. Brussels @ 1.05								
18	44	Foster Bros., City......	350 yds. Ingrain @ 65½	Check $300, balance		450.00					
			300 yds. Mette 1.50	due in 30 days....							
			500 yds. loth .19¾								
19		Cash sales......	For the day......		774.87	229.25		55.10			95.62
21		Cash sales......	500 yds. Wilton @$2.80	Check $500, balance	157.72	89.60		58.80		33.28	13.02
23	44	R. Roberts, City......	500 yds. Linoleum @ .60	in 10 days......	160.54	50.40			1,400.00	300.00	18.06
					1,700.00						
		To be Forwarded......			9,804.77	1,141.80	1,468.62	938.90	4,535.00	1,039.82	680.63

28

SALES BOOK—JANUARY, 1903—Continued

Date	Ledger Folio	Name and Address	Explanation	Terms	Amount Dr.	Ingrain	Mo-quette	Brussels	Wilton	Linoleum	Oilcloth
25 25	44	James Farott & Co., Troy, N. Y.	500 yds. Wilton @$2.80 500 yds. Linoleum @ .60 500 yds. oilcloth @ .19 For the day...	Brought forward	9,804.77	1,141.80	1,468.62	938.90	4,535.00	1,039.82	690.63
26 30	41	Cash sales........ Brolt & Co., Albany, N. Y.	300 yds. Brussels @$1.15 500 yds. Linoleum @ .60 500 yds. oilcloth @ .19 For the day	2/10, n/30......... Check $300, 30 ds. note with 6% interest for balance	1,795.00 87.15			60.90	1,400.00	300.00	95.00 26.25
29 30 31	45	Cash sales........ F. Peters & Bro., City....	300 yds. oilcloth @ .22½ 200 yds. Linoleum @ .65	2/10, n/30	740.00 36.25			345.00 36.25		300.00	95.00
31		Cash sales........	For the day......		197.50 181.90		105.45			130.00 57.96	67.50 18.49
		Total			12,842.57	1,141.80	1,574.07	1,381.05	5,935.00	1,827.78	992.87
						45	45	45	45	46	46

CASH RECEIVED JANUARY, 1908

Date	L. F	Name of Account to be Credited	Explanation	Net Cash	Discount	Customers	Sundries
2	46	A. Roberts, capital account	His investment on this date	$5,000.00			$5,000.00
5		Cash sales	For the day	59.06			59.06
7	43	B. Eckert & Son	On account	200.00		$200.00	
7		Cash sales	For the day	45.59			45.59
10	43	Girard & Co	For bill of the 6th inst	167.21	$3.41	170.62	
11	44	Eastern Rug & Carpet Co	For bill of the 11th inst	594.00		594.00	
11		Cash sales	For the day	141.92			141.92
13	43	B. Eckert & Son	Balance due me	324.13		324.13	
13		Cash sales	For the day	58.88			58.88
14	41	Wm. Johnson & Bro	On account	500.00		500.00	
16	46	Notes receivable discounted	Johnson's note less discount 28 days	995.33	4.67		1,000.00
16		Cash sales	For the day	18.69			18.69
18	44	Foster Bros	On account	300.00		300.00	
19		Cash sales	For the day	157.72			157.72
20	41	Notes payable	Discounted our 60 days note (6%)	1,980.00	20.00		2,000.00
21		Cash sales	For the day	160.54			160.54
23	44	R. Roberts	On account	500.00		500.00	
26		Cash sales	For the day	87.15			87.15
30	41	Brolt & Co	On account	300.00		300.00	
30		Cash sales	For the day	36.25			36.25
31	44	James Farrott & Co	For the bill of the 15th inst	1,759.10	35.90	1,795.00	
31		Cash sales	For the day	181.90			181.90
				$13,567.47	$63.98	$4,683.75	$8,947.70

Summary:
48 Cash Dr. $13,567.47
48 Discount Lost Dr. 39.31
48 Cash Discount Dr. 24.67
To Customers (posted) Cr. $4,683.75
Sundries (posted) Cr. 8,947.70

31

Date	L.F.	Name of Account to be Debited	Explanations	Net Cash	Discount	General Expense	Sundries
2	47	Rent account	For January, 1908	$150.00			$150.00
4	41	King & Co.	On account	2,000.00			2,000.00
4	47	Insurance	1 1/2% premium Han. Fire Ins. Co.	159.38			159.38
5	47	Furniture and fixtures	J. Walters	250.00			250.00
7	47	Office salaries	For the week ending the 7th	45.00			45.00
9	46	Purchases	At auction	540.00			540.00
9	47	A. Roberts drawing account	For private use	50.00			50.00
13		Advertising		28.50			28.50
13		Sundry expenses		12.39		12.39	
14	47	Office salaries	For the week ending the 14th	45.00			45.00
14	48	Freight outward	On deliveries	22.16			22.16
16	42	Hooker & Sons	For bill of the 12th inst	3,206.25	168.75		3,375.00
20	42	Jacobs & Sons	For bill of the 19th inst	2,721.75	143.25		2,865.00
20	47	Sundry printing		21.30		21.30	
20		Advertising		28.50			28.50
20		Petty expenses		11.85		11.85	
21	46	A. Roberts, D/A	For private use	100.00			100.00
21	47	Office salaries	For the week ending the 21st	55.00			55.00
21		Postage and petty expenses		4.72		4.72	
23	48	Commission (5%)	To Simpson on Robert's sale	85.00			85.00
25	48	Freight outward	On Farrott & Co.'s goods	18.65			18.65
26	48	Commission (5%)	To Simpson on Farrott's sales	89.75			89.75
26		Petty expenses		1.65		1.65	
27	41	King & Co.	On account	1,000.00			1,000.00
28	47	Office salaries	For the week ending the 28th	60.00			60.00
28		Sundry expense		2.96		2.96	
31		Balance	In office	2,857.66			
				$13,567.47	$312.00	$54.87	$10,966.94
				10,709.81			

Summary:
49 General expense Dr. $54.87
   Sundries (posted) Dr. 10,966.94
48   To Cash Cr.

31

12. *Analysis of transactions in January.*—(For entries in the books refer to pages 26 to 31.)   The transactions under date of January 2, are recorded in the journal and cashbook.   The cash invested is entered in the cashbook on debit side under the proprietor's name, because the $5,000.00 represent his investment. The cash debit appears in the net cash column, and the complement (credit) under sundries.   The record of the lease is shown in memorandum form in the journal. In this case there was no exchange and hence there is neither debit nor credit.   The opening of a bank account is not recorded in any of the financial books except in the stub of the check book, nor is it necessary to keep a separate record for deposits in and withdrawals from the bank.   The cashbook shows all cash receipts and all cash payments regardless as to whether such receipts are in our own possession or in that of the bank, or whether paid in cash or by check.   The engagement of employés, not being an exchange, need not be recorded as a transaction, but may be entered as a memorandum; here, it is left out entirely.

The exchange under date of January 3 is recorded in the purchase book, in accordance with the columnar provisions.   As no other terms are given, it is marked simply on account.

The transactions of the 4th are recorded as follows: The cash payment on account of the bill of the 3rd, is entered on the credit side of the cashbook, showing a credit to cash and a debit to the individual, personal account of King & Company.   The transaction relating to the note is recorded in the journal, where King & Company as receivers of the benefit of the exchange are debited, and the account, notes payable, as yielding the benefit is credited.   The promise of the 4 per cent interest is not shown in the entry proper, except in the explanatory text.   Interest is not an item that becomes due suddenly on a given date, but accrues daily.   At the time of issue there are no accretions and no journal entry is necessary.

The payment of insurance premiums is shown on credit side of the cashbook.   The insurance account is debited for the premium paid, while cash, having yielded the benefit, is credited.

It is sometimes advisable, where a complete record is required, to make also a memorandum entry in the journal, showing the amount of insurance, how distributed, important clauses, etc.

The last part of the transaction under this date is ignored entirely, for cash is debited when received or credited when paid regardless of its source.

On the 5th, cash was paid for furniture and fixtures and therefore the cashbook shows, on the credit side, a debit to furniture and fixtures and a credit to cash.

The cash sales are recorded in the sales book without any explanatory notes, but they are distributed with regard to the kind of goods sold in the proper columns. They are also recorded in the cashbook in order to show the cash received and, therefore, to debit cash. It suffices for the present to state that the entry in the sales book indicates credit to the respective merchandise sales accounts, while the entry showing cash sales in the cashbook indicates the debit to cash.

The sale of goods on the 6th we record in the sales book, with explanatory notes in regard to the sale.   It is not necessary to do this in the case of a purchase, as we have the invoice to which we can refer.   In the case of a sale, unless we have a copy of the bill forwarded to the buyer, we are at a loss as to quantities sold, or as to prices, etc. The entry in this case means a debit to Girard & Company and a credit to sales or merchandise sales, under the respective kinds of goods sold. The terms on which the sale was made are $^2/_{10}$ or $^n/_{30}$, which means, 2 per cent discount from the face of the bill if paid within ten days; net if paid in thirty days. At present, we merely consider that Girard & Company owe us the face of the bills, as it is within their discretion whether to pay in ten or in thirty days.

Under date of the 7th, we record the sale to Eckert & Son in the sales book, with complete explanation, by which they are debited for the face of the bill and the sales accounts are credited. The cash payment that we receive from them is shown in the cashbook, in which cash is debited and Eckert & Son credited, the balance being ignored entirely. As Eckert & Son have been debited, through the sales book, for the face of the bill, and credited, through the cashbook, for the cash they have paid, the balance that they owe us is already recorded and shown.

The cash sales are recorded as explained before. The salaries paid are entered in the cashbook under the heading "office salaries," and comprise the total mentioned in the data of January 2. The deposit is ignored entirely for reasons before mentioned.

The purchase of the 9th is recorded in the purchase book and also in the cashbook. The entry in the former indicates a debit to merchandise purchases, under the properly subdivided accounts, while the entry in the latter indicates a credit to cash. This purchase, differing from former purchases, is recorded in detail; e.g., the quantities and prices are given. The reason for this complete entry is that in auction purchases we do not always receive invoices.

The amount withdrawn by the proprietor, for private use, is shown on the cash paid side, being a debit to his account and a credit to cash.

On the 10th, Girard & Company remit for their bill by check. According to the terms of the sale they are entitled, if they pay within ten days, to a 2 per cent discount from the face of the bill. Their bill amounted to $170.62. They are, therefore, entitled to a discount amounting to $3.41. This is shown in the cash book by an entry in the net cash column for $167.21, and, in the discount column for $3.41, while in the customers' column the total, $170.62, is entered. By this record the cash is debited for the amount received, $167.21, and the discount, for $3.41, while the customer is credited for the full amount.

The sale to the Eastern Rug & Carpet Company is recorded in the sales book, as explained before.

The check received from the Eastern Rug Company, as well as the cash sales under the 11th, are recorded as explained in similar transactions.

On the 12th, we bought goods and made an entry in the purchase book as before, as we did not know at the time when a settlement would be made. The sale under this date is recorded in the same manner as before.

Eckert & Son's payment, as well as the cash sales, under date of the 13th are recorded as instructed before.

The advertising expense is entered in the cashbook under the head "advertising," so that we have a debit to this account and a credit to cash. The petty expenses, while recorded under petty expenses, are entered in the general expense column provided for minor expenditures. We have then a debit to general expense and a credit to cash.

The sale to Johnson & Bro., on the 14th, is first re-

corded in the sales book, as in previous cases. The
cash remitted is shown in the cashbook, as in former
cases, while the note is entered in the journal, notes receivable account being debited and Johnson & Bro.
credited. The balance is ignored for reasons mentioned
above.

The salaries are recorded as previously instructed.
The amount paid for freight is shown under the heading freight outward, i. e., it is debited to this account and
credited to cash. A technical distinction is made regarding freight inward, i. e., freight on incoming goods,
in order to be able more easily to show gross, ordinary
business, and net profit on trading.

The transactions under the 16th require a little attention. The average business man, who accepts notes
in settlement of accounts due to him, discounts them in
his bank. For this the bank usually charges him a discount of 6 per cent per annum for the unexpired time
that the note has to run. Roberts desires to have Johnson & Bro.'s note discounted. To do this, the bank
requires him to indorse the note. Since the note is
payable to him, he must, in order to negotiate it,
transfer the right and title to the note to this indorsee.
By doing this he guarantees that the note is genuine, not
a forged one, and that, in case of default by the maker,
he, the indorser, will make it good. In discounting this
note, Mr. Roberts assumes a contingent liability, for if
Johnson & Bro. fail to honor the note at maturity he
will be called upon by the bank to make it good. Therefore, we do not credit the notes receivable account, the
account which yields the benefit of the exchange, but a
similar account, viz., notes receivable discounted. By
this method we show the actual facts of the exchange—
the contingent or doubtful liability. When we receive

notice that the note is paid, the contingent liability being wiped out, we make a journal entry, debiting notes receivable discounted, and crediting notes receivable. The discount paid to the bank is being taken care of through the discount column in the cashbook.

In paying Hooker & Son's invoice of the 12th, deduct the discount to which we are entitled, as per terms of purchase, entering the net cash paid, $3,206.25, in the net cash column and the discount in the discount column, and debiting the seller for the face of the bill.

The cash sale is recorded as previously instructed.

The transactions under the 18th and the 19th are treated as similar ones in previous cases.

Under the 20th, we have discounted our own note with the bank, that is, we borrowed from the bank $2,000.00 on our sixty-days note, for which we paid the bank a discount. Record of this is made in our cashbook by a debit to cash for $1,980.00, the net proceeds of the note, a debit to discount in the discount column for $20.00, the amount of discount, and a credit to notes payable for the face of the note.

In the purchase of the 19th our terms were 3 per cent discount if paid in thirty days or net if paid in sixty days. Since Jacobs & Sons are willing to give us 5 per cent discount if immediate payment is made on the invoice, we pay the amount of the bill less the discount and record the transaction in the cashbook as before.

The printing and petty expenses are shown under general expense, while the advertising appears under its own heading, as similar items were treated in former cases.

The transactions on the 21st are recorded as previously instructed.

In the transactions of the 23rd we pay to Simpson a

5 per cent commission on the sale. Therefore, in addition to recording the sale through the proper channels, we make an entry in the cashbook under the heading commission for the amount paid. By this entry, cash yielding the benefit to the exchange is credited, while the commission account receiving the benefit is debited.

All the transactions from the 25th to the 31st, inclusive, will cause no difficulty, as they are repetitions of transactions which have occurred, and for the recording of which explicit instructions have been given.

In analyzing the books in use, note that the purchase book as well as the sales book are, at the request of the proprietor, so arranged as to show results for each class of merchandise dealt in. Each entry, when made, is classified by itself. Thus, when an entry is made in the amount credited column in the purchase book, it means a credit to the man from whom the goods were bought, while an entry in any of the distribution columns indicates a debit to each respective account.

The columns in the cashbook are self-explanatory. So far this month no use has been made of the petty cashbook. This will come in the transactions of next month.

13. *Posting the entries.*—The assumption is now made that all the records in the books of original entry are complete and ready to post.

The reader must appreciate that all the routine work gone through with in this set, while practical and in accordance with business customs, is not as minute as in actual procedure. There we might post daily, but here we are satisfied to post monthly.

Beginning with our journal each respective debit or credit is posted to an account opened under the same heading under which it appears in the journal. To illustrate, our first journal entry (we ignore, of course, the memorandum) shows a debit to King & Co. and a credit to notes payable account. We open an account in the ledger headed King & Co. and on the debit side (left hand side) enter the date, the initial letter of the book from which the posting is done (in this case "J"), and the page folio of the book, as well as the amount. Similarly we open an account for notes payable, and make an exact entry on the right-hand or credit side of the account. In the folio column in the journal we note the page of the ledger where the account is posted. Proceeding thus, we post all the accounts from the journal.

The reader can see at a glance how many lines would be required for each account. In posting our purchase book we foot and rule up the respective columns and then credit each individual creditor account, naturally omitting cash purchases as these are recorded in the cashbook. Having done this we have the credits, and we get the corresponding debits by opening separate accounts for each column of the purchase book. As we want each account to show definite results leading to some conclusion, we have separate accounts for purchases and for sales. Thus we open an "ingrain purchase account" for the total amount bought, placing the ledger page under the footing of each respective column.

The same process is followed with the sales book, but instead of crediting the individual personal accounts, we debit them, as they owe us for the sales, and credit "ingrain sales account," etc., showing sales in separate accounts from purchases. The cash sales are included in the sales columns, but are not posted with regard to cash received, as that appears in the cashbook.

In posting the items from the cashbook, notice that

the accounts appearing on the cash debit side yield a benefit and are credited; the accounts on the cash credit side receive a benefit and are debited.

All accounts, cash sales excepted, that appear on the cash debit side are posted, under appropriate headings, to the ledger, as previously instructed. All accounts, cash purchases and general expense items excepted, that appear on the cash credit side, are also posted under appropriate headings, to the ledger.

The next step is to close the cashbook. This is done by footing the net cash debit column and the net cash credit column. Subtracting the payments from the receipts we have the cash balance. The book is then ruled off and the balance carried forward, as shown on pages 30–31. So far the credits of the cash debit side and the debits of the cash credit side have been obtained, but not their respective complements. To get these we make a summary entry as shown on pages 30 and 31. We debit the total cash received as shown by the debit net cash column and debit the discount lost for the total amount of discount lost, as shown by the debit discount column, and credit the two following columns, that is, customers and sundries only respectively. In posting, however, we transfer the two debit items, as the credits are already individually posted.

The summary on the cash credit side shows a debit for general expense for the total shown in this column; and a debit to sundries for the total shown in this column. Of the two debit items, only the former is posted. The corresponding credits to this summary are cash, for the amount paid, not including, of course, the balance, and the discount gained, for the amount of discount gained as shown by the discount credit column; both credits are posted to the ledger.

KING AND COMPANY

1908					1908				
Jan.	4		J 26	$8,562 39	Jan.	3		P 27	$10,562.39
Jan.	27		J 26	1,260 00	Jan.	27		P 27	2,260 00
Jan.	4	Cash	C 31	2,000 00					
Jan.	27	Cash	C 31	1,000 00					

NOTES PAYABLE

					1908				
					Jan.	4		J 2	$8,562.
					Jan.	27		J 2	1,260 39
					Jan.	20	Cash	C 30	2,000.00

NOTES RECEIVABLE

1908				
Jan.	14		J 26	$1,000.00
Jan.	30		J 26	440.00

WM. JOHNSON & BRO., TROY, N. Y.

1908					1908				
Jan.	14		S 28	$2,972.50	Jan.	14		J 26	$1,000.00
					Jan.	14	Cash	C 30	500.00

BROLT & CO., ALBANY, N. Y.

1908					1908				
Jan.	30		S 29	$740.00	Jan.	30		J 26	$440.00
					Jan.	30	Cash	C 30	300.00

41

HOOKER & SONS, CITY

1908 Jan.	16	Cash	C 31	$3,375.00	1908 Jan.	12		P 27	$3,375 00

P. JACOBS & SONS, CITY

1908 Jan.	20	Cash	C 31	$2,865.00	1908 Jan.	19		P 27	$2,865 00

INGRAIN PURCHASES

1908 Jan.	1–31		P 27	$3,692.97					

MOQUETTE PURCHASES

1908 Jan.	1–31		P 27	$3,326.25					

BRUSSELS PURCHASES

1908 Jan.	1–31		P 27	$2,608.17					

WILTON PURCHASES

1908 Jan.	1-31		P 27	$5,600 00						

LINOLEUM PURCHASES

1908 Jan.	1-31		P 27	$2,805.00						

OILCLOTH PURCHASES

1908 Jan.	1-31		P 27	$1,570.00						

GIRARD & CO., BUFFALO, N. Y.

1908 Jan.	6		S 28	$170 62	1908 Jan.	10	Cash	C 30	$170 62

B. ECKERT & SON, CITY

1908 Jan.	7		S 28	$524.13	1908 Jan.	7	Cash	C 30	$200.00
Jan.	18		S 28	975.00	Jan.	13	Cash	C 30	324.13

EASTERN RUG & CARPET CO.

1908 Jan.	10		S 28	$594.00	1908 Jan.	11	Cash	C 30	$594 00

M. PHILLIPS, BUFFALO, N. Y.

1908 Jan.	12		S 28	$1,451 25					

FOSTER BROS., CITY

1908 Jan.	18		S 28	$774.87	1908 Jan.	18	Cash	C 30	$300 00

R. ROBERTS, CITY

1908 Jan.	23		S 28	$1,700.00	1908 Jan.	23	Cash	C 30	$500 00

JAMES FAROTT & CO., TROY, N. Y.

1908 Jan.	25		S 29	$1,795 00	1908 Jan.	31	Cash	C 30	$1,795.00

F. PETERS & BRO., CITY

1908 Jan.	31		S 29	$197 50					

INGRAIN SALES

					1908 Jan.	1–31		S 29	$1,141.80

MOQUETTE SALES

					1908 Jan.	1–31		S 29	$1,574.07

BRUSSELS SALES

					1908 Jan.	1–31		S 29	$1,381 05

WILTON SALES

					1908 Jan.	1–31		S 29	$5,935.00

LINOLEUM SALES

					1908 Jan.	1–31		S 29	$1,827.78

OILCLOTH SALES

					1908 Jan.	1–31		S 29	$982.87

A. ROBERTS C/A

					1908 Jan.	2	Cash	C 30	$5,000.00

A. ROBERTS D/A

1908 Jan.	6	Cash	C 31	$50.00					
Jan.	21	Cash	C 31	100.00					

NOTES RECEIVABLE DISCOUNTED

					1908 Jan.	16	Cash	C 30	$ 1,000.00

RENT

1908 Jan.	2	Cash	C 31	$150.00					

INSURANCE

1908 Jan.	1	Cash	C 31	$159.38					

FURNITURE AND FIXTURES

1908 Jan.	5	Cash	C 31	$250.00					

OFFICE SALARIES

1908 Jan.	7	Cash	C 31	$45.00					
Jan.	14	Cash	C 31	45.00					
Jan.	21	Cash	C 31	55.00					
Jan.	28	Cash	C 31	60.00					

ADVERTISING

1908 Jan.	13	Cash	C 31	$28.50					
Jan.	20	Cash	C 31	28.50					

FREIGHT OUTWARD

1908									
Jan.	14	Cash	C 31	$22.16					
Jan.	25	Cash	C 31	18.65					

COMMISSION

1908									
Jan.	23	Cash	C 31	$85.00					
Jan.	26	Cash	C 31	89.75					

CASH

1908					1908				
Jan.	31	Cash	C 30	$13,567.47	Jan.	31	Cash	C 31	$10,709 81

DISCOUNT LOST

1908									
Jan.	31	Cash	C 30	$39 31					

CASH DISCOUNT LOST

1908									
Jan.	31	Cash	C 30	$24.67					

GENERAL EXPENSE

1908 Jan.	31	Cash	C 31	$54.87					

DISCOUNT GAINED

					1908 Jan.	31	Cash	C 31	$312.00

14. Preparation of the trial balance.—Having posted all the accounts, we desire to test the accuracy of our posting. Errors may have been made and still the testing may not have disclosed them. If John Smith was credited instead of Frank Jones, the testing would not show this, but it, at least, would tell us whether our debits and credits agreed. For this purpose, then, we draw up what is known as a trial balance. At present we are satisfied to know that this trial balance is prepared so that we may find out whether the debits and credits are in equilibrium. If not, we want to discover where the error occurred and rectify it. Use ordinary journal ruling for this purpose and write down the names of all accounts that appear in the ledger and that show either a debit or a credit balance. The first column is used for debit balances and the second for credit balances. It is advisable to place the ledger folio in close proximity to each account, so that we may easily refer to any of the accounts. Those that do not show any balance are, of course, omitted. We then foot the trial balance to see whether the accounts balance, as shown on the following page.

III—4

TRIAL BALANCE FOR JANUARY, 1908.

Notes payable		$11,822.39
Notes receivable	$1,440.00	
Wm. Johnson & Bro.	1,472.50	
Ingrain purchases	3,692.97	
Moquette purchases	3,326.25	
Brussels purchases	2,608.17	
Wilton purchases	5,600.00	
Linoleum purchases	2,805.00	
Oilcloth purchases	1,570.00	
B. Eckert & Son	975.00	
M. Philips	1,451.25	
Foster Bros.	474.87	
R. Roberts	1,200.00	
F. Peter & Bro.	197.50	
Ingrain sales		1,141.80
Moquette sales		1,574.07
Brussels sales		1,381.05
Wilton sales		5,935.00
Linoleum sales		1,827.78
Oilcloth sales		982.87
A. Roberts C/A		5,000.00
A. Roberts D/A	150.00	
Notes receivable discounted		1,000.00
Rent	150.00	
Insurance	159.38	
Furniture and fixtures	250.00	
Office salaries	205.00	
Advertising	57.00	
Freight outward	40.81	
Commission	174.75	
Cash	2,857.66	
Discount lost	39.31	
Cash discount lost	24.67	
General expense	54.87	
Discount gained		312.00
	$30,976.96	$30,976.96

STATEMENT OF FEBRUARY TRANSACTIONS.

Now we are ready to continue next month's transactions, which are as follows:

FEBRUARY 1, 1908.

Paid February rent. Withdrew for petty cashier, $100.00. R. Roberts remits amount due me. Paid advertising bills,

$112.00. Paid for cleaning windows, $2.30. Cash sales to-day were as follows:

54 yds. Moquette	@	$1.89 per yd.
89 yds. Linoleum	@	.61 per yd.
42 yds. Oilcloth	@	.21 per yd.

2.

William Johnson & Bro. remit amount due me. Sold F. Peters & Bro., City, the following:

100 yds. Moquette	@	$1.50 per yd.
300 yds. Ingrain	@	.70 per yd.
300 yds. Oilcloth	@	.20 per yd.
200 yds. Linoleum	@	.55 per yd.

Terms $2/10$, $n/30$.

Sold Shaw & Co., Buffalo, N. Y.:

500 yds. Ingrain	@ $	.69 per yd.
200 yds. Moquette	@	1.50 per yd.
300 yds. Brussels	@	1.05 per yd.
1,000 yds. Oilcloth	@	.19$\frac{1}{8}$ per yd.

Received in payment check for $500.00, balance due in 10 days.

4.

F. Peters & Bro. remit check in full payment for bill of the 31st ult. Cash sales to-day are as follows:

153 yds. Ingrain	@ $	.75 per yd.
50 yds. Wilton	@	3.00 per yd.

Pay salaries $60.00. Sundry expenses $8.59.

6.

Foster Bros. have failed and compromised for 30¢ on the dollar in cash, balance lost. Prepay by check our note of the 27th ult., less 6% discount for unexpired time. Pay sundry stationery expenses, $6.05. Cash sales to-day are as follows:

100 yds. Ingrain	@ $	.73 per yd.
50 yds. Wilton	@	2.90 per yd.

97 yds. Oilcloth	@	.20 per yd.
88 yds. Linoleum	@	.57 per yd.

7.

Bought of Price & Co., City, the following :

1,000 yds. Wilton   @ $2.18 per yd.

Gave in payment my 30 days' note, with 5% interest.

9.

Sold to Wm. Johnson & Bro., Troy, N. Y.:

1,000 yds. Oilcloth	@ $	.19¼ per yd.
300 yds. Wilton	@	2.88 per yd.
400 yds. Ingrain	@	.66 per yd.
400 yds. Linoleum	@	.54 per yd.

Terms $2/10$, $n/30$. Pay Smithson commission on above sale, 5% in cash.

11.

Cash sales are as follows:

100 yds. Linoleum	@ $	.60 per yd.
100 yds. Ingrain	@	.70 per yd.

Pay salaries in cash, $65.00; for freight on goods sold, $29.85. Have withdrawn for private use, $100.00.

13.

Sold to Maxwell & Co., Albany, N. Y., the following:

1,000 yds. Ingrain	@ $	.66 per yd.
300 yds. Moquette	@	1.50 per yd.
300 yds. Brussels	@	1.05 per yd.
500 yds. Linoleum	@	.55 per yd.
500 yds. Oilcloth	@	.19¼ per yd.

Received in payment check for $500.00; a note dated January 14, 1908, given to them by B. Roberts of Albany, and amounting to $700.00, with 5% interest for 60 days, less 6% discount for unexpired time, balance due in ten days.

15.

The bank notifies us that Johnson & Bro. have honored their note. Have drawn on Shaw & Co. for amount due me and deposited the draft with the bank for collection.

Johnson & Bro. remit amount due me. Pay by check for freight on Price & Co.'s goods, $2.56.

17.

Sold King & Co., City, 500 yds. Wilton @ $2.50 per yd.

Terms $2/_{10}$, $\cdot^{os}/_u$ Paid in cash advertising bills, $21.85; sundry expenses, $8.96.

18.

Paid salaries, $65.00. Maxwell & Co. remit for balance due me.

20.

Cash sales to-day were as follows:

100 yds. Oilcloth	@ $ .21 per yd.
43 yds. Brussels	@ 1.20 per yd.

21.

Sold Brown & Co., Buffalo, N. Y., the following:

1,000 yds. Ingrain	@ $ .68 per yd.
500 yds. Wilton	@ 2.80 per yd.
200 yds. Moquette	@ 1.50 per yd.

Terms $2/_{10}$, $n/_{30}$.

24.

King & Co. remit amount due me. Pay Smithson 5% commission in cash on Brown & Co.'s sale.

25.

Pay salaries in cash, $65.00.

27.

Brown & Co. remit for bill of the 21st inst. The bank notifies us that Shaw & Co. have honored our draft of the 15th

28.

I have made a special agreement with **King & Co.** whereby I prepay my note of the 4th ult. as follows: I pay them in cash $5,000.00 and issue to them a 30 days' note for the balance; they are waiving their right to interest.

29.

Sold Peabody & Langman, Albany, N. Y., the following:

200 yds. Brussels	@ $1.05 per yd.
400 yds. Oilcloth	@ .21 per yd.
400 yds. Linoleum	@ .60 per yd.

Received in payment, $300.00; balance due in 10 days.

Cash sales were as follows:

38 yds. Moquette	@ $1.70 per yd.

Have withdrawn for my own personal use, $200.00 in cash.

15. *Illustration of entries for February.*—The tables on pages 55–61 and 66–76 show how the transactions above described are entered in the various books.

16. *Analysis of transactions in February.*—(For book entries refer to pages 55–61.) The first item under date of February 1 is recorded in the cashbook on cash paid side exactly as the item of January 2, which has already been explained.

The second item is recorded as follows: On the cash paid side an entry is made under the heading "petty cash," this account receiving the benefit of the exchange and hence being debited. In the petty cashbook the entry is made in column headed cash receipts. This column shows the amount of cash received by the petty cashier for his disbursements. The third and fourth items are recorded as before. The fifth item is shown in the petty cashbook in columns headed total payment and general expense, respectively. The total payment column shows

February, 1908	Ledger Folio	Dr. Column	Cr. Column
6			
Profit & Loss Account, Dr.	73	$332.41	
To Foster Bros., Cr.......................	70		$332.41
for 70% on $474 87, lost in compromising with them, due to failure.			
7			
Price & Company, Dr.........................	73	2,180.00	
To Notes Payable, Cr.....................	66		2,180.00
for my 30 daysynote with 5% interest.			
13			
Notes Receivable, Dr.	66	700.00	
Interest Lost, Dr.	70	5.83	
To Cash Discount Gained, Cr.	69		3.53
To Maxwell & Co., Cr	69		702.30
for a 60 days note given me by Maxwell & Co. dated Jan. 14, 1908, and signed by B. Roberts of Albany, bearing 5% interest, on which I am allowed 6% discount for unexpired time (30 days).			
15			
Notes Receivable Discounted, Dr..............	72	1,000.00	
To Notes Receivable, Cr...................	66		1,000.00
The bank notifies us that Johnson & Brothers have honored their note of the 14th inst.			
Have drawn on Shaw & Co. for amount due me $651.25 and deposited the draft with the bank for collection.			
28			
Notes payable, Dr............................	66	8,562.39	
To Cash (posted), Cr.	66		5,000.00
Notes Payable, Cr.......................			3,562.39
By agreement King & Co. waive their right to interest on my note of the 4th ult. and I pre-pay same by giving cash $5,000.00 and a 30 days note for the balance.			

PURCHASE BOOK—FEBRUARY, 1908

Date	Ledger Folio	Name and Address	Explanation	Terms	Amount Cr.	Ingrain	Moquette	Brussels	Wilton	Linoleum	Oilcloth
7	73	Price & Co., City...	Invoice dated..	30 days note with 5% interest.......	$2,180.00				$2,180.00		
					$2,180.00				$2,180.00		

68

56

Date	L. F.	Name and Address	Explanation	Terms	Amt. Dr.	Ingrain	Moquette	Brussels	Wilton	Linoleum	Oilcloth
1		Cash sales........	For the day....	....	165.17		102.06			54.29	8.82
2	71	F. Peters & Bros., City........	100 yds. Moquette @ $1.50......; 300 yds. Ingrain @ 70c....; 300 yds. Oilcloth @ 20c....; 200 yds. Linoleum @ 55c..	2/5, n/10....	530.00	210.00	150.00			110.00	60.00
2	73	Shaw & Co., Buffalo, N. Y........	500 yds. Ingrain @ 69c..; 200 yds. Moquette @ $1.50......; 300 yds. Brussels @ $1.05..; 1000 yds. Oilcloth @ 19½c	Check for $500, balance due in 10 days...	1,151.25	345.00	300.00	315.00	150.00		191.25
4		Cash sales........	For the day....	....	264.75	114.75			150.00		
6		Cash sales........	For the day....	....	287.56	73.00			145.00	50.16	19.40
9	66	Wm. Johnson & Bros Troy, N. Y......	1000 yds. Oilcloth @ 19¼c; 300 yds. Wilton @ $2.88......; 400 yds. Ingrain @ 66c....; 400 yds. Linoleum @ 54c..	2/10, n/30..	1,536.50	264.00			864.00	216.00	192.50
11		Cash sales........	For the day....		130.00	70.00				60.00	

SALES BOOK FEBRUARY, 1908—Continued

Date	L. F.	Name and Address	Explanation	Terms	Amt. Dr.	Ingrain	Moquette	Brussels	Wilton	Linoleum	Oilcloth
13	69	Maxwell & Co, Albany, N. Y......	1000 yds. Ingrain @ 66c.. 300 yds. Moquette @ $1.50....... 300 yds. Brussels @ $1.05.. 500 yds. Linoleum @ 55c.. 500 yds Oilcloth @ 19¼c...	Check for $500, a note aded Jan. 14, 1908 by B. Roberts for $700 bearing 5% int., bal. in 1 0 days.	1,796.25	660.00	450.00	315.00		275.00	96.25
17	66	King & Co., City....	500 yds. Wilton @ $2.50......	2/10, n/30....	1,250.00				1,250.00		
20		Cash sales......	For the day.....		72.60			51.60			21.00
21	67	Brown & Co., Buffalo, N. Y......	1000 yds. Ingrain @ 68c. 500 yds Wilton @ $2.80.. 200 yds. Moquette @ $1.50......	2/10, n/30...	2,380.00	680.00	300.00		1,400.00		
29		Peabody & Langman, Albany, N.Y.	200 yds. Brussels @ $1.05.. 400 yds Oilcloth @ 21c.. 400 yds. Linoleum @ 60c..	Check $300 balance due in 10 days..	534.00			210.50		240.00	84.00
29		Cash sales.....	For the day....		64.60		64.60				
					10,162.68	2,416.75	1,366.66	891.60	3,809.00	1,005.45	673.22
						71	71	71	71	72	72

CASH RECEIVED FEBRUARY, 1908

Date	L.F.	Name of Account to be Credited	Explanation	Net Cash	Discount	Customers	Sundries
1		Balance..........	Balance due........	$2,857 66			
1	70	R. Roberts........	For the day.........	1,200 00		$1,200 00	
1		Cash sales........	....	165.17			$165.17
2	66	Wm. Johnson & Bros.	Balance due........	1,472.50		1,472 50	
	73	Shaw & Co.........	On account.........	500.00		500.00	
4	71	F. Peters & Co....	For bill of 31st ult.	193.55	$3.95	197.50	
6		Cash sales........	For the day.........	264.75			264.75
6	70	Foster Bros.......	30% compromise.....	142.46		142 46	
11		Cash sales........	For the day.........	287.56			287.56
13		Cash sales........	For the day.........	130 00			130.00
15	69	Maxwell & Co......	On account.........	500 00		500.00	
18	66	Johnson & Bros....	Amount due me......	1,505.77	30.73	1,536 50	
20	69	Maxwell & Co......	Balance due........	593 95		593 95	
24		Cash sales........	For the day.........	72.60			72.60
27	66	King & Co.........	Amount due.........	1,225.00	25.00	1,250 00	
27	67	Brown & Co........	For bill of the 21st..	2,332.40	47.60	2,380 00	
29	73	Shaw & Co.........	For draft drawn....	651.25		651.25	
29	67	Peabody & Langman.	On account.........	300 00		300.00	
29	67	Cash sales........	For the day.........	64 60			64.60
				$14,459.22	$107.28	10,724 16	984.68

Summary:

```
75 Cash Dr......  $11,601.56
75 Discount Lost Dr..  107.28
     To Sundries (posted) Cr...   $10,724.16
        Customers (posted) Cr.       984.68
```

59

CASH PAID FEBRUARY, 1908

Date	L. F.	Name of Account to be Debited	Explanations	Net Cash	Discounts	General Expense	Sundries
1	73	Rent.............	For February........	$150.00			$150.00
1	76	Petty cash.........		100.00			100.00
1	74	Advertising........		112.00			112.00
4	74	Office salaries.....		60.00			60.00
6	66	Notes payable......	Prepayment of one note of the 27th ult. less 6% discount for unexpired time.	1,255.80	4.20		1,260. 0
9	74	Commission.........	5% to Smithson on Johnson's sale.	76.83			76.83
11	74	Office salaries.....		65.00			65.00
11	74	Freight ward...	On sales	29.85			29.85
11	74	A. Robert, D/A....		100.00			100.00
15	75	Freight inward.....	On Price's goods....	2.56			2.56
17	74	Advertising........		21.85			21.85
18	74	Office salaries.....		65.00			65.00
24	74	Commission.........	5% to Smithson on Brown's sale..	119.00			119. 0
25	74	Office salaries.....		65.00			65.00
28		Notes p age...	(posted J.....).....	5,00 000			5,000.00
29	72	A. Robert D/A.....		200. 0			200.00
		Balance...........		7,036.33			
				$14,459.22	$4.20		$7,427.09
			Summary: Sundries (posted) Dr. $7,427.09				
	75		To Cash, Cr.......	$7,422.89			
	69		Cash Discount Gained Cr........	4.20			

60

PETTY CASH BOOK—FEBRUARY, 1908

[Date	Cash Book Folio	Cash Receipts	Date	Particulars	Total Payment	General Expense	Postage	Stationery	Car Fares
1	60	$100.00	1	Cleaning windows..	$2.30	$2.30			
			4	Sundry expenses....	8.59	8.59			
			6	Stationery, etc....	6.05			$6.05	
			17	Sundry expense ...	8.96	8.96			
				Summary:					
				75 General expense Dr. 19.85					
				76 Stationery Dr. 6.05					
				75 Cash (returned					
				to general cash) Dr. 74.10					
				76 To petty cash		Cr. 100.00			

61

the credits of the petty cashier for his disbursements, while the general expense column as well as the other distributive columns show the various debits to the respective accounts.   All the transactions of the 2nd and 4th are entered in the various books as similar transactions were recorded in the month of January, the only exception being the last item on the 4th, sundry expense, $8.59.   This is recorded in the petty cashbook, as was the item of $2.30 on the 1st.

The history of the transactions under date of the 6th is as follows: According to our ledger, the account of Foster Bros. shows a debit balance of $474.87 due to us for goods sold to them under date of January 18. Since then this firm failed and compromised with us for 30 cents on the dollar, paid in cash.   That part of the entry which relates to the cash transaction, namely, the receipt of $142.46, is recorded in the cashbook on cash debit side under net cash and customers.   The part relating to the loss of $332.41 (70 per cent of the balance) is recorded in the journal.   As a direct loss it is charged directly to the profit and loss account, and credited, with proper explanation, to Foster Bros.

The second item under date of the 6th shows the prepayment of our note of the 27th ultimo.   Referring to the transactions of the 27th ultimo it will be noticed that we gave to King & Co. our thirty-days note amounting to $1,260 for a balance due on an invoice of that date.   This note is not due until the 26th of February, and King & Co. agree to give us a discount of 6 per cent on the unexpired time, namely, twenty days.   We make the entry in our cashbook on cash credit side, with proper explanation, entering the amounts as follows: Net cash paid in net cash column and the discount in discount column.   The total, the face of the note, is entered in the sundry column ($1,260). Payment for the stationery items is recorded in the petty cashbook under total payments and stationery.

All the other items up to and including the payment of salaries under date of the 11th are treated as were similar ones in January. Payment of freight on goods bought on the 15th, $2.56, is recorded in the cashbook under "freight inward." This account is different from the one used in January, and headed "freight outward." This distinction is important. While the former increases the cost of the goods bought, the latter is classified with selling expenses. The last item under the 11th is treated as in January.

On the 13th we sold to Maxwell & Co. merchandise amounting to $1,796.25. They paid, by check, $500 and gave a note dated January 14, 1908, drawn by B. Roberts. They, Maxwell & Co., received this note from Roberts in settlement of their account. The note amounts to $700, is to run for sixty days and bears 5 per cent interest. They allow us 6 per cent discount on the unexpired time of the note. The balance they promise to pay in ten days. The usual entry is made in the cashbook for the receipt of the cash. The note is recorded in the journal as follows: Debit notes receivable for the face of the note, $700; debit the interest lost account for $5.83, representing the 5 per cent interest for sixty days; and credit cash discount gained account with $3.53, representing the 6 per cent discount allowed on unexpired time (thirty days). This discount is computed on the amount of the note plus interest. Finally, credit Maxwell & Co. for the difference of $702.30. They have not only given us the note, the face of which is only $700, but they have also transferred to us the right to collect interest at maturity.

In the first item under date of the 15th there is a notice from the bank that Johnson and Bro. have honored their note. It will be recalled that under date of January 14 we received from Johnson & Bro. a note amounting to $1,000 to run for thirty days. This note we discounted under date of January 16 with the bank, and recorded the transaction by crediting notes receivable discounted. In the January analysis this transaction was fully explained. As Johnson & Bro. paid the note, we have no use for the notes receivable discounted account, which shows contingent liabilities. As there is no contingent liability with the Johnson & Bro.s' note, the former record is canceled by the following journal entry: debit in the journal notes receivable discounted, showing that the liability is wiped out, and credit notes receivable, as we have now no claim to the note. The second item on the 15th is not a direct exchange and therefore is not recorded as an entry, but as a memorandum, as was done in the journal under date of the 15th.

All the other transactions up to and including the remittance received from Brown & Co. on the 27th, are recorded as explained in the January analysis.

The last item under the 27th is a notification by the bank that Shaw & Co. honored our draft of the 15th and we show this record in our cashbook in the net cash and customers' columns.

The history of the transaction under the 28th is as follows: On the fourth of January, 1908, we gave to King & Co. a three-months note for $8,562.39, bearing 4 per cent interest. By a special arrangement with them they agree to waive their right to interest and we pay them in cash $5,000 and a new thirty-days note for $3,562.39, thus redeeming the note of the 4th ultimo.

The record for this transaction is in the journal debiting notes payable with the original note, for $8,562.39 and crediting notes payable with the new note, for $3,562.39, and cash for $5,000. The cash credited is marked "posted," e.g., it will not be posted from the journal, where it is merely recorded in order to explain properly the entire transaction. It is also entered on the cash paid side under the heading of notes payable, where it is marked "posted, Journal, p. 00." By this combination the notes payable account is debited for the full sum through the journal instead of the cashbook, and the cash recorded as posted with the total cash from the cashbook.

The transactions under the 29th are identical with the former ones which have been analyzed and explained with the January transactions.

The summaries in the cashbook are made exactly as in January, and all the other books footed and posted as before.

In the petty cashbook a summary is made similar to that in the general cashbook, as shown on page 61; the balance of cash on hand with the petty cashier is transferred to the general cash.

KING & CO., CITY

1908					1908				
Jan.	4		J 26	$8,562.39	Jan.	3		P 27	$10,562.39
Jan.	27		J 26	1,260.00	Jan.	27		P 27	2,260 00
Jan.	4	Cash	C 31	2,000.00					
Jan.	27	Cash	C 31	1,000.00					
Feb.	17		S 58	$1,250.00	Feb.	24	Cash	C 59	$1,250.00

NOTES PAYABLE

1908					1908				
Feb.	28	Cash	J 55	$8,562.39	Jan.	4		J 26	$8,562.39
Feb.	6	Cash	C 60	1,260.00	Jan.	27		J 26	1,260 00
					Jan.	20	Cash	C 30	2,000 00
					Feb.	7		J 55	2,180.00
					Feb.	28		J 55	3,562 39

NOTES RECEIVABLE

1908					1908				
Jan.	14		J 26	$1,000 00	Feb.	15		J 55	$1,000.00
Jan.	30		J 26	440 00					
Feb.	13		J 55	700.00					

WM. JOHNSON & BRO., TROY, N. Y.

1908					1908				
Jan.	14		S 28	$2,972.50	Jan.	14		J 26	$1,000 00
Feb.	9		S 57	1,536.50	Jan.	14	Cash	C 30	500 00
					Feb.	2	Cash	C 59	1,472.50
					Feb.	15	Cash	C 59	1,536 50

BROLT & CO., ALBANY, N. Y.

1908					1908				
Jan.	30		S 29	$740.00	Jan.	30		J 26	$440.00
					Jan.	30	Cash	C 30	300.00

HOOKER & SONS, CITY

1908 Jan.	'16	Cash	C 31	$3,375.00	1908 Jan.	12		P 27	$3,375.00

BROWN & CO., BUFFALO, N. Y.

1908 Feb.	21		S 58	$2,380 00	1908 Feb.	28	Cash	C 59	$2,380.00

P. JACOBS & SONS, CITY

1908 Jan.	20	Cash	C 31	$2,865.00	1908 Jan.	19		P 27	$2,865 00

PEABODY & LANGMAN, ALBANY, N. Y.

1908 Feb.	29		S 58	$534.00	1908 Feb.	29	Cash	C 59	$300.00

INGRAIN PURCHASES

1908 Jan.	1–31		P 27	$3,692.97					

MOQUETTE PURCHASES

1908 Jan.	1–31		P 27	$3,326.25					

BRUSSELS PURCHASES

1908 Jan.	1–31		P 27	$2,608.17					

WILTON PURCHASES

1908 Jan.	1–31		P 27	$5,600 00					
Feb.	1–29		P 56	$2,180 00					

LINOLEUM PURCHASES

1908 Jan.	1–31		P 27	$2,805 00					

OILCLOTH PURCHASES

1908 Jan.	1–31		P 27	$1,570.00					

GIRARD & CO., BUFFALO, N. Y.

1908 **Jan.**	6		S 28	$170.62	**1908** Jan.	10	Cash	C 30	$170.62

MAXWELL & CO.

1908 **Feb.**	13		S 58	$1,796.25	**1908** Feb. Feb. Feb.	13 13 18	 Cash Cash	J 55 C 59 C 59	$702.30 500.00 593.95

B. ECKERT & SON, CITY

1908 **Jan.** **Jan.**	7 18		S 28 S 28	$524.13 975.00	**1908** Jan. Jan.	7 13	Cash Cash	C 30 C 30	$200.00 324.13

EASTERN RUG & CARPET CO.

1908 **Jan.**	10		S 28	$594.00	**1908** Jan.	11	Cash	C 30	$594.00

CASH DISCOUNT GAINED

					1908 Feb. Feb.	13 29	 Cash	J 55 C 60	$3.53 4.20

M. PHILLIPS, BUFFALO, N. Y.

1908 Jan.	12		S 28	$1,451.25					

FOSTER BROS., CITY

1908 Jan.	18		S 28	$774.87	1908 Jan.	18	Cash	C 30	$300.00
					Feb.	6		J 55	332.41
					Feb.	6	Cash	C 59	142.46

R. ROBERTS, CITY

1908 Jan.	23		S 28	$1,700.00	1908 Jan.	23	Cash	C 30	$500.00
					Feb.	1	Cash	C 59	1,200.00

JAMES FAROTT & CO., TROY, N. Y.

1908 Jan.	25		S 29	$1,795 00	1908 Jan.	31	Cash	C 30	$1,795 00

INTEREST LOST

1908 Feb.	13		J 55	$5 83					

F. PETERS & BRO., CITY

1908 Jan. Feb.	31 2		S 29 S 57	$197.50 530.00	1908 Feb.	4	Cash	C 59	$197.50

INGRAIN SALES

					1908 Jan. Feb.	1–31 1–29		S 29 S 58	$1,141 80 2,416.75

MOQUETTE SALES

					1908 Jan. Feb.	1–31 1–29		S 29 S 58	$1,574.07 1,366.66

BRUSSELS SALES

					1908 Jan. Feb.	1–31 1–29		S 29 S 58	$1,381 05 891.60

WILTON SALES

					1908 Jan. Feb.	1–31 1–29		S 29 S 58	$5,935.00 3,809.00

LINOLEUM SALES

					1908				
					Jan.	1–31		S 29	$1,827.78
					Feb.	1–29		S 58	1,005.45

OILCLOTH SALES

					1908				
					Jan.	1–31		S 29	$982.87
					Feb.	1–29		S 58	673.22

A. ROBERTS C/A

					1908				
					Jan.	2	Cash	C 30	$5,000.00

A. ROBERTS D/A

1908									
Jan.	6	Cash	C 31	$50.00					
Jan.	21	Cash	C 31	100.00					
Feb.	11	Cash	C 60	100.00					
Feb.	29	Cash	C 60	200.00					

NOTES RECEIVABLE DISCOUNTED

1908					1908				
Feb.	15		J 55	$1,000.00	Jan.	15	Cash	C 30	$1,000.00

PRICE & CO

1908 Feb.	7		J 55	$2,180.00	1908 Feb.	7			P 56	$2,180.00

RENT

1908 Jan.	2	Cash	C 31	$150 00						
Feb.	1	Cash	C 60	150.00						

SHAW & CO., BUFFALO, N. Y.

1908 Feb.	2		S 57	$1,151.25	1908 Feb.	2	Cash	C 59	$500 00
					Feb.	27	Cash	C 59	651.25

INSURANCE

1908 Jan.	1	Cash	C 31	$159.38						

PROFIT AND LOSS ACCOUNT

1908 Feb.	6		J 55	$332.41						

FURNITURE AND FIXTURES

1908 Jan.	5	Cash	C 31	$250.00					

OFFICE SALARIES

1908									
Jan.	7	Cash	C 31	$45.00					
Jan.	14	Cash	C 31	45.00					
Jan.	21	Cash	C 31	55.00					
Jan.	28	Cash	C 31	60.00					
Feb.	4	Cash	C 60	60.00					
Feb.	11	Cash	C 60	65.00					
Feb.	18	Cash	C 60	65.00					
Feb.	25	Cash	C 60	65.00					

ADVERTISING

1908									
Jan.	13	Cash	C 31	$28.50					
Jan.	20	Cash	C 31	28.50					
Feb.	1	Cash	C 60	112.00					
Feb.	17	Cash	C 60	21.85					

FREIGHT OUTWARD

1908									
Jan	14	Cash	C 31	$22.16					
Jan.	25	Cash	C 31	18.65					
Feb.	11	Cash	C 60	29.85					

COMMISSION

1908									
Jan.	23	Cash	C 31	$85.00					
Jan.	26	Cash	C 31	89.75					
Feb.	9	Cash	C 60	76.83					
Feb.	24	Cash	C 60	119.00					

CASH

1908					1908				
Jan.	31	Cash	C 30	$13,567 47	Jan.	31	Cash	C 31	$10,709.81
Feb.	29	Cash	C 59	11,601.56	Feb.	29	Cash	C 60	7,422.89
Feb.	29		PC 61	74.10					

DISCOUNT LOST

1908				
Jan.	31	Cash	C 30	$39.31
Feb.	29	Cash	C 59	107.28

CASH DISCOUNT LOST

1908				
Jan.	31	Cash	C 30	$24.67

FREIGHT INWARD

1908				
Feb.	15	Cash	C 60	$2.56

GENERAL EXPENSE

1908				
Jan.	31	Cash	C 31	$54.87
Feb.	29		PC 61	19.85

PETTY CASH

1908 Feb.	1	Cash	C 60	$100.00	1908 Feb.	29		PC 61	$100.00

DISCOUNT GAINED

					1908 Jan	31	Cash	C 31	$312.00

STATIONERY AND PRINTING

1908 Feb.	29		PC 61	$6.05					

NOTES PAYABLE

1908 Feb.	28			$9,822.39	1908 Feb.	28			$17,564.78

NOTES RECEIVABLE

1908 Feb.	28			$2,140.00	1908 Feb	28			$1,000.00

PEABODY & LANGMAN, ALBANY, N. Y.

1908 Feb.	28			$534.00	1908 Feb.	28			$300.00

INGRAIN PURCHASES

1908 Feb.	28			$3,692 97	1908 Feb.	28	Trad- ing	J 105	$3,692.97

MOQUETTE PURCHASES

1908 Feb.	28			$3,326.25	1908 Feb	28	Trad- ing	J 105	$3,326 25

BRUSSELS PURCHASES

1908 Feb.	28			$2,608.17	1908 Feb.	28	Trading	J 105	$2,608.17

WILTON PURCHASES

1908 Feb.				$7,780 00	1908 Feb.	28	Trading	J 105	$7,780.00

LINOLEUM PURCHASES

1908 Feb.	28			$2,805 00	1908 Feb.	28	Trading	J 105	$2,805 00

OILCLOTH PURCHASES

1908 Feb.	28			$1,570.00	1908 Feb.	28	Trading	J 105	$1,570.00

B. ECKERT & SON, CITY

1908 Feb.	28			$1,499.13	1908 Feb.	28			$524.13

CASH DISCOUNT GAINED

1908 Feb.	28	Profit & loss	J 106	$7.73	1908 Feb.	28				$7.73

M. PHILLIPS, BUFFALO, N. Y.

1908 Feb.	28			$1,451.25						

INTEREST LOST

1908 Feb.	28			$5.83	1908 Feb.	28	Profit & loss	J 106	$5.83

F. PETERS & BRO., CITY

1908 Feb.	28			$727.50	1908 Feb.	28			$197.50

INGRAIN SALES

1908 Feb.	28	Trad- ing	J 106	$3,558 55	1908 Feb.	28			$3,558 55

MOQUETTE SALES

1908 Feb.	28	Trad-ing	J 106	$2,940.73	1908 Feb.	28			$2,940 73

BRUSSELS SALES

1908 Feb.	28	Trad-ing	J 106	$2,272.65	1908 Feb.	28			$2,272.65

WILTON SALES

1908 Feb.	28	Trad-ing	J 106	$9,744 00	1908 Feb.	28			$9,744 00

LINOLEUM SALES

1908 Feb.	28	Trad-ing	J 106	$2,833.23	1908 Feb.	28			$2,833.23

OILCLOTH SALES

1908 Feb.	28	Trad-ing	J 106	$1,656.09	1908 Feb.	28			$1,656.09

A. ROBERTS C/A

					1908 Feb.	28	Profit & loss	J 106	$5,000.00
									2,017.11

A. ROBERTS D/A

1908 Feb. Feb.	28 28	A Roberts C/A	J 106	$450.00 2,017.11	1908 Feb.	28	Profit & loss	J 106	$2,467.11
				$2,467.11					$2,467.11
									$2,467.11

RENT

1908 Feb.	28			$300.00	1908 Feb.	28	Profit & loss	J 106	$300.00

INSURANCE

1908 Feb.	28			$159.38	1908 Feb.	28	Profit & loss	J 106	$26.56

FURNITURE AND FIXTURES

1908 Feb.	28			$250.00					

OFFICE SALARIES

1908 Feb.	28			$460.00	1908 Feb.	28	Profit & loss	J 106	$460.00

ADVERTISING

1908 Feb.	28			$190.85	1908 Feb.	28	Trad- ing	J 105	$190.85

FREIGHT OUTWARD

1908 Feb.	28			$70.66	1908 Feb.	28	Trad- ing	J 105	$70 66

COMMISSION

1908 Feb.	28			$370.58	1908 Feb.	28	Trad- ing	J 105	$370.58

CASH

1908 Feb.	28			$25,243.13	1908 Feb.	28			$18,132.70

DISCOUNT LOST

1908 Feb.	28			$146.59	1908 Feb.	28	Trading	J 106	$146.59

CASH DISCOUNT LOST

1908 Feb.	28			$24 67	1908 Feb.	28	Profit & loss	J 106	$24.67

FREIGHT INWARD

1008 Feb.	28			$2 56	1008 Feb.	28	Trading	J 105	$2 56

GENERAL EXPENSES

1908 Feb.	28			$74 72	1908 Feb.	28	Profit & loss	J 106	$74.72

DISCOUNT GAINED

1908 Feb.	28	Trading	J 106	$312.00	1908 Feb.	28			$312.00

STATIONERY AND PRINTING

| 1908 Feb. | 28 | | | $6.05 | 1908 Feb. | 28 | Profit & loss | J 106 | $6.05 |

INGRAIN INVENTORY

| 1908 Feb. | 28 | | J 94 | $565.00 | | | | | |

MOQUETTE INVENTORY

| 1908 Feb. | 28 | | J 94 | $885.00 | | | | | |

BRUSSELS INVENTORY

| 1908 Feb. | 28 | | J 94 | $736.00 | | | | | |

WILTON INVENTORY

| 1908 Feb. | 28 | | J 94 | $150.00 | | | | | |

LINOLEUM INVENTORY

1908 Feb.	28		J 94	$350.00					

OILCLOTH INVENTORY

1908 Feb.	28		J 94	$250 00					

TRIAL BALANCE FOR FEBRUARY, 1908.

Cash	$7,110.43	
Notes receivable	1,140.00	
Furniture and fixtures	250.00	
Notes payable		$7,742.39
Ingrain purchases	3,692.97	
Moquette purchases	3,326.25	
Brussels purchases	2,608.17	
Wilton purchases	7,780.00	
Linoleum purchases	2,805.00	
Oilcloth purchases	1,570.00	
Ingrain sales		3,558.55
Moquette sales		2,940.73
Brussels sales		2,272.65
Wilton sales		9,744.00
Linoleum sales		2,833.23
Oilcloth sales		1,656.09
Rent	300.00	
Insurance	159.38	
Office salaries	460.00	
Advertising	190.85	
Freight outward	70.66	
Commission	370.58	
Freight inward	2.56	
General expense	74.72	
Stationery and printing	6.05	
Discount gained		312.00
Discount lost	146.59	
Interest lost	5.83	
Cash discount gained		7.73
Cash discount lost	24.67	
Profit and loss	332.41	
B. Eckert & Son	975.00	
Peabody & Langman	234.00	
M. Philips	1,451.25	
F. Peters & Bro.	530.00	
A. Roberts C/A		5,000.00
A. Roberts D/A	450.00	
	$36,067.37	$36,067.37

1908 Feb. 28				1908 Feb. 28			
Ingrain purchases	J 105	$3,692.97		Discount gained	J 106	$312.00
Moquette "	J 105	3,326.25		Ingrain inventory	J 106	565.00
Brussels "	J 105	2,608.17		Moquette "	J 106	885.00
Wilton "	J 105	7,780.00		Brussels "	J 106	736.00
Linoleum "	J 105	2,805.00		Wilton "	J 106	150.00
Oilcloth "	J 105	1,570.00		Linoleum "	J 106	350.00
Advertising	J 105	190.85		Oilcloth "	J 106	250.00
Freight outward	J 105	70.66		Ingrain sales	J 106	3,558.55
Freight inward	J 105	2.56		Moquette "	J 106	2,940.73
Commission	J 105	370.58		Brussels "	J 106	2,272.65
Discount lost	J 106	146.59		Wilton "	J 106	9,744.00
Profit and loss	J 106	3,689.62		Linoleum "	J 106	2,833.23
				Oilcloth "	J 106	1,656.09
		$26,253.25				$26,253.25

PROFIT AND LOSS ACCOUNT

1908 Feb.					1908 Feb.			
28	Rent.................	J 106	$332.41		28	Trading...............	J 106	$3,689.62
"	28	Insurance............	J 106	300.00		"	28	Cash discount gained......	J 106	7.73
"	28	Office salaries........	J 106	26.56					
"	28	General expense......	J 106	460.00					
"	28	Stationery and printing......	J 106	74.72					
"	28	Cash discount lost.....	J 106	6.05					
"	28	Interest lost.........	J 106	24.67					
"	28	A. Roberts D/A......	J 106	5.83					
				2,467.11				
				$ 3,697.35					$3,697.35

88

CHAPTER IV

TRIAL BALANCE, PROFIT AND LOSS STATEMENTS AND BALANCE SHEETS

17. Definition of the trial balance.—Lisle, in his "Accounting in Theory and Practice," defines a trial balance as follows:

A trial balance is a statement of ledger accounts prepared after the books of the concern have been posted, but before the closing entries are made, showing in two parallel money columns either the total debit and total credit side of each ledger account, or the difference between the debit side and the credit side of each ledger account.

Some writers distinguish between the trial balance before closing and the trial balance after closing the ledger accounts, but this differentiation is rather strained. The statement showing the balances after the closing of the ledger accounts exhibits definite balances, and absolute results, such as assets, liabilities and proprietorship. If the double-entry system is followed, such a statement should be spoken of as a balance sheet. The trial balance gives totals or balances of all ledger accounts containing items of a nominal nature. Hence what is properly a balance sheet should not be misnamed as a trial balance.

The only thing in favor of the first method of showing total debits and total credits of ledger accounts is that it helps to localize errors. As a rule, provided every debit has an equal credit and vice versa, the trial

89

balance will be in equilibrium, as is correct, because it is supposed to give a bird's-eye view of the contents of a ledger.   Where the first method is used it is easier to discover the error if the trial balance is out of balance, as is sometimes the case.

The second method has more advantages than the first, namely: (a) It facilitates the preparation of statements, business or financial; (b) the various ledger headings can be so arranged as to group nominal and real accounts; (c) we can further subdivide them into debit and credit balances.

By a systematic ordering of ledger accounts in the trial balance, the business man is enabled—leaving the inventory out of consideration—to tell approximately his financial position at any time.   No definite rule can be laid down for the order in which the accounts should appear on the trial balance.   It is, however, a good policy to place real accounts first, followed by nominal accounts, and finally proprietorship accounts, e.g., drawing and capital accounts.   This order has been adopted in the working of the various sets given in the text-book.   It facilitates the preparation of statements, as each section can be taken up separately.   The trial balance given on page 96 is a good illustration of the arrangement of ledger accounts.

18. *Explanation of the trial balance book.*—Trial balances are prepared monthly, and it is always advisable to enter them in a book made for the purpose which is known as a trial balance book.   Such a book consists of twelve double columns, debit and credit, for the entire year.   Each double column contains debit and credit balances of a month's transactions.   Accounts which have already appeared in one month

need not be repeated. Only new accounts should be added.

This trial balance book affords also statistical advantages. A merchant can readily compare his sales of one month with those of another. Similarly he can compare and contrast his floating or quick assets, as well as his floating or quick liabilities of different months.

It must be always borne in mind that the trial balance is not positive proof of the accuracy of the entries. There may be errors even though the trial balance is in equilibrium. The following errors will be revealed by a trial balance: (1) Omission of posting an entry; (2) posting an entry twice; (3) posting to the wrong side of an account.

The following errors will not be revealed by a trial balance: (1) An entry which, although posted to the right side of the ledger, is posted to the wrong account; (2) errors in mathematical operations which occurred on the books of original entry and have been carried so to the ledger; (3) posting of transposed figures to both sides of the ledger account; (4) the omission of entire business transactions; (5) over-debiting one account and under-debiting another (provided the amount of the over-debit equals the amount of the under-debit); (6) over-crediting one account and under-crediting another (provided the amount of the over-credit is equal to the amount of the under-credit).

19. *Relation of the trial balance to the business statements.*—The relation of the trial balance to the business or financial statements is such that one does not need to refer to the ledger in order to be able to tell the results of operations or the condition of finances, provided, of course, that the inventories are furnished. In-

deed, it would be very difficult to begin to prepare statements directly from the ledger. Leaving out of the question the time needed to do this, it would be an impossibility to avoid errors were this method adopted. The trial balance thus gives the material for the preparation of the various statements required. It is a feeder for the statements, and if it is without errors, even if the books of account are destroyed, can furnish the necessary information for carrying on the business.

Having completed the trial balance we usually have to make certain adjustment entries, and also to take into account, the value—generally at cost—of the stock on hand. Only then can we proceed to prepare statements showing the result of operations and the financial condition of the affairs at a given time.

20. *Preparation of profit and loss account.*—The profit and loss account, as a ledger account, is a summary of all the outlay and income. On the debit side are collected all the charges incurred in making the profit during a given period; on the credit side are gathered all the sources of profit for the same period. The remaining balance, if to the debit, indicates a loss; if to the credit, a profit.

One important feature is that no matter how complicated the affairs of the concern may be, the profit and loss account prepared for the benefit of the merchant or for any other person interested in the progress of the firm, should be so framed that a layman can grasp the salient points without difficulty. Whenever possible, the facts to be shown in the profit and loss account should be as follows: (1) Gross profit as a whole and in each department separately. (2) The expenditure as a whole and in each department separately, provided it is directly due to the volume of the business done.   (3) Expenditures not directly due to the volume of business done, but which depend more on the constitution of the business.   (4) Results of trading regardless of excess or insufficiency of capital employed in the business.   (5) Charges affecting capital, such as interest and discount.   (6) The net profit, apportionable to proprietorship.

In preparing the profit and loss statement, items which ordinarily are not shown on the books must be taken into consideration.   To illustrate: If a firm insures the stock of merchandise and fixtures on a given date, say the first of February, and pays the premium for a full year, it is obvious that if the accounts are closed on June 30 of the same year, the unexpired insurance for seven months represents an asset and not an expenditure.   Accrued salaries are of the same class, but, of course, show a liability.

Notice must also be taken of such items as interest accretions due to the firm, or advances made to salesmen on commissions or the like.   Such balances also represent assets of the firm at that particular time.

The profit and loss account should be so arranged as to give in complete and detailed, but at the same time summarized form, the information regarding the progress or retrogress of the business.   The method of division adopted in the preparation of profit and loss statements is of great importance.   Items of expenditures as well as incomes derived from independent sources should be so introduced in the profit and loss account as not to confuse the trading account.   Where the method of division is required to compare one year with another, the arrangement of one period should exactly agree with the arrangement of the other period, because otherwise the statistical advantages that could be afforded by the means of comparison are destroyed. The pro-forma profit and loss accounts given on pages 98–99 illustrate the division of the various sections of this account.

21. *Definition of the balance sheet.*—After preparing the summary of profits and losses we are in a position to test the arithmetical accuracy of the results shown in such statement by what is known as a balance sheet.

Some writers confuse a statement of assets and liabilities with a balance sheet. While a balance sheet contains the same items as the statement of assets and liabilities the sources of compilation are entirely different. A statement of assets and liabilities may be prepared from any data available, and not necessarily from books. "A statement of assets and liabilities" is the proper title under which the resources and liabilities of a concern whose books have been kept by single entry may be arranged. A balance sheet is a concise statement of ledger accounts after the collection of all the nominal balances in the profit and loss summary, compiled from a set of books kept by the double-entry principle, containing assets, liabilities and proprietorship of the concern at a particular moment.

22. *Arrangement of the balance sheet.*—The method of arrangement in a balance sheet, while not so important, is nevertheless a subject of controversy. With some writers the arrangement is unimportant. They will class both assets and liabilities in any shape or form. With others, the importance of the assets that yield income is prominently displayed on the balance sheet. These would begin with fixed assets, such as plant, machinery, buildings, tools and the like, winding up with cash as the last item. Some writers adopt the plan

of arranging the assets and liabilities in the order of their realization and liquidation. The assets that are most easily realized on or most quickly convertible into cash are placed first; such as cash, notes receivable and the like. The same plan is followed on the liability side: Bank overdrafts, loans payable, accounts payable and the like, winding up with immaterial assets, such as good will and franchises, on the asset side, and surplus and undivided profits on the liability side. The method to be adopted depends entirely upon what the balance sheet is intended to disclose. If the balance sheet is to show how strong the concern is for the purpose of earning revenue, it stands to reason that importance will be attached to assets which are the cause of the income, such as plant, machinery, tools, etc. On the other hand, if the balance sheet is to show how strong the concern is financially—and this is the general purpose for which balance sheets are prepared—the current assets should be classed first. The illustration on page 100 shows arrangement of assets in the order they would be realized upon and the liabilities in the order of liquidation. The last mentioned arrangement is followed throughout the text-book. The main distinction between a profit and loss account and a balance sheet is that while the profit and loss account shows the progress or the retrogression of the business during a certain period of time, the balance sheet shows the financial position of the concern at a particular moment of time.

English accountants and writers place the assets on the right-hand side of the balance sheet and the liabilities on the left-hand side. American practitioners and writers follow just the opposite plan. There can be little question about the correctness of the latter plan. Mr. Lisle, an English writer, summarizes his views in the following statement: "Why in the process the assets which are on the debit side and the liabilities, which are on the credit side, in the ledger as according to the principles of accounting they ought to be, should change places, it is impossible to justify." The custom undoubtedly arose as early as 1862, when the "English Companies Act" was passed, which must have been prepared by people unacquainted with the theory of accounts, for if the profit and loss account, which is also taken from the ledger, is not transposed, why should the balance sheet, taken from the same source, be treated differently?

23. Illustration of the trial balance, profit and loss account, etc.—We are now ready to take up the matter of closing our transactions for January and February. However, before we proceed to prepare from our sets the business and financial statements in which Roberts would be interested, we will take up this problem as an illustration.

PROBLEM.

From the following trial balance prepare a profit and loss account and a balance sheet:

Cash	$ 12,300.00	
Notes receivable	32,700.00	
Accounts receivable	47,000.00	
Merchandise inventory (beginning of period)	3,650.00	
Furniture and fixtures	3,000.00	
Buildings	13,000.00	
Real estate	50,000.00	
Notes payable	$	30,000.00
Accounts payable		13,100.00
Purchases	84,000.00	
Sales		152,000.00
Advertising	2,600.00	
Commissions	3,050.00	
General expense	12,900.00	
Office salaries	9,300.00	
Insurance (1 year)	625.00	

Postage 1,650.00
Discounts and allowances 550.00
Exchange 25.00
Interest 175.00
Cash discount 375.00
Jones's capital account 50,000.00
Smith's capital account 35,000.00
Jones's drawing account 2,400.00
Smith's drawing account 1,900.00

                                        $280,650.00 $280,650.00

Notations: Inventory on hand, $5,365.00; unexpired insurance, 4 months; unconsumed advertising, $165; office salaries due, $240; division of profits, Jones, five-eights; Smith, three-eighths.

It will be noticed that the trial balance contains the accounts classified as real, nominal and proprietorship accounts. This order facilitates the preparation of business and financial statements. The problem requires the preparation of a profit and loss account and of a balance sheet (illustrated on pages 98–100) which may be analyzed as follows:

24. *Explanation of profit and loss account.*—On January 1, 1908, the beginning of the period, we had an inventory of goods on hand amounting to $3,650.00. During the year we bought $84,000 worth of goods, making a total of $87,650. As we have received certain discounts and allowances and have not sold all the goods bought, but have some on hand, we deduct the two items from the total of $87,650, showing the cost of the goods sold to be $81,735.

On the credit side of the profit and loss account we have the sales for the year, amounting to $152,000. As there were no deductions from the sales the gross profit made on the goods sold is $70,265. That represents the turnover, without taking into consideration the selling or general administration expenses.

This turnover or gross profit is carried down to the credit side of the second section of the profit and loss

PROFIT AND LOSS ACCOUNT OF THE FIRM JONES AND SMITH FOR THE YEAR ENDING DEC. 31ST, 1908

Dr.				Cr.	
To Inventory Jan. 1	$3,650.00			By sales	$152,000.00
Purchases	84,000.00	$87,650.00			
Deduct:					
Discounts and allowances	550.00				
Inventory Dec. 31	5,365.00	5,915.00	$81,735.00		
Gross profit			70,265.00		
			$152,000.00		$152,000.00
Advertising	2,600.00			By gross profit	70,265.00
Less unconsumed	165.00	2,435.00			
Commissions		3,050.00			
Balance carried down		64,780.00			
		$70,265.00			$70,265.00
To General expense		12,900.00		By balance brought down	64,780.00
Office salaries	9,300.00				
Office salaries, accrued	240.00	9,540.00			
Insurance	625.00				
Less unexpired	208.33	416.67			
Postage		1,650.00			
Ordinary business profit		40,273.33			
		64,780.00			64,780.00
To Exchange	25.00			By ordinary business profit	40,273.33
Interest	175.00				
Cash discount	375.00	575.00			
Net profit for distribution		39,698.33			
		$40,273.33			$40,273.33

PROFIT AND LOSS APPROPRIATION ACCOUNT

To Jones' ⅝ of net profits...............	$24,811.46	By net profits...............	$39,698.33
Smith ⅜ of net profits....	14,886.87		
	$39,698.33		$39,698.33

BALANCE SHEET OF THE FIRM JONES AND SMITH, DECEMBER 31st, 1908

ASSETS:

Cash................................		$12,300.00
Notes receivable............	$32,700.00	
Accounts receivable........	47,000.00	79,700.00
Merchandise inventory..........	5,365.00	$97,365.00
Real estate........................	50,000.00	
Buildings..........................	13,000.00	
Furniture and fixtures............	3,000.00	66,000.00
Unexpired insurance............	208.33	
Unconsumed advertising.....	165.00	373.33
		$163,738.33

LIABILITIES:

Notes payable..................	$30,000.00	
Accounts payable..............	13,100.00	$43,100.00
Accrued salaries...............		240.00

PROPRIETORSHIP:

Jones, balance		
Jan. 1, 1908...........	$50,000.00	
⅝ of profits...........	24,811.46	
	74,811.46	
Less withdrawals........	2,400.00	$72,411.46
Smith, balance		
Jan. 1, 1908...........	35,000.00	
⅜ of profits...........	14,886.87	
	49,886.87	
Less withdrawals........	1,900.00	47,986.87
		120,398.33
		$163,738.33

account. Against this are charged the selling expenses; such as commission and advertising, deducting from the latter the amount of advertising expended during the period but not consumed, making a total charge of $5,-485. The subtraction of these amounts from the gross profit leaves a balance of $64,780, which shows the profit made before considering the administration expenses. This remainder is carried down to the credit side of the next section of the profit and loss account. Against this balance are charged the administration expenses, such as: General expenses, salaries, postage, insurance, deducting from the last the unexpired premium and adding to the office salaries, the amount accrued, making a total of $24,506.67. This, deducted from the profit carried down from the previous section, shows $40,273.33, which we call ordinary business profit to distinguish it from the net profit shown in the final section. This ordinary profit is shown regardless of such expenditures as result from insufficiency or excessiveness of capital. Before charging large items for interest and discount due to insufficiency of capital, it is of considerable advantage to have a classification showing the ordinary business profit.

The final section shows on the credit side the ordinary business profit, against which are charged such items as interest, discount and exchange on foreign checks, making a total of $575 and leaving a net profit for distribution among partners of $39,698.33.

In this problem no thought was expended on reserve for depreciation of furniture and fixtures or buildings, nor was there a provision made for reserve for bad debts. The consideration of these items was omitted in order to avoid confusion at this step, and they are mentioned now so that the reader may be able to reconcile the definition given of net profits, which states that it is the sum arrived at after all the charges have been provided for, including reserves for depreciation and bad debts.

The next account, headed profit and loss appropriation, shows on the credit side the net profits carried from the profit and loss account, and is apportioned according to the partnership provision of 5/8 to Jones and 3/8 to Smith.

25. *Preparation of the balance sheet.*—Having completed the profit and loss account, and having appropriated or allocated the profit, we must prepare a balance sheet or a financial statement. This statement not only shows the financial condition of the concern but also verifies the result given in the profit and loss account. As already stated, the balance sheet may be arranged to show fixed assets first, and then the current or floating assets; or current assets may be shown first, and then the fixed assets. The latter method is the one adopted in this balance sheet. The author believes that this should be the method always followed because the balance sheet, strictly speaking, is nothing else than a financial statement and as such should show the financial condition. The former method of placing fixed assets first, may be adopted where it is desirable to show the strength of the company in assets available for earning revenue. As will be noticed, the notes and accounts receivable are added together, both representing outstanding amounts due the firm, and the other two items on the asset side are added to them to show the current assets; the second group totaled represents the fixed assets; the third group, advanced or deferred assets. It will be noticed that the two items last mentioned—unexpired insurance and unconsumed advertising—were deducted in the

profit and loss account for the reason that they were advances made during the current period to be utilized at a future time, and hence were properly listed among the assets at the time the statements were prepared.

On the liability side we have the notes and accounts payable added together, showing the amount due by us to the trade. In addition, we have accrued salaries, forming a deferred liability created during this period, which is accrued but not as yet due. The final part of the balance sheet shows the proprietorship. As the problem does not call for separate partners' accounts, it is advisable to show the proprietorship in detail, accounting for the present capital. We therefore begin with Jones's balance on the first of January, adding to it the 5/8 of the profits and deducting his withdrawals, showing his present capital to be $72,411.46. We do the same thing with Smith's account, determining his capital to be $47,986.87, making the combined capital of the business $120,398.33. This makes the liability side equal to the asset side, and, therefore, verifies the result shown in the profit and loss account.

26. *"Closing" entries.*—We have already learned something about the preparation of a business, as well as of a financial statement. It will be recalled that we used this problem only preparatory to taking up the closing of the accounts of the January and February transactions given in the former chapter. By closing entries we mean classifying, in the form of a journal entry, all nominal accounts which, when posted to their respective accounts, will be closed out, leaving open on the ledger only such accounts as show an asset, a liability, or proprietorship.

In preparing a profit and loss account we were able to deduct certain items from others in order to show the results.   We cannot do this by means of journal entries.   In order to show deductions, reversed entries must be made.

Another proposition in the working of the set is that the owner desires to know apart from the total results shown the gain or loss on each class of goods carried. The first step is to determine the amount of goods on hand at the end of February.   In ordinary business houses such inventory is determined by actual count or measure, as the case may be.   Here we have to satisfy ourselves with an approximate estimate.   Our estimate, as nearly as can be determined, shows the following inventories:

Ingrain	$565.00
Moquette	885.00
Brussels	736.00
Wilton	150.00
Linoleum	350.00
Oilcloth	250.00

It will be borne in mind that all the nominal accounts that have a debit balance need necessarily a credit balance in the closing entries, and those having credit balances will have to have a debit balance.

27. *Illustration of the closing entries.*—The following are the closing entries:

Trading account $22,417.04.

To Ingrain purchases	$3,692.97
Moquette purchases	3,326.25
Brussels purchases	2,608.17
Wilton purchases	7,780.00
Linoleum purchases	2,805.00
Oilcloth purchases	1,570.00
Advertising	190.85
Freight outward	70.66
Commission	370.58
Freight inward	2.56

To close into trading all the accounts enumerated above.

Discount gained	312.00	
Ingrain inventory	565.00	
Moquette inventory	885.00	
Brussels inventory	736.00	
Wilton inventory	150.00	
Linoleum inventory	350.00	
Oilcloth inventory	250 00	
To trading account		$3,248.00

To close the first account and show the offsets in the trading account, against cost—appearing on the debit side.

Ingrain sales	3,558.55	
Moquette sales	2,940.73	
Brussels sales	2,272.65	
Wilton sales	9,744.00	
Linoleum sales	2,833.23	
Oilcloth sales	1,656.09	
To trading account		23,005.25

Transfer of former accounts and closing them at the same time.

Trading account	146.59	
To discount lost		146.59

To close the last named account.

Trading account	3,689.62	
To profit and loss account...............		3,689.62

Closing out of former account by transfer to the latter.

Profit and loss account.............	897.83	
To rent ....⌄.....................		300.00
Insurance		26.56
Office salaries		460.00
General expense		74.72
Stationery and printing..................		6.05
Cash discount lost......................		24.67
Interest lost		5.83

To close into profit and loss account all the accounts enumerated above.

Cash discount gained	$7.73	
To profit and loss account.................		$7.73

To close the first mentioned account.

Profit and loss account.............	2,467.11	
To A. Roberts D/A.......................		2,467.11

Transfer of final balance of the profit and loss account to the proprietor's account.

A. Roberts D/A....................	2,017.11	
To A. Roberts C/A.....................		2,017.11

Transfer of balance.

In analyzing the closing entries we see that the trading account has been charged with **$22,417.04**, comprising the cost of the purchases, as well as the necessary expenses in bringing the goods to market and disposing of them. In the closing entries we cannot very well show the profit and loss made on each kind of goods. It is also important to include such items as freight inward, because this increases the cost of the goods. The items of advertising, freight outward, and commission are included, as they represent the selling expense incurred in marketing the product.

The second entry closes first of all the discount gained account, as this is an offset to the debit of the trading. It also opens separate accounts for the inventories of the balance on hand at the end of the period. As our trading account has been charged for total purchases without regard to the sale of the goods, it is necessary to credit this account for inventories, in order to show cost of goods sold. These inventories are asset and not nominal accounts.

As we charged the trading account for the cost of the goods, we credit it with the sales. We transfer the subdivided sales accounts by debiting each account and crediting the trading. That closes the sales accounts and shows the returns against the goods in the trading account.

We then close the discount loss account into trading, as this decreases the sales. Subtracting the debit side of the trading account from the credit side, we find the difference to be $3,689.62, which we transfer to the profit and loss account, thus closing entirely the trading account. The trading account has now fulfilled its function, showing the profit realized on trade, exclusive of administration expenses.

The profit and loss account is then debited for all items of administration expenses. By means of this entry, all nominal accounts showing administration expenses are closed.

As cash discount gained is additional income it is closed into the profit and loss account.

Deducting the debit side of the profit and loss account (which also includes the item of $332.41 for bad debts) we find the net profit to be $2,467.11, which is closed by transferring it to the proprietor's drawing account.

As has already been said, we keep the drawing account separate from the capital account in order to show the capital investment intact. We do not want to disturb this account until the end of the fiscal period, when it is adjusted by transferring to it any remaining balance in the drawing account. Our next entry, then, is to debit the drawing account for the balance of $2,017.11. after deducting the withdrawals from the profits, and to credit the capital account for this amount. This closes all nominal accounts, leaving on the books of the concern only such accounts as show assets, liabilities or proprietorship.

On pages 77–85 are given the ledger accounts after having posted the closing entries. Instead of repeating the items appearing in the accounts in detail, the totals only are given. As the purpose of repeating the ledger accounts is to show them when closed, there is no necessity for including details.

28. *Illustration of the statement of profit and loss.*— As by the closing entries Roberts cannot tell very much with regard to the result of operation, and moreover cannot tell which class of merchandise was the more profitable, we prepare for him the following profit and loss statement:

FIRST SECTION OF PROFIT AND LOSS STATEMENT, SHOWING PROFIT OR LOSS3

	Ingrain	Moquette	Brussels	Wilton	Linoleum	Oilcloth	Total
Purchases during the period........	$3,692.97	$3,326.25	$2,608.17	$7,780.00	$2,805.00	$1,570.00	
Less inventory on hand............	565.00	885.00	736.00	150.00	350.00	250.00	
	$3,127.97	$2,441.25	$1,872.17	$7,630.00	$2,455.00	$1,320.00	$18,846.39
Prime profit....	430.58	499.48	400.48	2,114.00	378.23	336.09	4,158.86
	$3,558.55	$2,940.75	$2,272.65	$9,744.00	$2,833.23	$1,656.09	$23,005.25

ON EACH CLASS OF GOODS FOR THE PERIOD ENDING FEBRUARY 28, 1909

	Ingrain	Moquette	Brussels	Wilton	Linoleum	Oilcloth	Total
Sales for the period.....	$3,558.55	$2,940.73	$2,272.65	$9,744.00	$2,833.23	$1,656.09	$23,005.25
	$3,558.55	$2,940.73	$2,272.65	$9,744.00	$2,833.23	$1,656.09	$23,005.25

SECOND, THIRD AND FOURTH SECTIONS OF PROFIT AND LOSS STATEMENT FOR PERIOD ENDING

FEBRUARY 28, 1908

Advertising...................................	$190 85	Prime profit carried from first section.	$4,158.86
Freight outward..............................	70 66	Add discount gained...............	312.00
Commissions.................................	370 58		4,470.86
Discount lost................................	146.59	Less freight inward................	2.56	$4,468.30
Gross profit exclusive of administration expenses.....	3,689.62		
	$4,468 30		$4,468.30

Rent..		$300.00	Gross profit, exclusive of administration expenses.	$3,689.62
Insurance.................... $159.58			
Less unexpired (10 mos.)..... 132.82		26 56	
Office salaries..............................	460 00		
General expenses............................	74.72		
Stationery and printing......................	6.05		
Bad debts...................................	332.41		
Ordinary business profits....................	2,489 88		
	$3,689.62		$3,689.62

Cash discount lost....	24.67	Ordinary business profit.............	$2,489.88
Interest lost.........	5.83	Cash discount gained................	7.73
Net profit........	2,467.11		
	$2,497.61		$2,497.61

110

BALANCE SHEET THE FIRM A. ROBERTS AS ON FEBRUARY 28, 1908

ASSETS:			
Cash			$7,110.43
Notes receivable		$1,140.00	
Accounts receivable:			
Peabody & Langman	$234.00		
B. Ecket & Son	975.00		
M. Philips	1,451.25		
F. Peters & Bro.	530.00	3,190.25	4330.25
Furniture and fixtures		250.00	
Merchandise inventory		2,936.00	$14,626.68
Advances:			
Insurance premium prepaid			132.82
			$14,759.50

LIABILITIES:		
Notes payable		$7,742.39
PROPRIETORSHIP		
A. Roberts, as per Capital account in ledger		7,017.11
		$14,759.50

The first section, as the heading shows, is arranged merely to show the turnover or prime profit on goods sold, regardless of selling or administration expenses. The arrangement is self-explanatory and shows the respective prime profit made on each class of goods dealt in.

The second section shows on the credit side the prime profit carried down from the first section, to which the discount gained is added, and from which the freight inward is deducted, making this sum, $4,468.30. Against this appear all the selling expenses on the debit side, including discount lost, showing the gross profit, exclusive of administration expenses, to be $3,689.62. This is the same sum as shown in closing entries when the trading account is closed and the balance forwarded to the profit and loss account.

The third section shows on the credit side the gross profit carried down from the second section and on the debit side contains administration expenses. These are only such administration expenses as have nothing to do with the capital of the business, leaving out such items as cash discount or interest. The difference shows the ordinary business profit to be $2,489.88. It will be noticed that, as the insurance premium was paid for a full year, the unexpired premium, for ten months, is deducted from the insurance account.

The fourth section shows on the credit side the ordinary business profit carried down from the third section, to which is added cash discount gained. On the debit side we have the cash discount lost as well as the interest lost; in other words, those items which have not directly to do with the profits on the trading, but rather disclose sufficiency or insufficiency of capital. The difference shows the net profit for the period.

The reader must not overlook the fact that we could have apportioned the selling and administration expenses. If we had followed this method, we could have shown the net profit on each class of goods handled.

29. *Illustration of the balance sheet.*—As already stated, in double-entry bookkeeping we are able to verify the result shown in the profit and loss account. This is done by preparing the balance sheet, which also shows the financial condition of the concern at the time. Thus on the asset side of the balance sheet the total of the various assets of the firm, including the advances, is found to be $14,759. On the liability side we have the liability which consists only of the notes payable, and the proprietorship, amounting to $7,017.11. This amount is made up of Roberts's original investment, $5,000, plus $2,017.11, transferred from the drawing account. The last named figure is the difference in the drawing account between the net profit and withdrawals.

CHAPTER V

SINGLE ENTRY METHOD

30. *Distinction between single entry and double entry.*—As the reader already knows, in single entry, transactions or exchanges have a personal quality only, and therefore such exchanges as do not possess this quality are not recorded. In double entry each transaction or exchange has a double aspect, viz., personal and impersonal. Therefore, this twofold effect is recorded by having for each debit a complement—a credit. As a result of such records, the system—double entry—affords the following advantages over single entry. First, the arithmetical accuracy of the books can be tested by means of the trial balance. So long as there is a corresponding credit to each debit entry and vice versa, the totals of this arithmetical test, the trial balance, will be equal. Second, such impersonal accounts representing profit made or loss sustained, during a given period, can be collected, in classified form, into a summary known as the profit and loss account. One can always tell in what manner the profit or loss has been arrived at by means of a profit and loss statement. Third, the final result shown on the profit and loss account can be verified by the balance sheet, which again is another test of the accuracy of the accounts. Fourth, due to the fact that the books are subject to arithmetical tests, the chance of overlooking fraud is considerably reduced.

In the early days of double entry bookkeeping, people

imagined that each business transaction or exchange should be recorded twice and that this was the reason it was called double entry. They furthermore imagined that double entry required double the amount of labor of single entry. It is, therefore, important to emphasize the following points: (a) Double entry does not involve double the amount of labor demanded by single entry. (b) Double entry does not depend on keeping a journal, invoice book or the like, neither does it exclude the use of them, nor does the use of these books imply that they are kept by single entry. (c) Double entry does not mean keeping other people's accounts as well as your own.

Briefly summarized, we may say that while single entry records some facts it does not show results; whereas double entry bookkeeping records all the facts as well as their results.

The reader may ask why, if single entry bookkeeping is so incomplete and imperfect, intelligent business men keep their accounts by this method? The answer lies in the fact that these men are probably not familiar with the advantages offered by the double entry system and simply keep on in the old path, although none of them has the satisfaction of saying, "My accounts are correct; I have proven them to be so." Many times such people wake up too late and find their misfortune in not being able to tell precisely how their accounts stand, nor why they have not made much profit in a given year, although their sales were larger than in the year before.

Professor Hardcastle in an article which appeared in *The Journal of Accountancy,* Vol. II, No. 3, says:

In spite of this ...... it—single entry—must have considerable merit, especially in certain businesses, or it would have gone out of existence long ago.   It is generally used by the small retailer and very often by business carried on on a most extensive scale.

There is hardly a justification for this commendation. Many evils continue to exist although we know them to be such.   Single entry is certainly an evil in modern accountancy and accountants greatly discourage its use. No well-conducted business house of to-day keeps its accounts by the single entry plan.   The disadvantages of the system are not lessened if it is used by a small rather than by a large concern.

31. *Definition of proprietorship.*—The proprietorship of a firm is the term employed to signify the excess of assets over liabilities at a given date.   It is obvious that if the proprietorship at the close of a certain period exceeds proprietorship as stated at the beginning of that period, the excess will represent profits made during that period.   On the other hand, if the proprietorship at the end of the period is less than that given at the beginning, it will show a loss.   This principle is the base for the ascertainment of profit or loss, when the books are kept by the single entry method.   The procedure in such cases is best illustrated by the following problem:

PROBLEM I.

32. *The ascertainment of profits under single entry.* —On January 2, 1908, John Brown possesses the following assets: Cash in bank, $1,800.00; securities consisting of stocks and bonds amounting to $2,000.00; notes given to him by customers amounting to $1,500.00; merchandise on hand valued at $15,000.00.   He has out-

standing accounts to be collected, amounting to $2,000.00.

These assets are subject to the following liabilities: He owes to the trade for goods bought on notes, $1,900.00; on open accounts, $2,000.00. His books have been kept by single entry and at the end of the year he desires to find out whether he has made any profit or not. On December 31, 1908, he presents to us a list of all his assets as well as his liabilities and asks us to find out the progress or retrogression of the business for that year. The following is the list of his assets and liabilities: Assets: cash in bank, $2,000.00, cash on hand, $50.00. He has in his possession notes amounting to $3,500.00; his stock of goods on hand at this date is valued at $21,000.00 and the customers' accounts due to him amount to $2,500.00. Securities in the shape of stocks and bonds, $2,400.00. Liabilities: He owes on notes $2,500.00 and on accounts, $2,150.00. He withdrew during the year, for his personal use, $2,000.00.

The problem presented by Mr. Brown is solved as follows:

Our first step is the preparation of a statement showing assets and liabilities on January 2, 1908. By this statement, as given on page 118, the proprietorship is shown to be $18,400.

We then prepare a statement of assets and liabilities as of December 31, 1908 (page 118), and this shows Brown's capital to be $26,800, an increase of $8,400 over last year's capital. If we add to this amount the withdrawals made by Brown during the year ($2,000) there is left a net profit of $10,400 for the year. If we desire to verify the facts a comparative statement of assets and liabilities can be prepared as shown on page

STATEMENT OF ASSETS AND LIABILITIES OF THE FIRM OF JOHN BROWN AS ON JAN. 2, 1908

Assets

Cash		$1,800.00
Stocks and bonds		2,000.00
Notes receivable	$1,500.00	
Accounts receivable	2,000.00	3,500.00
Merchandise inventory		15,000.00
		$22,300.00

Liabilities

Notes payable	$1,900.00	
Accounts payable	2,000.00	$3,900.00
John Brown, proprietorship		18,400.00
		$22,300.00

STATEMENT OF THE ASSETS AND LIABILITIES OF THE FIRM OF JOHN BROWN AS ON DEC. 31, 1908

Assets

Cash in bank	$2,000.00	
Cash on hand	50.00	$2,050.00
Stocks and bonds		2,400.00
Notes receivable	$3,500.00	
Accounts receivable	2,500.00	6,000.00
Merchandise inventory		21,000.00
		$31,450.00

Liabilities

Notes payable	$2,500.00	
Accounts payable	2,150.00	$4,650.00
John Brown's capital made up thus:		
Capital at beginning of period	$18,400.00	
Less withdrawals	2,000.00	16,400.00
Net profit	10,400.00	26,800.00
		$31,450.00

COMPARATIVE STATEMENT OF ASSETS AND LIABILITIES OF THE FIRM OF JOHN BROWN FOR 1907-1908

Assets	1907	1908	Increase	Decrease
Cash	$1,800.00	$2,050.00	$250.00	
Stocks and bonds	2,000.00	2,400.00	400.00	
Notes Receivable	1,500.00	3,500.00	2,000.00	
Accounts Receivable	2,000.00	2,500.00	500.00	
Merchandise Inventory	15,000.00	21,000.00	6,000.00	
	$22,300.00	$31,450.00	$9,150.00	
Net increase				$9,150.00
	$22,300.00	$31,450.00	$9,150.00	$9,150.00

Liabilities	1907	1908	Increase	Decrease
Notes Payable	$1,900.00	$2,500.00	$600.00	
Accounts Payable	2,000.00	2,150.00	150.00	
	$3,900.00	$4,650.00	$750.00	$750.00
Net increase Proprietorship	18,400.00	26,800.00		
	$22,300.00	$31,450.00	$750.00	$750.00

The profits earned, are accounted for as follows:

Increase of assets		$9,150.00
Less increase of liabilities		750.00
		$8,400.00
Add withdrawals		2,000.00
		$10,400.00

119

119. This statement discloses the fact that the assets have increased $9,150, but that the liabilities have also increased at the same time by $750.00. If we deduct the increased liability from the increase of assets we find the difference to be $8,400. To this add the withdrawals, making a total of $10,400, the exact amount shown by the statement of assets and liabilities.

33. *Procedure in connection with a change from single entry to double entry bookkeeping.*—If it is desired to convert a set of books from single entry to the double entry method, first of all prepare a statement showing the condition of affairs at that particular time. It has already been shown that by the single entry method we deal, or at least should deal, with personal accounts only, and therefore in order to convert such a system to double entry it will be necessary to raise the additional impersonal accounts which are required by this latter system. The various adjustments in the personal accounts must also be made. Generally where the single entry method is used the books as a whole are found in a chaotic condition. They are in all stages of incompleteness. The results, therefore, can only be estimated and consequently the first balance sheet after such conversion is not very satisfactory.

It is preferable to introduce an entirely new set of books and arrange the system of accounts to meet the demands and needs of the business. If this is done, the business accounts appearing in the old ledger after proper adjustment, will be transferred to the new ledger, and in addition the other accounts showing assets or liabilities as well as proprietorship will be raised. This is done by means of a journal entry, in order to bring the ledger into equilibrium.

STATEMENT OF ASSETS AND LIABILITIES OF THE FIRM FYNES AND ALTHERR

ASSETS:

Cash		$5,500.00	
X. Y. Z. stock		2,000.00	
Bills receivable	$2,300.00		
Accounts receivable	8,500.00	10,800.00	
Merchandise inventory		18,000.00	
Real estate		5,000.00	
		$41,300.00	

LIABILITIES:

Bills payable		$2,000.00	
Accounts payable		6,000.00	$8,000.00

PROPRIETORSHIP

Made up thus:			
Capital at beginning, viz.:			
F. F. Fynes	$12,500.00		
Deduct withdrawals	2,500.00	$10,000 00	
W. J. Altherr	$12,500.00		
Less withdrawals	2,000.00	10,500 00	
		20,500.00	
Net profit for year, being amount required to make up proprietorship to	$33,300.00	12,800.00	
Proprietorship as above		33,300.00	33,300.00
			$41,300.00

This profit is to be allocated as follows:

F. F. Fynes .... $6,400.00, one-half of net profits
W. J. Altherr .... 6,400.00, one-half of net profits
making their respective capital to be $16,400 and $16,900

121

34. *Illustration of change from single to double entry.*—F. F. Fynes and W. J. Altherr are partners in business, sharing equally profits and losses.   Their books have been kept by single entry, but Fynes and Altherr desire to change to the double entry method.   The following accounts are shown by the ledger:

F. F. Fynes, investment, $12,500.00; withdrawals, $2,500.00; W. J. Altherr, investment, $12,500.00; withdrawals, $2,000.00.   Sundry accounts receivable, $8,500.00; sundry accounts payable, $6,000.00.

Assets and liabilities not shown in ledger: Merchandise per inventory, $18,000.00; cash in bank, $5,500.00; bills receivable, $2,300.00; bills payable, $2,000.00; X Y Z stock, $2,000.00; real estate, $5,000.00.

Determine the amount of gain or loss of each partner at this date, and formulate a journal entry that will convert the single entry ledger to one of double entry.

SOLUTION.

The following journal entry is made for the purpose of converting the single entry ledger to a double entry ledger:

Cash	$5,500.00	
X Y Z stock	2,000.00	
Bills receivable	2,300.00	
Accounts receivable (posted)	8,500.00	
Merchandise inventory	18,000.00	
Real estate	5,000.00	
F. F. Fynes drawing account (posted)	2,500.00	
W. J. Altherr drawing account (posted)	2,000.00	
To bills payable		$2,000.00
Accounts payable (posted)		6,000.00
F. F. Fynes capital account (posted)		12,500.00
W. J. Altherr capital account (posted)		12,500.00
F. F. Fynes drawing account		6,400.00
W. J. Altherr drawing account		6,400.00

for the purpose of converting the single entry ledger into double entry, posting only the new accounts.

With this problem as with the former, the first step was the preparation of a statement of assets and liabilites of the firm, as found at the end of the period. This statement (page 121) shows us a total of assets amounting to $41,300 and a total liability amounting to $8,000, leaving the proprietorship to be $33,300. As the proprietorship originally was $25,000, from which the partners have withdrawn $4,500, leaving a balance of $20,500, it is obvious that they must have made a profit of $12,800, the difference between the present capital and the former. As the problem tells us that the profits were to be allocated share and share alike, each partner will receive $6,400. If their withdrawals were equal as were their investments, their present capital would also be equal. Fynes having, however, withdrawn $500 more than Altherr, the capital accounts will necessarily be unequal, namely, Fynes, $16,400, and Altherr, $16,900.

We have so far solved one part of the problem, namely, the determination of the amount of gain or loss due each partner at this date. The second part of the problem asks us to formulate a journal entry that will convert the single entry to a double entry ledger. We, therefore, make the journal entry as shown on the preceding page, by means of which we convert the ledger as required.

It will be noticed that beside certain accounts the word "posted" is entered in parenthesis. As already stated in some previous chapter, where a single entry system is in use, the only accounts that should be operated are the personal accounts. This firm followed this method, but in addition had also the capital accounts of the partners. It is obvious that as the same ledger is to be used the accounts that appear there as already posted need not be repeated.   Alongside of these accounts is placed the word "posted."   This indicates that, in posting this journal entry to the ledger, only the new accounts are to be entered, omitting entirely those already posted.

CHAPTER VI

MANUFACTURING ACCOUNTS

35. *Definition of manufacturing accounts.*—In the early days when a manufacturer's establishment was under his personal supervision, he could, with a reasonable degree of accuracy, tell for how much he could sell a unit of his product in order to make a profit. To be able to tell this he did not require an elaborate system of cost accounting or even manufacturing accounts. There were also other reasons why he could make an estimate without any system at all, because consumers were not so exacting as they are to-day and competition was not so keen as it is at present. But under changed conditions large-scale production requires the employment of men upon whose report manufacturers must rely for their information.

It is advisable to emphasize, lest the reader misunderstand, the fact that we are not dealing with cost accounting, but with factory accounting. We are not devising or working a system of cost accounts, but are only considering the additional accounts that a manufacturer would keep in his ledger which are not ordinarily found in the ledger of a trader. We are trying to find out what results these additional accounts would show and whether they are indispensable.

What has been so far stated about trading accounts in general applies also to manufacturing accounts. In these, however, we have more elements to deal with,

especially in regard to finding and verifying the profit
or loss.

In considering trading accounts, it was necessary for
us to arrive at the cost of the sales as against the proceeds of the sales in order to find the relation between
the two.   In this new subject we have to arrive at the
cost of manufacture and naturally we must consider
many more items than before.

36. *Purposes of a manufacturing concern.*—A manufacturer's functions are twofold: viz., to manufacture
and to sell.   He may manufacture for the purpose
of obtaining the manufacturer's profit—being able
to manufacture cheaper than he can buy; or he may
manufacture for the purpose of maintaining a certain quality in the goods or for various other reasons.
As his business is of a twofold nature we should be able
to tell the manufacturer whether it is profitable for him
to buy in the open market or make for himself.   We
need, therefore, to keep the two branches of his business—the result of manufacturing and the result of
trading—separate and distinct.   We should be able to
tell him how much profit he has made in each branch
of his business as well as on the whole.

The average manufacturer, although he may not
know very much about accounting in general, knows
approximately how much the goods ought to cost him,
what they should be sold for, and what his profits should
be.   If the figures his bookkeeper submits to him are
not what he expects, the latter must be in a position to
prove his contentions.

In determining the price at which he can afford to
sell an article, a manufacturer would generally require
the following information: (1) Cost of the material
consumed; (2) cost of the labor, productive and unpro-

ductive, employed in the manufacture of the goods;
(3) cost of the general administration charges in connection with the manufacture.   When he has this information he can reasonably tell the profit over and above the
cost of getting the same article on the market.

37. *Treatment of manufacturing accounts.*—Bearing
in mind that in every manufacturing concern there are
two departments—manufacturing and selling—the
goods manufactured may be treated on the books of
the concern in two ways.   (a) They may be acquired
by the selling department at the manufactured cost without any profit, regardless of market conditions.   (b)
They may be acquired by the selling department at the
prevailing market price regardless of cost.   By the latter method it is easier to tell when manufacturing pays
and when it does not.   In other words, the factory is
put on a profit basis.   On this point many accountants
disagree.

In order to get all the information required for the
preparation of manufacturing accounts, additional accounts will necessarily have to be introduced.   Thus we
will have an account showing the cost of raw material;
separate accounts for productive labor, e.g., wages
paid to working men, and unproductive labor, such as
superintendence and management wages.   We will also
have an account for plant and machinery, one for tools,
etc.   All these are very important, as otherwise we cannot prepare an intelligent manufacturing account at the
end of any given period.

A manufacturing account should usually contain the
following items:

    1. Debit side.

        (a) Raw materials at beginning of given period.

   (b) Goods in process of manufacture at the
        beginning of a given period.
   (c) The net cost of goods purchased during a
        given period.
   (d) Freight inward paid on raw materials pur-
        chased.
   (e) Labor expenses. The total of these
        charges may be called the prime cost of
        the manufacturing account.
2. Against these charges the credit side of this account will show:
   (a) Raw material on hand at the end of the
        given period.
   (b) Cost value of the goods partly manufac-
        tured and remaining unfinished at the
        end of the given period.

After making all these deductions there will remain
the first cost of the goods completely manufactured during the given period. This balance is usually transferred to the second section of the manufacturing account; which contains the following items:

Debit side.
   (a) Transfer from prime cost (balance of first
        section of manufacturing account).
   (b) Factory expenses, such as rent and taxes of
        factory and buildings used for manufac-
        turing purposes, fire insurance on build-
        ings, etc.
   (c) Supervision; wages of factory workers,
        watchmen and other men whose wages
        cannot be applied to prime costs.
   (d) All such charges as repairs and renewals
        for machinery and tools, ordinary wear

and tear on machinery, tools and buildings (known as depreciation).

Against this, we will have on the credit side, as a deduction, the item of expense on partly manufactured
goods on hand at the end of a given period, which of
course is not a proper charge against this period's work.
The balance then remaining is called the first charge
against the cost of production.

38. *Illustration of the working of manufacturing
accounts.*—It will be noticed that the author has touched
only on the principles of manufacturing accounts, leaving out the consideration of cost accounts and cost systems, as this is treated exhaustively in another volume.

PROBLEM I.

From the following trial balance of Smart & Currie's
books, extracted on December 31, covering six months'
operations, prepare a manufacturing, trading and profit
and loss account and balance sheet:

Cash at bank	$3,000.00	
Petty cash in hand	15.00	
Bills receivable on hand	1,000.00	
Sundry debtors	36,825.00	
Buildings	20,000.00	
Plant and machinery	15,000.00	
Sundry creditors		9,850.00
Loan on mortgage		22,500.00
Material on hand, July 1 (raw material)	13,705.00	
Purchases	42,000.00	
Wages	7,020.00	
Discounts allowed on purchases		1,950.00
Discounts allowed customers	4,690.00	
Returns (customers' returns for half-year)	1,650.00	
Sales		$80,000.00
Patent rights (expenses)	250.00	
Rent and taxes	500.00	
Advertising	2,300.00	
Travelers' salary	2,150.00	
Carriage outward	1,950.00	
Bad debts written off	500.00	
Repairs	420.00	
Patent royalties received in advance		2,500.00
Royalties on patents attributed to half-year		200.00

III—9

Trade and general expenses	2,510.00	
Interest on loans	600.00	
Reserve for bad and doubtful debts		2,700.00
Reserve for discounts on book debts		985.00
Smart capital account		30,000.00
Smart drawing account	6,000.00	
Currie capital account		15,000.00
Currie drawing account	3,600.00	
	$165,685.00	$165,685.00

The goods on hand (raw material) on December 31 are valued at $17,500.00.

Write off 5 per cent from plant and machinery for depreciation for the half year. The profits are to be apportioned as follows:

Smart ....two-thirds

Currie ....one-third

39. *Analysis of transactions in manufacturing accounts.*—The first problem contains a trial balance of a manufacturing concern from which we are asked to prepare a manufacturing, a trading and a profit and loss account, as well as a balance sheet, covering the period of six months, ending December 31, 1908.

The manufacturing account on page 131 begins with the inventory of raw material on hand, amounting to $13,705, to which purchases of raw material, amounting to $42,000, are added. From the total is deducted the discount on purchases as well as the inventory of raw material on hand December 31, making a total deduction of $19,450 and showing the cost of the raw material consumed to be $36,250. The next item is that of wages, amounting to $7,020.00. In accordance with the wording of the problem, we are to write off 5 per cent from plant and machinery for depreciation—that is, the ordinary wear and tear—amounting to $750.00. As the plant and machinery is carried on the

MANUFACTURING ACCOUNT OF THE FIRM SMART AND CURRIE FOR THE PERIOD OF SIX MONTHS, ENDING DECEMBER 31, 1908

To inventory July 1			$13,705.00	
Purchases			42,000.00	
			$55,705.00	
Discount on purchases	$1,950.00			
Inventory Dec. 31	17,500.00	19,450.00	$36,255.00	
Wages			7,020.00	
Depreciation on plant and machinery 5%			750.00	
Repairs			420.00	
Patent rights			250.00	
			$44,695.00	

By royalties on patents		$200.00
Balance carried down to trading account		44,495.00
		$44,695.00

TRADING ACCOUNT OF THE FIRM SMART AND CURRIE FOR SIX MONTHS, ENDING DECEMBER 31, 1908

To balance brought down from manufacturing account	$44,495.00	
Advertising	2,300.00	
Traveler's salary	2,150.00	
Carriage outward	1,950.00	
Gross profit on trading	27,455.00	
	$78,350.00	

By sales	$80,000.00	
Less returns	1,650.00	$78,350.00
		$78,350.00

131

PROFIT AND LOSS ACCOUNT OF THE FIRM SMART AND CURRIE FOR SIX MONTHS, ENDING DECEMBER 31, 1908

To rent and taxes.................	$500 00	
Trade and general expenses........	2,510.00	
Bad debts written off.............	500.00	
Ordinary business profit..........	23,945.00	By gross profit on trading........... $27,455.00
	$27,455.00	$27,455.00

To interest on loans...............	$600.00	
Discount allowed customers........	4,690.00	By ordinary business profit.... $23,945.00
Net profit allocated thus:		
Smart, ⅔ of profits........ $12,436.67		
Currie, ⅓ of profits........ 6,218.33	18,655.00	
	$23,945.00	$23,945.00

132

BALANCE SHEET OF THE FIRM SMART AND CURRIE ON DECEMBER 31, 1908

ASSETS:

Cash at hand	$3,000.00	
Cash in hand	15 00	$3,015.00
Bills receivable	1,000.00	
Accounts receivable	36,825.00	
	$37,825.00	
Less reserve for bad and doubtful debts and reserve for discounts	3,685.00	34,140.00
Inventory of raw material		17,500.00
Buildings		20,000 00
Plant and machinery	15,000.00	
Less depreciation reserve	750.00	14,250 00
		$88,905.00

LIABILITIES:

Accounts payable		$9,850.00
Loan on mortgage		22,500.00
Patent royalties received in advance		2,500.00

PROPRIETORSHIP:

Smart C/A	$30,000.00	
⅓ of profit	12,436.67	
	42,436.67	
Less withdrawals	6,000.00	$36,436.67
Currie C/A	15,000.00	
⅓ of profit	6,218.33	
	21,218.33	
Less withdrawals	3,600.00	17,618.33
		54,055.00
		$88,905.00

books at a cost of $15,000, 5 per cent of this gives us the above-mentioned figure. The repairs and patent-right expenses are added, the latter because the patents are used in the manufacture of the product, making a total debit of $44,695.

On the credit side we have, first, the royalties on patents, attributed to this half year, amounting to $200, leaving a balance of $44,495, which is carried to the trading account, it being the first charge against trading.

The trading account begins with the balance mentioned before, brought down from the manufacturing account, to which is added selling expenses shown on page 131 in the trading account, making a total of $50,895. Against this we have on the credit side the gross sales amounting to $80,000, from which the return sales are deducted, leaving net sales of $78,350.00. Subtracting from this the debit of $50,895, we find the gross profit on trading, which amounts to $27,455.

We then prepare the profit and loss account as shown on page 132. It will be seen that the credit side of this account contains the gross profit on trading, carried forward from the trading account, and amounting to $27,455. On the debit side we have first of all rent and taxes. While this is an item which properly should be apportioned to the various departments, manufacturing, trading and general administration, in this case the problem merely gives us rent, without specifying the partienlar department, so we class it with general administration affairs. In the second item trade and general expenses should also be apportioned; that part belonging to trade going into the trading section, the balance into administration expenses, but according to the wording of the problem it is impossible to do this. The item of bad debts written off represents the losses on customers' accounts. The difference between the total debits and the credit side, shows the ordinary business profit regardless of such items as discount and interest.

The next section of the profit and loss account shows on the credit side the ordinary business profit carried down from the former section, and on the debit side the discount allowed to customers and interest on loans amounting to $5,290. Subtracting this from the ordinary business profit there is a net profit of $18,655, which is allocated in accordance with the provision given in the problem; namely, two-thirds or $12,436.67 to Smart and one-third or $6,218.33 to Currie.

Our next step in the solution is to prepare the balance sheet. It will be seen on page 133 that the items reserve for bad and doubtful debts and reserve for discounts, as given in the trial balance and amounting to $3,685, are deducted from the outstanding accounts. It will also be observed that neither of these reserves is brought into the profit and loss account, and rightly so, because they are balances calculated during previous periods and have nothing to do with the profits of this period.

In this connection it might be mentioned that if the problem should read "to provide proper reserves," and should specify only reserve for depreciation we would have to provide similar reserves for bad debts and discounts, as had been provided in former periods. The author followed in this instance the exact wording of the problem and, therefore, did not make any provision for such reserves. The depreciation reserve on machinery has been deducted from that account, which makes the total assets $88,905; the liabilities, amounting to $34,850, and the proprietorship, as itemized in the balance sheet amounting to $54,055, make the liability side equal the asset side.

40. *Further illustrations of manufacturing accounts.*
—A. Burt, a contractor, is constructing two houses. He has paid for labor: masons, $20,000.00; carpenters, $15,000.00; ordinary labor, $6,000.00; superintendent, $2,600.00; for materials, brick, cement and lime, $25,000.00; timber, flooring and trim, $10,000.00.

The superintendent (who had charge of both contracts) reports for contract No. 1: mason's labor, $8,000.00; carpenter's, $7,000.00; sundry labor, $2,-500.00; brick, $10,000.00; cement and lime, $1,000.00; hard pine flooring, $1,500.00; trim, $2,000.00; hardware, nails, etc., $400.00.

The number of day's labor amounted to 5,200 days on both contracts (2,500 days on No. 1; 2,700 days on No. 2), upon which basis the establishment charges are to be apportioned. Open an analytical ledger and allocate the items. Raise the operating account in the ledger.

SOLUTION:

In the second problem we are confronted with a contracting business where the contractor is constructing two houses, making certain payments for materials and labor consumed, and we are asked to open an analytical ledger and to raise the operating account in such ledger. The operating account, as shown on page 137, is self-explanatory. It shows the various expenditures allocated to the respective accounts, and each individual account columnarized in the operating account is shown separately, giving the total charge to such account, the amount consumed and the balance as inventory. The

OPERATING ACCOUNT

Voucher No.	Amount	Labor Masons	Labor Carpenters	Labor Ordinary	Materials Bricks Cement and Lime	Materials Timber Flooring and Trim	Superintend
1............	$20,000	$20,000					
2............	15,000		$15,000				
3............	6,000			$6,000			
4............	2,600						$2,600
5............	25,000				$25,000		
6............	10,000					$10,000	
	$78,600	$20,000	$15,000	$6,000	$25,000	$10,000	$2,600

137

MASON'S LABOR

Voucher No.	Total	Consumed	Balance
One..............	$20,000.00	....	....
Contract No. 1......	....	$8,000.00	....
Balance...........	....	....	$12,000.00
	$20,000.00	$8,000 00	$12,000.00
Inventory.....	$12,000.00	....	....

CARPENTER'S LABOR

Voucher No.	Total	Consumed	Balance
Two..............	$15,000.00	....	....
Contract No. 1......	....	$7,000.00	....
Inventory.........	....	....	$8,000.00
	$15,000 00	$7,000 00	$8,000.00
Inventory.........	$8,000.00	....	....

ORDINARY LABOR

Voucher No.	Total	Consumed	Balance
Three.............	$6,000.00	....	....
Contract No. 1......	....	$2,500.00	....
Balance...........	....	....	$3,500.00
	$6,000.00	$2,500.00	$3,500.00
Inventory.........	$3,500.00	....	....

SUPERINTENDENT — Overhead or Establishment.

Voucher No.	Total	Consumed	Balance
Four..............	$2,600.00	....	....
Contract No. 1......	....	$1,250.00	25/52
Contract No. 2......	....	1,350.00	27/52
	$2,600 00	$2,600.00	....

BRICK, CEMENT AND LIME

Voucher No.	Total	Consumed	Balance
Five................	$25,000.00	....	....
C. No. 1. Bricks....	....	$10,000.00	....
C. No. 1 Cement & L	....	1,000.00	....
Balance.............	....	....	$14,000.00
	$25,000.00	$11,000.00	$14,000.00
Inventory............	$14,000.00	....	....

TIMBER, FLOORING AND TRIM

Voucher No	Total	Consumed	Balance
Six................	$10,000.00	....	....
Contract No. 1	....	....	....
Flooring...	....	$1,500.00	....
Trim......	....	2,000.00	....
Nails......	....	400.00	....
Balance.............	....	....	$6,100 00
	$10,000 00	$3,900.00	$6,100 00
Inventory..........	$6,100.00	....	....

CONTRACT NO. 1

Mason's labor	$8,000.00
Carpenter's labor..	7,000.00
Ordinary labor..	2,500.00
Materials, brick..	10,000.00
Materials, cement and lime.......................................	1,000.00
Materials, flooring...	1,500.00
Materials, trim..	2,000.00
Materials, nails, etc..	400.00
Superintendence...	1,250.00
	$33,650.00

CONTRACT NO. 2

Superintendence	$1,350.00

summary is then made under contract 1, showing hc w much of the expenditure has been made to contract 1 ard how much to contract 2.   It will be seen that this problem is semi-complete because it is only intended to show in the case of a contracting concern, how to allocate the various items to the various contracts.

In the third problem given below we are asked to open the general ledger accounts that control cost accounts and to show the operation of each as well as the net profits resulting.   The accounts given are self-explanatory.   We are also asked in this problem to calculate the percentage that is to be added to each dollar of material and of labor, in order to give the total cost.   This is shown on pages 142–146.

PROBLEM III.

The books of a manufacturing concern, operating under a system of cost accounts, show the following conditions at the opening of the fiscal year: Raw materials in storeroom, $15,621.42; factory pay roll, applied and distributed but not paid, 2 days, $831.78; partly manufactured goods, at prime cost, $63,888.44; and the further value of $8,037.17, to cover factory burden, also $12,074.92, to cover management charges; finished wares in stock at total cost of $21,656.01.

The financial operations during the ensuing year include: purchases of raw materials, $80,416.45; factory pay rolls, $125,793.90; factory expense including wages not applied to cost accounts, $24,846; management expenses, $38,100; interest paid on loans, $1,200; income from investments $5,004.

The manufacturing operations during the same year comprehend: raw materials issued on requisition for consumption, $79,820.34; wages applied and distributed to manufacturing cost, $120,250.40, and to factory expenses, $5,959.39, included in the sum stated in preceding paragraph.

Finished goods transferred from factory to warerooms, at prime cost, covering materials, $78,542.58, and labor, $118,333.75. The trading operations during the same year comprehend: cost of goods sold, $251,949.90; proceeds from goods sold, $302,339.88.

At the close of the year the partly completed goods included, in addition to prime cost, the further elements of value to cover factory and management expenses in the amounts respectively of $8,439.02, and $12,678.66, and factory pay roll for three days amounting to $1,247.67, which has been applied and distributed, though not due till the close of the current week.

The basis of the apportionment On Cost or Overhead Charges was as follows: factory expense 20 per cent to materials and 80 per cent to labor; management expenses 30 per cent to materials and 70 per cent to labor.

The transactions of the previous year in round amounts were used in calculating the current year's apportionments, viz., materials, $75,000; labor, $115,000; factory expense, $24,000; management expense, $36,-000.

Open the general ledger accounts that control the cost accounts; show the operation of each and the net profits resulting; also calculate the percentage to be added to each $1 of material and of labor to give the total cost.

SOLUTION.

COST ACCOUNTS OF THE BLANK MANUFACTURING COMPANY.

Raw Materials.

Inventory at commencement	$15,621.42	Manufacturing account, being amount of requisitions for consumption	$79,820.34
Purchases during period	80,416.45	Balance carried down	16,217.53
	$96,037.87		$96,037.87
Balance ..	$16,217.53		

Factory Pay Roll.

Cash	$125,793.90	Balance at commencement, being two days' labor applied and distributed but not paid	$831.78
Balance, three days' labor applied and distributed but not due	1,247.67	Manufacturing acc't: Wages applied and distributed	120,250.40
		Factory general expense: Am't not applied to prime cost	5,959.39
	$127,041.57		$127,041.57
		Balance, three days' wages applied and distributed	$1,247.67

Factory General Expense.

Balance at commencement, proportion applicable to inventory of partly manufactured goods..... $24,846.00 .... $8,037.17

Cash $24,846.00

Less wages not applied to cost account .... 5,959.39 .... 18,886.61

Factory pay roll account, wages not applied to prime cost 5,959.39

         $32,883.17

Balance, inventory ... $8,433.87

Finished goods account $24,449.30

Transfer of the total expenditure under this account, less the proportion applied to partly manufactured goods as per inventory, being 98.40396% of $24,846.00.

Balance carried down, being the amount referred to above 8,433.87

         $32,883.17

Management Expense.

Balance at commencement $12,074.92

Proportion of expense applicable to partly manufactured goods included in inventory.

Cash 38,100.00

         $50,174.92

Balance, inventory ... $12,683.24

Finished goods account $37,491.68

Transfer of total expense under this caption less the proportion applicable to partly manufactured goods as per inventory, being 98.40396% of $38,100.00.

Balance carried down being the amount referred to above 12,683.24

         $50,174.92

MANUFACTURING ACCOUNT.

Balance at commencement		$63,888.44
Prime cost of partly manufactured goods		79,820.34
Raw material account		
Requisitions for consumption		
Factory pay roll account		120,250.40
Wages applied and distributed		
		$263,959.18
Balance, inventory at prime cost		$67,082.85

Finished goods account:		
Transfer of value of finished goods from factory to warerooms at prime cost, viz:		
Materials	$78,542.58	$196,876.33
Labor	118,333.75	
Balance, inventory at prime cost		67,082.85
		$263,959.18

FINISHED GOODS.

Balance at .... ent, being the total cost as per inventory		$21,656.01
Manufacturing ...... ant:		
Gds ...... d from ...... tory to wareroom at ...... st, viz:		
Mls	$78,542.58	
Labor	118,333.75	196,876.33
Factory general expense:		
Proportion of ...... tory expense ...... le to finished ogds, 98.40336% of $24,846	24,449.30	
Management ...... pe:		
Proportion of ...... gnt ...... pe applicable to ...... nd goods		37,491.68
		$280,473.32
Balance, inventory		$28,522.85

Trading account:		
Cost of goods sold		$251,949.90
Balance, inventory		28,523.43
		$280,472.75

Finished goods account:		
Cost of goods sold	...	$251,949.90
Balance, prime profit ...	...	50,389.98
		$302,339.88
Interest paid on loans	...	$1,200.00
Net profit to income account ...	...	54,193.98
		$55,393.98

Sales	...	$302,339.88
		$302,339.88
Balance	...	$50,389.98
Income from investments ...	...	5,004.00
		$55,393.98

Manufacturing operations during the year:
Raw material issued on requisitions $79,820.34
Labor applied and distributed to manufacturing cost 120,250.40

Year's charge to prime cost ....,...................... $200,070.74

Overhead charges during the year:
Factory expense $24,846.00
Management expense 38,100.00

Year's overhead charges $62,946.00

$$\frac{62,946}{200,070.74} = 31.46187\%$$ percentage to be added to prime cost to make cost of production.

Finished goods during the year at prime cost:
Raw material $78,542.58
Labor 118,333.75 $196,876.33

$$\frac{196,876.33}{200,070.74} = 98.40336\%$$ percentage of year's prime cost used in finished goods during year.

Therefore,
$24,846.00 × 98.40336% = 24,449.30 = factory expense, and
$38,100.00 × 98.40336% = 37,491.68 = management expense.

Proof: $196,876.33 × 31.46187% = 61,940.98,
          and 24,449.30 + 37,491.68 also = 61,940.98.

Hence, 31.46187% is to be added to each dollar of labor and material.

PART II: PARTNERSHIP AFFAIRS

CHAPTER VII

FORMATION AND MANAGEMENT OF PARTNERSHIPS

41. *The importance of partnership agreements.*— It is a very difficult task to undertake to trace the origin and development of partnerships. A partnership agreement is a contract of antiquity. Perhaps the earliest instance of a partnership on record is that narrated in Genesis, when Abraham and Lot entered into partnership as farmers and graziers, which before long resulted in a dissolution through a disagreement amongst their herdmen.

"And there was strife between the herdmen of Abraham's cattle and the herdmen of Lot's cattle." Gen. xiii.

There are various circumstances which make it beneficial, advantageous, profitable, sometimes even compulsory, for one man or class of men to join others in a lawful enterprise, for the purpose of making profits. The man with capital will seek the man with ability, ideas or patents. Two competitors, in order to do away with cut-throat competition, may unite for their mutual interest. Many people, however, do not realize the importance of a partnership agreement, as is evidenced by the frequent dissolutions, changes in partnerships, and numerous expensive court litigations, which are the best evidence of the correctness of the above statement.

Dr. Jackson, of England, in a paper read before the

Chartered Accountants Students' Society of Kingston-upon-Hull, England, said:

> Next to the contract of marriage the contract of partnership is perhaps the most far-reaching legal contract; it requires the utmost good faith between the parties. It deals not only with the status of the firm created by the partnership agreement; it treats not only of the relationship of the parties amongst themselves and with the firm, but it introduces the various combinations of rights and obligations which may arise between the firm or its respective partners and the world at large.

The average person entering into partnership relation does not stop to consider in what position he places himself. The subject is usually dismissed with the suggestion that the partnership can always be dissolved. At least it is argued that a provision to that effect suffices to enable the partners to relieve themselves from the relation into which circumstances may have placed them. An actual case will perhaps illustrate the false notion of such reasoning.

C, who was in the laundry business in partnership with X, and who by virtue of a clause in their articles of co-partnership, agreed not to enter into any other partnership relation, violated this clause. Due to trade depression the profits in this enterprise, for a time at least, were nominal. He, therefore, secretly entered into a partnership with S, a retail jeweler. C, having a good reputation in the business community, was a stimulant for S, as it enabled him to buy large quantities of merchandise on notes, which were signed S & Co.

After a few months the laundry business picked up again, while the jewelry business was continually on the decline. C then resolved to dissolve his partnership with S. Upon mutual agreement the latter (S) was *supposed* to meet the notes at their maturity, which he never did. C was sued as a partner and, as S became bankrupt, he, C, had either to pay out thousands of dollars, or prosecute S, who issued notes with the firm signature even after its dissolution, but antedated. Granted that C could get enough evidence to prove S defrauded him, he would by this act disclose that he had violated the agreement with X. In pecuniary terms the dissolution with X would have been a far greater loss to him than the paying of S's note, so he chose the latter of the two evils.

This was due to a hasty step taken by C, by which he underrated the position one is in from the moment he enters into a partnership relation. Partnership is a relation into which a person is easily tempted to enter, but from which it is often quite difficult to escape. If business men could have placed before them statistical figures of cases where partners' confidences have been greatly abused, they would think twice before hastily venturing into that relation.

42. *Qualifications of partners.*—A shrewd, competent business man may be able to take various precautions in selecting his employés, to get the most honest and faithful subordinates; even go further than that, install a system whereby to check up whatever happens in his business, but he cannot exercise too much precaution in the selection of his business associates.

It is not only present conditions and circumstances that he must take cognizance of, and bear in mind, but he must also take into consideration futurities, contingencies and possible remote circumstances.

These remarks may seem rather harsh, too emphatic, perhaps enough to discourage any reasonable man from entering into partnership relation with his fellowmen, yet they are in place, in order to stir up business men to carefully scrutinize the men with whom they intend to associate themselves.

In this connection Thomas Conyngton in his "Manual of Partnership Relations" says:

The financial responsibility of a partner is frequently as important an asset of a business as the money or other tangible property actually invested. A wealthy member may put into a firm only a strictly limited amount of capital, but since, owing to the unrestricted liability of the partnership relations, he is responsible for all its debts, it is evident that the extent of his responsibility has an important bearing on the credit of the new firm. Practically his entire property is behind the partnership undertakings, regardless of the amount of his actual investment. On the other hand, if a partner's financial responsibility is not equal to that of his associates, it is obvious that from a credit standpoint he is not so valuable a member of the firm, even though his cash investment may be the same. Also, it is quite possible that such a partner, having less at stake, might be willing to take risks with the partnership business and property from which his associates would shrink. For both these reasons, other things being equal, the desirability of a prospective partner varies directly as his financial responsibility, regardless of the amount of his contemplated investment.

Only after they have fully satisfied themselves about their would-be co-partners should they proceed to take such other precautions as circumstances and conditions warrant, to protect their rights.

43. *Certain essential legal provisions of partnership agreements.*—The majority of business men, not being familiar with legal technicalities, often wonder why certain provisions are incorporated in their articles of co-partnership. Others, in many instances, fail to see the necessity of having written agreements at all, although

in some cases this may be a legal requirement. Thus the Statute of Frauds provides that a partnership contract that is to last for more than one year must be in writing in order to be valid.

Another class of men think that as long as the law does not require the agreement to be in writing there is no necessity for its being written, while others believe that if a partnership agreement is not in writing it cannot be enforced.

In this connection it will, perhaps, not be amiss to quote the Statute of Frauds with relation to partnerships, and to illustrate its application by some particular case or cases.

The statute provision, commonly called "the fourth section of the Statute of Frauds," contains the following:

> No action shall be brought whereby to charge any executor or administrator upon any special promise to answer damages out of his own estate; or whereby to charge the defendant upon any special promise to answer for the debt, default, or miscarriage of another person; or to charge any person upon any agreement made in consideration of marriage; or upon any contract for sale of lands, tenements, or hereditaments or any interest in or concerning them; or upon any agreement that is not to be performed within the space of one year from the making thereof, unless the agreement upon which such action shall be brought or some memorandum or note thereof, shall be in writing and signed by the party to be charged therewith or some person thereunto by him lawfully authorized.

This statute had its origin in England as early as 1676, under the title, "An Act for the Prevention of Frauds and Perjuries," and its object was, as the heading suggests, to lessen the perjury in the testimony of witnesses. It is of importance not to misunderstand the statute; it does not render oral contracts void, but debars any action on them.   In other words, it takes away the remedy that an injured party would otherwise have.

Although the statute does not specifically refer to partnerships this is inferred from the clause relating to *agreements that are not to be performed within the space of one year.*   The following cases will illustrate that this inference is a correct one:

In Morris v. Peckham, 51 Conn. 128, plaintiff agreed orally to assign to defendant a one-half interest in an invention for making patent screw-drivers, upon the defendant's agreement to furnish the capital to procure the patent, and to purchase the machinery, stock, etc., and they were then to engage in manufacturing the screw-drivers.   After conducting the business one year defendant refused to continue and to furnish more funds. The plaintiff thereupon sued to compel specific performance of the partnership agreement, claiming that the partnership was to continue for seventeen years, the life of the patent, but the court held that such an agreement, not being by its terms to be performed within one year, is void under the Statute of Frauds, unless in writing.

Similarly in Wahl v. Barum, 116 N. Y. 87, the court held that a contract of partnership to continue for three years was void under the Statute of Frauds unless in writing.

Aside from the two ways of forming a partnership, oral or written, a partnership may in some cases be implied from transactions and relations although the term "partnership" has never been used, but from which the law will imply a partnership, whether it was so intended by the parties or not.   The following quotation, however, elucidates how far implication would be construed:

The intention of the parties will be determined from the effect of the whole contract regardless of special expressions, and if the actual relation which the parties have assumed towards each other, and the rights and obligations which have been created by them, are those of partners, the actual intention of the parties or their declared purpose, cannot suspend the consequences.   Even if the parties have used the word partnership in their contract and called themselves partners, this will not make them such if the contract is not consistent with such relation.— Bates on Partnerships.

As far as third parties (outsiders) are concerned, the mere passive acquiescence in presentation will suffice to establish partnership liabilities. This, however, is not the case between the parties themselves. The early test whether a partnership existed or not was sharing of profits, but now the intention of the parties governs. Whether a partnership relation was intended depends upon the facts in each case. In an action of Powell v. Moore, 79 Ga. 524, under circumstances noted below, it was held that this constituted a partnership as to third parties:

Powell and Marbut were doing business under the firm name of S. P. Marbut. Powell denied that he was a partner; his contribution to the firm property was the use of a dwelling, storehouse, and $200, which he called a loan, and Marbut contributed his time to the business and $200. No agreement was made as to the rent of the house or the interest on the money, but Powell was to receive one-half of the profits of the business as profit, and not as compensation for the use of the house and money.

On the other hand, in the case of Meehan v. Valentine, 145 U. S. 611, it was held that one who lends a sum of money to a partnership, under an agreement that in addition to the interest he is to receive thereon, he shall also be paid one-tenth of the yearly profits of the partnership business, if those exceed the sum lent, does not become liable as a partner for the debts of the firm.

Justice Gray in deciding the above case says: "In whatever form the rule is expressed, it is universally held that an agent or servant, whose compensation is measured by a certain proportion of the profits of the partnership business is not thereby made a partner in any sense. . . . And it is now equally well settled that the receiving of part of the profits of a commercial partnership in lieu of or in addition to interest, by way of compensation for a loan of money has of itself no greater effect."

In order to form a legal partnership relation the following elements are essential:

(a) An agreement (verbal or written).

(b) Competent parties to enter into the agreement. (Minors, aliens, insane persons, etc., are incompetent parties.)

(c) A lawful enterprise.

(d) Profit sharing as a motive.

With regard to (d) Justice Lindley, in his work on Partnerships, states the following:

Nothing, perhaps, can be said to be absolutely essential to the existence of a partnership except a community of interest in profits, resulting from an agreement to share them.

44. *Adjustment of partnership accounts.*—In no branch of accounting (executors' accounts excepted) is a knowledge of law so essential as in partnership affairs, especially in the adjustment of partnership accounts. From the formation to the dissolution one must necessarily be guided by the statutes. In order to carry out the exact intentions of the partners, it is necessary that there be a written rather than an oral agreement. While the "statute of frauds" requires the agreement to be in writing only when the partnership is to continue for more than one year, business men, however, recognize the necessity that such an agreement be in writing regardless of the time that the partnership is to last.

A drawback usually met in adjusting partnership accounts is that business men do not, at the formation of the partnership, provide sufficiently for the contingencies which may occur during the existence of the partnership or at its dissolution. The intention of the partners at the formation of the agreement is to be the sole guide in adjusting the partnership affairs, even though the wording may not warrant it, provided, of course, that it is for the benefit of the whole concern.

Lord Justice Lindley, in his work on "Partnership and Companies," says in regard to this:

In order to solve questions arising at an adjustment, regard must always be had to the terms of the partnership articles; but an expressed agreement with reference to the taking of accounts may be, and frequently is, only applicable to the case of a continuing partnership, and may not be intended to be observed on a final dissolution of the firm or even on the retirement of one of its members. . . . That which has been done for the purpose of sharing annual profits or losses is by no means necessarily a precedent to be followed when a partnership account is to be finally adjusted.

It must, however, be understood, that a verbal agreement is absolutely as binding as a written one, provided, of course, that it does not come within the limitations of the statute of frauds. However, disputes arising out of misunderstanding are not as frequent where written agreements exist.

45. *Various classes of partnerships.*—Partnerships may be divided into the following main classes, with proper subdivisions:

(1) General partnerships, subdivided as follows:
  (a) Trading partnerships, formed for the purpose of buying, vending, etc.
  (b) Non-trading partnerships, which do not buy, manufacture or vend as a principal part of their undertaking.

(2) Special partnerships, formed for special enterprise, such as: joint ventures or adventures.

(3) Mining partnerships; the chief feature of this class of partnerships is that while the co-owners are partners to the profits earned, the partnership does not extend to the property.

(4) Limited partnerships, formed only under special statutes; the dominant feature of this class of partnerships is that as long as certain of its members are inactive, their liability is limited to the amount actually invested by them.

(5) Joint stock companies; being ordinary partnerships with this distinction, however, that the members thereof may transfer their interests without dissolution of the firm, as proprietorship is proven by the possession of shares of stock similar to the shares of corporations.

46. *Kinds of partners.*—There are also various kinds of partners, and hence the difficulty arises as to who are partners.

The number of persons who may unite for the purpose of forming a partnership is not limited in any of the states, while in England the Limited Partnership Act of 1907 provides that the number of persons who may form either a "general" or "limited" partnership is restricted to ten in the case of a banking business, and to twenty in the case of any other business.

(1) Public or Ostensible Partner; an active and known member of the partnership.

(2) Secret Partner; although in reality a partner, he conceals the fact from the public.

(3) Nominal Partner; having no partnership relation with the other members of the firm, yet held forth as such by his own consent, because he has given his credit to the firm.

(4) Silent Partner; taking no active part in the business of the firm, but sharing profits.

(5) Dormant Partner; he is both unknown as a partner and inactive in the business.

(6) Special or Limited Partner; where the statute provides for limited partnerships, he contributes a certain sum of money and is not liable for the debts of the firm beyond the sum he contributed.

With regard to the last kind of partners mentioned, it is important to notice that no absolute immunity is assured in any event to the special partners in a limited partnership. These relations are the creations of statute, but the members are real partners, and by slight irregularities may become general partners. Great caution, therefore, should be observed in entering upon such relations, to see that due safeguards are taken in contracts of limited partnerships.

47. *Distinctive characteristics of partnerships.*—(1) Each partner is an agent for his co-partners in all the transactions falling within the scope of the partnership, and therefore, binds all the members of the firm to any contract he may enter.

(2) In the absence of an agreement to the contrary, each partner shares equally in the profits or losses of the business. The partnership investment does not determine the partners' interests in the business. There is no necessary relation between a partner's investment

and his participation in the profits or losses of the firm.

(3) In case of insolvency each partner is personally liable for the firm's obligations. It is in this most important feature that a partnership is so distinctly different from a corporation.

(4) All firm property, including goodwill or other intangible possessions, forms the common fund of the partnership. This is also true of any subsequent acquisitions of property with partnership funds.

(5) A new member cannot be introduced into the firm unless *all* partners agree to it. This is in fact the creation of a new partnership.

(6) A partner may on dissolution demand an accounting to ascertain his interests in the business.

(7) A partner cannot claim any interest either on his required investment, or on any excess, unless expressly so agreed. Nor can he claim any interests on profits left in the business.

(8) If a firm dissolves and no disposition is made as to the use of the firm's name, each partner has an equal right to its use, and may engage in business thereunder.

(9) Each partner has the same power over the property of the firm.

(10) A firm cannot hold real estate, as the law does not recognize it as a legal entity, capable of holding real property.

(11) A person who is admitted as a partner in an existing firm does not thereby become liable for debts incurred previous to his admission into the partnership.

(12) The retirement of a partner does not release him from debts of the firm incurred previous to his retirement. A retiring partner may be so released by an agreement between the new firm, the creditors, and him-

self. The assent of the creditors is important; such assent, however, may be implied and need not be expressly given.

(13) A retiring partner remains liable not only for existing debts, but may also be held liable for debts incurred after his retirement unless he has given due notice thereof to all those who had dealings with the firm.

(14) The acts of each partner, in the usual business relating to the firm, are the acts of all, even if contrary to the partnership agreement, unless the party with whom he is dealing has knowledge of his want of authority. Thus when a partner sells the goods of the firm, and misapplies the proceeds of the sale, he nevertheless gives a good title to the buyer.

(15) No services, ordinary or extraordinary, can be charged against the firm.

(16) A partner cannot bind the firm by a guarantee of the debt of a third person, unless such has been the practice of the firm.

In connection with the sixth essential mentioned above, there is an interesting case reported in *The Accountant's Journal,* Vol. XVIII, page 280. Briefly stated, the contents are as follows:

One of the members of a partnership, about to sell his interest in the firm of his co-partners, in order to determine the value of his share of interest in the business, demanded an investigation by a professional accountant, upon article 16 of their partnership agreement, which read:

Proper books of account shall be kept by the managing partners for the time being, in which all transactions relating to the partnership business shall be duly entered, and such books, together with all bills, letters, and other writings which shall from time to time reach the said partnership business, shall be kept at the counting house of the partnership, and each of the partners shall have free access, examine and copy, or take extracts from any of the books and writings of the partnership at all reasonable times.

This the co-partners refused, claiming that it was sufficient that the firm auditor should present proper statements, or that the partner himself, but not through a professional accountant, investigate and examine the correctness of the accounts. While the first court sustained the contention of the co-partners, stating that it was a novelty, the Court of Appeals reversed the decision, remarking:

When a right to do an act was conferred by a written instrument, in the absence of any limitation of the right to a merely personal right, it could not be said that the act might not be done by means of an agent.

48. *Provisions of English Partnership Acts.*—It may perhaps be interesting to note how favorably the English Partnership Acts of 1890, by which, in the absence of an agreement to the contrary, the rights, interest and duties of the partners are determined, compares with our laws. This act provides:

(1) Equal distribution of profits or contribution to losses.

(2) No interest payable in respect of capital, but interest allowed at 5 per cent on distinct advances.

(3) Every partner entitled to be indemnified in respect of payments properly made for the firm.

(4) No partner entitled to remuneration for his services.

(5) Every partner may take part in the management of the business.

(6) No person to be introduced as a partner without the consent of all the partners.

(7) Differences on ordinary matters to be decided by a majority of the partners, but no change to be made in the nature of the business without the consent of all the partners.

(8) Partnership books to be kept at the principal place of business and every partner to have access to them and a right to make copies thereof.

The difficulties attending a proper understanding of partnership arise mainly from the following causes:

(a) The nomenclature in connection with partnerships is used in ambiguous senses.

(b) Business men have a conception of partnership which is at variance with the legal decisions.

(c) In entering into partnership relations merchants do not sufficiently provide in their articles of co-partnership for the various contingencies which may arise during the existence of the partnership or at its dissolution.

49. *Business men's ideas of partnership.*—(1) The average merchant considers a partnership as an entity, a sort of corporation. To him the accounts of the partnership are always the accounts of the firm. He even regards the accounts of the individual partners as that of debtors or creditors of the firm.

(2) In his accounts he considers the firm always solvent, as the partners are sureties for its solvency.

(3) All the property contributed by each individual partner forever loses its separate ownership and belongs to the firm as a firm.

(4) He does not distinguish in his accounts between personal property, real estate, and personal accounts.

(5) To him the firm is perpetual, unless the in-

solvency of the members composing the firm render it impossible to continue the business.

(6) He believes that the firm may take in new partners or retire old ones without in any way destroying the firm entity.

(7) He believes that the courts should be open to settle all business disputes among the partners, without appointing a receiver to wind up the affairs of the partnership.

50. *Legal view of partnership.*—(1) According to the interpretation of the legal definition of partnerships, it has no survivorship as between the partners themselves, but has survivorship in regard to third persons.

(2) The ownership of the partnership property is a joint tenancy, e.g., each partner owns the whole of the partnership and therefore may dispose of it in any way he sees fit.

(3) The exact intention of the partners, although not exactly worded in the agreement, but shown by their continued approval, will control the provisions of the written articles.

(4) A person holding himself out as a partner or permitting his name to be used in a partnership becomes liable to third persons (outsiders), who may have been induced thereby to grant credit to the firm, provided, however, that the following three elements are present:

(a) Express or implied holding out.

(b) Reasonable reliance by the second party.

(c) Parting with value.

51. *Usual clauses in co-partnership articles.*—The usual clauses in articles of co-partnership are as follows:

1. Name of firm.
2. Place of business.
3. Nature of business.
4. Date of commencement and the duration of the partnership.
5. Capital to be invested.
6. Provision in regard to interest on capital invested, if such be agreed upon.
7. Provision in regard to sharing of profit or loss.
8. Provision in regard to withdrawals and how to treat them.
9. Provision in regard to admitting a new partner and how to adjust the affairs on admission; especially if the goodwill is to be taken into consideration.
10. Provision for the accurate keeping of records of all business transactions and the making of periodical balance sheets.
11. Provision for procedure in case of dissolution.

Professor Hardcastle, in his pamphlet on "Partnership," as well as in various articles upon this subject contributed by him from time to time, calls attention to certain points to be noted in drawing up articles of co-partnership, a summary of which follows:

IN GENERAL.

(1) That the partners shall be true and just to each other.

(2) That they shall diligently employ themselves, or apportion their services, deciding which shall take the managing part, and which the other parts.

(3) That they shall promptly communicate all partnership transactions to each other.

(4) That they shall not engage in any other business.

(5) That they shall employ the firm's property for the exclusive benefit of the firm.

(6) That they shall not engage the firm's credit for their private use.

(7) That they shall not buy any kind of merchandise or goods, beyond a certain amount, without the consent of the others.

(8) That they shall not transact any business that is against the wishes of the majority of the members composing the firm.

(9) Nor lend money of the firm.

(10) Nor file petitions in bankruptcy.

(11) Nor draw bills or accept drafts, except in the usual course of business.

(12) Nor extend excessive credit without the consent of the others.

(13) Nor speculate in stocks or otherwise, except in such speculations as pertain to the business.

(14) That they shall not become bondsmen or sureties.

(15) That they shall not assign their interests in the business.

(16) Nor withdraw their capital or any part thereof.

(17) Nor do anything by which the firm's property may be taken in execution.

ACCOUNTING CLAUSES.

(18) That proper books of entry be kept.

(19) That the entries be made by each partner.

(20) That the books and partnership documents be kept at the place of business and be open for the inspection of all the partners.

(21) That the books be kept under the direction of the acting partner.

(22) That all checks, drafts, acceptances, etc., be signed by the acting partner, except in the case of his sickness or absence.

(23) That all drafts, acceptances, or securities be made and taken in the name of the firm.

(24) That real estate purchased be bought by the acting partner in trust for the firm.

(25) That the (give name) bank be used by the firm.

(26) That the cashbook be made up . . . (state time—monthly, quarterly, etc.).

(27) That the cash collected be deposited daily.

(28) That all moneys received by each partner be duly paid in.

(29) That a general accounting be made yearly or half-yearly.

(30) That the inventory and the balance sheet be signed by each partner and be conclusive.

(31) That the ledger, among other accounts, shall contain

    (a) An account for each partner's partnership obligations, which shall be debited with the amount the partner obligates himself to put in the business, and credited with what he actually puts in.

    (b) A drawing account for each partner to keep separately his withdrawals.

    (c) If there be advances made by any partner to the firm as a temporary loan, an account should be kept under the title "A. B.'s Loan to Firm Account."

    (d) Before a division of profits be declared the

profit and loss account shall be debited with say 10 per cent on diminishing balances on the fixed capital subject to depreciation, and depreciation account to be credited with same. The depreciation account shall in the balance sheet be always treated as an offset to the fixed capital subject to depreciation.

(e) There shall also be two reserve accounts—one, the reserve accounts for doubtful debts, and the other the general reserve account. The former shall be credited with . . . per cent of the debts due the firm and remaining unpaid at the time of closing up the accounts, as a contingent fund to meet bad debts; and the latter, the general reserve account, shall be credited with . . . per cent of the balance remaining in the profit and loss, and the profit and loss account debited.

(f) Extraordinary profits and losses, i. e., such as do not usually occur, but are accidental, shall, as they arise, be carried to the general reserve account. The remaining profit and loss should now be duly divided and carried into each partner's drawing account (credit side). This drawing account to be then closed and balance carried to each partner's capital account.

52. *Explanation of "goodwill."*—The goodwill of a firm, under which commonly is meant the benefit arising from the connection and reputation of the firm be it personal or trade, passes with a sale of the business as a whole to the vendee. The contract of sale may not specify this, but it is impliedly assumed.

In drawing up articles of co-partnership, care must be taken with regard to the clause treating of goodwill. In a recent English case (Smith v. Nelson) on account of a poorly constructed clause in the partnership agreement, it was decided that the outgoing partner was not entitled to anything for goodwill.

It is needless, perhaps, to say that the subject of goodwill will arise only when a business is bought outright or a new partner is admitted. It is absurd for a merchant to assume that the goodwill of his business has any value unless he has paid for such goodwill; yet there are merchants that think that goodwill should be valued in the yearly business statements of the partnership. The following case will illustrate this extreme and also the court's ruling on this false notion.

The case mentioned is Stewart v. Gladstone (England, 1897) and relates to the making out of annual accounts. A clause in their articles of co-partnership stated that the annual accounts were to comprise "all particulars that might be susceptible of valuation," and the contention of one of the partners was that it included goodwill also. The presiding justice remarked:

> Then is it a fair construction of these articles to assume that, in taking the annual accounts of the profits of the concern, the partners were going to put a value upon the goodwill, so as to allow each partner to take year by year out of the partnership the amount of his share of the increase in the value of the goodwill? That is really what it comes to. Now one cannot help feeling that no mercantile man ever dreamt of such a thing. The goodwill is not an available asset in the sense that you can draw upon it, or that you can turn it into money, or pay it out to the partners, and I should say with some confidence, not only relying upon my own experience, but having appealed to the

Bar in this case, that no one ever saw such a thing in a merchant's accounts.

.While it is quite common to list an immaterial asset in a business statement, there is no doubt that such listing of a non-existing or overvalued goodwill is not only immaterial, but imaginary. From the viewpoint of accounting, there is no more justification for such a procedure than there is for listing any asset which has no existence.

In the case of Camden v. Stuart, 144 U. S. 104, the United States Supreme Court held that goodwill is a legitimate asset where it is *actually existent,* but it must not be something shadowy; it must be capable of pecuniary estimation.

In this connection it is worthy of notice that often the question arises whether goodwill, after having once been properly entered in the book at its cost price, should be continued at that figure, or whether it should be periodically revalued or written off. Opinions differ as to the course to be pursued. Pixley, Cooper and Guthrie represent a type of English accountants who favor regularly writing off the goodwill placed on the books; while Dicksee, Caldocott and James, representing another type of English accountants, argue that it be continned at its original figure regardless of changes in its pecuniary value. It is, perhaps, better to follow the former class and write off, considering it as a kind of premium paid for the privilege of earning profits.

53. *Definition of partnership settlement.*—What has already been remarked about partnerships should serve as a guide to a careful understanding of the intricate and peculiar relation in which one places himself by forming a partnership. The sole object of its existence being to make and share profits, it necessarily follows

that the difficulties that partners may encounter will not be so much in the management of affairs, nor in the over-extension of credits by one or another of the partners, as in the settlement of their own accounts, that is, partnership settlements. By partnership settlement we mean the adjustment of the financial standing of partners at the close of business, e.g., finding the monetary value of net capital or net insolvency of each partner at the time the statement is made, and the adjustment thereof on the books of account. That is the time when trouble arises, especially when there are losses. In most of the partnership agreements the legal points are the only ones that are, to some extent, well taken care of, while the business points are nearly always lacking.

Only in exceptional cases, does a partnership agreement contain proper accounting clauses. Yet any accountant can recall numerous confusions that are caused by not having a proper opening entry at the formation of a partnership—an entry which should embody all the essential features of the agreement as far as the account-keeping is concerned.

The books of account should show the proper valuation of existing assets at the time of the formation of the partnerships; otherwise the firm is likely to have imaginary profits, as is illustrated in the case of Robinson v. Ashton, L. R. 20 Eq. 28. The court said:

> In the absence of special agreement, the rise or fall in the value of fixed capital or real estate belonging to a partnership is as much profit or loss of the partnership as anything else.

The absurdity of such a decision is self-evident. We can not show any profit or loss not actually realized on our books, because we can not show anything that is not a fact, unless a trade has been made. To illustrate the preposterousness of such reasoning we will take the following instance:

A is in partnership with B, and on January 1, 1907, they buy a parcel of real estate for $5,000.00. In December, 1907, when closing their books, this parcel is worth only $3,000.00. Their profit and loss account will have to show a loss of $2,000.00. Next year the value of real estate rises to $8,000.00, showing a profit for this year of $5,000.00. Offsetting the loss of $2,000.00 of last year against the gain of $5,000.00 of this year, there still remains an *imaginary* net profit of $3,000.00. In accordance with the above quoted decision, if there were no other profits or losses, and A, would, at this stage, desire to retire from the partnership, he would be entitled to $1,500.00, his equal share of the profits; while as a matter of fact there was no profit at all. There can not be a profit or a loss made, unless there is a purchase and a sale.

54. *General miscomprehension of financial statements.*—Perhaps one of the greatest drawbacks in partnerships is the fact that business men often misunderstand financial and business statements; first, because of a lack of knowledge of the nomenclature of the statements and their exact meaning; second, because of incomplete articles of co-partnership. Thus they often say that they have an interest in a business. This may mean that they have an interest in the capital as having loaned money, or that they have an interest in the profits as part of their salaries. It may also, and most of the time does, mean an interest in both capital and profits, as partners. Agreements with employés are quite often drawn loosely and it is difficult to determine whether the employé is a partner or not.

Business men, sometimes at least, do not quite comprehend what are and what are not profits. To some merchants the term depreciation is strange, and, consequently, is never used in connection with their profit and loss statements. This is true not only of business men but also of our attorneys. In the case of Eyster v. Centennial Board of Finance, 94 U. S. 503, the Supreme Court of the United States decided that profits are receipts over expenditures, with no consideration given to depreciation. This decision strongly illustrates how far behind we are in our laws, so far as proper accounting of depreciation is concerned, especially so in this particular case, as the buildings had very little value after the exhibition.

Most of our court decisions are based on confused terminology. In one case, for instance, the court decided that all debts must be paid before the profits can be ascertained—a notion that is not only absurd to the accountant, but is against common sense.

Some merchants, on the other hand, go to the other extreme, believing that a financial statement is an absolute exhibition of the exact status of the firm, at the time it is prepared; a fallacy also due perhaps to the terminology. It is interesting to note that Dicksee, in this connection says: "A balance sheet is not a statement of fact, but rather an expression of opinion." Rehm, in this connection is also of the same opinion; he states: "Not more than 10 per cent of the items in any average balance sheet are or can possibly be facts that are capable of being absolutely tested."

55. *Advantages of a fixed rate of interest on capital.* —It is advisable that a fixed rate of interest be charged per annum in respect of capital employed in the business. This is based on the assumption that the money if employed somewhere else would earn a similar rate of

interest.   Where there are few partners it gives to those holding the larger proportion of capital an advantage prior to the division of profits.   Where the capital invested by each partner is fixed and the share of profits is in exact proportion to the capital, the effect of charging interest will make no difference with the final amount which will be credited to each partner.   Nevertheless it is advisable to follow this rule so as to provide for all happenings and to distribute to interest its share, aside from profits.

The effect of an omission to charge interest on capital is as follows: (1) If the capital contributed by each partner is equal, but if they share profits unequally, the partner entitled to the smaller share will lose.   (2) If the profits are shared equally, but the capital contributed is unequal, the partner with the larger amount invested will lose.

Where partners by their partnership agreement are entitled to salaries in lieu of services to the firm, such salaries should be charged to the profit and loss account and credited to the partners' current or drawing account. If it is paid regularly in cash, it should be charged directly as an expense item or to some other proper nominal account.

56. *Treatment of partnership accounts.*—The treatment of partnership accounts does not materially differ from the general principles that are applied to a business carried on by a single individual.   Each partner's account is treated separately; e.g., each is credited for his share of investment in the enterprise.   Profits or losses at the end of a given period are adjusted and carried to the partners' accounts in accordance with their partnership agreement.   The excess of the assets over the liabilities at any time still represents proprietorship,

with this distinction, however, that the transactions between the business proper and its partners must also be taken into consideration.

57. *Illustration of division of profits in proportion to the capital invested and the time such capital has been employed.*—

PROBLEM I.

McDonald and Smith form a co-partnership January 2, 1908, each investing $7,500.00. March 1, Smith makes an additional investment of $2,400.00 and McDonald withdraws $1,200.00. July 1, McDonald invests $2,500.00 and Smith withdraws $2,500.00. Profits for the year are $4,800.00. Show each partner's average investment and share of profits, the latter being divided in proportion to the capital invested and the time it is employed.

SOLUTION.

It will be noticed that the problem calls for two things; the average investment of each partner and the share of profits due each partner. On page 174 it will be seen that the average investment of McDonald was $7,750.00. As the investment and withdrawals were by months, we reduce the entire operation to months, basing the calculations on the interest that the money would earn, thus: the interest on $7,500.00 for twelve months would be the equivalent of the interest on $90,000.00 for one month. The interest on $2,500.00 for six months is equivalent to the interest on $15,000.00 for one month. That gives us a gross product for the credit side, amounting to $105,000.00, from which we deduct the

McDONALD.

January 2, 1908	Investment	$7,500 × 12 = 90,000.
July 1, 1908	"	2,500 × 6 = 15,000. 105,000.
March 1, 1908	Withdrawals	1,200 × 10 = 12,000. 93,000.

93,000 ÷ 12 = $7,750.00 average investment.

SMITH.

January 2, 1908	Investment	7,500 × 12 = 90,000.
March 1, 1908	"	2,400 × 10 = 24,000. 114,000.
July 1, 1908	Withdrawals	2,500 × 6 = 15,000. 99,000.

99,000 ÷ 12 = $8,250.00 average investment.

McDonald's share of investment .... $= \dfrac{93,000}{192,000} = \dfrac{31}{64}$ of profits $4,800 = $2,325.00.

Smith's share of investment ... . $= \dfrac{99,000}{192,000} = \dfrac{33}{64}$ of profits $4,800 = $2,475.00.

or

$7,750.00 + $8,250.00 = 16,000.00 ∴ 4,800.00 ÷ 16,000 = 30% return on investment.

174

McDONALD'S CAPITAL ACCOUNT.

March 1, 1908, Cash withdrawals ...	$1,200.00	January 2, 1908, Cash investment ...		$7,500.00
January 1, 1909, Balance ...	11,125.00	July 1, 1908, Cash investment		2,500.00
		January 1, 1909, Profit		2,325.00
	$12,325.00			$12,325.00
		January 1, 1909, Balance ...	..	$11,125.00

SMITH'S CAPITAL ACCOUNT.

March 1, 1908, Cash withdrawals ...	$2,500.00	January 2, 1908, Cash investment ...		$7,500.00
January 1, 1909, Balance ...	9,875.00	March 1, 1908, Cash investment ...		2,400.00
		January 1, 1909, Profit		2,475.00
	$12,373.00			$12,373.00
		January 1, 1909, Balance ...	.	$9,875.00

product of the withdrawals $12,000.00, showing the average product of the investment to be $93,000.00. This product we divide by the number of months in operation (12) and it gives us an average investment of $7,750.00. The same process we follow in Smith's account. We find, however, that his average investment was $8,250.00. As the combined investment was $16,000.00 and the profits earned for the year were $4,800.00, dividing the amount of the profits by the combined average investment, we find that the return on the capital was 30 per cent. Thirty per cent of $7,750.00 (McDonald's investment) gives $2,325.00, which is his share of the profits, and 30 per cent of $8,250.00 gives $2,475.00, or Smith's share of profits.

This completed, we show McDonald's and Smith's respective capital accounts. After crediting them for their share of profits we show the balance or the present worth of the respective accounts at the beginning of the new period.

PROBLEM II.

58. *Preparation of partnership accounts.*—From the following trial balance of the books of James and Herbert taken on December 31, 1907, and other information given, prepare: (a) Trading account, showing in concise form the gross results in each department; (b) profit and loss account; (c) balance sheet.

TRIAL BALANCE.

Cash	$ 90.00	
Notes receivable	1,250.00	
Accounts receivable	27,500.00	
Furniture and fixtures	2,250.00	
Notes payable		3,600.00
Accounts payable		10,000.00
Inventory on Jan. 1, 1907, dept. A.	12,500.00	
Inventory on Jan. 1, 1907, dept. B.	8,000.00	
Inventory on Jan. 1, 1907, dept. C.	9,000.00	
Purchases, dept. A.	37,000.00	

Purchases, dept. B.	10,500.00	
Purchases, dept. C.	13,500.00	
Bank overdrafts		2,800.00
Sales, dept. A.		43,500.00
Sales, dept. B.		13,750.00
Sales, dept. C.		16,500.00
Wages, dept. A.	1,750.00	
Wages, dept. B.	750.00	
Wages, dept. C.	950.00	
Trade expense	1,500.00	
Office salaries	2,250.00	
Rent, taxes and insurance	1,300.00	
Bad debts	430.00	
Discounts allowed customers	630.00	
D. James, capital account		25,000.00
W. Herbert, capital account		20,000.00
D. James, drawing account	2,500.00	
W. Herbert, drawing account	1,500.00	
	$135,150.00	$135,150.00

The inventory of goods on hand on December 31, 1907, is as follows:

Department A	$15,000.00
Department B	9,000.00
Department C	8,000.00

During the year goods were transferred from Department A to Department B at cost price amounting to $1,000.00; also to Department C at cost price amounting to $750.00, neither of these transfers being through the books. Discount on customers' accounts has to be allowed at 2 per cent on the amount outstanding. A reserve of $500.00 is to be set aside for doubtful and bad debts. Depreciation at the rate of 10 per cent is to be written off on furniture and fixtures. There is accrued rent amounting to $100.00. Each partner is entitled to interest on his capital at the rate of 4 per cent (interest on drawings being ignored) after which the profit is to be divided in proportion to the capital as stated in the trial balance.

TRADING ACCOUNT OF THE FIRM OF JAMES AND HERBERT FOR THE YEAR ENDING DECEMBER 31, 1907.

Debit Side:

	Dept. A.	Dept. B.	Dept. C.	Total.
To inventory January 1, 1907	$12,500.00	$8,000.00	$9,000.00	
Purchases during the year	33,000.00	10,500.00	13,500.00	
	49,500.00	18,500.00	22,500.00	
Deduct inventory on hand December 31, 1907	15,000.00	9,000.00	8,000.00	
	34,500.00	9,500.00	14,500.00	
Transfer during the year from Department A to B at cost	1,000.00	1,000.00		
	33,500.00	10,500.00	14,500.00	
Transfer during the year from Department A to C at cost	750.00		750.00	
	32,750.00	10,500.00	15,250.00	
Wages	1,750.00	750.00	950.00	$61,950.00
Gross profit	9,000.00	2,500.00	300.00	11,800.00
	$43,500.00	$13,750.00	$16,500.00	$73,750.00

Credit Side:

	Dept. A.	Dept. B.	Dept. C.	Total.
By sales during the year	$43,500.00	$13,750.00	$16,500.00	$73,750.00
	$43,500.00	$13,750.00	$16,500.00	$73,750.00

PROFIT AND LOSS ACCOUNT OF THE FIRM JAMES AND HERBERT FOR THE YEAR ENDING DECEMBER 31, 1907.

To trade expenses		$1,500.00		By gross profit on trading, viz:	
Office salaries		2,250.00		Department A.	$9,000.00
Rent, taxes and insurance	$1,300.00			Department B.	2,500.00
Accrued rent	100.00	1,400.00		Department C.	300.00 $11,800.00
Bad debts		430.00			
Depreciation on furniture and fixtures (10%)		225.00			
Ordinary business profit		5,995.00			
		$11,800.00			$11,800.00
To discount allowed customers	630.00			By ordinary business profit ..	5,995.00
Reserve for discount on outstanding accounts (2%)	550.00	1,180.00			
Balance carried down to appropriation account		4,815.00			
		5,995.00			$5,995.00

PROFIT AND LOSS APPROPRIATION ACCOUNT.

To reserve for bad and doubtful debts		$500.00
Interest on capital:		
D. James 4% on 25,000.00	$1,000.00	
W. Herbert 4% on 20,000.00 ..	800.00	1,800.00
Net profit allocated as per partnership provision, viz:		
D. James ⅔ of profits	1,397.22	
W. Herbert ⅘ of profits	1,117.78	2,515.00
		$4,815.00
By balance brought down from profit and loss account		$4,815.00
		$4,815.00

BALANCE SHEET OF THE FIRM JAMES AND HERBERT AS ON DECEMBER 31, 1907.

ASSETS:

Cash			$90.00
Notes receivable		$1,250.00	
Accounts receivable	$27,500.00		
Less reserve for bad debts	500.00	26,450.00	27,700.00
Reserve for discount	550.00	1,050.00	
Inventory			32,000.00
Furniture and fixtures		2,250.00	
Less reserve for depreciation		225.00	2,025.00
			$61,815.00

LIABILITIES:

Bank overdrafts		$2,800.00
Notes payable	$3,600.00	
Accounts payable	10,000.00	13,600.00
Accrued rent		100.00

PROPRIETORSHIP.

D. James	24,897.22	
W. Herbert	20,417.78	45,315.00
		$61,815.00

59. *Analysis of transactions.*—In this problem we are asked for a trading account to show in concise form the gross results in each department, for a profit and loss account and a balance sheet.

In order to make the trading account show the gross result in each department we columnarize the trading account, heading it department A, B and C, and make a separate column for the totals. The debit side of this account, as shown on page 178, gives, first, the prime cost of the goods sold, after deducting the inventory. The transfers made from one department to another are then adjusted, showing a total cost to Department A of $32,750.00, Department B $10,500.00 and Department C $15,250.00. To these sums we add the wages expended respectively in each department making a total of $61,950.00.

On the credit side of the trading account, on page 178, we have the sales during the year for each department, making a total of $73,750.00. Subtracting the cost, as shown on debit side, from the sales, shown on the credit, there is a gross profit of $11,800.00. The proportion of profit for each department, as shown on the same page, is $9,000 for department A; $2,500 for Department B and $300 for Department C.

In our profit and loss account, page 179, we enter on the credit side the gross profit of trade $11,800.00 and charge against this on the debit side all expenses of general administration, leaving a balance of $5,995.00, which is ordinary business profit.

It will be noticed that the item "accrued rent $100.00" is added to the amount shown in the trial balance, as per instructions in the problem, and that 10 per cent has been charged off for depreciation on furniture and fixtures.

We then carry this ordinary business profit to credit side of the following section in the profit and loss account, against which is charged the discount allowed to customers as well as reserve for discount on outstanding accounts. The balance of $4,815.00 is carried down to the appropriation account.

That reserve for discount mentioned in the former paragraph is used for the purpose of burdening each respective period for its share of loss. Thus, if no reserve for discount were provided, the discount that the customers might deduct at the next period, and which represents transactions of a former period, would be charged against that next period. This second period, therefore, would be charged with the discount of the former as well as with that of the current period. To avoid this, a reserve for discounts is provided and all of those deducted that applied to the former period are charged against that reserve, while the discounts of the current period are charged against the discount lost account.

The next account, given on page 180, is the profit and loss appropriation account or that section of the profit and loss account which shows the allocation of profits.

On the credit side of this account there is the balance brought down from the profit and loss account, viz., $4,815.00. We allocate this profit by charging against it the reserve for bad debts $500.00, as explained in the problem. We also charge against it the interest on capital invested. The total of such charges is $2,300.00, which, deducted from the balance on the credit side, leaves a net profit of $2,515.00 for division among the partners. As profit and loss is to be apportioned in accordance with the capital stated in the trial balance,

James is entitled to 25/45 or to $1,397.22 and Herbert to 20/45 or $1,117.78.

Having completed that part of the work the results shown must be verified and a balance sheet prepared, as shown on page 181.   After deducting all reserves, the assets are all stated at net value, making a total of $61,815.00.   The liabilities are all given, including ac-'erued liabilities and the total amounts $16,500.00.   The balance of $45,315.00 represents the proprietorship. That is made up of James' capital in the business amounting to $24,897.22; viz., his original investment, $25,000.00, to which is added $1,397.22 profits and $1,000.00 credited for interest, making a total of $27,-397.22.   From this sum his withdrawal of $2,500.00 is deducted.   It further consists of Herbert's capital in the business amounting to $20,417.78; viz., his original investment $20,000.00, to which is added $1,117.78 profits and $800.00 for interest on investment, making a total of $21,917.78.   From this sum is deducted his withdrawal of $1,500.00.

CHAPTER VIII

PARTNERSHIP DISSOLUTION

60. *Reasons for dissolution of a partnership.*—Having dealt more or less with the principles governing the formation of partnerships and having also treated of the principles of bookkeeping in general, there is no necessity for going any further into the details of the mechanism of actual business operations, as these will vary according to the line of business.

The adjustment of partnership accounts is the fundamental principle of all partnership dealings and therefore some space must be devoted to this part of our subject.

A partnership may be dissolved for one of the following reasons:

(1) Expiration of the time originally fixed for the continuation or by completion of the act for which the partnership was created.

(2) Later agreement, annulling the first agreement by which the partnership was created.

(3) The objects of the partnership becoming illegal or impossible.

(4) Assignment of a partner's interest, unless it be with the consent of all partners. (Partnership being a personal relation, only the parties that originally entered into that relation can continue, but they cannot assign any of their interests without the other partners' consent.)

(5) Death of any one of the partners.

(6) Other occurrences, while not dissolving the firm, *ipso facto,* give the right to certain partners to dissolve, if they so desire. Such cases are: insolvency or bankruptcy of one or more partners; insanity; etc.

61. *Application of partnership assets after a dissolution.*—In adjusting accounts of partners, losses are to be made good, first, out of profits of the firm, next out of capital of the firm and finally by the partners individually contributing to the deficit, according to their respective shares.

The assets of a partnership are, at a dissolution, to be applied as follows: (1) firm debts to outsiders, (2) advances on loans made by the partners to the firm, (3) settlement of capital, (4) ultimate residue, if any, to be divided as profits in accordance with the terms of the partnership agreement for sharing the profit and loss. If there be no agreement to this effect, then equally.

That in the absence of an agreement for sharing profits and losses such profits or losses are to be divided equally we infer from the wording of the statutes of the various states, which in substance is as follows (New York):

A partnership as between the members thereof is an association, not incorporated, of two or more persons who have agreed to combine their labor, property and skill, or some of them, for the purpose of engaging in any lawful trade or business and sharing the profits and losses as well between them.

62. *Illustration of the adjustment of partnership accounts.*—The points connected with an adjustment will most clearly be brought out by an illustration. Dicksee in his "Advanced Accounting" does not recommend that the books of a partnership concern be kept by the single-entry method. Yet, as such cases frequently arise, he

gives the following interesting problem, showing how the adjustment should be made. It is needless to say that the monetary system as well as some of the details have been changed and modified, in order to adapt the problem to American readers:

On December 31, 1901, A's liabilities amounted to $10,-000.00, and his assets to $17,000.00. On January 1, 1902, he admitted B into partnership on the terms that A's capital was to be agreed at $7,500.00; that B should not be called upon to find any capital; that profits should be divided between the partners in the proportions of two-thirds to A, and one-third to B; that B's drawings should be limited to $2,000.00 a year until such time as A had been paid the premium which it was agreed that he should receive in consideration of the partnership. This premium was fixed at $2,875.00, to be paid from year to year out of the excess of B's share of profits over his drawings, interest at the rate of 5% per annum, being charged by A on the balance outstanding from time to time. The firm kept their books by single-entry, but statements of their assets and liabilities were prepared at the end of each year as follows:—

Time	Assets	Liabilities
1902 ....\$26,500.00		\$18,000.00
1903 .... 20,000.00		12,000.00
1904 .... 26,000.00		17,500.00
1905 .... 33,500.00		16,000.00
1906 .... 30,000.00		15,000.00

A's drawings during the five years were as follows:
1902	....\$3,625.00
1903	.... 4,250.00
1904	.... 5,000.00
1905	.... 5,000.00
1906	.... 8,000.00

SOLUTION

Statement of Affairs (Condensed) 1902–1906.

Liabilities side

	1906	1905	1904	1903	1902
LIABILITIES Balance down (being Capital of the firm at close of the year)	$15,000.00	$16,000.00	$17,500.00	$12,000.00	$18,000.00
	15,000.00	17,500.00	8,500.00	8,000.00	8,500.00
	$30,000.00	$33,500.00	$26,500.00	$20,000.00	$26,500.00
Capital at commencement of the year	$17,500.00	$8,500.00	$8,000.00	$8,500.00	$7,500.00
Interest on Capital	875.00	425.00	400.00	425.00	375.00
Balance (net profit)	6,625.00	15,575.00	7,100.00	5,325.00	6,250.00
	$25,000.00	$24,500.00	$15,500.00	$14,250.00	$14,125.00
Division of above profits: A	$ 4,416.67	$10,383.34	$ 4,733.34	$ 3,550.00	$ 4,166.67
B	2,208.33	5,191.66	2,366.66	1,775.00	2,083.33

Assets side

	1902	1903	1904	1905	1906
ASSETS	$26,500	$20,000	$26,500	$33,500	$30,000
	$26,500	$20,000	$26,300	$33,500	$30,000
Bal. carried down	$ 8,500	$ 8,000	$ 8,500	$17,500	$15,000
A's withdrawals	3,625	4,250	5,000	5,000	8,000
B's withdrawals	2,000	2,000	2,000	2,000	2,000
	$14,125	$14,250	$15,500	$24,500	$25,000

A'S CAPITAL ACCOUNT (Condensed)

Dr.

	1902	1903	1904	1905	1906
To drawings	$ 3,625.00	$ 4,250.00	$ 5,000.00	$5,000.00	$ 8,000.00
To balance; Dec. 31....	8,500.00	8,225.00	8,500.00	17,500.00	14,864.67
	$12,125.00	$12,475.00	$13,500.00	$22,500.00	$22,864.67

Cr.

	1902	1903	1904	1905	1906
By balance Jan. 1......	$ 7,500.00	$ 8,500.00	$ 8,225.00	$ 8,500.00	$17,500.00
By interest on capital.	375.00	425.00	411.25	425.00	875.00
By share of profits.....	4,166.67	3,550.00	4,733.34	10,383.34	4,416.67
By transfer from B. on account of goodwill...	83.33	......	130.41	3,191.66	73.00
	$12,125.00	$12,475.00	$13,500.00	$22,500.00	$22,864.67

1907, Jan. 1, By balance.................$14,864.67

189

B'S CAPITAL ACCOUNT (Condensed)

Dr.

	1902	1903	1904	1905	1906
To bal. Jan. 1	......	......	$225.00	......	......
To withdrawals	$2,000.00	$2,000.00	2,000.00	2,000.00	$2,000.00
To int. on overdraft	......	......	11.25	......	......
To transfer to A	83.33	......	130.41	3,191.66	73.00
To bal Dec. 31					135.33
	$2,083.33	$2,000.00	$2,366.66	$5,191.66	$2,208.33

Cr.

	1902	1903	1904	1905	1906
By Share of profits	$2,083.33	$1,775.00	$2,366.66	$5,191.66	$2,208.33
To bal. Dec. 31	......	225.00			......
	$2,083.33	$2,000.00	$2,366.66	$5,191.66	$2,208.33
Jan. 1, 1907 By bal	......	......	......	......	$ 135.33

B" IN %c WITH "A" IN RESPECT OF GOODWILL (Condensed)

Dr.

	1902	1903	1904	1905	1906
To agreed premium.	$2,875.00	....	....	....	....
To balance Jan. 1....		$2,935.42	$3,082.19	$3,105.89	69.52
To int. for the year..	143.75	146.77	154.11	155.29	3.48
	$3,018.75	$3,082.19	$3,236.30	$3,261.18	$73.00

Cr.

	1902	1903	1904	1905	1906
By amount credited as paid on account..	$83.33	....	$130.41	$3,191.66	$73.00
By balance Dec. 31....	2,935.42	$3,082.19	3,105.89	69.52	....
	$3,018.75	$3,082.19	$3,236.30	$3,261.18	$73.00

B drew out only his agreed maximum of $2,000.00. Required to show (*a*) the capital accounts of the partners for the five years, allowing interest at the rate of 5% per annum, and (*b*) a statement showing the account between A and B, in respect of goodwill.

Solution given on pages 188–191.

Problems of this kind are rather troublesome to solve, as the smallest error vitiates the figures of every subsequent year. It is best, therefore, to complete the statement of affairs for the whole period before attempting to compile the capital accounts of the partners. These should then be compiled, taking care to see that the closing balances added together agree each year with the total capital of the firm, as shown in the statement of affairs.

The account of B with A in respect to goodwill is compiled as a memorandum in order to know, from time to time, the amount due from "B" to "A" in respect of goodwill, and also to know when the whole amount is cleared off; but it cannot be included in the books of the firm.

PROBLEM II.

The following problem in partnership settlement is a quasi-partnership agreement between an employer and employé by which, in addition to salary, such employé is to receive a certain percentage of profits, if such profits reach a certain minimum sum. The problem reads thus:

On January 1, 1908, F. Mathews engaged J. Phillips as bookkeeper on the following conditions:

(1) Phillips is to keep the books and manage the sales department.

(2) He is to get a fixed salary of $75 per month.

(3) If the sales average $8,000 per month, Phillips is to receive 10% of the net profits.

(4) If the sales average $12,000 per month and 18% is cleared, Phillips is to receive 15% of the net profits.

(5) If the sales average $15,000 and 20% is cleared, Phillips is to receive 18% of the net profits.

(6) The sales must average as much as $8,000 per month in order to entitle Phillips to share in the profits. Phillips' salary is to be deducted with the other expenses of operation before the profits are allocated. It is on the remainder of profit (net profit) that the percentage earned is to be calculated.

(7) Discounts allowed or received are not to be considered. On August 15, 1908, the business was closed, and an extract of the books reveals the following condition:

Merchandise on hand January 1, 1908...$ 3,765.89

Purchases to August 15, 1908.......... 84,210.00

Sales to August 15, 1908.............. 96,048.00

Inventory August 15, 1908............ 2,089.48

General expenses 4,290.45

Cash discounts allowed................ 315.86

Cash discounts received............... 875.19

Bookkeeper's salary paid up to August 1, 1908.

It is desired to find the balance due to Phillips on final settlement, August 15, 1908.

STATEMENT OF PROFITS AND PERCENTAGE OF PROFITS FOR
PURPOSE OF DETERMINING PHILLIPS'
SHARE OF PROFITS.

Net profits as shown by profit and loss account $5,867.97

Less difference between discount allowed and discount received, viz.:

Discount received ....$875.19 less

Discount allowed 315.86   559.33

$5,308.64

Dividing the cost of goods sold into the profit realized we arrive at % .0618+.

III—13

SOLUTION

Profit and Loss Account, for the period January 1, to August 15, 1908

To inventory (January 1)............	$ 3,765.89			
Purchases..........................	84,210.00			
	$87,975.89		By sales.....	$96,048.00
Less inventory (August 15).....	2,089.48			
		$85,886 41		
Gross profit.................		10,161 59		
		$96,048 00		$96,048.00
To general expenses...........	$4,290.45		By gross profit.....	$10,161.59
Bookkeeper's salary paid.....	$525.00			
Bookkeeper's salary due........	37.50			
		562 50		
Ordinary business profit.....		5,308 64		
		$10,161.59		$10,161.59
To discounts allowed.....		$315 86	By ordinary business profit....	$5,308 64
Net profit...........		5,867 97	Discounts received.......	875 19
		$6,183 83		$6,183.83

In accordance with the original agreement, Phillips cannot claim a share of the profits as per clause 4, but only as per clause 3, because, although the sales average more than $12,000 per month, the profit cleared does not reach the minimum percentage required.

The sum due Phillips is as follows:

One-half month's salary ($75 per month)...$ 37.50

10% of net profits ($5,308.64)........... 530.86

$568.36

PROBLEM III.

63. *Adjustment of partnership affairs, on the retirement of a partner.*—A, B, C and D, were partners having a partnership agreement in writing which provided among the ordinary clauses usually found in partnership agreements the following special provisions:—(1) The capital of the firm is to be $100,000.00 and is to be contributed by the members, as follows: A one-half, B one-fourth, C one-fifth and D one-twentieth. (2) Interest is to be allowed at the rate of 6 per cent per annum on any amount contributed by a member of the firm in excess of the required investment and charged on any deficiencies. (3) No extra withdrawals are to be made by any partner except the salary allowance mentioned below. (4) Each partner is to be allowed a yearly salary, which he may withdraw monthly or otherwise: namely, A $3,500.00, B $2,500.00, C $2,000.00, and D $1,000.00. Such salary allowance is to be credited at the end of the year to the drawing account of each partner—an offset against his monthly withdrawals of such salary. (5) All adjustments among the partners, for interest on capital, drawings, etc., are to be made at the end of each year after the trial balance of the ledger accounts has been taken. The amounts appearing on the trial balance with all the other necessary data for such adjustments is to be the basis of the settlement. (6) In case of the retirement of one or more of the members of the firm, such member is to be entitled, in addition to the amount appearing on the credit side of his ledger account, to goodwill. The valuation of the goodwill is to be one-half the sum of the last two years' net profits of the business for each retiring member. (7) Profits and losses are to be divided as follows: A, 50 per cent; B, 25 per cent; C, 15 per cent; D, 10 per cent.

64. *Preparation of necessary statements for adjustments.*—On December 31, after the partnership had existed for four years, A expresses his desire to retire from the business. The partners therefore ask their bookkeeper to prepare a list of the ledger accounts as well as all the facts and notations necessary for the adjustment in accordance with the partnership agreement. The list gives the following information:

Plant and machinery	$50,000.00
Purchases of raw materials	200,000.00
Land and buildings	49,600.00
Advertising	1,800.00
Wages (productive)	240,000.00
Accounts receivable	20,000.00
Supplies for factory	2,450.00
Light, heat and power (factory)	20,000.00
Superintendence (unproductive labor)	10,000.00
Light, heat and power (office)	1,000.00
Cash	87,500.00
Packing materials	1,300.00
Salesmen's travelling expenses	6,000.00
Accounts payable	161,000.00
Insurance on buildings and plant	1,200.00
Interest lost	1,200.00
Reserve for bad debts	5,400.00
A, capital account	52,500.00
B, capital account	23,275.00
C, capital account	13,400.00
D, capital account	4,125.00
Bills receivable	76,000.00
Raw material inventory Jan. 1, 1908	13,500.00

Finished goods inventory Jan. 1, 1908 .... 19,000.00
Supplies inventory Jan. 1, 1908 .... 16,000.00
Sundry factory expense 7,200.00
Commissions 1,500.00
Bills payable 21,000.00
Taxes on land and buildings 500.00
Trade discount gained 4,000.00
Reserve for depreciation on plant and machinery 5,000.00
Reserve for depreciation on buildings 2,000.00
Reserve for depreciation on furniture and fixtures 1,000.00
Mortgage on buildings (5 per cent interest) 15,000.00
Allowances on sales 1,500.00
Insurance on stock and fixtures 1,000.00
Freight, outward 1,600.00
Freight, inward 900.00
Cash discount gained 2,800.00
Interest on mortgage 750.00
Finished goods sales 550,000.00
Salaries (including partners) 20,000.00
Furniture and fixtures 7,000.00
A, drawing account 500.00
B, drawing account 500.00
C, drawing account 500.00
D, drawing account 500.00

The net profits for previous three years were $8,-500.00, $9,300.00, $6,700.00 respectively.

The semi-annual interest on the mortgage is payable in January, and July respectively.

Of the premium paid on insurance of buildings and plant, and stock and fixtures there is unexpired insurance amounting to $200.00 and $100.00, respectively.

The inventories are as follows:

Raw material $16,750.00
Factory supplies 930.00
Goods in process of manufacture 5,450.00
Packing materials 150.00
Finished goods 20,300.00

It is agreed that the depreciation of various assets at the present should be at the following percentages, on the net balance shown on the respective ledger accounts, after deducting the depreciation of former years as shown by the various depreciation accounts:

On plant and machinery...................5 %

Buildings ....2 %

Furniture and fixtures...................10 %

It is also agreed upon that a reserve of 5 per cent be provided for bad and doubtful accounts under notes and accounts receivable outstanding.

In the first year of the enterprise the capital contributed by the partners was as follows: A, $60,000.00; B, $20,000.00; C, $14,000.00; D, $6,000.00.   Contrary to the partnership provision, no interest adjustments were made covering the transactions between the partners, and so they unanimously agree that such an adjustment be made at this time.   The items shown as drawings to B's and C's accounts are not all to be considered as overdrafts on salary.   On the contrary, an abstract shows that B and C have not taken out all their salaries and that there is due to each after deducting the withdrawals of $500.00, another $500.00 on account of salary not withdrawn, while A and D have each overdrawn $500.00.

We are asked to (a) determine the result of the year's operations; (b) make the proper adjustment entries consistent with the intentions of the partners; (c) prepare final balance sheet; and (d) show partners' respective capital accounts.

After completing the foregoing, the partners decide in accordance with the partnership agreement (clauses 5 and 6) that A is to get in cash one-half of the sum due him and the other half in four notes of equal amounts, payable within two years' time; one note every six months.

SOLUTION.

The first step is to find out if the books are in equilibrium and in order to do this we prepare the trial balance given on page 199.

It stands to reason that, before any adjustments can be made or before the dissolution agreement of the part-

Cash	$87,500.00	
Bills receivable	76,000.00	
Accounts receivable	20,000.00	
Raw material inventory (January 1)	13,500.00	
Finished goods inventory (January 1)	19,000.00	
Supplies inventory (January 1)	16,000.00	
Plant and machinery	50,000.00	
Land and buildings	49,600.00	
Furniture and fixtures	7,000.00	
Bills payable		$21,000.00
Accounts payable		161,000.00
Mortgage on buildings (5% interest)		15,000.00
Purchases of raw materials	200,000.00	
Wages (productive)	240,000.00	
Light, heat and power (factory)	20,000.00	
Supplies for factory	2,450.00	
Superintendence (unproductive labor)	10,000.00	
Packing materials	1,300.00	
Salesmen's travelling expenses	6,000.00	
Advertising	1,800.00	
Insurance on buildings and plant	1,200.00	
Sundry factory expense	7,200.00	
Commissions	1,500.00	
Taxes on land and buildings	500.00	
Trade discounts gained		4,000.00
Allowance on sales	1,500.00	
Insurance on stock and fixtures	1,000.00	
Freight outward	1,600.00	
Freight inward	900.00	
Cash discount gained		2,800 00
Interest on mortgage	750.00	
Finished goods sales		550,000.00
Salaries (including partners')	20,000.00	
Light, heat and power (office)	1,000.00	
Interest lost	1,200.00	
Reserve for bad debt		5,400.00
Reserve for depreciation on plant and machinery		5,000.00
Reserve for depreciation on buildings		2,000.00
Reserve for depreciation on furniture and fixtures		1,000.00
A, capital account		52,500.00
B, capital account		23,275.00
C, capital account		13,400.00
D, capital account		4,125.00
A, drawing account	500.00	
B, drawing account	500.00	
C, drawing account	500.00	
D, drawing account	500.00	
	$860,500.00	$860,500.00

PROFIT AND LOSS ACCOUNT OF THE FIRM A., B., C. AND D., DECEMBER 31, 1908

To raw material inventory, Jan. 1			$13,500.00	
Purchases			200,000.00	
			213,500.00	
Deduct:				
Raw material inventory				
Dec. 31	$16,750.00			
Trade discount	4,000.00		20,750.00	$192,750.00
Productive labor			240,000.00	
Unproductive labor			10,000.00	
Light, heat and power (factory)			20,000.00	
Supplies inventory, Jan. 1		16,000.00		
Supplies purchases		2,450.00		
		18,450.00		
Less inventory, Dec. 31		930.00	17,520.00	
Insurance on building				
and plant	1,200.00			
Less unexpired	200.00		1,000.00	
Freight inward			900.00	
Factory expenses			7,200.00	
Taxes on land and buildings			500.00	
Depreciation reserves:				
Plant and machinery (5% on 45,000)		2,250.00		
Land and buildings (2% on 47,600)		952.00	3,202.00	
			$493,072.00	

By goods in process of manufacture		$5,450.00
Balance carried down, being first charge against trading		487,622.00
		$493,072.00

To				By		
Balance brought down, being prime charge against trading		$487,622.00		gross sales of finished goods	$550,000.00	
Finished goods inventory January 1		19,000.00		Less allowances	1,500.00	
Packing materials	$1,300.00					548,500.00
Less inventory Dec. 31	150.00	1,150.00		Finished goods on hand unsold	20,300.00	$568,800.00
Salesmen's travelling expenses		6,000.00				
Advertising		1,800.00				
Commissions		1,500.00				
Freight outward		1,600.00				
Gross profit on trading		50,128.00				
		$568,800.00				$568,800.00

To				By	
Salaries (including partners)		$22,000.00		gross profit on trading	$50,128.00
Light heat and power (office)		1,000.00			
Insurance on stock and fixtures	$1,000.00				
Less unexpired	100.00	900.00			
Reserve for depreciation on furniture and fixtures (10% on $6,000)		600.00			
Ordinary business profit		25,628.00			
		$50,128.00			

To		By	
Interest on mortgage (1 year)	$750.00	ordinary business profit	$25,628.00
General interest lost	1,200.00	Cash discount gained	2,800.00
Net profit exclusive of interest on investment and reserve for bad debts	26,478.00		
	$28,428.00		$28,428.00

PROFIT AND LOSS APPROPRIATION ACCOUNT

To reserve for bad debts (5% on notes and accounts receivable, $20,000.00+$76,000.00)....			$4,800.00	By net profits... Interest debit on partners' deficiencies of investment:	$26,478.00
Interest credit on excess investment, viz.:					
A., excess investment......	$2,500.00			B., Deficiency investment.... $1,725.00	
Less excess withdrawal....	500.00			Less deficiency withdrawal. 500.00	
Net excess.............	2,000.00 @ 6%		120.00	Net deficiency............. 1,225.00	
Allocation of net profits:				@ 6% interest per annum.........	73.50
A., 50%.................	11,040.00			C., Deficiency investment.... $6,600.00	
B., 25%.................	5,520.00			Less deficiency withdrawal.. 500.00	
C., 15%.................	3,312.00			$6,100.00 @ 6 %	366.00
D., 10%.................	2,208.00		22,080.00	D., Deficiency investment... 875.00	
				Add excess withdrawals. 500.00	
				$1,375.00 @ 6 %	82.50
			$27,000.00		$27,000.00

BALANCE SHEET OF THE FIRM A., B., C., AND D., ON DECEMBER 31, 1908

CURRENT ASSETS:			
Cash..........................		$87,500.00	
Bills receivable...........	$76,000.00		
Accounts receivable.......	20,000.00		
	$96,000.00		
Less 5% reserve for bad debts..................	4,800.00	$91,200.00	$178,700.00
Inventories:			
Raw materials.............	16,750.00		
Goods in process..........	5,450.00		
Finished goods............	20,300.00		
Factory supplies..........	930.00		
Packing materials.........	150.00		43,580.00
FIXED ASSETS:			
Plant and machinery.... $50,000.00			
Less 5% depreciation on balance of $45,000....	2,250.00	47,750.00	
Land and buildings...... 49,600.00			
Less 2% depreciation on balance of $47,600....	952.00	48,648.00	
Furniture and fixtures.... 7,000.00			
Less 10% depreciation on balance of $6,000.00..	600.00	6,400.00	102,798.00
DEFERRED ASSETS:			
Insurance premium (unexpired)...............			300.00
			$325,378.00

CURRENT LIABILITIES:		
Bills payable..................	$21,000.00	
Accounts payable...............	161,000.00	$182,000.00
FIXED LIABILITIES:		
Mortgage on buildings................		15,000.00
PROPRIETORSHIP & RESERVES:		
Reserve for depreciation on plant and machinery......................	$5,000.00	
Reserve for bad debts.............	5,400.00	
Reserve for depreciation on buildings..	2,000.00	
Reserve for depreciation on furniture and fixtures.................	1,000.00	$13,400.00
A., Capital account.............	63,160.00	
B., Capital account.............	29,221.50	
C., Capital account.............	16,846.00	
D., Capital account.............	5,750.50	114,978.00
		$325,378.00

A'S CAPITAL ACCOUNT

Dr.			Cr.		
1908			**1908**		
December 3—To personal drawings in excess of salary..........	$500.00		January 2—By balance..........	$52,500.00	
Balance..........	63,160.00		December 31—By 50% of profits..........	11,040.00	
			—By 6% interest on excess investment..........	120	00
		$63,660.00			$63,660.00
1909			**1909**		
January 2—To cash..........	$39,075.00		January 2—By balance..........	$63,160.00	
Notes payable (4 notes each for $9,768.75, payable one each and every six months)......	39,075.00		Adjustment of interest on first year's excess investment......	600.00	
			Goodwill as per clause 6 of the partnership agreement.......	14,390.00	
		$78,150.00			$78,150.00

B.'S CAPITAL ACCOUNT

1908		
December 31—To 6% interest on deficient investment..................	$73.50	
Balance.........	$29,221.50	
	$29,295 00	

1908		
January 2—By balance..........	$23,275.00
December 31 — 25% of profits....	5,520.00
Unpaid salary.....	500.00
	$29,295.00

1909		
January 2—To adjustment of interest on first year's deficient investment.....	$300.00	

1909		
January 2 —By balance.....	$29,221.50

C's CAPITAL ACCOUNT

1908			1908		
December 31	To 6% interest on deficient investment.....	$366.00	January 2	By balance.....	$13,400.00
December 31	balance.....	16,846.00	December 31	15 % of profits.....	3,312.00
			December 31	unpaid salary.....	500.00
		$17,212.00			$17,212.00
1909			1909		
January 2	To adjustment of interest in first year's deficient investment...	$360.00	January 2	By balance.....	$16,846.00

D'S CAPITAL ACCOUNT

1908			1908		
December 31	To personal drawings.....	$500.00	January 2	By balance.....	$4,125.00
December 31	6% interest on deficient investment.....	82.50	December 31	10% of profits.....	2,208.00
December 31	balance.....	5,750.50			
		$6,333.00			$6,333.00
			1909		
			January 2	By balance.....	$5,750.00
			January 2	adjustment of interest on first year's excess investment.....	60.00

ADJUSTMENT ENTRIES

Adjustment account...................................$660.00
   To A, capital account.. $600.00
   To D, capital account..   60.00
   Adjustment of interest on first year's investments
     as per unanimous agreement.

B, capital account $300.00
C, capital account 360.00
To adjustment account........................ $660.00
   Adjustment of interest on first year's invest-
    ments as per unanimous agreement.

BALANCE SHEET OF THE FIRM B, C AND D, AFTER DISSOLUTION OF PARTNERSHIP

CURRENT ASSETS:			
Cash..............................		$48,425.00	
Bills receivable....	$76,000.00		
Accounts receivable	20,000.00	$96,000.00	
Less provision for bad debts..	10,200.00	85,800.00	
Inventories of raw material, goods in process, finished goods, etc		43,580.00	$177,805.00
FIXED ASSETS:			
Plant and machinery........	$50,000.00		
Land and buildings...........	49,600.00		
Furniture and fixtures....	7,000.00	$106,600.00	
Less depreciation provisions.............		11,802.00	94,798.00
Goodwill.........................			14,390.00
DEFERRED ASSETS:			
Unexpired insurance premium..........			300.00
			$287,293.00

CURRENT LIABILITIES:			
Bills payable........................		$60,075.00	
Accounts payable....................		161,000.00	$221,075.00
FIXED LIABILITIES:			
Mortgage on buildings.............			15,000.00
PROPRIETORSHIP:			
B, capital account................		$28,921.50	
C, capital account................		16,486.00	
D, capital account................		5,810.50	51,218.00
			$287,293.00

ners can be carried out, the books must be in balancing order. The trial balance shows that they are. This statement is drawn up systematically. Real accounts are placed first, then nominal accounts, followed by reserves and finally the proprietorship accounts— capital and drawing accounts. As has been explained, it is important that the trial balance be so arranged as to render easier the preparation of business and financial statements.

Our next step is the preparation of a profit and loss account for the firm for the year ending December 31, 1908. It will be noticed that the debit side of this account, in the first section, shows the cost of the material used during the year's operation, e.g., the raw material, inventory and the purchases. From this we deduct the raw material inventory as well as the trade discount allowed us on purchases, showing a net cost of \$192,750.00. This is followed by other charges, such as labor (productive and unproductive) as well as supplies, light, heat, power and other direct charges incurred for manufacturing, including depreciations for plant and machinery and for buildings used for manufacturing purposes.

The inventory of raw material on hand at the end of the period is shown as a deduction from the purchases, but instead of treating it in this manner, it could be entered on the credit side of the same section. The result would be the same, but if we desired to find the percentage of the cost against proceeds, or to compare percentages of different periods, the deduction of these inventories is preferable to entering them on the credit side.

We enter the goods in process of manufacture on the credit side, because correct results would not be obtained were we to charge the expenditure on these goods

III —14

to the current period, when they are not utilized nor even completed during such period. The balance is carried down as a first charge against the trading section of the profit and loss account. The second section, known as the trading section, contains on debit side; first, the balance brought down from the first, or manufacturing section, followed by the inventory of finished goods on hand at the beginning of the period, as well as by all the other items pertaining to the trade, such as advertising, commissions, etc.

On the credit side we show gross sales from which proper deductions are made for the allowances, leaving net sales of $548,500.00. We also show the amount of finished goods on hand at the end of the period, giving a gross profit of $50,128.00 on trading. This balance we carry forward to the credit side of the third section of the profit and loss account. Against this is charged all general items of expenditure, such as salaries (including the unpaid salaries due B and C), general insurance, etc., showing the ordinary business profit to be $25,-628.00. This we carry to the credit side of the final section of the profit and loss account, and adding the cash discount gained, we make a total of $28,428.00. Against this amount we charge the interest on the mortgage and general interest, thus leaving a net profit, exclusive of interest on investment and reserve for bad debts, amounting to $26,478.00.

The reason for dividing the profit and loss account into various sections is to show to the best advantage the result of each section. The author believes that a factory is not to show a profit, but the cost of manufacturing, and hence the reason for the first section giving only the cost of production.

The trading section is to show the gross profit realized

on the trade, the turnover. This should be shown regardless of the general expenditures of the business. The balance showing business profit is separate from the other items, such as interest or discount, because the latter disclose sufficient or insufficient capital employed in the business. A business may show a fair ordinary profit and yet half of this may be eaten up by excessive interest and discount charges and it is obvious that such facts should be disclosed and shown prominently.

Having completed the profit and loss account we prepare the profit and loss appropriation account. This account, as the name suggests, shows the net profit to be distributed among the partners, after provision has been made for reserve for bad debts. The credit side shows the net profits brought forward from the profit and loss account, and amounts to $26,478.00. Under this section we also show interest charged to B, C and D on account of their deficient investment as well as withdrawals, making a total of $27,000.00. Against this we show, on the debit side, the 5 per cent reserve for bad debts on notes and accounts receivable, amounting to $4,800.00; also the interest accrued on A's excess investment, after deducting withdrawals, amounting to $120.00, leaving a balance of $22,080.00 for allocation among partners. This net profit is allocated according to the provision for dividing profits and losses, namely, to A, 50 per cent, or $11.040.00; to B, 25 per cent, or $5,520.00; to C, 15 per cent, or $3,312.00, and to D 10 per cent, or $2,208.00.

Next we must verify the results shown by the profit and loss account, as well as disclose the financial condition of the concern. The balance sheet on page 203 shows this condition. It will be noticed that the assets are divided into current, fixed and deferred. By deferred assets we mean outlays made under one period for the benefit of a future period. The item here is the unexpired insurance premium amounting to $300.00. The total assets are $325,378.00 The total liabilities (divided into current and fixed) amount to $197,000.00. The last division of the balance sheet shows the proprietorship and reserves. The reserves deducted for the current period are taken off from each asset, while the general reserves created in previous periods are entered on the liability side. The capital left in the business, after adding the profits made during the period, as well as accrued salaries of B and C, and deducting the excess withdrawals of the other partners, amounts to $114,978.00. The problem now requires us to show the partners' individual capital accounts, and these are shown on pages 204–206, respectively. B, C and D's capital accounts are self-explanatory. They show the credit balances to each partner at the beginning of the period, January 1, 1908, to which is added the share of profit made during the period, including in B's and C's accounts the unpaid salary, and against which is charged interest. The interest is debited, if there is a deficiency, or credited if there is an excess of capital. At the end appears the balance of capital on each partner's account.

65. *Analysis of transactions.*—An analysis of Problem III discloses the following: While the partnership clause (5) provided that all adjustments among the partners for interest on capital, drawings, etc., should be made at the end of each year, yet, contrary to that provision, none were made covering transactions between the partners, and by their unanimous agreement we made the adjustment now shown on page 207. This adjustment entry shows

a debit of $660.00 to the adjustment account, and a credit to A for $600.00 and to D for $60.00. It also shows a debit to B for $300.00, and one to C for $360.00, and a credit to the adjustment account for the $660.00. These entries represent the adjustment of interest on the first year's investments. This is not carried through the profit and loss account because it has nothing to do with the profits. In this case, if we debit B and C, and credited A and D for the respective amounts mentioned in the adjustment entry, the result is the same as if we debited and credited the adjustment account for the same amounts. Nevertheless, if the figures disclosed a balance in the adjustment account, if it were debited for only $600.00 instead of $660.00, and credited for $660.00, that balance of $60.00 would have to be apportioned among the partners in accordance with the provision for sharing profits and losses. In such case the partner or partners who are charged with interest would share in the apportionment, and rightly so. To the business it does not, and should not, make any difference whether the interest is earned by reason of a partner's deficiency of investment or because the money has been loaned at interest to an outsider.

After having made the adjustment entries necessary to correct omissions made during the first year, we debit or credit each partner's respective account in accordance with the adjustments. We then find the value of the goodwill to which A is entitled, as per clause 6, which reads, that in case of the retirement of a member of the firm he is to receive for goodwill one-half the sum of the last two years' net profits of the business. On page 197 we are told that the net profit for the year 1907 was $6,700.00, to which we add the net profit of this year, $22,080.00, making a total of $28,780.00. Therefore,

A is entitled to one-half of this, $14,390.00, and we credit this sum to his account. As we issue to A four notes for $39,075.00 and pay him a like amount in cash to make up his net capital in the business, which is $78,150.00, we debit his account for such notes and cash, thus making it balance.

This completes the solution of the problem, but it is advisable to show also the position of the firm of B, C, and D, who are continuing the business after the dissolution. We prepare, therefore, the balance sheet shown on page 208. It will be seen that the item of goodwill is added to the assets. On the other hand, the total reserves are deducted, as for this purpose it is not necessary to extend them. This balance sheet shows the total assets to be $326,368.00. On the liability side we add the notes payable given to A for his share in the business, making the total liabilities to be $275,150.00. The respective proprietorship of the partners is slightly less than the one shown on the balance sheet, before dissolution, because of the subsequent adjustments with regard to interest, which were omitted during the first year.

PROBLEM IV.

66. *Another illustration of a partnership dissolution with certain special provisions.*—X, Y & Z are partners with equal capital and share equally in the profits. After trading for three years Z wishes to retire and Y and X elect to remain and purchase the share of the former. The partnership agreement provides that the retiring partner shall receive a share of the goodwill, the value of the latter to be equal to two-thirds of the average of the profits of the last three years preceding his retirement.

The following are the figures and we are requested to prepare a balance sheet and a profit and loss account as of June 30, 1906, and an account showing the amount due to Z from the remaining partners:

Capital account X	$8,000.00
Capital account Y	8,000.00
Capital account Z	8,000.00
Plant and equipment	14,840.00
Trade marks	4,500.00
Inventory June 30, 1906	7,600.00
Inventory July 1, 1905	4,800.00
Accounts receivable	19,400.00
Merchandise creditors	13,402.00
Sales	55,188.00
Purchases	27,804.00
Wages and salaries	4,600.00
General expenses	1,560.00
Partners' drawing accounts:	
X debit balance	5,500.00
Y debit balance	5,500.00
Z debit balance	5,500.00
Cash in bank and on hand	3,974.00

The following adjustments are to be made for the year just closed. Ten per cent depreciation on the plant and equipment; 15 per cent on the trade-marks; 10 per cent reserve for bad and doubtful debts.

There is on the books a special reserve account to cover depreciation of the stock on hand which is of a very perishable nature. The reserve amounts to $5,388.00 and must be equitably dealt with in the dissolution of the partnership.

The previous two years' profits were $17,816.00 and $22,020.00 respectively.

SOLUTION.

In the problem just stated, we are to notice the following special provisions:

First, the retiring partner is to receive a share of the goodwill, which is to be a sum equal to two-thirds of the average profits earned during the last three years preceding the retirement.

Second, the depreciation is to be deducted on the balance sheet, as mentioned in the problem.

Cash on hand and in bank	$3,974.00	
Inventory July 1, 1905	4,800.00	
Plant & equipment	14,840.00	
Trade marks	4,500.00	
Accounts receivable	19,400.00	
Accounts payable		$13,402.00
Special reserve for merchandise		5,388.00
Purchases	27,804.00	
Wages & salaries	4,600.00	
General expense	1,560.00	
Sales		55,188.00
X capital account		8,000.00
Y capital account		8,000.00
Z capital account		8,000.00
X drawing account	5,500.00	
Y drawing account	5,500.00	
Z drawing account	5,500.00	
	$97,978.00	$97,978.00

Third, the question of dealing with the reserve of $5,388.00, which has been set aside to cover depreciation on stock on hand, such stock being of a very perishable nature, is to be decided.

Our first step in solving this problem is the drawing up of a trial balance, as shown on page 216. The special reserve for merchandise appears on the credit side as all reserves of profits should go on the same side on which they originated. As profits are entered on the credit side of the profit and loss account, reserves created from profits must be arrived at by debiting the profit and loss, and crediting reserves.

Our next step is the preparation of a profit and loss account as shown on page 217. Carrying out the provisions of depreciation we find the net profit available for appropriation amounting to $21,865.

We now prepare the appropriation section, showing on the credit side the available profit for distribution and appropriate it by charging a 10 per cent reserve for bad and doubtful debts, and one-third of the balance to each partner respectively. It will be seen that in

PROFIT AND LOSS ACCOUNT OF THE FIRM X, Y, AND Z, FOR THE YEAR ENDING JUNE 30th, 1906.

To inventory July 1, 1905	$4,800.00		By sales		$55,188.00
Purchases	27,804.00				
	$32,604.00				
Less inventory June 30, 1906	7,600.00	$25,004.00			
Wages and salaries		4,600.00			
General expense		1,560.00			
Depreciation on plant and machinery (10%)		1,484.00			
Depreciation on trade marks (15%)		675.00			
Net profit for the year available for appropriation		21,865.00			
		$55,188 00			$55,188.00

PROFIT AND LOSS APPROPRIATION ACCOUNT

To Reserve for bad and doubtful debts (10%)	$1,940.00	By Net profit for the year available for distribution	$21,865.00
X., ⅓ of net profits	6,641.67		
Y., ⅓ of net profits	6,641.66		
Z., ⅓ of net profits	6,641.67		
	21,865.00		$21,865.00

217

BALANCE SHEET OF THE FIRM X, Y AND Z, ON JUNE 30, 1906

Assets:

Cash on hand and in bank			$3,974.00
Accounts receivable	$19,400.00		
Less reserve for bad debts	1,940.00		17,460.00
Merchandise inventory		7,600.00	
Less special reserve		5,388 00	2,212.00
Plant and equipment		14,840 00	
Less depreciation (10%)		1,484 00	13,356.00
Trade marks		4,500.00	
Less depreciation (15%)		675.00	3,825.00
			$40,827.00

Liabilities:

Accounts payable			$13,402.00
PROPRIETORSHIP:			
X, C/A	$8,000.00		
⅓ of profits	6,641.67	$14,641 67	
Less withdrawals		5,500.00	9,141.67
Y, C/A	8,000.00		
⅓ of profits	6,641.67	$14,641 67	
Less withdrawals		5,500 00	9,141.67
Z, C/A	8,000.00		
⅓ of profits	6,641 66	14,641 66	
Less withdrawals		5,500 00	9,141.66
			$27,425.00
			$40,827.00

Z'S DRAWING ACCOUNT

1905–1906		1906	
July 1—June 30, To withdrawals........	$5,500.00	June 30, By ⅓ net profits....	$6,641.67
1906			
June 30 To capital account...........	1,141.67		
	$6,641.67		$6,641.67

Z'S CAPITAL ACCOUNT

1906		1905	
June 30—To balance....	$22,421.89	July 1—By balance.........	$8,000.00
		1906	
		June 30—By drawing account..........	$1,141.67
		June 30—By ⅓ of total value of goodwill based on two years' purchase of the average of the last three years' profits......	13,280.22
	$22,421.89		$22,421.89
		1907	
		July 1—By balance....	$22,421.89

making up the profit and loss account no attention whatever is paid to the special reserve on merchandise. As long as we are not told whether there was any loss sustained on the merchandise the reserve remains untouched.

Having completed this we prepare the balance sheet as shown on page 218. The special reserve for merchandise is deducted from the merchandise inventory, because the reserve has to be used to make up any losses in connection with that inventory. All the other assets are shown at their net value, after deducting reserves for depreciation or reserves of any other nature, making the total valuation of the assets $40,827. As the liabilities are only $13,402 there is a balance of capital in the business, amounting to $27,425. The balance sheet clearly shows the apportionment of this capital among the partners.

As the investment was of an equal amount and the profits are divided share and share alike, and furthermore as the withdrawals were also of the same amounts, necessarily the proprietorship is divided into three equal parts.

So far we have completed only part of the problem; namely, we have determined profits for the year; we have made the adjustment pertaining to reserves, and have verified the results by the balance sheet. One part of the problem remains to be completed and that is to show the amount due Z from the partners according to the partnership agreement. This states that the retiring partner is to receive his share of the goodwill of the business.

The problem gives us the profits for the previous two years $17,816.00 and $22,020.00, respectively. The profits for this current year, after deducting reserves for bad debts, as shown on page 217, amount to $19,925.-00, making a total of $59,761.00 for the three years. Two-thirds of this (as stated in the problem) would be $39,840.67. This would represent a total value of the goodwill. As Z's share in the business is only one-third, he is entitled to one-third of this sum, or to $13,280.22. On page 219 where Z's account is given there is shown a balance due to Z, by the remaining partners, amounting to $22,421.89. This total is made up of the balance to his credit in the business, amounting to $8,000, and the balance transferred from the drawing account after deducting his withdrawals from the net profits, amounting to $1,141.67, plus his one-third of the total value of the goodwill.

The special reserve for merchandise amounting to $5,388 was not considered in settling with the retiring partner, because as long as he receives such a large share of the goodwill this reserve is to remain with the partners staying with the firm in order to compensate them for any possible loss on the goods, which in accordance with the wording of the problem, are of a very perishable nature.

Problem V.

A and B are partners in a mercantile business sharing profits and losses equally. At the end of five years the partnership terminates and the balance sheet shows the following financial condition:

BALANCE SHEET.

ASSETS:

Cash	$3,000.00
Accounts receivable	15,000.00
Merchandise inventory	2,000.00
Plant and fixtures	20,000.00
	$40,000.00

LIABILITIES:

Notes payable	$5,000.00
Accounts payable	15,000.00

PROPRIETORSHIP:

A	15,000.00
B	5,000.00
	$40,000.00

Subsequently the business as it stands (except cash) was sold for $37,500.00. We are asked to make final adjustments and closing entries showing the amount each partner receives.

FINAL ADJUSTMENT AND CLOSING ENTRIES.

Realization and liquidation account...............	37,000.00	
To accounts receivable		15,000.00
Merchandise inventory		2,000.00
Plant and fixtures		20,000.00
charging the realization account with the total book value of assets sold, for the purpose of closing out the asset accounts.		
Vendee	37,500.00	
To realization and liquidation		37,500.00
for the sale and transfer of right, title and interest in all the assets of the firm, consisting of merchandise, plant, fixtures and Accounts receivable.		
Cash	37,500.00	
To vendee		37,500.00
cash payment for assets acquired.		
Notes payable	5,000.00	
Accounts payable	15,000.00	
To cash		20,000.00
settlement of all liabilities.		
Realization and liquidation account	500.00	
To A, ...		250.00
B, ...		250.00
dividing between A and B the surplus value received for assets sold.		
A, ...	15,250.00	
B, ...	5,250.00	
To cash		20,500.00
distribution of cash between the partners.		

In this problem we are asked to make, first, final adjustment entries and then the closing entries and to show the amount that each partner is to receive.

We prepare, first, the final adjustment, and closing entries, as shown above. We debit there an account headed realization and liquidation account. For the present it may be stated that a realization and liquidation account is an account showing the result of the liquidation of a business concern. The reader will find in some other chapter a full discussion of the realization and liquidation account.

The entries shown on page 223 close out all assets that have been sold and liquidate all the liabilities. The difference between the debit and credit side of the

A'S CAPITAL ACCOUNT.

To cash ...	...	$15,250.00	By balance	..	$15,000.00
			50% of surplus profits on assets sold	250.00
		$15,250.00		$15,250.00

B'S CAPITAL ACCOUNT.

To cash ...	....	$5,250.00	By balance	..	$5,000.00
			50% of surplus profits on assets sold	250.00
		$5,250.00		$5,250.00

realization and liquidation account is $500.00. The debit side of the realization is charged with the value of assets, as shown on the books, and it is credited with the sales made to the vendee, amounting to $37,500.00. These records account for the difference of $500.00. This difference is closed out when it is transferred to the proprietors' accounts, and divided among them as a surplus value received for assets sold. As A and B withdrew the cash, having sold the business, we debit each partner's respective account for the amount to which he is entitled; namely, A $15,000.00 capital, plus $250.00 profits and B $5,000.00 capital and $250.00 profits. On page 224 the partners' respective accounts are shown; as they have withdrawn the cash, their accounts balance.

CHAPTER IX

PROBLEMS IN PARTNERSHIP ACCOUNTS

PROBLEM I.

Three men, located respectively at New York, Chicago, and Minneapolis, conducted a business as partners. The partnership agreement recited that the New York partner was to receive a salary of $5,000 a year, the Chicago partner a salary of $3,000 a year and one-third of the profits of that branch, and the Minneapolis partner a salary of $2,000 a year and one-fourth of the profits of that branch. Six per cent interest was to be allowed on the capital used in the business, $500,000 which was employed one-half at New York, one-third at Chicago and one-sixth at Minneapolis. Repairs and renewals were to be charged to plant, and a depreciation of 6 per cent per annum was to be allowed. Interest on borrowed money was to be distributed according to the invested capital at each branch. Plant account at the beginning of the period showed as follows: New York, $250,000; Chicago, $200,000; Minneapolis, $150,000. Repairs and renewals paid during the year amounted to $25,000 at New York, $30,000 at Chicago, and $15,000 at Minneapolis; interest on borrowed money, $15,000. Subject to these items, the profits of the year amounted to $50,000 at New York, $35,000 at Chicago, and $25,000 at Minneapolis. Complete the profit and loss account for the year.

In the solution of this problem, given on pages 228–

229, it will be observed that repairs and renewals on the plant were added to the plant account and from this total ($250,000, original cost, plus $25,000, repairs and renewals, New York, etc.) the depreciation was deducted. This is not a very accurate method for the reason that as repairs and renewals replace parts worn out through operation and so represent expenditures of, and not additions to, the asset, they should be charged as a revenue and not as a capital expenditure. However, as the problem reads that repairs and renewals are to be charged to the plant and then to allow depreciation at 6 per cent, the wording of the problem was followed.

The interest on loans in this problem was distributed between New York, Chicago and Minneapolis, on the same basis as the interest on capital. While this division of interest on loans may be questioned, yet from the wording of the problem nothing else could be inferred. The problem distinctly states that "interest on borrowed money was to be distributed according to the invested capital at each branch." Whether the capital on which that interest is charged was divided according to the original investment or not the problem does not state.

Solution given on pages 228 and 229.

PROFIT AND LOSS ACCOUNT for

Accounts	New York	Chicago	Minneapolis	Total
To depreciation of plant	$16,500 00	$13,800 00	$9,900 00	$40,200 00
Partners' salaries..	5,000 00	3,000 00	2,000 00	10,000 00
Interest on capitals:				
6% on........ $250,000 00	15,000.00			15 000.00
6% on......... 166,666 66		10,000.00		10 000.00
6% on......... 83,333.34			5,000.00	5 000.00
$500,000 00				
To interest on loans:				
50% on...... $15,000.00	7,500.00			7,500.00
33.33% on...... 15,000.00		5,000.00		5,000.00
16.67% on...... 15,000.00			2,500.00	2,500.00
100%				
Being net profits.....	50,000 00	35,000.00	25,000 00	110,000.00
Balance down.	$6,000.00	$3,200 00	$5,600 00	$14,800 00

Division of Profits

	New York	Chicago	Minneapolis	Total
To Chicago partner:				
Profits ⅓ of $3,200 00		$1,066.67		$1,066.67
Minneapolis partner:				
Profits ¼ of.. .... $5,600 00			$1,400 00	1,400.00
New York branch capital ⅓ ..	$2,000 00	711 11	1,400 00	4,111 11
Chicago branch capital ⅓ . ..	2,000 00	711 11	1,400 00	4,111.11
Minneapolis branch capital ⅓.	2,000 00	711 11	1,400 00	4,111 11
	$6,000 00	$3,200 00	$5,600 00	$14,800 00

	NEW YORK	CHICAGO	MINNEAPOLIS	TOTAL
By profits......................	$50,000.00	$35,000.00	$25,000.00	$110,000 00

	$50,000 00	$35,000.00	$25,000 00	$110,000 00
By net profit.................	$6,000 00	$3,200 00	$5,600 00	$14,800.00
	$6,000 00	$3,200 00	$5,600 00	$14,800.00

PROBLEM II.

A, the senior partner of a firm, dies May 9, at the close of which day the trial balance of the co-partnership ledger shows the following items:

Cash	$3,794	
Fixed assets	21,036	
Trade debtors	92,766	
Trade creditors		$93,206
Inventory, January 1	12,005	
Purchases	14,160	
Sales		19,658
Expenses	5,213	
Capital, A		20,000
Capital, B		10,000
Capital, C		5,000
Personal, A		2,310
Personal, B	750	
Personal, C	450	
	$150,174	$150,174

· The inventory of mdse. stock May 9, is computed at $15,200, the unexpired insurance at $149, and accrued expenses at $207.   The division of profits between partners is as follows: A, 57 per cent; B, 28 per cent; C, 15 per cent.   No interest is credited on capital, but interest is credited on A, personal $115, and charged to B, personal $6.25, and to C, personal $3.75.

The partnership agreement provides in case of A's death for the sale of A's interest to B and C on the execution of a bond by them in favor of A's estate, payable in five yearly installments, and stipulates that the assets are to be taken at book value, excepting one-half per cent reserve for bad debts, in compliance with which provision a reserve of $500 is made.

A new firm of B, C, and D is formed, in which D invests $5,000 cash for a one-fourth interest in the business.   B withdraws all in excess of $10,000 and C pays

SOLUTION

LIQUIDATION OF THE FIRM OF A, B AND C

May 9, 1907

TRADING ACCOUNT

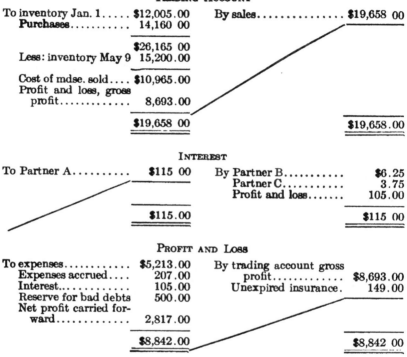

To inventory Jan. 1.....	$12,005.00	By sales..............	$19,658 00
Purchases..........	14,160 00		
	$26,165 00		
Less: inventory May 9	15,200.00		
Cost of mdse. sold....	$10,965.00		
Profit and loss, gross profit............	8,693.00		
	$19,658 00		$19,658.00

INTEREST

To Partner A..........	$115 00	By Partner B..........	$6.25
		Partner C..........	3.75
		Profit and loss.......	105.00
	$115.00		$115 00

PROFIT AND LOSS

To expenses............	$5,213.00	By trading account gross profit............	$8,693.00
Expenses accrued....	207.00	Unexpired insurance.	149.00
Interest.............	105.00		
Reserve for bad debts	500.00		
Net profit carried forward.............	2,817.00		
	$8,842.00		$8,842 00

To profits allocated to partners, thus:		By net profit brought forward.............	$2,817.00
A 57 per cent........	$1,605.69		
B 28 per cent........	788.76		
C 15 per cent........	422.55		
	$2,817.00		$2,817.00

PARTNER A

To balance.............	$24,030.69	By investment..........	$20,000.00
		Personal account........	2,310.00
		Interest	115.00
		Net profits, 57 per cent..	1,605.69
	$24,030.69		$24,030.69
		By balance.............	$24,030.69

PARTNER B

To personal account.....	$750 00	By investment..........	$10,000.00
Interest..............	6 25	Net profits, 28 per cent.............	788.76
Balance.............	10,032.51		
	$10,788.76		$10,788.76
		Balance.............	$10,032.51

PARTNER C

To personal account.....	$450.00	By investment..........	$5,000.00
Interest..............	3.75	Net profits, 15 per cent.............	422.55
Balance.............	4,968.80		
	$5,422.55		$5,422.55
		Balance.............	$4,968.80

AFFAIRS OF B, C AND D
PARTNER B

To cash withdrawn......	$32.51	By capital, firm A, B and C.............	$10,032.51
Balance.............	10,000 00		
	$10,032.51		$10,032.51
		Balance.............	$10,000.00

Partner C

To balance..............$5,000 00	By	capital, firm A, B and C..........	$4,968.80
		Cash invested......	31.20
$5,000.00			$5,000.00
		Balance..........	$5,000.00

Partner D

	By cash invested......	$5,000.00

Cash Account

To balance, firm A,B and C $3,794.00	By B, withdrawal.....	$32.51
C, additional invest-		Estate of A........	4,030.69
ment............... 31.20		Balance..........	4,762.00
D, investment........ 5,000.00			
$8,825.20			$8,825.20
To balance..............$4,762.00			

Firm of B, C and D

Balance Sheet

May 10, 1907

Assets:			Liabilities:		
Cash.....................$4,762.00			Accounts payable.....	$93,206.00	
Accounts			Accrued expenses......	207.00	
Receivable.....$92,766			Bond and mortgage		
Less: Reserve for			payable to estate of		
bad debts...... 500	92,266.00		A in five yearly in-		
Merchandise......	15,200.00		stallments..........	20,000 00	
Unexpired insur-			Capital:		
ance	149.00		Partner B..$10,000		
Fixed assets......	21,036.00		Partner C... 5,000		
			Partner D.. 5,000	20,000 00	
	$133,413.00			$133,413.00	

233

in a sum sufficient to bring his capital up to $5,000. The future profits are to be shared in the following stated proportions, viz.: B one-half, C one-fourth and D one-fourth. The new firm executes a purchase mortgage with bond as provided in favor of A's estate for $20,000, and pays over balance of his interest in cash.

Prepare the necessary accounts to give expression to the foregoing liquidation of the firm of A, B and C, and a balance sheet of the firm of B, C and D, as at the beginning of their enterprise.

In solving this problem on pages 231–233, the exact wording of the problem was followed. We first show the liquidation of the firm of A, B and C, by preparing the trading account in order to determine the gross profit realized on the trading proper. We follow this by the interest account which is credited for the interest due from B and C, and charged for the interest due to A. The profit and loss account shows, on the credit side, the gross profit carried forward from the trading account, and the unexpired insurance, making a total of $8,842.00. Against this we charge on the debit side all expenses including accrued items and reserves, leaving a balance of $2,817.00, or the net profit. This is carried forward to the new section, showing the allocation of the net profit, in accordance with the profit-sharing provision; 57 per cent to A, 28 per cent to B and 15 per cent to C. The partners' capital accounts, following the profit and loss account, show the balance of each partner in the business. This part concludes the liquidation of A, B and C. The second part shows the affairs of the new firm of B, C and D. In accordance with the profit-sharing agreement of the new firm, B withdraws $32.51, this being the excess of $10,000.00 as per his account. C invests an additional $31.20 to make up the $5,000 which he was supposed to invest, while D invests in cash one-fourth of the capital, namely, $5,000, as shown by their respective accounts on pages 232 and 233.

The cash account is given here to show the cash balance on hand at the beginning of the partnership of B, C and D. This account is debited for the balance taken over from the old firm, and also for C's and D's additional investments, making the total receipts $8,825.20. It is then credited for the withdrawal by B, of $32.51, as well as for the amount paid to the estate of A, $4,030.69, leaving a cash balance for the new firm, amounting to $4,762.00.

The balance sheet, which completes the solution, shows the assets of the new firm as well as their liabilities, including, of course, the bond and mortgage, amounting to $20,000.00, payable to the estate of A in five yearly installments, as per agreement.

The solution to problem III. is so similar to other solutions that there is not much to be said, except to call attention to the various items appearing in the manufacturing accounts, all of which are direct charges in manufacturing. As shown on page 237 the manufacturing account gives on the debit side, the cost of the goods manufactured, and on the credit side, the sales less discounts and allowances, the difference being the gross profit on goods manufactured and sold. The profit and loss account discloses a net loss which is allocated in accordance with the wording of the problem, in proportion to the capital on January the 1st. The balance sheet on page 239 verifies the condition of affairs, and shows the proprietorship of the members of the firm, which is arrived at by adding the withdrawals and losses, and deducting the total from the partners' capital.

PROBLEM III

From the following particulars of the business of Jamieson & Robb, Timber Merchants and Wood Turners, prepare a manufacturing and profit and loss account, and a balance sheet as at the close of the year.

TRIAL BALANCE AS ON DECEMBER 31, 1908

J. Jamieson, capital account..................		$25,000.00
R. Robb, capital account......................		20,000 00
Sales		50,000 00
Stock on January 1............................	$12,500.00	
Purchases (timber)............................	40,000.00	
Bills payable.................................		15,000.00
Debtors.......................................	21,000.00	
Creditors.....................................		10,000.00
Carriage, cartage and horse expenses............	2,500.00	
Repairs and maintenance.............	500.00	
Coal...	350.00	
Gas and water...............................	100.00	
Oil, grease, and waste........................	450.00	
Taxes and insurance..........................	350.00	
Bank interest................................	100.00	
Discounts and allowances......................	1,000.00	
Bad debts....................................	300.00	
Buildings, fixed machinery, and plant.......... ..	20,000.00	
Horses, carts, harness, etc....................	2,000.00	
Loose tools, utensils, and furniture..............	750.00	
Wages.......................................	5,000.00	
Salaries......................................	2,000.00	
Incidental expenses...........................	500.00	
Partners' salaries.............................	1,500.00	
Cash at bank.................................	4,000.00	
Cash in hand.................................	100.00	
Bills receivable...............................	5,000.00	
	$120,000.00	$120,000.00

Stock on December 31........................ $15,000.00

Make provision for the following:

> Depreciation on buildings, etc., $1,000.00.
> Accrued incidental expenses, $250.00.
> Discount 5 % on debtors' balances.
> Loss on debtors' balances, $200.00.

The net profit is divisible between the partners in proportion to their capital on January 1st.

MANUFACTURING ACCOUNT OF THE FIRM JAMIESON AND ROBB, DECEMBER 31, 1908

To inventory January 1, 1908	$12,500.00		
Purchases	40,000.00		
	52,500.00		
Less inventory December 31	15,000.00	$37,500.00	
Repairs and maintenance		500.00	
Coal		350.00	
Gas and water		100.00	
Oil, grease and waste		450.00	
Taxes and insurance		350.00	
Wages		5,000.00	
Depreciation buildings, etc.		1,000.00	
Gross profit carried down to profit and loss account		3,750.00	
		$49,000.00	
By sales		$50,000.00	
Less discount and allowances		1,000.00	$49,000.00
			$49,000.00

237

PROFIT AND LOSS ACCOUNT OF THE FIRM JAMIESON AND ROBB, DECEMBER 31, 1908

To carriage, cartage and horse expenses	$500.00	$2,500 00	By gross profit from manufacturing account		$3,750.00
Incidental expenses	250.00		Net loss, allocated thus:		
Accrued expenses		750.00	Jamieson	$2,583.33	
			Robb	2,066.67	4,650.00
Bad debts		300 00			
Salaries		2,000 00			
Partners' salaries		1,500 00			
Bank interest		100 00			
Reserve for bad debts		200 00			
Reserve for discount		1,050 00			
		$8,400.00			$8,400.00

BALANCE SHEET OF THE FIRM JAMIESON AND ROBB, DECEMBER 31, 1908

Cash at bank...........	$4,000.00			
Cash in hand..........	100.00		$4,100.00	
Bills receivable.........	$5,000.00			
Accounts receivable......	21,000.00			
		$26,000.00		
Reserve for losses and bad debts........	$200.00			
Reserve for discounts	1,050.00	1,250.00		
			24,750.00	
Merchandise inventory..........			15,000.00	
Buildings etc...... $20,000.00				
Less depreciation.... 1,000.00			19,000.00	
Horses, carts and harness........			2,000.00	
Loose tools, etc.........			750.00	
			$65,600.00	

Bills payable.........	$15,000.00	
Accounts payable......	10,000.00	$25,000.00
Accrued expenses.........		250.00
PROPRIETORSHIP:		
J. Jamieson......	$22,416.67	
R. Robb.........	17,933.33	$40,350.00
		$65,600.00

A, B and C agree to purchase and sell coffee for their joint account.

They purchase 3,000 bags of coffee for $58,500.00, and one month thereafter sell the same at 16 cents per lb. (say 130 lbs. to the bag). The warehouse charges, labor, cartage, weighing, brokerage, etc., amount to $600.00.

A contributes cash			$20,000.00
B contributes note at 4 months	$19,000.00		
Discount at 6% on same	?		?
C contributes cash		$18,900.00	
Also a note at 3 months	2,500.00		
Discount at 6% on same	?	?	?
			$59,982.50

It was arranged that each should contribute equally to the requisite purchase money, in default of which, interest at 6 per cent per annum for the month covering the transactions was to be calculated so as to equalize their respective contributions.

Prepare an account of the venture; also separate accounts of A, B and C, showing the share of each in the final net proceeds.

In this problem we are asked to supply certain missing figures, namely, the net value of the note and discount on same, etc.

In the solution on pages 241 and 242 the venture account is given, showing the total cost of the enterprise, including also charges for interest on the amount invested. It is credited for the proceeds realized from the sale of the goods as well as for the interest charged against B's account, leaving a profit on the transaction of $3,292.59, which is apportioned one-third to each member of the enterprise.

VENTURE ACCOUNT 3,000 BAGS OF COFFEE FOR A/C OF A, B AND C.

To purchase 3,000 bags of Coffee			$58,500.00
Warehouse charges, labor, cartage, weighing, brokerage			600.00
Interest, 1 mo. @ 6% on $1,8662.50 a/c of C			9.31
Interest, 1 mo. @ 6% on $500 a/c of A			2.50
			$59,111.81
A, $\frac{1}{3}$ profit		$1,097.53	
B, $\frac{1}{3}$ profit		1,097.53	
C, $\frac{1}{3}$ profit		1,097.53	
			3,292.59
			$62,404.40

By proceeds 3,000 bags of Coffee, 300,000 lbs. @ 16c			$62,400.00
Interest, 1 mo. @ 6% on $880 a/c of B			4.40
			$62,404.40

A'S ACCOUNT, VENTURE 3,000 BAGS COFFEE.

To balance carried down			$21,100.03
			$21,100.03

By cash, a/c $\frac{1}{3}$ interest		$19,500.00	$20,000.00
Interest, 1 mo. @ 6% on ...		500.00	2.50
$\frac{1}{3}$ share of profit		....	1,097.53
			$21,100.03
By balance brought down ...			$21,100.03

III—16

241

B'S ACCOUNT, VENTURE 3,000 BAGS COFFEE.

To interest on $880, 1 mo. @ 6%	$4.40	
Balance, carried down	19,713.13	
	$19,717.53	

By note @ 4 mos.	$19,000.00	
Deduct 6% discount, 4 mos. ..	380.00	$18,620.00
⅓ share profit		1,097.53
		19,717.53
		$19,717.53
By balance brought down ...	..	$19,713.13

C'S ACCOUNT, VENTURE 3000 BAGS COFFEE.

To balance, carried down ...	...	$22,469.34
		$22,469.34

By cash		$18,900.00
Note @ 3 mos.	$2,500.00	
Deduct 6% discount, 3 mos. ..	37.50	2,462.50
Interest, 1 mo. @ 6% on $1,862.50		9.31
⅓ share of profit		1,097.53
		$22,469.34
By balance brought down ..	.	$22,469.34

PROBLEM V.

A, B and C have been partners in a manufacturing enterprise since January 1, 1907. Their books have been kept by the double-entry principle, but the nominal accounts have not been closed at all.

On December 31, 1908 (after two years), their books disclose the following:

A, capital account	$9,500.00
B, capital account	6,000.00
C, capital account	4,500.00
Cash	21,500.00
Plant and machinery	14,000.00
Rent of factory	4,000.00
Tools	1,500.00
Productive labor	24,000.00
Factory expense	3,200.00
Unproductive labor	8,000.00
Power, light and heat (factory)	8,800.00
Raw material	31,000.00
General expenses	3,000.00
Rent of salesrooms	3,000.00
Commission	1,800.00
Salesmen	3,000.00
Advertising	1,000.00
Freight (inward)	500.00
Freight (outward)	1,200.00
Factory supplies	900.00
Discount on purchases	1,500.00
Discount on sales	1,100.00
Sales	152,000.00
Office salaries	6,000.00
Office rent	1,200.00
Discount lost	300.00
Discount gained	800.00
Interest lost	400.00
Return sales	200.00
Packing materials	700.00
Insurance on factory	1,400.00
General insurance	900.00
Heat and light (office)	800.00
Postage and expressage	500.00
Stationery and printing	300.00
Repairs to machinery	1,500.00
Accounts receivable	19,500.00
Notes receivable	16,300.00
Furniture and fixtures	1,500.00
Factory fixtures	2,000.00
Furniture and fixtures in salesrooms	3,000.00
Accounts payable	18,700.00
Notes payable	4,000.00
A, drawing account	4,275.00
B, drawing account	2,700.00
C, drawing account	2,025.00

Close the nominal accounts, prepare for them manufacturing, trading, and profit and loss accounts. Verify your results by a balance sheet accompanied by the partners' capital accounts.

NOTATIONS.

Profits and losses are to be divided in proportion to the original investment.

The partners agree that their personal withdrawals shall be charged as an expense of the business before apportioning profits or losses.

The inventories on hand are as follows:

Raw material	$5,300.00
Goods in process of manufacture	3,200.00
Finished goods	3,000.00
Unexpired insurance, (factory)	150.00
Unexpired insurance, (general)	100.00

There are accrued wages amounting to $350.00.

Make proper provision for depreciation charges and other reserves.

SOLUTION.

TRIAL BALANCE, DECEMBER 31, 1908.

Plant and machinery	$14,000.00	
Factory fixtures	2,000.00	
Furniture and fixtures in salesrooms	3,000.00	
Furniture and fixtures	1,500.00	
Tools	1,500.00	
Accounts receivable	19,500.00	
Notes receivable	16,300.00	
Cash	21,500.00	
Accounts payable		18,700.00
Notes payable		4,000.00
Rent of factory	4,000.00	
Productive labor	24,000.00	
Factory expense	3,200.00	
Unproductive labor	8,000.00	
Power, light and heat (factory)	8,800.00	
Raw material purchases	31,000.00	
Freight inward	500.00	
Factory supplies	900.00	
Discount on purchases		1,500.00

Discount on sales	1,100.00	
Sales		152,000.00
Returned sales	200.00	
Insurance on factory	1,400.00	
Repairs to machinery	1,500.00	
Rent of salesrooms	3,000.00	
Commission	1,800.00	
Salesmen	3,000.00	
Advertising	1,000.00	
Freight outward	1,200.00	
Packing materials	700.00	
General expense	3,000.00	
Office salaries	6,000.00	
Office rent	1,200.00	
General insurance	900.00	
Heat and light (office)..	800.00	
Postage and expressage	500.00	
Stationery and printing	300.00	
Discount lost	300.00	
Discount gained		800.00
Interest lost	400.00	
A, drawing account	4,275.00	
B, drawing account	2,700.00	
C, drawing account	2,025.00	
A, capital account		9,500.00
B, capital account		6,000.00
C, capital account		4,500.00
	$197,00.00	$197,000.00

CLOSING ENTRIES:

Manufacturing account	$85,500.00	
To raw material purchases		$31,000.00
Rent of factory		4,000.00
Productive labor		24,350.00
Unproductive labor		8,000.00
Power, light and heat		8,800.00
Freight inward		500.00
Factory supplies		900.00
Insurance of factory		1,250.00
Repairs to machinery		1,500.00
Factory expense		3,200.00
Reserve for depreciation on plant and machinery		1,400.00
Reserve for depreciation on factory fixtures		300.00
Reserve for depreciation on tools		300.00
Discount gained on purchases	$1,500.00	
Inventory of raw material	5,300.00	
Goods in process of manufacture	3,200.00	
Trading account (first charge against sales)	75,500.00	
To manufacturing account		85,500.00
Sales account	1,300.00	
To discount on sales		1,100.00
Returned sales		200.00

Trading Account $11,000.00
  To rent of salesrooms $3,000.00
    Commission 1,800.00
    Salesmen 3,000.00
    Advertising 1,000.00
    Freight outward 1,200.00
    Packing material 700.00
    Reserve for depreciation on furniture and fixtures used in
      salesrooms 300.00
Sales Account 150,700.00
  To trading account 150,700.00
Finished goods inventory 3,000.00
  To trading account...................................... 3,000.00
Trading account 67,200.00
  To profit and loss account 67,200.00

Profit and loss account 23,425.00
  To General expense 3,000.00
    Office salaries 6,000.00
    A, drawing account 4,275.00
    B, drawing account 2,700.00
    C, drawing account 2,025.00
    Office rent 1,200.00
    General insurance 800.00
    Heat and light (office) 800.00
    Postage and expressage 500.00
    Stationery and printing 300.00
    Discount lost 300.00
    Interest lost 400.00
    Reserve for depreciation on furniture and fixtures 150.00
    Reserve for bad debts 975.00
Discount gained 800.00
  To profit and loss 800.00

Profit and loss account 44,575.00
  To A, ... 21,173.12
  To B, ... 13,372.50
  To C, ... 10,029.38

In the solution of this problem, as given on pages 247–252 it will be seen that the first thing was the preparation of a trial balance. The closing entries were then made, as shown above, by means of which all the items were classified to their respective departments, manufacturing, trading or general administration. This is followed by the manufacturing, trading and profit and loss accounts as well as profit and loss appropriation account with the final balance sheet of the firm. As the problem also requires the partners' capital accounts, such are given on page 252.

MANUFACTURING ACCOUNT OF THE FIRM A, B AND C, FOR THE PERIOD OF TWO YEARS FROM

JANUARY 1, 1907, TO DECEMBER 31, 1908.

To raw material, purchases		$31,000.00	
Deduct:			
Discount on purchases	$1,500		
Inventory	5,300	6,800.00	$24,200.00
Rent of factory			4,000.00
Productive labor		24,000.00	
Accrued labor		350.00	24,350.00
Unproductive labor			8,000.00
Power, light and heat			8,800.00
Freight inward			500.00
Factory supplies			900.00
Factory expense			3,200.00
Insurance on factory	1,400		
Less unexpired pre-			
mium	150		1,250.00
Repairs to machinery			1,500.00
Depreciations:			
Plant and machinery (10%)		1,400.00	
Factory fixtures (15%)		300.00	
Tools (20%)		300.00	2,000.00
			$78,700.00

By goods in process of manufacture		$3,200.00
Balance carried forward to trading account ..		75,500.00
		$78,700.00

TRADING ACCOUNT OF THE FIRM A, B AND C, COVERING TWO YEARS FROM JANUARY 1, 1907, TO DECEMBER 31, 1908.

To balance brought forward from manufacturing account			$75,500.00
Rent of salesrooms			3,000.00
Commission			1,800.00
Salesmen			3,000.00
Advertising			1,000.00
Freight outward			1,200.00
Packing materials			700.00
Depreciation on furniture and fixtures in salesrooms (10%)			300.00
Gross profit on trading			67,200.00
			$153,700.00

By gross sales of finished goods			$152,000.00
Less:			
Returned sales	$200		
Discount on sales	1,100		
		1,300.00	$150,700.00
Finished goods inventory			3,000.00
			$153,700.00

248

PROFIT AND LOSS ACCOUNT OF THE FIRM A, B AND C, COVERING TWO YEARS FROM JANUARY 1, 1907, TO DECEMBER 31, 1908.

1907, TO DECEMBER 31, 1908.

Debit				Credit	
To general expenses			$3,000.00	By gross profit on trading ..	$67,200.00
Office salaries		$6,000.00			
Partners' withdrawals:					
A, ...	$4,275				
B, ...	2,700				
C, ...	2,025	9,000	15,000.00		
Office rent			1,200.00		
General insurance		900			
Less unexpired		100	800.00		
Heat and light (office)			800.00		
Postage and expressage			500.00		
Stationery and printing			300.00		
Depreciation on furniture and fixtures (10%)			150.00		
Ordinary business profit			45,450.00		
			$67,200.00		$67,200.00
To discount lost			300.00	By ordinary business profit ..	45,450.00
Interest lost			400.00	Discount gained	800.00
Net profit for allocation ...			45,550.00		
			$46,250.00		$46,250.00

PROFIT AND LOSS APPROPRIATION ACCOUNT.

To reserve for bad debts (5%) on accounts receivable		$975.00	
A, 19/40 of profits	$21,173.12		
B, 12/40 of profits	13,372.50		
C, 9/40 of profits	10,029.38	44,575.00	
		$45,550.00	

By net profits brought forward for allocation .. $45,550.00

$45,550.00

BALANCE SHEET OF THE FIRM A, B AND C AS ON DECEMBER, 1908.

ASSETS:

Cash		$21,500.00
Notes receivable	$16,300.00	
Accounts receivable $19,500.00		
Less reserve for bad debts 975.00	18,525.00	34,825.00
Inventories:		
Raw material 5,300.00		
Goods in process 3,200.00		
Finished goods 3,000.00		11,500.00
Plant and machinery 14,000.00		
Less depreciation reserve 1,400.00	12,600.00	
Factory fixtures 2,000.00		
Less depreciation reserve 300.00	1,700.00	
Tools 1,500.00		
Less depreciation reserve 300.00	1,200.00	
Furniture and fixtures		
Salesroom and office 4,500.00		
Less depreciation 450.00	4,050.00	
Unexpired insurance (Factory and general)	250.00	
		$87,625.00

LIABILITIES:

Notes payable	$4,000.00	
Accounts payable	18,700.00	$22,700.00
Accrued labor		350.00

PROPRIETORSHIP:

A, as per capital account	$30,673.12	
B, as per capital account	19,372.50	
C, as per capital account	14,529.38	$64,575.00
		$87,625.00

A'S CAPITAL ACCOUNT.

To balance ..	$30,673.12	By investment		$9,500.00
		By 19/40 of profits ...		21,173.12
	$30,673.12			$30,673.12
		By balance ..		$30,673.12

B'S CAPITAL ACCOUNT.

To balance ...	$19,372.50	By investment		$6,000.00
		By 12/40 of profits ...		13,372.50
	$19,372.50			$19,372.50
		By balance ..		$19,372.50

C'S CAPITAL ACCOUNT.

To balance ...	$14,529.38	By investment		$4,500.00
		By 9/40 of profits		10,029.38
	$14,529.38			$14,529.38
		By balance ...		$14,529.38

PART III: CORPORATION ACCOUNTING

CHAPTER X

CLASSIFICATION OF CORPORATIONS

67. *Limited partnerships.*—In the chapters on partnership affairs we saw something of the difficulty of arranging satisfactory partnerships. We learned also something of the responsibilities and liabilities of partners and of the difficulty caused by the withdrawal of any of the capital invested. It is largely due to these defects that the corporation came into prominence. The advantages of limited liability and of comparative ease in withdrawing the investment by selling one's stock, give confidence to the prospective investor; if careful in the selection of a sound enterprise, he may now feel reasonably sure of a fair return on his investment.

The first step in this country toward a change of the ordinary partnership form was taken in Pennsylvania in the introduction of a new system of capital grouping known as the "limited partnership."

A limited partnership is one in which a man can limit his liability to the amount invested. Such limitation applies not only to the settlement among partners but to outsiders as well. The idea was conceived in Italy whence it was transplanted into France and then into the United States. In France, and later in Pennsylvania, the law allowed shares—certificates of stock—to be issued against the interest of the partners, so that this form of limited partnership became a sort of quasi-corporation.

As might have been expected, this system of limited partnerships resulted in extensive litigation. Nor was it adequate to meet the needs of advancing commerce. Accordingly the commercial corporation of to-day was instituted.

The commercial corporation as it exists to-day was not fully developed in this country prior to 1848, although the first corporation act was passed by the Connecticut Legislature in 1837. It was in 1848 that the Legislature of the State of New York passed the first corporation law of modern cast in the act known as the "Manufacturing Act."

68. *Classification of corporations.*—A definition of a corporation and a description of the articles of incorporation are given in the volume on CORPORATION FINANCE and need not be repeated here. We should, however, note the classification of corporations laid down by the New York statute, which is substantially followed by the other states. It gives four general classes of corporations, viz.: (a) municipal corporations; (b) stock corporations; (c) non-stock corporations; (d) mixed corporations.

Municipal corporations include counties, cities, school districts, villages and other territorial divisions of the state established by law with powers of local government.

A stock corporation may be (a) a moneyed corporation, which is one formed under or subject to the Banking or Insurance Law; (b) a transportation corporation; or (c) a business corporation.

A non-stock corporation is either (a) a religious corporation; or (b) a membership corporation.

A mixed corporation may be (a) a cemetery corporation; (b) a library corporation; (c) a coöperative corporation; (d) a board of trade; or (e) an agricultural corporation.

A stock corporation is a corporation having capital stock divided into shares, to the holders of which it is authorized by law to distribute the surplus profits of the corporation by means of dividends on the shares. But a corporation is not a stock corporation because of having issued certificates of stock. These are merely certificates of membership, and do not necessarily imply the distribution to their holders of any dividends arising from operations of the corporation.

The term non-stock corporation includes every corporation other than a stock corporation.

Another kind of business association similar in some respects to the quasi-corporation is the joint-stock company. This organization is obsolete in America. We should, however, note the difference between a joint-stock company and a corporation. The joint-stock company is a partnership composed of many partners, but it has the following elements in common with the corporation:

(a) Continuousness. Partnership in this case is evidenced by shares similar to the corporation's, and any partner in the company may transfer his shares, with or without the consent of the other partners, and thus introduce a new partner without dissolving the original organization.

(b) Management. A board of trustees or directors controls the body and no member of the company has agency to act for the company as a whole.

The joint-stock company differs from the corporation in that its members are liable, jointly and severally, for the debts of the company, as in the case of the simple partnership, while the stockholders in a corporation are not so liable.

The joint-stock company sues and is sued in the name of an officer empowered to sue and defend, whereas the corporation sues and is sued in its corporate name.

69. *Books incidental to corporations.*—In addition to the ordinary books used in mercantile houses, which vary according to the nature of the business, all or some of the following auxiliary books are necessary in order to record properly the transactions of a corporation:

(a) Minute book.

(b) Subscription book.

(c) Installment book.

(d) Installment scrip book.

(e) Stock certificate book.

(f) Stock ledger.

(g) Stock transfer book.

(h) Dividend book.

The minute book contains a record of all the meetings of the stockholders and of all the meetings of the board of directors, although in some cases it is advisable to have a separate minute book for the meetings of directors.   The minute book is usually kept by the secretary of the corporation.   It is important to emphasize that the wording of the resolutions recorded in the minute book should be such as to avoid ambiguity or misinterpretation.

The subscription book is used for the purpose of recording the subscriptions of stockholders.   It should contain the date of each subscription, the name and address of the subscriber, and the number of shares which each agrees to take.   This book records the contract existing with the subscribers, whereby each binds himself to take the amount of stock for which he has subscribed.

The installment book is made up from the records of the subscription book and contains the name of each subscriber with the amount paid on each installment. A separate record should be kept for each installment. It is hardly necessary to state that the use of the installment book and the installment scrip book is limited to cases where the stock is to be paid for by installments.

The installment scrip book is the receipt book for installments paid by stockholders. It is a book of blank receipts to be filled out and signed by the secretary and treasurer as the installments are paid, the receipt being given to the subscriber and a stub retained by the secretary. In some cases the by-laws of a corporation provide that the president and secretary, instead of the treasurer and secretary, should sign such receipts. Upon the payment of the last installment the scrip should be taken up and a certificate of stock issued in its place.

The stock certificate book, or, as it is sometimes called, certificate book, contains blank certificates to be filled out and signed in accordance with the provisions of the by-laws of the corporation either by the secretary, president and treasurer, or by the secretary and treasurer. For convenience these certificates are numbered consecutively. A transfer form is usually printed on the back of the certificate in order to facilitate the transfer or sale of the stock. For sample certificate form see the volume on CORPORATION FINANCE in this series.

The stock ledger contains an account entitled capital stock, which is debited with the par value of all stock issued. It also contains an account for each stockholder, which is credited with the par value of the stock issued to him. When stock for any reason is transferred from one owner to another, the transferer is debited and the transferee is credited with the par value of the stock transferred. Thus, this ledger is always self-balancing, and its account for capital stock is exactly the reverse of the capital stock account in the general ledger, which is credited with the par value of stock issued to record the liability of the corporation thereon. Furthermore, this ledger shows the detail of the capital stock account in the general ledger.

The laws of the State of New York call for the keeping of a stock book or a stock ledger which shall contain the following information: (1) names of stockholders arranged alphabetically; (2) residence of each stockholder; (3) number of shares held by each; (4) time the stock was acquired; (5) amount paid thereon; (6) a record of all transfers showing from whom the stock was received and to whom it was transferred.

The stock transfer book is used to record the transfer of stock and contains the original entries which are posted to the stock ledger. In some cases the stock ledger and the stock transfer book are combined. But both books in some form are absolutely required by the laws of a number of the states.

The dividend book, or more properly the dividend receipt book, is used for the purpose of recording each dividend declared and paid. It contains a record of each dividend, the number of shares held by each stockholder and the amount of dividend paid thereon, with the signature of the stockholder as a receipt for the dividend paid to him.

The form given on page 259 is an illustration of a stock transfer book. The left side of the page records

WE, the persons named below, recorded owners of the   Capital Stock of

represented by the certificate described below, do by the undersigned Attorney, hereby sell, assign and transfer the number of Shares

of said stock set opposite our respective names, to the persons indicated:

Date	Certificates Surrendered		From Whom Transferred	Ledger Folio	Certificates Issued		To Whom Transferred	Ledger Folio	Address	Signature of Attorney
	Nos.	Shares			Nos.	Shares				

NAME.. ADDRESS..

Date of Transfer of Shares by the Above Named	Transfer No.	To Whom Shares Are Transferred	Ledger Folio	Certificates Surrendered		Date of Acquisition of Shares	From Whom Shares Were Transferred (If original issue enter as such)	Ledger Folio	Certificates Issued		Balance Remaining Cr. of Above
				Certif. Nos.	No. Shares				Certif. Nos.	No. Shares	

260

the transfer of the stock and the right side attests its validity.   The number of certificates surrendered and the number of shares each certificate represents, are entered; the name of the person from whom they have been transferred and, for convenience, the folio of his account in the stock ledger, are also shown.   The number of the new certificate, how many shares it represents, to whom it is issued, i.e., the transferee, the address of the transferee and, again for convenience, the folio of his accounts in the stock ledger, are given to close the page, except for the signature of the stockholder's attorney authorized to make the transfer, who is the secretary of the corporation.

The form given on page 260, illustrates a stock ledger. It shows the name and address of the stockholder, the date when any transfer or surrender of stock was made, the number of the transfer, and the person to whom the transfer has been made.   It also shows the number of the certificate surrendered and the number of shares it represents.   On the right side of the account is shown the date of acquisition of stock and whether it is an original issue or a transfer from a prior holder.   If the latter, the name of that prior holder, is recorded.   Columns are provided for the number of the new certificate issued and the number of shares it represents.   The balance of shares held at any time is shown in the last column.

As stated on page 257, stock is often sold to be paid for in installments, and the installment book and the installment scrip book are used in such a case.   In addition, it is sometimes advisable to use an installment ledger in order to keep track of the various payments. On the following page is given an illustration of an installment ledger.   In this example it will be noticed that the original subscription was made January 15. On that date James Smith subscribed to one hundred shares at $100 each, making a total of $10,000.00, on which he paid nothing. On February 1 he paid the first installment of 25 per cent and his account in the installment ledger was credited for that payment, installment scrip for that amount being issued to him.

On March 1 F. Brown transfers to Smith his subscription to 50 shares of stock, on which the first installment had already been paid. Smith's account is, therefore, charged for that transfer, showing the unpaid amount of $3,750.00. On March 15 Smith transferred to A. Peters 25 shares. In order to complete that transfer Smith surrendered the installment scrip for 50 shares issued to him on Brown's transfer and received two new scrips, each for 25 shares, to enable him to give to Peters the scrip that he then transferred. On April 15 Smith paid the second installment on all his subscriptions and this was credited to his account.

By adding the shares debited on the left side of the account and subtracting from it the shares credited on the right side, we find the number of shares on which there remains an unpaid balance. We find that Smith's subscriptions at the present are 125 shares on which two installments have already been paid. By comparing the total debits with the total credits in the monetary columns we find a debit balance of $6,250.00, which Smith still owes. That balance represents the 50 per cent for two installments due by him on the 125 shares which he at present owns.

The reader has already been given on page 260 an illustration of a stock ledger. This is not by any means the only form of stock ledger commonly used. Special forms are adopted to meet special cases. Some-

INSTALLMENT LEDGER

JAMES SMITH, 320 BROADWAY, NEW YORK, N. Y.

Date	Shares	How Acquired	% Unpaid	Certificate No. of Scrip	Amount	Date	Shares Transferred	How Settled	% Unpaid	Certificate No. of Scrip	On How Many Shares Paid	Install-ment	%	Amount
1909 Jan. 15	100	Subscribed....	100	25	$10,000.00	1909 Feb. 1		Paid........		1	100	1	25	$2,500.00
Mch. 1	50	F. Brown.....	75	26	3750.00	Mch. 15	50	Surrendered...	75	25				3,750.00
Mch. 15	25	Reissued......	75	27	1,875.00	Mch. 15	25	A. Peters......	75	26				1,875.00
Mch. 15	25	Reissued......	75		1,875.00	April 15		Paid.........		50	125	2	25	3,125.00

STOCKHOLDERS' LEDGER

A. B. NICHOLS, 480 WEST BROADWAY, NEW YORK, N. Y.

Date	Shares	How Acquired	Certificate No.	Amount
1909				
Jan. 20	500	Original issue........	1	$100,000.00
Feb. 1	200	J Smith.............	10	20,000.00
Mch. 1	300	F. Brown...........	50	30,000.00
Mch. 12	100	Reissued............	75	10,000.00
Mch. 12	200	Reissued............	76	20,000.00

Date	Shares	How Disposed	Certificate No.	Amount
1909				
Feb. 25	200	M. Alexander........	10	$20,000.00
Mch. 10	300	Surrendered.........	50	30,000.00

times a combination of stock transfer book and stock ledger is used and sometimes there is a combination of the installment ledger and the stockholders' ledger.   On the preceding page is given an illustration of a common form of stockholders' ledger.   As will be seen, the credit or right side shows the credit to the stockholder's account for all the stock issued to him.   This credit may represent original issues or subsequent acquisitions of stock.   The debit side shows any surrender to the corporation or transfer to others of the stock which he owns.   The difference between the total of the credit column "shares" and the total of the debit column "shares" is the number of shares owned by the stockholder, and the difference between the corresponding monetary columns is the par value of those shares.   If the latter figure can not be obtained by multiplying the par of the stock by the number of shares shown by the former figure, there has been an error in the keeping of the book.

CHAPTER XI

DEFINITIONS OF CORPORATE TERMS

70. *Use of word "capital."*—The importance of careful definition of terms has already been emphasized. A prominent writer on scientific subjects says: "Sensible men always define things in the way they use them." We find, however, in the study of accountancy many terms used by one writer as meaning one thing and by another as meaning an entirely different thing. In the first place, one must be careful to note that the meaning of terms commonly used in other sciences is often different from their meaning when used in accountancy. Thus, the economist uses the term "capital" as denoting that portion of wealth which is set aside for the production of additional wealth. To him, therefore, the capital of a business is the whole amount of assets employed, regardless of whether or not it all be proprietorship. What the economist calls capital is represented on books of account on the debit or asset side; as used by accountants, however, the term "capital" appears on the credit or liability side of books of account. The accountant uses the term "capital" only for the difference between the value of the assets and the amount of the liabilities which must be satisfied out of them. That difference represents the proprietorship.

The method of treating investments made in individual or partnership enterprises has already been outlined. The contribution made by the individual is credited to his account, which at the end of the fiscal

266

period is credited with net gains or charged with net losses to reflect the outcome of the operation of the business, in accordance with the terms of the investment. The case is not so simple, however, with corporations. In some instances the original entry does not necessarily represent the amount of capital contributed; changes in the net wealth are not carried to the investor's account as in the case of partnerships. The capital account of a corporation represents the par value of the stock issued and outstanding. In separate accounts are shown the various changes—the increases or decreases in the proprietorship. This would not cause much trouble in recording simple transactions, but usually the transactions in financing a corporation are complex. Sometimes corporations do not receive the full value for their stock, especially when sold for cash, although this in some states is prohibited by law. Then there are intricate underwriting agreements, explained elsewhere. The accountant's business, of course, is not to conceal any matters, however intricate, but on the contrary to bring out all important facts.

71. *Increase or decrease of capital stock.*—Under a partnership, the capital invested may be decreased or increased at the will of the partners themselves and their decision does not concern the public at large. This is not the case, however, with corporations. A decrease or increase of capital stock can be made only by means of certain legal formalities for the protection of investors and creditors. For instance, under the laws of the State of New Jersey, in the case of a decrease in the capital stock, a certificate of such a decrease must be published in the county where the principal office is located once a week for three successive weeks. The first publication must be made within fifteen days after

the certificate of reduction is filed with the secretary of state under penalty of personal liability of directors for corporate debts contracted before compliance and liability on the part of stockholders for any amount of capital received by them under such reduction. Under the New York corporation laws the capital stock of a corporation may be increased or decreased, either with or without a meeting, by unanimous consent of the stockholders in person or by proxy, or by a vote of a majority in interest of the stockholders cast at a meeting specially called for that purpose. Notice of such meeting stating the time, place, object and the amount of increase or decrease proposed, signed by the president or vice-president or secretary must be published once a week for at least two successive weeks in a local newspaper. A copy of such notice must be mailed to each stockholder at least two weeks before the meeting or be served on him personally at least five days before the meeting. There are also certain other requirements.

72. *Surplus and deficiency accounts.*—It has already been stated that the profits or losses of a corporation are treated in accounts other than "capital stock." Some corporations, banks especially, use the term "undivided profits" instead of "surplus," while others use a combination of both terms, "surplus and undivided profits." Whatever term is used, however, the account represents simply the balance of net profits left after dividends, if any, have been declared.

If the assets of a business are insufficient to meet its liabilities, a deficiency results. In some cases we find an account called "surplus and deficiency account." As the name implies, this account is to record a surplus of the business as well as a deficiency, it being credited with the former and charged with the latter. It is, however, preferable to have two accounts, one for surplus and one for deficiency.

In addition to the surplus account corporations use other accounts to which undivided profits are credited. Corporations as a rule do not pay out all their profits in dividends, but make provisions for possible losses, depreciations or liabilities. Such provisions are made by means of accounts called "reserves" which show the profits which the corporation deems unwise at present to distribute to stockholders or even to credit to surplus account for future distribution.

73. Reserve account and reserve fund distinguished. —Reserve is the term used for an amount set aside out of profits either for some specific purpose or for the general purpose of strengthening the business by way of accumulation of working capital. When reserves are set aside for specific purposes the account should so state; for instance, reserve for bad debts, reserve for discount, or reserve for depreciation.

Care must be taken not to confuse reserve accounts with reserve funds. By the latter term is meant a fund actually created, out of appropriations of profit, and represented by an investment outside of the business. Such funds may also be for specific or general purposes. Sinking funds, depreciation funds, and redemption funds are illustrations of specific reserve funds.

There is considerable difference of opinion as to the exact meaning of the term reserve fund. Some persons use this term even where there is no specific investment representing such fund outside of the business. It is advisable, however, that the use of the word *fund* should be limited to cases where there is an outside investment of such nature that it can easily be converted into cash. Unless there are profits earned, no reserve fund can be created, while a reserve account can be set up whether or not there are any profits. If profits have been made, they are decreased by this charge. If losses have been sustained, the losses are increased by the amount set aside in the reserve account. Excessive losses would wipe out a reserve account, whereas they would not affect a reserve fund. An accountant has quite often to examine an account very closely to know its nature, and to look at the intention of the parties creating it, as frequently the account was set up by someone who did not have a clear understanding of the difference between a reserve and a reserve fund.

74. *What the sinking fund denotes.*—Sinking fund is the term used to denote the setting apart and accumulation of funds to make provision for discharging indebtedness at some future, usually remote, period. The payments into it are generally fixed in amount. They are made at regular intervals and usually to a trustee. Such payments are invested and the interest accruing thereon added to the fund, so that the amounts paid in, together with the accumulated income thereon, will provide a certain required amount at a given date.

Dr. Price of England was the originator of the sinking fund idea and he recommended it to the elder Pitt as a means of paying off the national debt of England. Briefly stated it is as follows:

Set aside such sum which if invested periodically at a fixed rate per cent of interest will at the maturity of the indebtedness exactly amount to that indebtedness. It must be borne in mind that the term sinking fund is applied to the *sum periodically set aside* and not to the amount of the indebtedness to be liquidated. Its account shows a debit balance representing the total of the individual deposits.

75. *Redemption and contingent funds.*—The term redemption fund represents an amount periodically set aside out of profits which by the time a certain funded debt or other obligation matures will provide an accumulated surplus for the redemption of it. It is created by a charge to revenue and a credit to redemption fund account. It is practically the payment of a time loan out of revenue by charging against the profits of each year a proportion of said loan. It is similar in character to a reserve fund as it represents undivided profits.

The term contingent fund represents a stated sum or a portion of the general receipts set aside to provide for the payment of incidental expenses not anticipated or provided for in other ways. It is used especially by government institutions and charitable and social organizations. It always shows a debit balance, as it represents an accumulation of funds and is therefore similar to a sinking fund.

By investment fund is meant an amount set aside out of profits for the purpose of purchasing securities that can be quickly realized upon, in times of monetary stringency when the ordinary assets of the business may not be convertible quickly enough to meet current liabilities. There are two methods of treating this fund on the books of the corporation. One method is for the investment fund account to appear among the liabilities as a sort of reserve account, and the corresponding securities purchased to appear among the assets. The other method is to charge the securities purchased out of this fund to the fund itself and to show on the balance sheet among the liabilities only the balance of the fund remaining uninvested.

The term loan capital is generally applied to money borrowed by a corporation upon its bonds secured by a mortgage upon its property, which mortgage, however, does not give to the mortgagee any proprietary rights or voting privileges in the management of the affairs of the corporation.

The dividend account on the books of a corporation is that to which each dividend when declared is credited and against which is charged the payments thereof made to the stockholders.   It is quite advisable to open a separate account for each dividend declared, as for example, Dividend Number I, June, 1909.

The term treasury stock represents issued stock that has come again into the possession of the corporation which issued it, by gift or donation or in liquidation of a debt.   Many use the term treasury stock loosely and apply it to unissued stock, but this is not correct. Treasury stock is an asset and represents value received, while unissued or unsubscribed stock does not; hence the latter should not be called by the same name. Treasury stock, as long as it is held by the corporation, does not participate in the meetings of the corporation as voting stock nor is it entitled to dividends.   It, however, represents a paid-for interest in the property of the corporation.   The creation of treasury stock by donation from the incorporators, to whom the stock was originally issued as consideration for the purchase of the assets of the corporation from them or for services performed by them, is often made a device for giving away stock as a bonus with bonds or for selling stock below par.   This is perfectly legal procedure because treasury stock is a purchased asset of the corporation for which value has been given and as such an asset it may be given away or sold at any price upon which the directors may decide. It should be remembered always that stock can be issued originally only for its equivalent value, because to issue it for anything less would work a misrepresentation upon subsequent investors and creditors in that the capital stock outstanding would not then be equaled by assets of the corporation which upon dissolution could be used to redeem such stock.

There is no necessity of giving the definitions of the various classes of bonds, as such definitions are discussed in the volume on CORPORATION FINANCE.

CHAPTER XII

PROCEDURE IN CHANGING A SET OF BOOKS FROM PARTNERSHIP TO CORPORATE FORM

76. *Procedure in the case of a new corporation.*— When a corporation is organized, the opening entries, while different from ordinary partnership entries, are not as involved as the entries when an existing partnership is converted into a corporation. It frequently happens that partners in an existing firm decide to incorporate, either with or without the admission of new members to the enterprise. We will consider first the initial entries for a corporation starting business for itself. The following problem will illustrate them.

PROBLEM I.

John Smith, Alfred Brown, Peter Marks and Adam Friend decide to enter into a manufacturing business and for that purpose desire to incorporate under the laws of the State of New York under the corporate name of The Brown Manufacturing Company. They agree that the capital stock of the company is to be $25,000.00, divided into 1000 shares at the par value of $25.00 each. The subscription to such stock is as follows: J. Smith, 200 shares; Alfred Brown, 300; Peter Marks, 250, and Adam Friend, 250.

They duly sign a subscription agreement and after the articles of incorporation are approved by the secretary of state, each pays one-half of his subscription in cash and gives a note payable in sixty days for the balance. The organization expenses in connection with the formation of the corporation amount to $350.00.

Required: (a) the entries in the various corporation books; (b) the initial balance sheet.

SOLUTION.

The initial entry should be a memorandum to show the organization of the corporation, in some form such as this:

THE BROWN MANUFACTURING COMPANY

Incorporated under the Laws of the
State of New York, with an
Authorized Capital
of
$25,000.00
divided into One Thousand Shares of $25.00 each.

This entry would, of course, be made in the journal of the corporation.

The subscription to the stock should appear in the subscription book. We then make in the journal the following entry:

Subscription Account $25,000.00
    To Capital Stock $25,000.00
        Representing the subscriptions
            to the Capital Stock of
            the Company, viz.:
        J. Smith 200 shares
        A. Brown 300   "
        P. Marks 250   "
        A. Friend 250   "

As one-half of the subscription is paid in cash an entry should be made in the cashbook, on the debit side, shown on the following page:

Attention is called to the fact that while in this form

of cashbook only one monetary column is shown, as we are interested only in recording this particular transaction, the usual form of cashbook contains more than one monetary column.

Dr.   CASH BOOK .... 190...

(Date)	To subscription account	J. Smith 50% on stock subscribed	$2,500.00
(Date)	To subscription account	A. Brown 50% on stock subscribed	3,750.00
(Date)	To subscription account	P. Marks 50% on stock subscribed	3,125.00
(Date)	To subscription account	A. Friend 50% on stock subscribed	3,125.00

As the subscribers pay the other 50 per cent of their subscriptions by notes we make the following entry in the journal:

Notes Receivable $12,500.00
   To Subscription Account $12,500.00
     Representing four 60 day
     notes, given by S m i t h,
     Brown, Marks and Friend
     respectively, in payment for
     50% of their subscriptions.

The organization expenses in connection with the formation of the company amounting to $350.00 are shown on the credit side of the cashbook, as follows:

CASH BOOK   Cr.

Date	Organization Expenses	Expenses incurred in connection with the organization of the Company	$350.00

In these entries in the books of the company, those pertaining to the issue of the stock are omitted because in a former chapter the method of entering in the stock ledger the issue of stock was given.

The initial balance sheet of the corporation is as follows:

Balance Sheet of the Brown Manufacturing Company as on

. . . .*190*. .

Assets:			Liabilities:	
Cash	$12,150.00		Capital Stock	$25,000.00
Notes receiv-able	12,500.00	$24,650.00		
Organization Expenses		350.00		
		$25,000.00		$25,000.00

This balance sheet shows the cash on hand to be $12,-150.00. It will be recalled that we received from the subscribers $12,500.00 in cash, from which we paid organization expenses of $350.00, leaving the balance as shown above. The notes receivable are the notes given by the subscribers in payment for the second half of their subscriptions. These two items represent the available assets of the company and accordingly they are grouped together. The item of organization expenses is treated for the present as an asset for the reason that it will be met out of the profits that the company expects to earn during the year. As it is not an asset that can be converted into cash at present, it is entered separately from the other assets. The credit side of the balance sheet does not contain any liabilities because none have been incurred. Capital stock is treated as a liability because it represents the amount which on dissolution would be due to the holders of the stock issued.

77. *Procedure when a partnership is converted into a corporation.*—The last problem illustrated the initial entries in the original organization of a corporation which starts business for itself. The following prob-

lem will illustrate the conversion of an existing partnership into a corporation:

PROBLEM II.

A, B and C constitute a firm engaged in a manufacturing business which they have decided to incorporate with a capital stock of $100,000.00 equally divided into common and preferred stock, the par value of each share to be $100.00.

The agreement among the partners is that each partner is to take 75 per cent preferred and 25 per cent common stock to the amount of his net investment in the business. The remaining shares authorized are to be offered for sale.

The partnership books show the following balances in the ledger accounts:

```
Real estate ..........................$25,000.00
Accounts payable ....................  5,000.00
Accounts receivable .................  9,000.00
Cash ................................  5,000.00
Machinery and tools.................. 10,000.00
Merchandise ......................... 15,000.00
Notes receivable ....................  3,000.00
Notes payable ....................... 10,000.00
Materials and supplies...............  8,000.00
```

The capital of the partners consists of $60,000.00 divided as follows: A, five-twelfths; B, four-twelfths and C, three-twelfths.

Required: (a) closing entries for the partnership books; (b) opening entries for the corporation books.

BALANCE SHEET OF THE FIRM A, B & C.

ASSETS:

Cash		$5,000.00
Notes receivable	$3,000.00	
Accounts receivable	9,000.00	
Merchandise inventory ..	12,000.00	
Materials and supplies	15,000.00	
	8,000.00	$40,000.00
Real estate	25,000.00	
Machinery and tools	10,000.00	35,000.00
		$75,000.00

LIABILITIES:

Notes payable	$10,000.00	
Accounts payable	5,000.00	$15,000.00

PROPRIETORSHIP:

A's Capital Account	$25,000.00	
B's Capital Account	20,000.00	
C's Capital Account	15,000.00	60,000.00
		$75,000.00

SOLUTION.

Before we can proceed to make any entries we must arrange the facts given in the problem in some systematic order. As there are no nominal accounts, we can prepare the balance sheet shown on the preceding page.

While as far as the partners are concerned there is no material change for the reason that they will share in the dividends of the firm on the same basis that they have shared in the profits of the partnership, each partner receiving stock to the amount of his capital in the partnership, in law the A B C Manufacturing Co. is entirely different from the former firm of A, B & C, although owned and controlled by the same persons. This is due to the fact that the nature of a corporation is entirely different from that of a partnership. We, therefore, assume that the old firm, A, B & C, sells to the A B C Manufacturing Co. all its assets and that the company assumes to pay all the liabilities of the old firm. The consideration to be paid by the company for this purchase would be the value of the assets less the liabilities, or the amount of the proprietorship in the partnership. This will be done by the issue of stock. Our first entry then in the books of the firm of A, B & C will be in the journal as follows:

The A B C Manufacturing Co....$75,000.00

    To cash .... $ 5,000.00

        Notes receivable 3,000.00

        Accounts receivable 9,000.00

        Merchandise 15,000.00

        Materials and supplies......   8,000.00

        Machinery and tools.........   10,000.00

        Real estate 25,000.00

        For the sale of all the assets
        enumerated above.

This entry records the sale of the assets which creates a debit or charge against the A B C Manufacturing Co. and a credit to respective asset accounts. It is obvious that when this entry is posted the various asset accounts will be closed out, and rightly so, as we have transferred these assets to the A B C Manufacturing Co.

Our next entry, also made in the journal, will show the assumption of the liabilities of the old firm by the corporation, and will be as follows:

```
Notes  payable ................$10,000.00
Accounts  payable ............  5,000.00
    To A B C Manufacturing Co...              $15,000.00
        For  the  assumption  of  the
        above  mentioned  liabilities,
        by  the  vendee,  the  A  B  C
        Manufacturing Co.
```

We have so far charged the A B C Manufacturing Co. with the assets acquired, amounting to $75,000.00 and we have credited it with the liabilities assumed, amounting $15,000.00. By this second entry the liability accounts have been closed out in the books of A, B & C. The A B C Manufacturing Co.'s account shows a debit balance of $60,000.00 due to the partnership. In accordance with the agreement the corporation is to issue to the partnership 75 per cent of this amount in preferred stock and 25 per cent of it in common stock. When this has been done, we make in the partnership journal the following entry:

```
Preferred  capital  stock..........$45,000.00
Common  capital  stock.......... 15,000.00
    To  the  A  B  C  Manufacturing
        Co, ...................              $60,000.00
```

This represents the issue of
stock, it being the balance of
the purchase price of all the
assets after the assumption
of the liabilities.

As this stock is to be apportioned to the respective
members of the firm in accordance with their investment
accounts, we make the following entry in the partnership journal:

A's capital account.............$25,000.00
 To preferred capital stock..... $18,750.00
  Common capital stock.....   6,250.00
  For his share in the net
   capital of the partner-
   ship.
B's capital account.............$20,000.00
 To preferred capital stock.....   15,000.00
  Common capital stock.....   5,000.00
  For his share in the net
   capital of the partner-
   ship.
C's capital account.............$15,000.00
 To preferred capital stock.......   11,250.00
  Common capital stock......   3,750.00
  For his share in the net
   capital of the partner-
   ship.

This last entry closes all the accounts that have appeared on the books of the partnership, because the
firm has sold its assets, its liabilities have been assumed
by another concern and the partners have received stock
for their investments.

This completes the first part of the problem, namely,

the closing of the books of the partnership. The second part deals with the opening entries in the corporation books. The first entry will be a memorandum in the journal, showing the organization of the company, as follows:

THE A B C MANUFACTURING CO.
Incorporated under the laws of the
State of ...... with an
Authorized Capital
of
$ 1 0 0 , 0 0 0 . 0 0 .
Divided into $50,000.00 Common and
$50,000.00 Preferred Stock
of One Hundred Dollars par value each.

The next entry should also be in the journal to show the subscription to the capital stock as follows:

Subscription to preferred capital stock.$45,000.00
Unsubscribed preferred capital stock... 5,000,00
Subscribed common capital stock...... 15,000.00
Unsubscribed common capital stock.... 35,000.00
   To authorized preferred capital stock $50.000.00
    Authorized common capital stock..   50,000.00
     For the capital stock subscribed
      as follows:
     A 250 shares, common and preferred.
     B 200 shares, common and preferred.
     C 150 shares, common and preferred.

It will be noticed that in the first problem the entire amount of authorized capital stock was subscribed to, while in this only part of it is so taken. As it is advisable to show in the capital stock account the full amount of capital stock authorized, we debit an account "unsubscribed capital stock" for the amount that is unsubscribed, in order to justify the placing of the full authorized issue of stock on the books. But in preparing a financial statement it is not advisable to list this unsubscribed stock on the debit side, because it is not in any sense an asset. This account should be deducted from the capital stock which should be stated in the balance sheet thus:

Authorized preferred capital stock.....$50,000.00
   Less unsubscribed 5,000.00 $45,000.00

Authorized common capital stock...... 50,000.00
   Less unsubscribed 35,000.00 15,000.00

The next journal entry should show the acquisition of the various assets as follows:

Plant and sundry assets..............$70,000.00
Cash (also entered in the cashbook).... 5,000.00

   To A, B and C................. $75,000.00
   For the transfer to this company
   by the above mentioned vendors of
   their right, title and interest in all
   of their assets, including cash, as
   scheduled in the bill of sale, dated
   ....190..

As the company has assumed the liabilities of the firm we make in the journal the following entry:

A, B and C........................$15,000.00
    To notes payable.................   **$10,000.00**
       Accounts payable..............   **5,000.00**
    For the assumption of their liabil-
       ities by this company as part con-
       sideration of the purchase of
       their assets.

The next step is to issue the stock to the firm, so we make in the journal the following entry:

A, B and C........................$60,000.00
    To subscription to preferred capital
       stock **$45,000.00**
       Subscription to common stock....   **15,000.00**
    For 450 shares of preferred stock
       and 150 shares of common stock,
       issued to them as per their sub-
       scription, for which they pay in
       property instead of cash.

It will be noticed that we have recorded the purchase of the assets by merely debiting the account entitled "plant and sundry assets." This is the policy generally followed for the reason that the assets may be acquired at one value and placed on the books of the corporation at a different value. What we have to do now is to close out the account "plant and sundry assets," and to place the various assets on the books of the company. We do this by means of the following journal entry:

BALANCE SHEET OF THE A, B, C MANUFACTURING COMPANY, AS ON ....190..

ASSETS:

Cash		$5,000.00
Notes receivable	$3,000.00	
Accounts receivable	9,000.00	12,000.00
Merchandise inventory	15,000.00	
Materials and supplies	8,000.00	$40,000.00
Real estate	25,000.00	
Machinery and tools	10,000.00	$35,000.00
		$75,000.00

LIABILITIES:

Notes payable	$10,000.00	
Accounts payable	5,000.00	$15,000.00
Capital Stock:		
Authorized:—		
Preferred	$50,000.00	
Less unsubscribed	5,000.00	$45,000.00
Authorized:—		
Common	50,000.00	
Less unsubscribed	35,000.00	15,000.00	60,000.00
		$75,000.00

286

Real estate $25,000.00
Machinery and tools................ 10,000.00
Merchandise inventory 15,000.00
Materials and supplies.............. 8,000.00
Notes receivable 3,000.00
Accounts receivable 9,000.00
   To plant and sundry assets......... $70,000.00
     For the purpose of placing the re-
     spective assets on the books of
     the company.

This completes the solution of the problem. It is advisable in all such cases to test the accuracy of the work accomplished and for this purpose a balance sheet should be prepared. It is preferable to prepare a balance sheet rather than a trial balance because there are no nominal accounts. The balance sheet would be as shown on the preceding page.

PROBLEM III.

The Western Grain Co. has this day been incorporated under the laws of this state by the following incorporators: C. H. Benton, J. W. Walters, F. Rowland, and A. B. Miller, all of this city, with an authorized capital of $25,000.00, divided into 250 shares of $100.00 each.

The purpose of this corporation is to buy and sell all kinds of grain, and the subscriptions to the stock of the company are as follows:

C. H. Benton 60 shares, J. W. Walters 60 shares, F. Rowland 100 shares, and A. B. Miller 30 shares.

Pursuant to an agreement between the firms of Benton and Walters and F. Rowland, and the Western Grain Co., the former two individual concerns agree to sell to the latter all their assets, consisting of stock

BENTON AND WALTER'S BALANCE-SHEET.

Cash		$2,300.00	Notes payable	$4,160.33	$2,300.00
Notes receivable	$2,300		Accounts payable	839.67	$5,000.00
Accounts receivable	8,600	10,900.00	Notes receivable discounted ...		1,300.00
Furniture and fixtures ..		200.00	C. H. Benton C/A		4,000.00
Unexpired insurance		68.75	J. W. Walters C/A		4,100.00
Merchandise (inventory) .		931.25			
		$14,400.00			$14,400.00

F. ROWLAND'S BALANCE-SHEET.

Real estate		$5,159.00	Notes payable	$1,250	
Furniture and fixtures ..		495.00	Accounts payable	1,750	$3,000.00
Merchandise (inventory) .		1,196.00	F. Rowland C/A		9,200.00
Notes receivable	$800.00				
Accounts receivable	1,350.00	2,150.00			
Cash		3,200.00			
		$12,200.00			$12,200.00

of merchandise, real estate, accounts and notes receivable, goodwill, etc., etc., in consideration of the assumption by the Western Grain Co. of all the liabilities of the two individual concerns as well as for the payment in capital stock of the company for the balance which the assets may exceed the liabilities. The balance sheet of each individual concern is taken as exhibiting the exact value of each plant, as given on the preceding page.

The goodwill of Benton and Walters is valued at $1,-500.00, while that of F. Rowland is valued at $2,000.00.

To enable the corporation to carry out this agreement the original subscriptions of Benton, Walters and Rowland are therefore amended as follows:

C. H. Benton subscribing 20 shares, Walters 20 shares, and Rowland 27 shares. A. B. Miller pays in cash for his subscription, and Benton, Walters and Rowland donate each five shares of the capital stock of the company to provide a reserve for contingencies.

Draft the necessary journal entries for the opening of the corporation books and all the other facts mentioned above, and create the ledger accounts.

SOLUTION:

THE WESTERN GRAIN COMPANY
INCORPORATED UNDER THE LAWS OF THE
STATE OF MICHIGAN WITH AN

AUTHORIZED CAPITAL
OF
$25,000.00,

DIVIDED INTO 250 SHARES OF $100 EACH.

SUBSCRIBERS:

C. H. Benton	$6,000.00	
J. W. Walters	6,000.00	
F. Rowland	10,000.00	
A. B. Miller	3,000.00	
To subscription		$25,000.00

for their respective subscriptions to the capital stock of the Co., as follows: C. H. Benton and J. W. Walters, 60 shares each; F. Rowland, 100 shares; and A. B. Miller, 30 shares.

III—19

PLANT AND SUNDRY ASSETS $24,600.00
   To Vendors $24,600.00
     for the surrender to this Co., of their right, title and inter-
     est in all of the assets of their respective firms, including
     the Goodwill.
SUBSCRIPTION $15,300.00
   To C. H. Benton $4,000.00
     J. W. Walters 4,000.00
     F. Rowland 7,300.00
     To enable the Co. to purchase the assets of the vendors the
     original subscriptions are amended to read as follows: C.
     H. Benton, 20 shares; J. W. Walters, 20 shares; F. Row-
     land, 27 shares.
VENDORS $9,300.00
   To sundry liabilities $9,300.00
     for the assumption by this Co. of all the liabilities on open
     accounts and notes payable, as part consideration for as-
     sets acquired.
VENDORS $15,300.00
   To Capital stock $15,300.00
     for 153 shares of the capital stock of this Co., issued to
     vendors in payment of balance of consideration for assets
     bought as per bill of sale dated ————.
SUBSCRIPTION, ... $9,700.00
   To Capital stock $9,700.00
     for 97 shares of capital stock issued to the subscribers in
     accordance with amended subscription, viz:—C. H. Benton
     and J. W. Walters, 20 shares each; F. Rowland, 27 shares,
     and A. B. Miller, 30 shares.
NOTES RECEIVABLE $3,100.00
ACCOUNTS RECEIVABLE 9,950.00
MERCHANDISE (Inventory) 2,127.25
FURNITURE AND FIXTURES 695.00
REAL ESTATE 5,159.00
UNEXPIRED INSURANCE 68.75
GOODWILL 3,500.00
   To Plant and sundry assets $24,600.00
     for the purpose of placing the respective assets, under ap-
     propriate headings, on the books of the Co.
SUNDRY LIABILITIES $9,300.00
   To Notes payable $5,410.33
     Accounts payable 2,589.67
     Notes receivable discounted 1,300.00
     for the purpose of placing the respective liabilities, under
     appropriate headings, on the books of the Co.
CASH $3,000.00
   To A. B. Miller $3,000.00
     cash payment for subscription to the stock of the Co.
TREASURY STOCK $1,500.00
   To Reserve for contingencies............................ $1,500.00
     Benton, Walters and Rowland donate each five shares of
     the capital stock of the Co., issued to them, to serve as a
     reserve for contingencies.

LEDGER.

C. H. Benton.

To subscription .... | $6,000.00 | By subscription .... | $4,000.00

J. W. Walters.

To subscription .... | $6,000.00 | By subscription .... | $4,000.00

F. Rowland.

To subscription .... | $10,000.00 | By subscription .... | $7,300.00

A. B. Miller.

To subscription.......... | $3,000.00 | By cash.......... | $3,000.00

Subscription.

To subscribers:
C. H. Benton (40 shares)
J. W. Walters (40 shares)
F. Rowland (73 shares) ...... | $15,300.00
To capital stock .... | 9,700.00

$25,000.00

By subscribers:
C. H. Benton (60 shares)
J. W. Walters (60 shares)
F. Rowland (100 shares)
A. B. Miller (30 shares) .... | $25,000.00

$25,000.00

Plant and Sundry Assets.

To vendors (assets bought) .. | $24,600.00 | — By assets (enumerated) .. | $24,600.00

VENDORS.

To liabilities (assumed) ..	$9,300.00	By sale of assets ... $24,600.00
Capital stock	15,300.00	
	$24,600.00	$24,600.00

SUNDRY LIABILITIES.

To liabilities (enumerated) ..	$9,300.00	By vendors (assumed) .. $9,300.00

CAPITAL STOCK.

	By vendors $15,300.00
	Subscription ... 9,700.00

NOTES RECEIVABLE.

To plant, etc. ...	$3,100.00

ACCOUNTS RECEIVABLE.

To plant, etc. ...	$9,950.00

MERCHANDISE INVENTORY.

To plant, etc. ...	$2,127.25

FURNITURE AND FIXTURES.

To plant, etc. ...	$695.00

REAL ESTATE.

To plant, etc. ... | $5,159.00

INSURANCE (Unexpired).

To plant, etc. ... | $68.75

GOODWILL.

To plant, etc. ... | $3,500.00

NOTES PAYABLE.

| By sundry liabilities ... | $5,410.98

ACCOUNTS PAYABLE.

| By sundry liabilities ... | $2,589.67

NOTES RECEIVABLE DISCOUNTED.

| By sundry liabilities ... | $1,300.00

CASH.

To cash book .... | $3,000.00

TREASURY STOCK.

To reserve for contingencies ... | $1,500.00

RESERVE FOR CONTINGENCIES.

| By treasury stock ... | $1,500.00

293

Cash	$3,000.00	
Notes receivable	3,100.00	
Real estate	5,159.00	
Furniture and fixtures	695.00	
Merchandise (inventory)	2,127.25	
Insurance (unexpired)	68.75	
Goodwill	3,500.00	
Treasury stock	1,500.00	
Notes payable		$5,410.33
Reserve for contingencies		1,500.00
Notes receivable discounted		1,300.00
Capital stock		25,000.00
Accounts receivable	9,950.00	
C. H. Benton	2,000.00	
J. W. Walters	2,000.00	
F. Rowland	2,700.00	
Accounts payable		2,589.67
	$35,800.00	$35,800.00

In this problem we are asked to draft the journal entries for opening of the corporation books and to create the ledger accounts.

In solving the problem, after giving the initial memorandum, showing the organization of the corporation, we debit the respective subscribers for their subscriptions and we credit the subscription account as shown on page 289. This entry is somewhat different from the former entries where the subscription account has been debited and the capital stock account credited. The reason for it is to show another way of making such entries. All the other entries shown on page 290 are self-explanatory.

We are told in the problem that Benton, Walters & Rowland each donate five shares of the stock to the company to provide for contingencies. We have shown this donation by debiting treasury stock and crediting the account headed "reserve for contingencies." All the ledger accounts given on pages 291–293, as well as the final trial balance shown above are self-explanatory.

78. *Special features of entries in corporation books.*—
A corporation may increase its capital stock by comply-
ing with certain provisions of the laws of the state under
which it is organized. Suppose, for illustration, that
a corporation having a capital stock of $50,000.00 has
decided to increase it to $100,000.00. Assume also that
it has complied with all the legal requirements and we
are asked to record the transaction in the books. The
method of procedure in such a case would be to debit the
subscription account, as a controlling account, for the
total amount of subscription to the capital stock, and to
credit the capital stock account for such subscribed capital. When the subscription is subsequently paid for,
the procedure would be to debit the cash received and to
credit the subscription account through the cashbook,
thus wiping out the subscription account.

The methods advocated by some accountants of debiting an account headed "new stock issue" and crediting
an account headed "capital stock," or of debiting an
account headed "nominal capital" and crediting an account headed "capital stock," or of debiting "treasury
stock" and crediting "capital stock" are believed to be
wrong. The capital stock account shows the liability
of the corporation for the stock issued. The corresponding entry to this account must be one showing the
receipt of an asset, cash or its equivalent, for such
liability. One can hardly classify an account headed
"new stock issue," "nominal capital" or "treasury stock"
as representing an asset for the liability created. The
best way to treat such an increase is to regard it in the
same light as an original issue.

The legal procedure in the case of a decrease of the
capital stock is generally similar to that in the case of
an increase; that is, the same notice is required and the

same vote of stockholders is necessary. But it must be borne in mind that the capital stock of a corporation may never be reduced below the actual indebtedness of the company.

The bookkeeping entries in a case of decrease would depend altogether on the circumstances. It is usually safe to assume that no corporation voluntarily decreases its capital stock. It generally does so only when the capital stock has been greatly impaired and there are no immediate prospects of its rehabilitation. Assume that a corporation having a deficiency of $20,000.00 wishes to reduce its capital stock, which has been impaired to that extent. The company will generally do more than merely wipe out the deficit; it will decrease its stock to a greater degree so as to leave a surplus. Assuming that the original capital stock of the company was $100,000.00, the corporation presumably would decrease its capital stock $30,000.00, thus leaving a surplus of $10,000.00. The entry would be a very simple one, namely, a debit to capital stock of $30,000.00 and credits to deficiency account of $20,000.00 and surplus account of $10,000.00. By this entry the capital stock is reduced to $70,000.00, the deficiency account closed out and a surplus account created to show a credit balance of $10,000.00.

Sometimes instead of carrying an impairment to capital to a deficiency account a new account is opened entitled "impairment to capital stock" and debited with the amount of the impairment. In such case the entry would be a debit to capital stock of $30,000.00, and credits to "impairment to capital" of $20,000.00 and to surplus of $10,000.00. It is, however, more advisable in such cases to credit the $10,000.00 to a special reserve account than to surplus. This would prevent the paying out of such amount in dividends.

Where stock is donated to a company by its stockholders who have received such stock for value for the purpose of creating working capital for the company, the entries should be as follows: on the receipt of the stock an account entitled "treasury stock" should be debited and "working capital suspense" account should be credited. This stock received by the company has been fully paid for by the stockholders and therefore when it is donated to the company the company receives an actual asset which it can sell and hence it is correct to debit the treasury stock account for such donation. The reason why a new account, "working capital suspense," should be credited is that it is impossible to foretell for how much this treasury stock can be sold. If on the sale of such stock the amount realized is less than the par value, the difference between actual cash received and the amount at which the treasury stock is placed on the books should be charged against the working capital suspense, so that the difference between the debit and credit side of this latter account would be the actual amount of working capital which this treasury stock realized.

CHAPTER XIII

PREMIUMS AND DISCOUNTS ON THE SALE OR PURCHASE OF STOCKS OR BONDS

79. Complications due to premiums and discounts.—
When stocks or bonds are issued for property it may
be assumed that the exchange is an equal one, i.e., that
the property is worth the par value of the securities so
issued. It often, happens, however, especially where
such securities are sold for cash, that the consideration
is worth less than the par value of the securities issued,
and complicated questions then arise.

Leaving out of consideration the legality of the issue
of stock at a discount, a distinction should be made between the case where such discount is collectible and the
case where it is not. If the discount may be recovered
from the person to whom the stock has been issued, the
discount is a contingent asset; otherwise it is not an
asset at all, but a charge to profit and loss.

Premiums on stock are a source of profit to the corporation. They are cash receipts in excess of the
liability on the capital stock which has been issued.
They are not, however, profits on operation and therefore should not be credited to the profit and loss account, but carried to a reserve account. They may, of
course, be applied to liquidate losses of an extraordinary
nature.

Where bonds are sold at a premium or discount, the
case is, of course, entirely different because these are
deductions or additions to the rate of interest which the

bonds bear. If the credit of the corporation is good and the money market is normal, a corporation may be able to issue its bonds at par, provided the rate of interest is a fair one. This, of course, would depend entirely on circumstances and conditions of a general nature as well as on the credit of the company issuing the bonds. A change in any of these factors—rate of bond interest, money market or credit of the corporation—will cause the sale of the bonds to be either above or below par. The nominal rate of interest, however, that is, the rate which the bonds bear, is fixed and is a proper periodical charge to the profit and loss account, while the premium or discount should be spread over the term of years which the bonds have to run and the annual proportion thereof should be debited or credited, as the case may require, to the profit and loss account.

80. *Bonds at a discount.*—Let us take first the case of bonds issued at a discount. Up to quite recent times it was the general practice of corporations—railroad and industrial—to treat such a discount as a capital charge, particularly in newly organized corporations. In the early years of a corporation's existence the earnings are rarely more than enough to meet the fixed interest charges. But in such cases the nominal rate of interest paid on the bonds is not sufficient inducement to prospective purchasers to buy such bonds at par, because the bonds being issued for the whole cash cost of the enterprise, leave no margin of security for the bond purchaser. Therefore, in order to add to the attractiveness of these bonds, the stockholders, who are looking for their profits in a future enhancement of the value of the property of the company, surrender a portion of such anticipated profits by selling the bonds at a discount. The future liability for the difference be-

tween the amount realized on the sale of the bonds and the amount for which these bonds will have to be redeemed at maturity constitutes the surrendered portion of profits. If the corporation is successful, its profits will more than offset the discount which was allowed.

The present tendency, however, is more towards conservatism and it is usual now to provide out of income for charges which formerly were borne by capital. This policy is followed in the discounts on bond sales. Such discounts are distributed over the life of the bonds and each year the proportionate share of them is charged to the profit and loss account. In some cases such discounts are provided for out of the profits of prosperous years only so as to prevent charges for them falling during lean years.

Assume that a corporation issues $1,000,000.00 of twenty-year bonds which are sold for cash at ninety, the corporation thus receiving $900,000.00. The $100,-000.00 lost in discount should be distributed over twenty years and the profit and loss account charged each year with one-twentieth of the discount or with $5,000.00.

A little thought will show that this conservative procedure is not only proper, but is absolutely fair. One of the most potent influences causing these bonds to sell at a discount is likely to be a low rate of bond interest that they bear. The credit of the corporation is also an element. If one corporation can sell bonds which bear 4 per cent interest at par, and another corporation is forced to sell its bonds bearing the same rate of interest at 95, the credit of the second corporation is evidently not as good as the credit of the first corporation. A discount on the sale of bonds is equivalent to the payment of a higher rate of interest, and as interest is a fixed yearly charge against the profit and loss account, so the discount allowed on the sale of bonds should be distributed over the period for which the bonds have to run and be charged yearly to the profit and loss account.

81. *Bonds sold at a premium.*—The case where bonds are sold at a premium is simple except that such premium should not be carried to the profit and loss or surplus account to be distributed in dividends. The most effective way to prevent such a premium being paid out in dividends is to carry it to a permanent reserve, or to apply it in writing off doubtful assets or expenses of an extraordinary nature. To be sure, when treating a premium in this way we are indirectly crediting it to income. It should not, however, be credited to the income of the year in which it is received.

Summarizing, then, the discount or premium on the sale of bonds is practically an increase or decrease of the rate of interest and therefore should be treated as follows:

(a) Discount should be charged to income over the term for which the bonds have to run.

(b) A premium should be either carried to a reserve account or applied to writing off doubtful assets such as goodwill or extraordinary expenses such as those of organization.

When bonds or stocks are bought by a corporation at a discount or premium it is advisable to treat such purchase as follows:

82. *Treatment of securities purchased.*—Stocks purchased should be carried at the cost. They are in nature similar to any other asset bought for the purpose of selling. Just as we debit the merchandise purchases for the cost of the goods bought, so we debit the stocks with their cost. The proceeds realized on the sale should be credited to them. The difference will represent the loss or gain on the venture. This, however, does not apply to bonds. If bonds are purchased at a premium the premium paid ,should be written off against the income during the term of the bond in such way that each year's income will be credited only with the true yield on the investment. For example, if the nominal interest on the bond is 5 per cent and by reason of such high rate of interest the bond sells at a premium, the actual yield of the bond is a lower rate of interest. Assume that a corporation purchases $1,000,000.00 of bonds bearing interest at 5 per cent payable semi-annually, with five years to run before maturity, and that the premium paid amounts to $1,000.00. The corporation should amortize that premium during the five years that the bonds have to run. Although it receives for interest at the semi-annual period, the sum of $2,500.00, its actual income from the bonds is only $2,400.00 and it should deduct from the interest received at each period the sum of $100.00. The effective interest rate in this case would be only 4.8 per cent instead of 5 per cent. There has been a loss of 0.2 per cent of interest by reason of the premium paid.

With regard to a discount on bond purchases, the general practice is not to credit such discount directly to income. No wrong is done to the person ultimately entitled to this extraordinary income because of such procedure, but to insure such person's rights in it, a discount reserve account should be opened and credited with the discount received.

CHAPTER XIV

PROBLEMS IN CORPORATION ACCOUNTING

PROBLEM I.

A corporation is organized to conduct a manufacturing business with a declared capital of $2,000,000.00 divided into 20,000 shares of the par value of $100.00, of which 15,000 shares or $1,500,000.00 shall be preferred stock and 5,000 shares or $500,000.00 common stock. The corporation purposes to issue $500,000.00 in consolidated mortgage bonds to be used toward the purchase of sundry properties. The amount of capital with which the corporation begins business is $50,000.00, being the proceeds of subscription of 500 shares preferred stock.

To carry out the purposes of said corporation, the real estate, water-power, machinery, goodwill, etc., of certain existing corporations have been purchased at an appraised valuation of $2,000,000.00, viz., Diamond Mfg. Co., $200,000.00; Eureka Mfg. Co., $300,000.00; Champion Mfg. Co., $500,000.00; American Mfg. Co., $600,000.00; and Ætna Mfg. Co., $400,000.00; and in payment full paid stocks and bonds have been issued at par on a basis of 60 per cent in preferred stock, 20 per cent in common stock, and 20 per cent in bonds. Materials and supplies are to be paid for when their value is determined. Formulate the entry necessary to open the books of the new corporation.

SOLUTION:

THE X, Y, Z COMPANY

INCORPORATED UNDER THE LAWS OF THE
STATE OF ———, WITH AN

AUTHORIZED CAPITAL

OF

$2,000,000.00.

DIVIDED INTO FIFTEEN THOUSAND SHARES OF PREFERRED AND FIVE THOUSAND
SHARES OF COMMON CAPITAL STOCK, PAR VALUE $100.00 EACH.

Subscription to preferred capital stock $50,000.00
   To preferred capital stock $50 000.00
      Representing the subscription to 500 shares of
      preferred stock of this company.
Cash $50,000.00
   To subscription $50,000.00
      Payment by subscribers for their respective
      subscriptions.

Plant and sundry assets 2,000.000.00
   To Diamond Manufacturing Company 200,000.00
      Eureka Manufacturing Company 300,000.00
      Champion Manufacturing Company 500,000.00
      American Manufacturing Company 600,000.00
      Aetna Manufacturing Company 400,000.00
      For the purchase of all assets including good-
      will of the above mentioned companies by this
      corporation in accordance with the resolution
      of the Board of Directors, dated ....
      190...
Diamond Manufacturing Company $200,000.00
Eureka Manufacturing Company 300,000.00
Champion Manufacturing Company 500,000.00
American Manufacturing Company 600,000.00
Aetna Manufacturing Company 400,000.00
   To preferred capital stock $1,200,000.00
      Common capital stock 400,000.00
      Consolidated mortgage bonds 400,000.00
      Payment to the above mentioned companies
      for the various assets acquired as per bill
      of sale, dated ...., 60% in pre-
      ferred capital stock, 20% in common capital
      stock, 20% in bonds.

In solving this problem we have debited the plant and sundry asset account for the assets acquired, and have credited the various companies whose assets we have bought. We cannot raise separate accounts on the books of the X, Y, Z Co. for the reason that the assets are not given in itemized form. As the company was authorized to issue $1,500,000.00 preferred stock but has issued only $1,200,000.00, to the respective companies whose assets it has acquired and $50,000.00 on subscription, making a total of $1,250,000.00, the company has unsubscribed preferred stock amounting to $250,000.00. The common stock that the company was authorized to issue was $500,000.00 of which it has issued $400,000.00, having unsubscribed common stock amounting to $100,-000.00.   In accordance with the wording of the problem the company determined to issue $500,000.00 of consolidated mortgage bonds.   In payment for the assets acquired from the respective corporations it has issued $400,000.00 of such bonds, and therefore has the right yet to issue $100,000.00 of bonds.   We cannot make any entry for the item of materials and supplies as no price has yet been determined.

In the second problem we are given the balance sheets of 1907 and 1908 and are asked to prepare tabulations, accounting for the profit earned.   It will be seen that the profit and loss balance in 1907 was $20,500.00 while the profit and loss balance in 1908 was $38,900.00, showing an increase of $18,400.00 for which the comparative balance sheet accounts.   As was stated earlier in this book, a profit is always the result of either an increase of assets or a decrease of liabilities, or both.   By means of this comparative balance sheet we show net increases of the assets as well as net decreases of the liabilities. Each represents a profit made and the sum of the two makes the $18,400.00 increase in profits for which we were to account.   (Pages 306–307.)

PROBLEM III.

A and B were partners trading under the name of A, B & Co.   On June 30, 1908, the following balances appear on their ledger:

PROBLEM II.

On December 31, 1907, the Balance Sheet of a certain corporation showed the following assets and liabilities:

Real estate.........	$55,000 00	Capital stock.........	$200,000.00	
Plant.........	95,000.00	Creditors' accounts.........	20,000.00	
Inventory.........	59,000 00	Bills payable.........	26,000.00	
Accounts receivable.........	45,500 00		$246,000.00	
Cash on hand.........	12,000.00			
		Profit and loss.....	20,500.00	

On December 31, 1908, one year later, the balance sheet showed the following:

Real estate.........	$57,000.00	Capital stock.........	$200,000.00	
Plant.........	85,500.00	Mortgage	20,000.00	
Inventory.........	73,750.00	Creditors' accounts....	22,000.00	
Accounts receivable.........	43,500.00		$242,000.00	
Other investments.........	10,000.00			
Cash on hand.........	11,150.00	Profit and loss.....	38,900.00	

Prepare tabulations showing what has become of the profits.

COMPARATIVE BALANCE SHEET OF THE X. Y. Z. COMPANY

ASSETS:

	1907	1908	Increase	Decrease
Cash.................	$12,000.00	$11,150.00		$850.00
Other Investments..		10,000.00	$10,000.00	
Accounts receivable.	45,500.00	43,500.00		2,000.00
Inventory...........	59,000.00	73,750.00	14,750.00	
Plant...............	95,000.00	85,500.00		9,500.00
Real estate.........	55,000.00	57,000.00	2,000.00	
	$266,500.00	$280,900.00	$26,750.00	$12,350.00
Net increase of assets				14,400.00
	$266,500.00	$280,900.00	$26,750.00	$26,750.00

LIABILITIES:

	1907	1908	Increase	Decrease
Bills payable.....	$26,000.00			$26,000.00
Accounts payable.	20,000.00	$22,000.00	$2,000.00	
Mortgage payable		20,000.00	20,000.00	
Capital stock....	200,000.00	200,000.00		
Profit and loss....	20,500.00	38,900.00		
	$266,500.00	$280,900.00	$22,000.00	$26,000.00
Net decrease of liabilities			4,000.00	
	$266,500.00	$280,900.00	$26,000.00	$26,000.00

Net profit amounting to $18,400.00 are accounted for as follows:

Net increase of assets................ $14,400.00
Net decrease of liabilities............ 4,000.00
$18,400.00

A, capital account	$70,000.00
B, capital account	50,000.00
Real estate	22,000.00
Buildings	20,000.00
Machinery and tools	44,000.00
Furniture and fixtures	2,000.00
Accounts receivable	50,000.00
Cash	7,000.00
Materials and merchandise	53,000.00
Accounts payable	35,000.00
Bills payable	48,000.00
Bills receivable	5,000.00

On June 30, 1908, the business is incorporated as the X Co., on the following plan:

1. Capital stock, $150,000.00.

2. X Co. takes over the assets and liabilities of A, B & Co., at the book figures as above, except (a) real estate of the book value of $5,000.00, which is retained by A, B & Co.; (b) the accounts receivable, which are taken over at $48,000.00.

3. X Co. pays A, B & Co. $30,000.00 for the goodwill of the business.

4. Payments to A, B & Co. are made as follows: viz., $50,000.00 in first mortgage bonds and the balance in capital stock of the X Co.

5. After paying off A, B & Co., the remainder of the capital stock is sold for cash to sundry persons.

6. The real estate which is retained by A, B & Co. is bought from A, B & Co., by A, for $7,000.00 and is to be charged to A's capital account.

After the completion of the foregoing described transactions A and B dissolve partnership.

REQUIRED.

(a) Closing entries for the books of A, B & Co.

(b) A statement setting forth the partners' accounts down to their final closing, beginning with the balances shown by the books on June 30, 1908.

(c) Opening entries for the X Co.

BALANCE SHEET OF THE FIRM A, B & COMPANY AS ON JUNE 30, 1908.

ASSETS:

Cash		$7,000.00
Bills receivable	$5,000.00	
Accounts receivable	50,000.00	55,000.00
Materials and merchandise		53,000.00	115,000.00
Real estate	22,000.00	
Buildings	20,000.00	
Machinery and tools	44,000.00	
Furniture and fixtures	2,000.00	88,000.00
		$203,000.00

LIABILITIES:

Bills payable	$48,000.00	
Accounts payable	35,000.00	$83,000.00

PROPRIETORSHIP:

A's capital account	70,000.00	
B's capital account	50,000.00	120,000.00
		$203,000.00

SOLUTION

In solving this problem we begin with the preparation of the balance sheet shown on the preceding page setting forth the accounts of the firm of A, B & Co.:

This balance sheet discloses a total value of assets of $203,000.00. The liabilities amount to $83,000.00, leaving a balance to proprietorship of $120,000.00 which, in accordance with the wording of the problem, is divided $70,000.00 to A, and $50,000.00 to B.

Our next step is to prepare the closing entries for the books of A, B & Co., which are as follows:

The X Co. (vendee)	$219,000.00	
For the purchase of the assets enumerated,		
To bills receivable		$5,000.00
Accounts receivable		48,000.00
Materials and merchandise		53,000.00
Machinery and tools		44,000.00
Furniture and fixtures		2,000.00
Buildings		20,000.00
Real estate		17,000.00
Goodwill		30,000.00
For the sale of the above mentioned assets, including goodwill, to the X Co., as per bill of sale dated .... 190...		
Bills payable	48,000.00	
Accounts payable	35,000.00	
To X Co. (vendee)		83,000.00
Assumed by the X Co., as part consideration for the assets bought.		
First mortgage bonds	50,000.00	
Part payment for assets sold to the X Co.		
Capital stock	86,000.00	
Balance of payment received from the X Co., as final settlement for assets acquired.		
To X Co.		136,000.00
Settlement in accordance with terms of sale.		

It will be noticed that the X Co. is debited for $219,000.00. The accounts receivable were to be taken over at $48,000.00 which is a decrease of $2,000.00 from the book value; part of the buildings were sold for $17,000.00 which is a decrease from the book value of $5,000.00. The cash is left out of consideration entirely for the reason that in selling the assets to the company the firm did not sell the cash as one of them. The problem might be so worded as to mean a transfer of *all* the assets, including cash, but in this case the wording does not necessarily include the cash among the assets sold. The cash then will be divided among the partners. Adding the cash item $7,000.00 to the deduction of $7,000.00 noted above, we have a total of $14,000.00. The total assets on the balance sheet amounted to $203,000.00, from which we deduct $14,000.00, leaving a balance of $189,000.00. To this we add the $30,000.00 for goodwill, which will account for the journal entry debiting the company for $219,000.00.

As the vendee has assumed the liabilities we close those accounts out by debiting them and crediting the company. Deducting the assumed liabilities from the assets sold we have a balance of $136,000.00. The company pays this sum by giving mortgage bonds amounting to $50,000.00 and capital stock for the balance of $86,000.00. We, therefore, debit the assets received, bonds and stocks respectively, and credit the X Co.

The real estate which is retained by A, B & Co. ($5,000.00) is sold by the firm to A, a member of the firm, for $7,000.00. It is accordingly charged to his account by the following journal entry:

```
A's capital account ............................... $7,000.00
   To real estate ............................................    $7,000.00
        For part of real estate sold by the firm to A.
```

It will be observed that the accounts receivable realized $2,000.00 less than their book value as given in the balance sheet, while the real estate realized $2,000.00 more than its book value. There was also realized $30,000.00 in excess of the valuation of the assets by reason of the sale of goodwill. It is not advisable to open a profit and loss account, to carry through the respective losses and gains realized on the sale of the assets because a profit and loss account deals with profits made or losses sustained in the ordinary course of trade, which is not the case here. The best plan to follow is to open an adjustment account and to debit it for all the losses and credit it for all the profits, transferring the balance to the respective partners' accounts. We, therefore, make the following entry:

```
Adjustment account ...........................  $2,000.00
    For the purpose of closing out the ac-
    counts showing a loss on realization.
    To accounts receivable .........,..................         $2,000.00
    For allowances made to the X Co., on
    transfer and sale of assets.
        Goodwill ..................... $30,000.00
        Real estate ...................   2,000.00
        For the purpose of closing out ac-
        counts showing an additional profit
        on realization.
    To adjustment account ......................  $32,000.00
    For additional profits realized.
Adjustment account ...........................   30,000.00
    To A's capital account ..............................         15,000.00
       B's capital account ..............................         15,000.00
       Transfer of additional profits made on re-
       alization in equal parts to the partners' ac-
       counts.
```

While the partners' capital accounts show a greater investment to A than to B, nevertheless, nothing being said to the contrary, we assume that the partners share profits and losses equally and as the balance of the adjustment account is a profit, it is equally divided.

We have so far closed all but five accounts, namely, cash, mortgage bonds, capital stock and the partners' capital accounts. We, therefore, make the following entry:

```
A's capital account .............................  $78,000.00
B's capital account .............................   65,000.00
    To cash ............................................         $7,000.00
    First mortgage bonds .................................         50,000.00
    Capital stock .......................................         86,000.00
        For the purpose of closing final accounts and
        distributing the remaining assets among part-
        ners, the partnership having been dissolved.
```

A'S CAPITAL ACCOUNT.

1908			1908		
June 30.	To sale of real estate	$7,000.00	June 30.	By balance	$70,000.00
30.	Sundry items, viz.:		30.	Adjustment Account ...	15,000.00
	Cash, bonds and stock ...	78,000.00			
		$85,000.00			$85,000.00

B'S CAPITAL ACCOUNT.

1908			1908		
June 30.	To sundry items, viz.:		June 30.	By balance	$50,000.00
	Cash, bonds and stock ...	$65,000.00	30.	Adjustment Account ...	15,000.00
		$65,000.00			$65,000.00

A's capital account is debited for $78,000.00 as follows: his investment $70,000.00 plus $15,000.00 profits, makes a total of $85,000.00, from which we deduct $7,000.00 due for real estate purchased, leaving a balance of $78,000.00. B's capital account is debited for $65,000.00, made up of the capital invested, $50,000.00 plus $15,000.00 profits. As the partners retained the cash and are entitled to the bonds and stock these assets are now distributed between them and the asset accounts credited.

This completes the first part of the problem, namely, the closing entries for the books of A, B & Co. The second part of the problem calls for a statement setting forth the partners' accounts down to their final closing. We, therefore, prepare the partners' accounts, shown on preceding page, which are self-explanatory.

We have now to give the opening entries for the X Co. They are as follows:

THE X COMPANY

INCORPORATED UNDER THE LAWS OF THE
STATE OF ———, WITH AN

AUTHORIZED CAPITAL
OF
$150,000.00,
DIVIDED INTO ...... SHARES OF $.... PAR VALUE.

Subscription $64,000.00
  To capital stock $64,000.00
    For subscription to shares of the capital stock
    of the company.
Cash $64,000.00
  To subscription $64,000.00
    Proceeds of sale of .... shares of stock
    as per subscription.
Plant and sundry assets ....:................. $219,000.00
    For sundry assets acquired of the firm of A,
    B & Co.
  To A, B & Co. (vendors) $219,000.00
    For the surrender to the company of their
    right, title and interest in all the assets enu-
    merated in the bill of sale, dated ....

```
A, B & Co. (vendors) ...........................   83,000.00
      For the assumption by the company of their
      liabilities.
   To sundry liabilities .......................................   $83,000.00
      Assumed by this company and enumerated in
      bill of sale, dated ...........
A, B & Co. (vendors) ........................ $136,000.00
      For final settlement for assets bought.
   To first mortgage bonds ...............................   50,000.00
      Capital stock ....................................   86,000.00
      For .......... @ .......... and ..........
      shares of stock.
Bills receivable ...................................    5,000.00
Accounts receivable ..............................   48,000.00
Materials and merchandise ......................   53,000.00
Machinery and tools .............................   44,000.00
Furniture and fixtures ...........................    2,000.00
Buildings .........................................   20,000.00
Real estate .......................................   17,000.00
Goodwill ..........................................   30,000.00
   To plant and sundry assets .............................   219,000.00
      This entry is made for the purpose of placing
      all the assets acquired on the books of the
      company.
Sundry liabilities ...............................   83,000.00
   To bills payable .........................................   48,000.00
      Accounts payable .....................................   35,000.00
      This entry is made for the purpose of placing
      the liabilities assumed on the books of the
      company.
```

As the par value of the stock is not mentioned in the problem, it has been omitted in the solution.

PROBLEM IV.

The Martin Co. was incorporated with a capital of $500,000.00 divided into 5,000 shares of $100.00 each, to take over the assets and liabilities of the firms of Martin & Scott, and Burton & James.

The subscriptions to the stock are as follows:

John Martin and Henry Scott, composing the firm of Martin & Scott, 200 shares each.

Charles Burton and Thomas James, composing the firm of Burton & James, 150 shares each.

The subscriptions were paid in cash and the stock was issued to the respective subscribers.

The net assets of the firm of Martin & Scott were

purchased by the company at 75 per cent of their ledger values and full paid stock of the company was given therefor. The net assets of the firm of Burton & James were purchased by the company at 60 per cent of their ledger values, and full stock given by the company in payment therefor.

The condition of affairs of the respective concerns was as follows:

Assets, liabilities and proprietorship of the firm of Martin & Scott:

ASSETS:

Cash	$5,000.00	
Accounts receivable	80,000.00	
Raw stock, lumber, etc.	1,000.00	
Raw stock, steel, brass, wire, etc.	8,000.00	
Machinery and tools	7,500.00	
Real estate (factory site)	15,000.00	
Goodwill	4,500.00	$121,000.00

LIABILITIES:

Bills payable	$70,000.00	
Accounts payable	27,000.00	97,000.00

PROPRIETORSHIP:

John Martin, capital account	$18,000.00	
Henry Scott, capital account	6,000.00	$24,000.00

ASSETS AND PROPRIETORSHIP OF THE FIRM OF BURTON & JAMES.

ASSETS:

Accounts receivable	110,000.00	
Manufactured stock	20,000.00	
Raw stock	25,000.00	
Goodwill	45,000.00	$200,000.00

PROPRIETORSHIP:

Charles Burton, capital account	150,000.00	
Thomas James, capital account	50,000.00	$200,000.00

It was agreed that all the assets and liabilities acquired by purchase should appear upon the books of the company at the values shown in the vendors' ledgers until the close of the third year, at which time goodwill should be charged to profit and loss account. And it was stipulated that in the event that the legitimate profit of any year from trading exceeded $20,000.00, the individual members of the firm of Burton & James were to receive 30 per cent of said excess, and expense account should be charged therewith, but if the profits were less than $20,000.00 they were to pay the deficiency to the company, and expense account credited therewith. The profit and loss account showed legitimate profits from trading for the first year amounting to $27,000.00, for the second year amounting to $40,000.00, and for the third year amounting to $15,000.00, before adjusting the claim arising from above stipulation as to the $20,000.00. The entire profits, irrespective of their source, were then paid to stockholders of issue, as dividends in full paid stock.

Required:

First: The aggregate of net assets at the close of the first, second and third years, assuming all debts to have been paid.

Second: The amount due to each of the parties in interest, in stock and undivided profits at the end of the first and second years respectively, assuming that the profit and loss account has been adjusted at these periods; and the amount of stock held by each stockholder after the actual adjustment of the profit and loss and dividend accounts, at the end of the year.

Third: Balance sheets for the close of each period, using given assets and liabilities throughout, with an additional account entitled "increase."

SOLUTION.

This solution conforms with the ideas of those accountants who desire to show the full amount of the authorized capital stock, regardless of whether or not such stock has been subscribed. (See page 284.) We show in a memorandum the organization of the corporation as follows:

THE MARTIN COMPANY
INCORPORATED UNDER THE LAWS OF THE
STATE OF ———, WITH AN

AUTHORIZED CAPITAL
OF
$500,000.00,
DIVIDED INTO 5,000 SHARES PAR VALUE OF $100.00 EACH.

OUR NEXT ENTRY WILL BE:

Subscriptions $70,000.00
Unsubscribed stock 430,000.00

    To authorized capital stock $500,000.00
      JohnMartin   subscribes 200 shares @ $100.00 par,
      Henry Scott   subscribes 200 shares @ $100.00 par,
      Charles Burton subscribes 150 shares @ $100.00 par,
      Thomas James   subscribes 150 shares @ $100.00 par,

Attention is called to the fact that while the account entitled "unsubscribed stock" will appear in the ledger, its balance should never be listed on the asset side of the balance sheet for the reason that it does not represent an asset; it should be deducted from the authorized capital stock.

The second entry shows the payment of cash for such subscription:

Cash $70,000.00
    To subscription $70,000 00
      Subscribers pay for their respective subscriptions.

Our next entry is to show the acquisition of the assets as follows:

Plant and sundry assets $231,250.00
   To Martin & Scott 111,250.00
   Burton & James 120,000.00
      For the transfer of their right, title and in-
      terest in assets sold, in accordance with agree-
      ment, dated ...., and resolution of the
      Board of Directors, dated ....

Plant and sundry assets account is debited for $231,250.00 which is made up of the following items: The value of the assets of the firm of Martin & Scott, as given in the problem, amounted to $121,000.00 including cash. As cash is not an asset to be sold, especially in view of the fact that the firm of Burton & James has no cash, that cash is treated as retained by the members of the firm of Martin & Scott. Deducting the cash, then, the assets amount to $116,000.00. Of this $97,000.00 worth are paid for in full by assumption of liabilities to that amount. The balance of $19,000.00 worth of assets is purchased at 75 per cent or $14,250.00. Adding this sum to the $97,000.00 paid by the assumption of liabilities makes the total price fixed or the assets of the firm of Martin & Scott $111,250.00 for which Martin & Scott are credited. The assets of Burton & James amount to $200,000.00, 60 per cent of which is $120,000.00; $120,000.00 plus $111,250.00 amounts to $231,250.00, the amount charged to plant and sundry assets.

The next entry is to show the assumption of the liabilities by the corporation, namely:

Martin & Scott $97,000.00
   To bills payable $70,000.00
   Accounts payable 27,000.00
      Liabilities assumed by the company represent-
      ing part consideration for the assets that were
      acquired from this firm.

Our next entry to show the payment by the company in stock for the assets acquired is as follows:

```
Martin & Scott ................................. $14,250.00
Burton & James ............................... $120,000.00
    To subscription ........................................... $134,250.00
        For the subscription to ........ shares of
        the capital stock of the company.
Subscription ................................... 134,250.00
    To unsubscribed stock ...................................... 134,250.00
        Representing the issue of stock to the parties
        mentioned in the preceding entry in settle-
        ment for assets acquired from them.
```

The company desires to place the assets on its books at the same values as shown in the vendors' ledgers. We, therefore, make the following entry:

```
Real estate ...................................... $15,000.00
Machinery and tools ............................ 7,500.00
Raw stock ....................................... 34,000.00
Goodwill ........................................ 49,500.00
Accounts receivable ............................ 190,000.00
Manufactured stock ............................ 20,000.00
    To plant and sundry assets ............................ $231,250.00
    Reserve for contingencies ............................. $84,750.00
        For the purpose of placing the assets on the
        books of the company, as per resolution, of
        the Board of Directors, dated .......... 19...
```

The problem requires us to state the amount of stock given to each member. In this connection there are several things to be noticed. There is nothing mentioned about the agreement which must exist between Martin & Scott and Burton & James as to the division of profits or losses in connection with the sale. The firms have sold their assets at a value less than that shown on the books, and have consequently sustained a loss. As nothing, however, is stated as to how that loss is to be apportioned, we assume that it is to be divided equally among the partners. Martin & Scott have suffered a loss of $4,750.00 in the sale of their assets. Assuming that the $5,000.00 cash was divided equally between them the capital of each partner would be as shown on page 323.

FIRST YEAR

Expense—Burton & James....................		$2,100.00
30% excess profits of 7,000.00, due to:		
James, ⅓........................	$1,050.00	
Burton, ⅓........................	1,050.00	
Net profit for the year..............		24,900.00
		$27,000.00

By profit from trading (first year).....	$27,000.00
	$27,000.00

SECOND YEAR

Expense—Burton & James..................		6,000.00
30% of $20,000 excess profit due to:		
James, ⅓..........................	$3,000.00	
Burton, ⅓........................	3,000.00	
Net profit at end of second year....		58,900.00
		$64,900.00

Balance...........................	$24,900.00
Profit from trading (second year)....	40,000.00
	$64,900.00

321

THIRD YEAR

Goodwill.................		$49,500.00
Net profit at the expiration of the third year.....		114,150.00
		$163,650.00

Balance........................		$58,900.00
Profit from trading (third year)........		15,000.00
Burton & James........		5,000.00
Representing contribution which they agreed to make in case of deficiency in profits below $20,000.00:		
Burton..........	$ 2,500.00	
James..........	2,500.00	
Reserve for contingencies.................		$84,750.00
		$163,650.00

PROFIT AND LOSS ACCOUNT (Continued)

To Stock Dividend:			
John Martin..........	185 shares	$18,500 00	
Henry Scott..........	118 shres	11,800 00	
Chas. Burton..........	698 shares	69,800 00	
Thos. James..........	139 shares	13,900.00	
	1,140 shres	1$4,000.00	
Cash Dividend (for fractional amounts due)			
John Martin..........	$12.70		
Henry Scott..........	6.21		
Chas. Burton..........	59.25		
Ms. James..........	71.84	150.00	
		$114,150.00	

By Balance.......... · $114,150.00

$114,150.00

Martin:
Former Capital		$18,000.00
Deduct cash received	$2,500.00	
Loss on sale of assets	2,375.00	4,875.00

Balance due him $13,125.00

Scott:
Former capital		6,000.00
Deduct cash received	$2,500.00	
Loss on sale of assets	2,375.00	4,875.00

Balance due him $1,125.00

Burton & James have sustained a loss of $80,000.00
and their accounts would, therefore, stand as follows:

Burton:
Former capital	150,000.00
Deduct loss on sale of assets	40,000.00

Balance due him $110,000.00

James:
Former capital	50,000.00
Deduct loss on sale of assets	40,000.00

Balance due him $10,000.00

That accounts for the total of $134,250.00 for which stock was issued and shows how that is to be apportioned among the members of the two firms. It was important for us to determine this as we had to know the holdings of each member on account of the stock dividend which is to be apportioned at the end of the third year.

The next point in solving the problem is to take up the matter of the profit and loss adjustment with regard to the clause relative to the $20,000.00 profit each year and the treatment of excesses and deficiencies over and under this amount. We therefore prepare the profit and loss account shown on pages 321–322.

It will be seen that the reserve for dividends amounted to $84,750.00, as created originally and now transferred to the credit of the profit and loss account, while goodwill of $49,500.00 has been debited at the end of the third year to that account in accordance with the wording of the problem.   Our next step is to show how this profit of $114,150.00 should be distributed, which is done as follows in a continuation of the profit and loss account, the stock dividend being shown separately from the cash dividend, which represents fractional payments.

It will be recalled that the shares of stock are of the par value of $100.00.   We therefore apportion $114,000.00 in stock dividends and we arrange for the balance of $150.00 to be paid as a cash dividend in fractional amounts.

Our next step is to prepare a statement of the undivided profits as they appear at the end of each year, as follows:

STATEMENT OF UNDIVIDED PROFITS AT THE END OF EACH

YEAR.

	1st Year.	2nd Year.	3rd Year.
John Martin	$4,038.25	$5,514.07	$8,960.29
Henry Scott	2,575.34	3,516.53	5,714.34
Charles Burton ....,..	15,238.67	20,807.84	33,812.82
Thomas James	3,047.74	4,161.56	6,762.55
	$24,900 00	$34,000.00	$55,250.00

We now prepare a comparative balance sheet (on following page) showing the condition of the corporation at the close of each year, stating each important fact in detail:

We have so far issued the following amounts of capital stock:

John Martin:	Cash subscription	200	shares	
	For excess of assets over liabilities	131¼	shares	
	Stock dividends	185	shares	516¼ shares

COMPARATIVE BALANCE SHEET OF THE MARTIN COMPANY

ASSETS:	1st Year	2nd Year	3rd Year
Cash..................	$70,000.00	$70,000.00	$69,850.00
Accounts receivable...	190,000.00	190,000.00	190,000.00
Manufactured stock...	20,000.00	20,000.00	20,000.00
Raw stock............	34,000.00	34,000.00	34,000.00
Real estate...........	15,000.00	15,000.00	15,000.00
Machinery and Tools.	7,500.00	7,500.00	7,500.00
	$336,500.00	$336,500.00	$336,350.00
Increase.............	27,000.00	67,000.00	82,000.00
	$363,500.00	$403,500.00	$418,350.00
Less old debts paid...	97,000.00	97,000.00	97,000.00
	$266,500.00	$306,500.00	$321,350.00
Less Burton's and James' claim......	2,100.00	8,100.00	3,100.00
Net value of our assets excluding goodwill..	$264,400.00	$298,400.00	$318,250.00
Goodwill.............	49,500.00	49,500.00	
	$313,900.00	$347,900.00	$318,250.00
Unsubscribed stock to be deducted from authorized capital stock.............	$295,750.00	$295,750.00	$181,750.00
	$609,650.00	$643,650.00	$500,000.00

LIABILITIES:	1st Year	2nd Year	3rd Year
Capital stock authorized.............	$500,000.00	$500,000.00	$500,000.00
Reserve for contingencies............	84,750.00	84,750.00	
Surplus..............	24,900.00	58,900.00	
	$609,650.00	$643,650.00	$500,000.00

Henry Scott:	Cash subscription	200	shares		
	For excess of assets over liabilities	11¼	shares		
	Stock dividend	118	shares	329¼	shares
Charles Burton:	Cash subscription	150	shares		
	For assets	1100	shares		
	Stock dividend	698	shares	1948	shares
Thos. James·	Cash subscription	150	shares		
	For assets	100	shares		
	Stock dividend	139	shares	389	shares
			Total	3,182½	shares

The amount of stock that each received represents the excess of assets over liabilities; in the cases of Martin & Scott this is 131¼ and 11¼ shares respectively. This fractional share may be taken to have been issued to them in scrip. Of course, it might have been assumed that they received cash for that sum.

PROBLEM V.

The A Co. went into liquidation, and its statement of affairs was as follows:

ASSETS:

Land and buildings, plant and machinery, etc.	$50,000.00
Stock in trade	12,500.00
Sundry debtors, after providing for bad debts and discounts ...	7,500.00
	$70,000.00
Profit and loss account, debit balance	25,000.00
	95,000.00

LIABILITIES:

Sundry creditors	20,000.00
Capital stock	75,000.00
	$95,000.00

The assets were purchased by the B Co. for $60,000.00, paid, as to $37,500.00, by the issue of 5,000 shares of $5.00 each, fully paid, in the B Co., taken at their then market price of $7.50 per share, and as to $22,500.00, in cash. The costs of winding up were $2,500.00. Make the journal and cashbook entries for the above transactions in the books of the A Co., and post and close the books of the company.

In solving this problem we have first of all to set up a realization account and to charge to it the sale of the assets so as to be able to determine any deficiency that may arise. We, therefore, make the following journal entry:

```
Realization account ............................. $70,000.00
  To land and buildings, etc. ................................  $50,000.00
     Stock in trade ........................................   12,500.00
     Sundry debtors ........................................    7,500.00
        For value of assets taken over by the B
        Co., as per resolution, dated ..........
        190...
```

This entry charges the realization account for the assets shown on our books. As we sold the assets to the B Co. for $60,000.00 we make the following entry:

```
The B Co. ....................................... $60,000.00
  To realization account ...................................  $60,000.00
     For transfer of the right, title and interest
     in assets enumerated in purchases agreement
     dated .......... 190.., approved by resolu-
     tion dated .......... 190...
```

As will be seen, the B Co. which acquires the assets is debited and the realization account is credited.

The cost of winding up the affairs was $2,500.00. As this cost must have been incurred from time to time and not at once, for the reason that the problem does not tell us of any cash in the possession of the company, we make the following journal entry:

```
Realization account ............................. 2,500.00
  To liquidation expenses ..................................  2,500.00
     For cost of winding up affairs.
```

The B Co. pays for the assets acquired 5,000 shares of stock the market price of which is $7.50 per share and cash to the amount of $22,500.00. The cash payment is shown in the cashbook as follows:

CASH BOOK.

Dr.			Cr.
To B Co. (for assets acquired)	$22,500.00	By accounts payable in full	$20,000.00
		Liquidation expenses	2,500.00
	$22,500.00		$22,500.00

The stock received is shown in the following journal entry:

B Co.'s stock $37,500.00
  To B Co. $37,500.00
    For 5,000 shares par value $5.00, received by
    us in payment for assets at $7.50 per share.

As will be seen the realization account has been debited for $70,000.00 in connection with the sale of the assets and has also been debited for $2,500.00 for the liquidation expenses. As the sale of the assets realized only $60,000.00, which has been credited to realization account, there is a balance of $12,500.00 in that account. In the profit and loss account, as we are told in the problem, there is a debit balance of $25,000.00. We, therefore, make the following journal entry:

Deficiency account $37,500.00
  For impairment of the capital of this com-
  pany.
  To realization account $12,500.00
  Profit and loss account 25,000.00
    For losses on realization and sundry trade
    losses.

We still have on our books the accounts of the capital stock of the company, the stock received from the B Co. and the deficiency account. As the deficiency

REALIZATION ACCOUNT.

To sundry assets	$70,000.00	By B. Co.		$60,000.00
Liquidation expenses ...	2,500.00	Deficiency account ...	...	12,500.00
	$72,500.00			$72,500.00

LIQUIDATION EXPENSE ACCOUNT.

To cash	$2,500.00	By realization account	$2,500.00

PROFIT AND LOSS ACCOUNT.

To balance	$25,000.00	By deficiency account	$25,000.00

ACCOUNTS PAYABLE.

To cash	$20,000.00	By balance	$20,000.00

CAPITAL STOCK.

To deficiency account	$37,500.00	By balance	$75,000.00
B Co.'s stock	37,500.00		
	$75,000.00		$75,000.00

THE B CO.

To realization account	$60,000.00	By B Co.'s stock $37,500.00
		Cash 22,500.00

B CO.'S STOCK.

To B. Co.	$37,500.00	By capital stock $37,500.00

DEFICIENCY ACCOUNT.

To profit and loss	$25,000.00	By capital stock $37,500.00
Realization account	12,500.00	
	$37,500.00	$37,500.00

account shows an impairment of the capital stock we make the following final entry, which when posted closes all the accounts.

```
Capital stock ..................................... $75,000.00
  To deficiency account ...................................... $37,500.00
  B Co.'s stock ............................................. $37,500.00
      For issue of B Co.'s stock pro rata, to our
      stockholders, charging against their holdings
      the losses of the company.
```

The ledger accounts of the firm now appear as shown on the preceding pages.

.PROBLEM VI.

A corporation is formed under the laws of the State of Pennsylvania with an authorized capital of $1,000,000.00 divided into 10,000 shares of the par value of $100.00 each.

The date of charter is January 1, 1900, at which time it starts business with 5,000 shares subscribed for upon which a payment of 20 per cent has been made, the balance to be paid in monthly installments of 10 per cent on the first day of each succeeding month, 90 per cent of the first installment being invested in plant.

On February 1, 1900, the corporation purchased the goodwill, plant and assets of a manufacturing concern, doing the same kind of business and assumed the liabilities of the same, for 2,500 shares of the capital stock of the company full paid and non-assessable.

The floating assets of the purchased company were as follows:

```
Book accounts receivable ..................................... $15,000.00
Bills receivable ............................................. 18,000.00
Material and supplies ........................................ 42,000.00
THE LIABILITIES ASSUMED CONSISTED OF:
Book accounts payable ........................................ $23,000.00
Bills payable ................................................ 10,000.00
```

The value of the plant acquired from this company was $158,000.00.

On July 1, 1900, a dividend of 5 per cent on the par value of the stock was paid to the stockholders of the company in proportion to their holdings.

On December 1, 1900, by resolution of the stockholders of the company it was determined to purchase another concern in a similar business and issue bonds in payment thereof.

The amount of bonds authorized to be issued was $1,000,000.00 and the price to be paid for the concern was $650,000.00 in mortgage bonds, bearing interest at 5 per cent, dated December 1, 1900, and due December 1, 1910.

The new company was to take over all assets and assume all liabilities of the concern purchased.

The assets consisted of:

Book accounts receivable $150,000.00
Bills receivable 26,000.00
Materials and supplies 82,000.00

The liabilities were book accounts payable, $8,000.00.

On December 31, 1900, a dividend of 5 per cent on the par value of stock was declared out of the earnings of the corporation, payable to the stockholders in proportion to their interests.

During this year the company purchased on credit material and supplies to the amount of $1,550,000.00, and for cash $38,150.00. It paid for organization expenses of the company $3,800.00, as well as the usual taxes incidental to corporations, counsel fees of $5,-000.00, commissions of $50,000.00, wages of $516,-100.00, and salaries of $110,000.00. It sold products to the amount of $2,510,000.00, and it received in cash from sundry debtors $2,000,000.00. It accepted drafts for $1,450,000.00.   Of the notes and acceptances $1,-240,000.00 became due and was paid and in addition there has been paid to creditors $50,000.00 in cash.   The discount allowed sundry debtors was $18,250.00, and the discount received from sundry creditors was $14,500.00. It is determined to write off 5 per cent on plant valnation, and $5,000.00 for bad debts.   The value of the stock of material and supplies on hand is $50,000.00.

Make entries showing the cash transactions, and prepare a balance sheet as on December 31, 1900.   In your cashbook show also the amount of taxes the company had to pay.

SOLUTION.

The cashbook is shown on the following page:

ANALYSIS OF SOLUTION.

On the debit side of the cashbook are entered all the receipts of cash on the installments as well as the amounts collected on the accounts receivable during the year.   On the credit side the second item is that of the taxes.   This amount of $3,375.83 is made up of the following items:

⅛ of 1% of the authorized issue of stock	$3,333.33
Cost of filing certificate	30.00
Payment to the Secretary of State	10.00
Recording of certificate, 25 cents per folio (about)	2.50
	$3,375.83

The various other payments made include the first semi-annual dividend of 5 per cent on outstanding stock. The cash balance on hand at the end of the year amounted to $356,074.17.

We then prepare the balance sheet shown on page 335.

CASH BOOK.

Dr.			Cr.
1900		**1900**	
Jan. 1. To subscription $100,000.00		Jan. 1. By plant $90,000.00
20% on 5000 shares.		Taxes 3,375.83
Feb. 1. subscription 50,000.00		Feb. 1. Organization expenses 3,800.00
2nd installment.		Counsel fees 5,000.00
Mar. 1. subscription 50,000.00		July 1. First semi-annual 5% dividend ... 37,500.00
3rd installment.		Jan.–Dec. Purchases of material 38,150.00
Apr. 1. subscription 50,000.00		Jan.–Dec. Wages 516,100.00
4th installment.		Jan.–Dec. Salaries 110,000.00
May. 1. subscription 50,000.00		Jan.–Dec. Commission 50,000.00
5th installment.		Jan.–Dec. Notes payable 1,240,000.00
June 1. subscription 50,000.00		Jan.–Dec. Accounts payable 50,000.00
6th installment.		Jan.–Dec. Balance 356,074.17
July 1. subscription 50,000.00		
7th installment.		
Aug. 1. subscription 50,000.00		
8th installment.		
Sept. 1. subscription 50,000.00		
9th installment.		
Jan.–Dec. Accounts receivable 2,000,000.00		
$2,500,000.00		$2,500,000.00
1901		
Jan. 1. To balance .. 356,074.17		

334

BALANCE SHEET

ASSETS:

Cash		$356,074.17
Notes receivable ...	$44,000.00	
Accounts receivable ...	656,750.00	
	700,750.00	
Less reserve for bad debts ...	5,000.00	695,750.00
Materials and supplies ...		50,000.00
Plant purchased ...	90,000.00	
Plant acquired ...	158,000.00	
	248,000.00	
Less depreciation 5% ..	12,400.00	235,600.00
Goodwill		450,000.00
		$1,787,424.17

LIABILITIES:

Bills payable ...	$220,000.00	
Accounts payable ...	66,500.00	$286,500.00
Bonds payable:		
Authorized	1,000,000.00	
Less unissued ...	350,000.00	650,000.00
Interest accrued ..		2,708.33
Capital stock:		
Authorized	1,000,000.00	
Unissued	250,000.00	750,000.00
Second semi-annual dividend declared		37,500.00
Surplus		60,715.84
		$1,787,424.17

It will be noticed that in giving the item of plant on the asset side, the plant purchased and the plant acquired from the company were added, giving a total of $248,000.00. From this total a depreciation of 5 per cent, according to the problem, has been deducted, showing the net value of the plant at the end of the year as $235,600.00. The last asset on the balance sheet is the item of goodwill amounting to $450,000.00. This is made up of the goodwill allowed to the first company amounting to $50,000.00 and of $400,000.00, representing the excess payment made to Company B over and above the valuation of its assets. The assets of Company B amounted to only $250,000.00, yet $650,000.00 in bonds were issued for them, which was $400,000.00 in excess of their valuation. Some companies in such cases would add this goodwill with the plant and carry the plant at the full sum, but this is not advisable for the reason that it would mis-state the facts. One who sees such a balance sheet might think that the amount of the asset was represented by an *actual* plant, which would not be the case. It is therefore preferable to state the plant at its actual valuation and to state the goodwill separately.

The liability side is self-explanatory excepting three items. First: interest accrued. This represents one month's interest on the bonds, which are dated December 1 and bear 5 per cent interest. As our balance sheet is prepared as for December 31 we must make allowance for this one month's accrued interest which at 5 per cent amounts to $2,708.33.

Second: semi-annual dividend declared. As this dividend has been declared on the 31st and has not been paid, it is a liability of the company.

Third: surplus. This represents the difference between the assets and liabilities, including the capital stock, and amounts to $60,715.84.

In order to show that surplus we must prepare a trading statement, although that was not expressly required by the problem. This is shown on the following page.

This trading account, page 338, shows a balance on trade to be carried to the surplus account amounting to $135,715.84. We prepare the surplus account:

SURPLUS ACCOUNT.

To 1st semi-annual dividend	$37,500.00	By balance from trading statement	$135,715.84
2nd semi-annual dividend	37,500.00		
Balance	60,715.84		
	$135,715.84		$135,715.84
		By balance	60,715.84

Having completed the surplus account we have yet to show the dividend account, which is shown on page 339.

PROBLEM VII.

Assuming that $1,000,000.00 a year is required to pay interest and dividends on the following:

(a) An issue of preferred stock at 4½% (amount not given)
(b) Common stock at 3% $300,000.00
(c) Bonds $350,000.00
(d) 2nd issue of preferred stock at 5% 100,000.00

and that there is a balance of $680,000.00 to meet this payment, show how this amount should be divided.

SOLUTION.

Adding the three given amounts makes a total of $750,000.00, which is required for the payment of the second, third and fourth items. As the total amount

To inventories	$124,000.00		By sales	$2,510,000.00	
Purchases	1,588,150.00		Less discounts allowed	18,250.00	
	$1,712,150.00				2,491,750.00
Less inventory Dec. 31	$50,000.00				
Discount	14,500.00	64,500.00			
Cost of goods sold		1,647,650.00			
Wages		516,100.00			
Depreciation on plant		12,400.00			
Gross profit		315,600.00			
		$2,491,750.00			$2,491,750.00

To commissions		50,000.00	By gross profit ...	315,600.00
Profit on trading		265,600.00		
		$315,600.00		$315,600.00

To salaries	110,000.00	By profit on trading ...	265,600.00
Taxes	3,375.83		
Organization expenses (including counsel fees)	8,800.00		
Reserve for bad debts	5,000.00		
Interest accrued on bonds	2,708.33		
Balance to surplus account	135,715.84		
	265,600.00		265,600.00

DIVIDEND ACCOUNT

To cash payment of dividend	$37,500.00	By 1st semi-annual dividend	$37,500.00
Balance	37,500.00	2nd semi-annual dividend	37,500.00
	$75,000.00		$75,000.00
		Balance	$37,500.00

required is $1,000,000.00, it is obvious that the amount required for the payment of dividends on the first issue of preferred stock must be $250,000.00. The first thing to be provided for is the interest on the bonds, and next in order is the dividend on the first issue of preferred stock. They together require $600,000.00, which leaves a balance of $80,000.00. As $100,000.00 is needed to pay the dividend on the second issue of preferred stock, and as there is only $80,000.00 left, the company could pay only 4 per cent, instead of 5 per cent, on this stock. The $680,000.00, therefore, would be applied as follows:

(a)	Interest on bonds	$350,000.00
(b)	Dividend on first issue of preferred stock ..	250,000.00
(c)	4% dividend on second issue of preferred stock	80,000.00
	Making a total of	$680,000.00

The holders of the common stock do not receive any dividends.

If this second issue of preferred stock is cumulative the holders of it would at some future period receive the 1 per cent that was not paid to them at this time, before the common stockholders would receive anything. If, however, the issue of the second preferred stock is non-cumulative, they would have no such right but would be forced to accept a 4 per cent instead of the expected 5 per cent dividend.

PROBLEM VIII.

A corporation issues bonds, the proceeds of which are to be used for construction purposes. If the bonds are sold at a discount, to what account should the discount be charged; if they sold at a premium, to what account should the premium be credited?

If the bonds are sold at a discount, the cost of the construction is not only the actual amount that must be paid out but also the discount incurred when thus acquiring capital. As the amount that has to be paid to get capital with which to construct the property is an additional cost, the discount on an issue of bonds, the proceeds of which are used for construction purposes, should be charged to the construction account and that is the policy usually followed.

If the bonds are sold at a premium, the cost of construction is not thereby reduced. Securing the premium resulted simply from the fact that the corporation was in a position to find capital cheaply and the premium is merely an offset against the interest that has to be paid on the bonds. The accounting procedure in such a case has been discussed on page 301.

CHAPTER XV

CORPORATION FORMS

83. *Waiver of notice.*—The form of the certificate of incorporation is given in the volume on CORPORATION FINANCE. The next form in order is the waiver of notice of meeting of incorporators and subscribers. The following is generally used:

WAIVER OF NOTICE
OF
Meeting of Incorporators and Subscribers
to the
.........................Company.

We, the undersigned, being all of the incorporators named in the certificate of incorporation of the .... Company, do hereby waive notice of the first meeting of the incorporators and subscribers to the capital stock of said company and do hereby fix the .... day of ...., 190.., at .... o'clock in the .... noon as the time, No. .... Street, in the .... (being the location given in the certificate of incorporation), as the place for holding said first meeting, and we do consent that the purpose of said meeting be the organization of said company and the transaction of such other business as may come before it.

Dated, ...

The importance of this notice is apparent when one considers that the law requires that each subscriber be given reasonable notice of the time and place of such meeting. Without such notice the business transacted at such meeting may be declared illegal. The law, however, permits the stockholders to sign a form waiving such notice and agreeing in such waiver to the time and place of the meeting. This waiver must be signed by all the subscribers and incorporators.

84. *Proxy.*—Where a subscriber and incorporator finds it impossible to attend the first meeting he may substitute another person to attend such meeting for him. Such substitute must produce at the meeting a proxy authorizing him to take the place of the subscriber and incorporator. The following is a form of such proxy.

PROXY

for

First Meeting of Incorporators and Subscribers

of

. . . .

Know all Men by these Presents, That I, ..., the undersigned, one of the incorporators and subscribers to the capital stock of the . . . . Company, do hereby make, constitute and appoint . . . . my true and lawful attorney and proxy in my name, place and stead, to vote and cast such ballots as I may be entitled to vote or cast by reason of the . . . . shares of stock in the . . . . Company subscribed for or owned by me and to otherwise represent and act for me and in my behalf at the meeting of the incorporators and subscribers of said company, to be held on the . . . . day of . . . ., 190. ., and to take all such action at such meeting, or any adjournment thereof, and to act at such meeting as fully as I could do if personally present, with full power of substitution and revocation, hereby ratifying and confirming all that my said attorney or proxy or his substitute lawfully appointed may lawfully do by virtue hereof.

In Witness Whereof, I have hereunto set my hand and seal this .... day of ...., 190..

In PRESENCE OF:

. ...

No proxy is valid in New York after the expiration of eleven months from the date of its execution unless the member executing it shall have specified therein the length of time it is to continue in force, which shall be for some limited period.—N. Y. General Corp. Law, # 21.

85. *Waivers and proxies for subsequent meetings.*— Waivers of notice and proxies may be executed for any of the subsequent meetings of the stockholders, and waivers of notice may also be executed for the meetings of the board of directors. The following is a form of waiver of notice of meeting of directors:

WAIVER OF NOTICE
of
MEETING OF DIRECTORS

We, the undersigned, being all the directors of ....

....

Do hereby waive all notice whatsoever of the first meeting of the board of directors of the said company and do consent that the .... day of ...., 190.., at .... o'clock in the .... noon be and hereby is fixed as the time and the [1] .... office of the company, at .... in the .... of ...., New York, as the place for holding the same and that all such business be transacted thereat as may lawfully come before said meeting.

Dated the .... day of ...., 190..

[1] " Permanent" or " temporary" as the case may be.

86. *Annual meeting.*—At least ten days before each annual meeting, the secretary of the corporation must mail a notice of the time and place of such meeting to each stockholder of record to the last address given to the corporation by such stockholder. Such notice is usually in this form:

NOTICE OF ANNUAL MEETING.

Please take notice that the annual meeting of the stockholders of ....
....
for the purpose of electing .... directors and inspectors of election and transacting such other business as may properly come before the meeting will be held on the .... day of ...., 190.., at .... o'clock in the .... noon, at the office of the company, ... in the .... of ...., county of .... and State of New York. The transfer books will remain closed from the .... day of ...., 19.., until the .... day of ...., 19..

Dated the .... day of ...., 19..

...................., Secretary.

A stockholder who can not attend an annual meeting has a right to be represented at it by a proxy. This proxy does not differ materially from the proxy of the incorporators and subscribers for the first meeting. The following is a form in general use:

PROXY

of

Stockholders' Meeting

of the

. . . . Company.

Know all Men by These Presents, That I, ...

. . . ., the undersigned, a stockholder

in the . . . . Company,

do hereby make, constitute and appoint . . . .

. . . . my true and lawful attorney and proxy, for

me and in my name, place and stead to vote upon all stock held

by me in the . . . . Com-

pany at the meeting of the stockholders of the said company to

be held on the . . . . day of . . . .,

1. . . ., for the election of directors and inspectors of election

and for such other business as may come before the meeting

or at any adjournment of said meeting, and to take all such ac-

tion at said meeting or any adjournment thereof, and to act at

such meeting as fully as I could do if personally present, with

full power of substitution and revocation, hereby ratifying and

confirming all that my said attorney or proxy or his substitute,

lawfully appointed, may lawfully do by virtue hereof and here-

by revoking any and all former proxies or powers of attorney

by me in this behalf made.

Dated . . . ., I. . . .

. . . .

(Witness) . . . .

A proxy must be executed in writing by the member
himself or by his duly authorized attorney.

No proxy is valid after the expiration of eleven
months from the date of its execution, unless the member executing it shall have specified therein the length
of time it is to continue in force, which shall be for some
limited period.

Every proxy is revocable at the pleasure of the person executing it.

A proxy holder need not be a stockholder.

No person shall vote or issue a proxy to vote at any meeting of stockholders upon any stock which has not been owned by him for at least ten days next preceding such meeting notwithstanding such stock may stand in his name on the books of the corporation.

87. *Certificate as to paid-up stock.*—In the majority of the states corporations are required upon the payment of the capital stock to forward a certificate signed by the president and secretary or president and treasurer to the secretary of state stating that the capital stock of the company has been fully paid and whether it has been paid in cash or in property. This certificate also states the location of the principal office and the agent in charge of such office upon whom process against the company may be served. The following is a form of such certificate with the acknowledgment:

CERTIFICATE UPON PAYMENT OF CAPITAL STOCK
of
.... Company.

We, the undersigned, being the president and the [1] ....
.... of the .... Company,
a corporation duly organized and existing under the laws of the State of New Jersey, do hereby certify that ....
.... dollars, being the full amount of the capital stock of said company, as authorized by its certificate of incorporation, recorded in the office of the clerk of the county of
....................., on the .... day of
..................., 1...., and also filed in the office of the Secretary of State on the .... day of ....
........, 1...., has been fully paid in, ...

------

[1] Secretary or treasurer.

.... dollars in cash and .... ,[1]
.... dollars in the purchase of property.

That no amount of capital stock has been previously paid in or reported.

And we further certify, that the location of the principal office in this State is at No. .... street in ....
.................., county of ....

That the agent therein and in charge thereof, and upon whom process against this company may be served, is ....
....

Witness our hands on the .... day of ......
.........., 1....

..........................,

President.

State of New Jersey, ⎫
County of .... ⎬ ss.:
                    ⎭

...., president, and
.... of the
.... Company,
being duly severally sworn upon their respective oaths, depose and say that the foregoing certificate signed by them is true.

Subscribed and sworn to before me this ....
day of ...., 1....

88. *Treasurer's report.*—A very important form for accountants is the treasurer's report. The following form is one in general use, although we do not approve of it:

REPORT OF TREASURER.

For the year——————, 1——, to——————, 1——

CAPITAL STOCK

Capital Stock Authorized.

——Shares @——————, par value............... ═══════

---

[1] Secretary or treasurer.

Capital Stock Issued.

> Paid up.

>> ——shares entirely paid up in cash........ ————
>> —— " partly paid up in cash......... ————
>> —— " issued for——————— .... ————
>>> Total paid up.................. ————

Subscribed.

>> ——shares subscribed for and issued but not
>> paid up............................... ————
>> ——shares issued, Total.............................. ————

TREASURY STOCK.

> ——shares not issued and not subscribed for .... ————
>> Total amount authorized...... ————

CASH STATEMENT.

For the year——————, 1——, to———————, 1——
Cash on hand———————————day of———————, 1——, ————

Cash Receipts.

Cash Receipts for month of ———————1——— ————
" " " " ———————1——— ————
" " " " ———————1——— ————
" " " " ———————1——— ————
" " " " ———————1——— ————
" " " " " ———————1——— ————
" " " " " ———————1——— ————
" " " " " ———————1——— ————
" " " " " ———————1——— ————
" " " " " ———————1——— ————
" " " " " ———————1——— ————

Total Cash Receipts.......... ════════

Total Cash Debit............. ————
Cash Disbursements.

Cash Disbursements for month of ———————1——— ————
" " " " " ———————1——— ————
" " " " " ———————1——— ————
" " " " ———————1——— ————
" " " " ———————1——— ————
" " " " ———————1——— ————
" " " " ———————1——— ————
" " " " ———————1——— ————
" " " " ———————1——— ————
" " " " ———————1——— ————
" " " " ———————F——— ————
" " " " ———————1——— ————

Total Cash Disbursements...... ————

Cash on hand the————————day of————————1——, .. ————

Total Cash Credit.............. ————

STATEMENT OF PROFIT AND LOSS.

For one year from————, 1——, to————, 1——

Sales less returns, ... ————

————————, ... ————

————————, ... ————

Contra.

Inventory at beginning of year,................... ————

Purchases, less returns,................. ————

Freight and Express,................... ————

Labor, ... ————

Manufacturing Expenses,............... ————

———————— .... ————

———————— .... ————

———————— .... ————

Total .... ————

Less Inventory at end of year................... ————

Gross Profit on Merchandise,................................ ————

———————— .... ————

———————— .... ————

Total Gross Profits,............ ————

Selling Expenses, including Salaries, etc.,........... ————

Worthless Accounts written off,................... ————

Interest and Discount,........................... ————

———————— .... ————

———————— .... ————

———————— .... ————

Net Profits for year........... ————

BALANCE SHEET.

————————, 1——,

Assets.

Patent Rights, Franchises, Good Will, etc........... ————

Land and Buildings,.............................. ————

Plant, including Machinery, Tools and Fixtures,.... ————

Cash in hands of the Treasurer,................... ————

Cash on Deposit,................................. ————

Notes Receivable,................................ ————

Accounts Receivable,............................... ————

Merchandise Inventory,............................ ————

———————————————— .... ————

———————————————— .... ————

Total Assets,................. ————

Liabilities.

Bonds, ... ————

Notes Payable,.................................. ————

Accounts Payable,............................... ————

———————————— .... ————

Total Liabilities,.............. ————

Surplus of Assets over Liabilities, ————

Capital.

Capital Stock Issued (authorized $————————),........ ————

Surplus.

Surplus at the beginning of fiscal year,............ ————

Less Dividends,................................. ————

———————————— .... ————

Profit for year.................................. ————

Total Surplus,................. ————

Total Capitalization and surplus, ————

On the first page of this report under the heading "treasury stock" are listed shares not issued or subscribed. This is erroneous. Unissued and unsubscribed stock should be carried under such name to distinguish it from actual treasury stock, which is *stock that has already been issued* but which the corporation has in some way re-acquired.

The statement of profit and loss is not in accordance with accounting principles for the reason that it does not give complete and full information and its classification is not scientific.

PART IV: SPECIAL TOPICS

CHAPTER XVI

DISTINCTION BETWEEN CAPITAL AND REVENUE

89. *Capital receipts and expenditures and revenue receipts.*—Nothing in accountancy requires more emphatic distinction than the expenditure of money as capital or as revenue.

"Capital receipts" represent sums contributed to a business with the intention that they be used to carry on the enterprise.

"Capital expenditures" is a term given to expenditures incurred for the purpose of acquiring and extending or completing the equipment of an enterprise in order to place it on a revenue earning basis or to increase its earning capacity.

"Revenue receipts" are the receipts of business operations, e.g., earnings. The cash revenue receipts will generally be less than the actual earnings, as practically no line of business is on a strictly cash basis and therefore the credit to revenue account, and not the receipts in cash, will show the true earnings for the period.

90. *Revenue receipts more than cash receipts.*—There are a number of cases on record, where this important fact has been entirely overlooked. The cash receipts are often mistakenly construed to represent all the revenue income. In illustration of this error is the case of Eyster v. Centennial Board of Finance (94 U.S. 503).

In this connection the Supreme Court of the United States put itself on record as follows:

> The receipts of the exhibition, over and above its current expenses, are the profits of the business. . . . They are, in fact, the net receipts, which, according to the common understanding, ordinarily represent the profits of the business. The public, when referring to the profits of the business of a merchant, rarely ever take into account the depreciation of the buildings in which the business is carried on, notwithstanding that they may have been erected out of the capital invested. Properly speaking, the net receipts of a business are its profits. So here, as the business to be carried on was that of an exhibition and its profits were t be derived only from its receipts, to the popular mind the net eceipts would represent the net profit.

Such a decision is, beyond question, against all proper accounting principles. It emphasizes the fact that many legal practitioners do not know the correct definition of "net profits."

91. *Intentional confusion of capital and revenue expenditures.*—How some corporations juggle their accounts by charging to capital expenditures what properly should go to revenue expenditures, or vice versa, depending on what they intend to conceal, may be illustrated by a supposed case: A corporation has an issue of income bonds bearing interest. As the reader will learn from the volume on corporation finance, the particular feature of income bonds is that the interest is not a fixed charge as with other bonds, but that such interest is only a lien against the income of the corporation; only when there are earnings left after all the fixed charges are defrayed will the income bondholder receive his interest. If the board of directors charges renewals and improvements, which increase materially the earning capacity of the corporation, against

III—23

the earnings, instead of to capital, there will be nothing left for the income bondholder, and as his income is only payable when there are earnings, one can readily see the difference such a charge makes.

92. *Surplus produced by wrong classification.*—Take the reverse illustration: A corporation makes repairs and improvements which do not increase the earning capacity of the company, but are actual replacements of assets wasted during the operation. Due to business depression the board of directors fear that they will not be able to declare the usual yearly dividend. But withholding the dividend, might cause serious fluctuation of the market quotations of the company's stock. So they order such repairs and improvements charged to capital, treating it as though it were an acquisition of property and hence an asset. Such procedure leaves the corporation a surplus which may be used for the payment of dividends. The author does not discuss here the propriety or impropriety of such action; he merely cites these illustrations to emphasize and impress the importance of proper classification of such cases.

93. *Capital expenditures are extended or acquired assets.*—We may safely say that most of such errors in principle and practice, show either lack of ability or lack of desire to discriminate strictly between capital and revenue items. All one needs to bear in mind is that all expenditures that can be recorded as capital expenditures must be represented by actual assets. There never remains anything to represent expenditures which have been incurred upon revenue account. Has the particular expenditure, incurred in any individual case, been for the sake of improving the earning capacity of the enterprise? If so, it is a charge against capital and should be classed as a capital expenditure.

If, however, the result of the expenditure has been such as merely to put the earning capacity of the undertaking on the same footing as before a decline—such decline being due to the ordinary wear and tear—then it must be charged against revenue. Not mere renewals but only the extension or acquisition of new assets can be recorded as capital expenditures.

94. *How to charge replacements.*—Many times an apportionment of expenditures is necessary when it is difficult to tell how much of the expenditure should be charged to capital and how much against revenue expenditure. Where new works, for instance, replace old works, such replacement increasing materially the earning capacity (especially true in the case of railroad corporations where old wooden bridges are replaced by new modern steel bridges), the accountant is then confronted with a difficult problem. Were he to treat the entire expenditures for such new assets as acquisitions, he would have ignored the ordinary wear and tear of the old assets. On the other hand, were he to treat the entire expenditure as a replacement, it would be an unfair charge against revenue as the cost may be many times more than the actual wear and tear. The best rule in such cases is to charge the ordinary cost of the old works, less the value of old materials, against revenue and to charge the remainder against capital.

95. *Acquisitions and not renewals capitalized.*—Some accountants, however, claim that inasmuch as variations in cost are to be expected, therefore only bona fide betterments should be capitalized. To illustrate: If assets which ordinarily cost $200,000 were to cost in renewals $250,000, the whole cost of such renewals would be a revenue charge. If, however, the assets which ordinarily cost $200,000 were replaced by as-

sets of a higher revenue earning capacity, due to the superior quality of the material used for the making of such assets, the method of apportioning should be as follows: Ascertain what the exact replacing of the ordinary assets would have cost and then charge only that sum to revenue and capitalize the excess.

Many accountants follow the policy of considering the "last cost" as a capital charge. If assets which ordinarily cost $10,000 are replaced at a cost of $12,000 the excess is charged against capital. In other words, they claim that the cost is the only correct basis because each concern will replace its plant at the least possible cost.

96. *No accounting of shrinkage.*—Capital assets, however, may decrease in value without revenue being affected by such decrease. A shrinkage in the value of assets may occur, owing to causes outside of the ordinary operations of the business. Therefore, as long as these assets are not disposed of, such shrinkage can be only an estimated item and may properly be ignored in the accounts.

Summarizing, we may say that if the item for which the expenditure was made exists at the end of the current period as an asset, such expenditure should be charged to capital. If, on the other hand, it is consumed during the current earning period, it must then be charged against the revenue of that period.

CHAPTER XVII

DEPRECIATION AND OTHER RESERVES

97. *Depreciation.*—The term depreciation is well known to all who are familiar with accounts. Nevertheless, the term is somewhat loosely employed. To some it means fluctuation of assets—a wrong conception. By depreciation is meant the ordinary wear and tear bound to occur to assets used in any enterprise. Unless proper provision is made for depreciation the true result of the enterprise is not shown. The fact that proper or improper provision for depreciation often makes the difference between a satisfactory and an unsatisfactory financial result has at all times tended to the abuse of the term. In some instances this is often done deliberately. It is quite obvious that those who are interested to show large profits or profits where they do not exist, will argue against any provision for depreciation. They will claim that under certain circumstances a direct charge for depreciation is unnecessary, especially where a large amount has been expended for repairs and renewals.

98. *Wear and tear a cost of production.*—That such arguments are usually based on false premises is self-evident. No matter how much is expended on repairs and renewals, the ordinary wear and tear will accrue just the same, and it is that ordinary wear and tear that we are trying to provide for by means of depreciation.

That the wear and tear of an asset is a part of the cost of production of any factory is also obvious.· The damage upon an asset by reason of an accident must be taken into consideration also. If a modern invention forces out a comparatively new machine, to be replaced by an improved one, there is then a waste, and that forms a part of the cost of production. We must therefore conclude that a part of the income is a part of the transformation of the assets, and most naturally we must provide for the replacing of the assets so transformed.

A difficulty arises from the fact that depreciation is largely a question of individual discrimination. The main thing therefore is to bear in mind that we have to estimate the extent of depreciation as closely as possible and charge the amount to profit and loss. This means that the net profit will be decreased by that amount and consequently the assets will, in the long run, be replaced out of earnings.

99. *Depreciations not offset by appreciations.*—The question is then raised, whether depreciation charges should be made, even if at the same time other appreciations of assets offset them. Mr. Teichman, in the *Journal of Accountancy,* Vol. 3, page 101, claims that even when the natural growth of population will increase the earning power of the plant sufficiently to offset any deterioration of its physical condition, the proper amount of depreciation should be written off. While this seems an over-scrupulous policy, it is in the main, the correct one. He says: "The fallacy of these contentions (that appreciations offset depreciations) is clearly visible and hardly needs any further elucidation."

100. *Argument against opposite opinion.*—Others take exactly the opposite stand, claiming that as the sole function of the balance sheet is to reflect the finan-

cial value of the property, it should express the profit neither over nor under. In other words when appreciation charges offset depreciation charges the latter should be ignored.

An argument that can forcibly be raised against the second opinion is that while depreciation is an actual fact whether the rate provided is correct or not, the depreciation takes place while the appreciation is a sum which at the time of the sale of the asset may not be realized at all. We cannot say that the appreciation of an asset causes a profit because a profit is the result of a trade. Unless a trade takes place and such a sale produces an excess over the cost of the asset, there is no profit.

101. *Depreciation of current assets.*—So far we have spoken of the subject of depreciation only with reference to fixed assets. The reader must, however, bear in mind that current assets are just as subject to depreciation as are fixed assets. The raw material on hand, the inventory of finished goods or the goods in process of manufacture are just as subject to depreciation as the plant, machinery or tools.

102. *How to provide for depreciation.*—Conceding the importance of making due provision for depreciation, the next question arises as to the exact method to be adopted in order to achieve that purpose. The essential point is that the profit and loss account be charged with a proper sum to cover the depreciation in the value of the assets and that the apportionment of such charge between one year and another should be upon some equitable basis. This of course involves a debit to profit and loss and a corresponding credit to some other account.

In England it is the practice to credit the asset directly with the sum charged to the profit and loss as depreciation. In America such charge made to the profit and loss account is credited to a new account headed "reserve for depreciation." Generally the reserve is ear-marked to indicate to which asset it applies, thus: "reserve for depreciation on plant and machinery;" "reserve for depreciation on horses and trucks," etc., etc.

By the English method the value of the asset is gradually written down in the books to correspond with the depreciation in its intrinsic value. By the American method the asset account remains unaltered, as any deductions from the assets are shown under a separate account. In framing a balance sheet, however, it is advisable that the depreciation be deducted from the asset rather than stated as a liability upon the opposite side of the balance sheet, thus:

Plant and machinery	$50,000.00	
Less 5% depreciation	2,500.00	$47,500.00

103. *Four ways of charging depreciation.*—There are various methods by which the charge against profits to cover depreciation may be apportioned, to cover the period of years constituting the life of the assets, namely:

1. An equal proportion of the cost may be written off each year.

2. The asset may be written down from year to year by deducting depreciation at a fixed rate percent upon the balance remaining to the debit side of the account at the beginning of the year.

3. By writing off to revenue each year an equal sum sufficient at the expiration of the life of the asset to reduce such asset to zero or its residual value, after deb-

iting the asset and crediting revenue each year with interest at an agreed rate, upon the amount for the time being invested in the asset in question.

4. By revaluing the asset from time to time and treating any decrease in value as the realized depreciation for the year.

The first method is usually used where the life of the asset is known and where the asset has no residual value. Patents or leasehold property are examples of assets where the first method may be adopted.

In the second method the charges against revenue become gradually less as time goes on and therefore the method is often called the reducing installment or fixed percentage method. With this system the installments charged against revenue are heaviest in the early years and are gradually automatically reduced. This method of depreciation may be used for plant and machinery, horses and trucks, etc.

The third method is also known as the annuity system, calculated so that after increasing the amount of such asset by interest at a fixed rate percent the depreciation installments will suffice to reduce it to zero at the end of the prescribed time. As the gross charge in respect of depreciation is constant, whereas the credits to revenue in respect of interest diminish as the asset is written down, the net effect of this method is to charge an increasing sum to revenue as years go on. The reason and justification for charging an increasing sum to revenue is that the depreciation installments remaining in the business increase the working capital of the enterprise. The increase in the installments represents the amount of interest that might have been earned on the former installments during the period in question if such installments had been taken out of the business and invested at a fixed rate percent. This method is usually adopted with regard to buildings or long term leasehold properties.

In the fourth method the charges against revenue in successive years will be very unequal, as a reduction in the market value of most articles must correspond with true depreciation as measured by the amount of use that has been made of the asset during the period under the review. That method is usually adopted with loose tools, etc.

104. *Different rates of depreciation.*—We have discussed the depreciation on plant and machinery without taking cognizance of the fact that this item is composed of many individual parts, such as engines and boilers, shafting, general machinery and special machinery.

The rate to be charged off as depreciation on each respective part of the plant will vary. Thus, the minimum rate of depreciation on engines should be 7 per cent, the maximum rate of depreciation 12½ per cent per annum.

On boilers, assuming all the conditions to be favorable, the minimum rate of depreciation should be 10 per cent upon the reducing of annual balance and the maximum rate 15 per cent.

The depreciation rate of shafting if properly constructed so as to avoid undue friction should be 5 per cent per annum on the reducing balance. It should not exceed, however, 7½ per cent. Belting is to be excluded from this category and treated separately.

105. *Out-of-date machinery.*—Coming to the item of general machinery there are numerous types of machines, some of which are never likely to be entirely superseded, and others which are likely to be replaced by modern inventions at an early date. As a general rule,

however, the last mentioned class of machines would go under "special machinery." In an average factory if all machinery be classed together, a 7½ per cent rate on the reducing balance will, as a rule, be sufficient for wear and tear, if the machinery be carefully worked—not on over-pressure—and kept constantly in thorough repair. The maximum rate to be charged should be 10 per cent. Special machinery, as a rule, requires a very heavy depreciation, a minimum rate of 20 per cent and a maximum rate of 30 per cent.

106. *Tools, moulds and patterns, patents and copyrights.*—Tools, as a general rule, which are also part of the plant, should be revalued, while moulds and patterns should be depreciated at a minimum rate of 25 per cent and a maximum rate of 33 1/3 per cent. Patents and copyrights, while they have a legal existence for a specified period of years, nevertheless, due to modern inventions, and the rapid changes, they rarely are used throughout the legal life. As a rule they are superseded after a period of a few years. The best plan to follow is to limit, on the books at least, their existence to half the legal life.

107. *Depreciation of good will.*—With regard to good will, while the arguments raised by a good many that good will does not depreciate are to some extent justified, nevertheless the best policy is to write it down. The fact must be borne in mind that good will represents the sum paid for benefits that accrue and which are utilized for a period of years to come and every year is to share part of the cost of the good will.

108. *Reserves.*—A reserve may be defined as a bookkeeping provision setting aside from profits a given sum to meet depreciation on property, or to provide for loss upon bad debts. It therefore covers a range far wider

than mere depreciations. A reserve may be said to be provided whenever a charge against revenue is made without the corresponding credit operating as a reduction of the debit balance upon an asset account. Thus, if a personal account be written off as bad, the ordinary entry is to credit the insolvent customer and to debit either a bad debt account or the profit and loss account directly. By this method no reserve is created.

If, however, a debt or series of debts are only doubtful and not bad, it is not advisable to extinguish the debt or debts; yet at the same time it is not necessary to debit the revenue with any loss which may not occur. Under such circumstances the course to pursue is to debit the revenue account with the assumed loss and to credit the corresponding sum to an account headed "reserve for bad and doubtful debts." This loss account is, as its name shows, in the nature of a reserve account, having to do with profits only, it being a reservation out of profits. Various other similar reserves may occur; reserves for depreciation, reserves for discount, etc., etc.

109. *When the reserve applies to general or to special assets.*—Where the reserve is ear-marked and applies to particular assets, in such cases the reserve should be deducted from the asset to which it belongs and not entered as a liability on the liability side of the balance sheet. Where, however, a reserve has been created for general purposes, in respect of all assets, this procedure is not longer practicable and therefore under such circumstances the reserve should appear on the liability side of the balance sheet. It is important that it be so stated and clearly ear-marked as a reserve to cover loss in respect of whatever the case may be.

110. *Secret reserves.*—When a reserve is deliberately

calculated in excess of the assumed loss or depreciation that is likely to occur under that particular heading, such excess constitutes "a secret reserve." This reserve is made to cover future hypothetical losses, and may be created by the under-valuation of assets or by the over-stating of liabilities. Occasionally, however, reserves are provided for losses to exceed the expectations of the greatest pessimist. Such reserves are theoretically indefensible, because it is as improper to understate as it is to overstate the profitable nature of an undertaking. However, although it would be difficult to find sufficient theoretical arguments to justify the deliberate provision of reserves in excess of expected requirements, it must be admitted that the practice is—within reasonable limits—prudent and moreover generally countenanced by thorough, sound business men.

111. *Authorities dispute the propriety of secret reserves.*—The propriety of creating a secret reserve is a matter of dispute among the highest authorities. Thus, Mr. Pixley in a chapter read before the Congress of Accountants at the World's Fair at St. Louis in 1904, states the following:

I am of the opinion that what are known as secret reserves are right and proper and tend toward the maintenance of the company as a permanent institution and that in fact without these secret reserves it is quite impossible, having regard to the fluctuations of both financial and trading operations to exist beyond a very limited period. At the same time these reserves must be honestly made and in the interests of the company. For directors to create secret reserves with the object of withholding profits legitimately earned without distribution to the stockholders, so as to induce them to dispose of their holdings, is as flagrant an act of dishonesty as can be conceived of.

If a concern is properly and conservatively managed

it will provide reserves yearly to meet the peculiarities of its business. Secret reserves, as a rule, do not appear in trading or manufacturing concerns, but do often exist in the case of banks or insurance companies.

112. *Sinking funds or debt extinguishment funds.*— There is a class of reserves which has caused a great deal of discussion and probably will cause more for some time to come—that is sinking funds or debt extinguishment funds. Lisle says that a sinking fund is one set aside out of assets and calculated at interest for the purpose of meeting a debt. Dicksee, on the other hand, makes a distinction between the sinking fund and the sinking fund account. He makes the latter a credit and the sinking fund a debit. He does not, however, explain why the debit is not just as much an account as the credit item is. Mr. A. Lowes Dickinson, in this connection, remarks as follows: "Sinking funds are not in theory a charge against profit and loss for the reason that they do not represent a loss or expense but the extinction of an existing liability. However, as in most cases the only source out of which such redemption fund can be provided is the surplus earnings, it is usual to insert a provision in trust deeds that the sinking fund is to be provided out of the profits of the year."

A good many criticise the policy of charging sinking fund instalments against the profits, among them Mr. Seymour Walton. He writes as follows:[1]

There is no essential accounting difference between bonds and ordinary bills payable secured by the deposit of collateral. The bonds run for a longer time and are more formal in character so that they may be easily transferred, but they are both promises to pay at a future time and nothing else. No one would

[1] *Journal of Accountancy,* Vol. VI, p. 397.

think of charging the partial payments of a six months' note to revenue and there seems no adequate reason why such charge should be made when the note is divided into bonds and runs for perhaps forty times six months.

113. *Theory and practice of charging sinking fund at variance.*—So far as theory is concerned, the general practice of charging the sinking fund against revenue is questionable, if not wrong. Nevertheless, there may well be doubts as to the propriety of changing this practice. The fact is that the majority of sinking fund mortgage agreements contain clauses to the effect that the fund be set aside out of profits. The accountant may object to the clause and may do his best to get away from it but he is in reality bound hand and foot. The clause is there and not only has he to conform to its provisions but he must see that the provision is carried out. Ignoring the conventional principles of accounting, the author is inclined to believe that it is a desirable practice because it tends to prevent directors from declaring excessive dividends out of profits, without making proper allowance for sinking fund payments.

Then too, since accountants are not living in a scientific world of their own construction, wherein everything is arranged according to their own ideas, but in a commercial world which as yet knows very little about accounting principles, the shrewd accountant will make concessions, and base his practice upon business and legal principles as they now are, not as in theory they should be.

114. *Place of a sinking fund in a company's books.*—Mr. Anyon clearly illustrates the position of a sinking fund in the books of a company. He gives the following illustration:[1]

[1] *Journal of Accountancy,* Vol. VII, p. 188.

A company starts business with a capital of $1,000,000.00, a bonded debtedness of $250,000.00 and requisite plant, machinery and working capital, to enable it to do a profitable business. The bonds are 20 year bonds, bear 5 per cent per annum and the deed of trust stipulates that there shall be a sinking fund for the redemption of such bonds to be provided out of the profits of the company, of such an amount each year as invested at 4 per cent along with the interest accumulation will aggregate a fund at the end of the twenty years sufficient to redeem the bonds. According to this the company must invest out of its profits each year for sinking fund purposes the sum of $8,395.00, which is the correct amount on a 4 per cent basis and which becomes the annual sinking fund charge or installment. The company works successfully, earns an average profit of $90,000.00 per annum, after providing for depreciation, bad debt reserve, and all other expenses, pays dividends of 6 per cent per annum on its capital stock, and regularly invests its sinking fund installments as provided in the deed of trust. At the end of the twenty years it stands in the position as shown on the following page.

This balance sheet clearly shows that the annual sinking fund installments of $8,395.00 per annum have been regularly invested; that the income from these investments has in turn been invested; and that the aggregate of these is enough to pay the bonds at maturity. When this is done the balance sheet in other respects will stand just the same except that the sinking fund account and surplus will appear as one account, as shown on page 370.

The whole trouble arises from the fact that a general idea prevails that when profits are used for the benefit of a sinking fund they disappear forever, like payments for interest or for other fixed charges. That is incorrect. The profits have not gone, they have been used merely to pay a debt and as profits exist just the same only in another form of asset.

BALANCE SHEET

ASSETS:

Patent rights, goodwill, etc.		$520,000.00
Real estate, machinery, plant, etc.		650,000.00
Inventory, accounts and cash.		330,000.00
Sinking fund investment account.		
Investments out of earnings.	$167,900.00	
Investments out of income.	80,600.00	
Cash not invested.	1,500.00	250,000.00
		$1,750,000.00

LIABILITIES

Capital.	$1,000,000.00
Bonds.	250,000.00
Accounts payable.	150,000.00
Sinking fund account.	250,000.00
Surplus profits.	100,000.00
	$1,750,000.00

BALANCE SHEET.

ASSETS:

Patent rights, goodwill, etc.	$520,000.00
Real estate, plant, etc.	650,000.00
Inventory, accounts and cash	330,000.00
	$1,500,00.00

LIABILITIES:

Capital	$1,000,000.00
Accounts payable	150,000.00
Surplus	350,000.00
	$1,500,00.00

370

CHAPTER XVIII

CONSIGNMENTS AND VENTURES

115. *Consignments inward and outward.*—There are some accounts which present a certain amount of difficulty. These are consignments of goods either inward or outward. Some distinguish by calling outward consignments "shipments," while inward shipments they term "consignments." There is no necessity, however, of such distinction as the term inward or outward will designate whether we receive the goods or whether we ship the goods. The principle involved in this class of transaction is that one merchant acts as agent for the other. He may receive in compensation a commission only, and he may also share in the profits of the particular enterprise. Therefore, we may say that consignments inward may be for the account of another—the merchant receiving the goods having an interest in same, or they may be exclusively for the risk and benefit of another. In the former case the merchant is one of the principals, in the latter he acts as agent.

Consignments outward are generally on account of the consignor or as co-partner with others. Where the merchant is interested with others in a shipment of goods, it is generally known as a joint account or venture.

116. *Treatment of consignments.*—With regard to the method of treating consignments it is best to follow the rules mentioned below: In the case of consignments received to be sold for and on behalf of another, no entry should be made on the receipt of the goods except when charges have been paid by the consignee. The goods are the property of the consignor and therefore do not form a portion of the assets of the consignee. A memorandum may be made in some book, say the stock book, or on a book set aside for that purpose so as to show the receipt of the goods. All charges paid on the consignment should be debited to a consignment account. To this account should also be debited all advances made to the consignor. All sales of the consignment should be credited to a consignment sales account.

When the sales are completed the consignee will desire to render to the consignor an account of his sales showing the proceeds due the consignor. In such case he would debit the consignment sales account for all charges as well as for the net proceeds and he would credit the general consignment account for items transferred to the consignment sales account, crediting at the same time the consignor's account for the net proceeds.

We have so far discussed the entries with regard to the consignee's books. The consignor on shipping goods debits an account headed merely "consignment outward or consignment to ....," for the cost of the goods shipped and any charges paid thereon, such as freight, cartage, insurance, etc. When he receives the account sales rendered him by the consignee he then debits the cash that he receives or, if the cash is not remitted, the consignee personally, and credits the consignment outward account for such proceeds. The difference, if any, is either his profit or loss on the venture.

117. *How to enter joint transactions.*—A joint adventure is when two or more parties combine to participate in some particular enterprise; thus a person may

consign goods in which he deals to a merchant in another city or country, both parties participating in such shipment. It often also happens that two or more merchants combine to ship to another city or country an article in which they deal on a joint account. It is usual in such cases for one called the manager, to handle the transaction, he being sometimes allowed a small percentage on the sales to remunerate him for his time and trouble, taken by him individually for the benefit of all. The best method of dealing with such joint transaction is as follows:

The manager should open an account entitled "joint adventure to ...." and debit this account with the cost of the goods, shipping and other charges, including even interest on money invested and credit it with the gross amount realized. The balance of this account is transferred to the partners' personal accounts for their respective shares of profits or losses, and to his own profit and loss account for his respective share in the venture.

Let us assume a hypothetical case to illustrate the principles involved.

The X Y Z Company of New York City consigned to James & Co., of San Francisco, Cal., on the 31st of October, 1907, 400 machines as follows:

Size	Number
0	100
1	100
2	100
3	50
4	50

The list prices of the machines are as follows:

Size	Price
0	$1.00
1	$1.25
2	$1.50
3	$1.75
4	$2.00

They were to be sold subject to a trade discount of 25 per cent and 5 per cent discount for cash. On the 15th of January the company received an account of the sales to December 31, 1907, James & Co. having sold twenty of each of the following numbers: 0, 1, 2, and ten of number 3.

James & Co. deducted for cash discount $25.00, for insurance $3.00 on the whole consignment, also for expenses and postage $2.50 and remitted a note at sixty days for the balance. Make out the account rendered by James & Co.

SOLUTION:

ACCOUNT SALES of 400 machines, consigned by the X, Y, Z Co., New York.

1908			
Jan. 15.	Sold 20 # 0 machines at	$1.00	$20.00
	Sold 20 # 1 machines at	$1.25	$25.00
	Sold 20 # 2 machines at	$1.50	$30.00
	Sold 10 # 3 machines at	$1.75	$17.50
			$92.50
	Less 25% trade discount	$23.12	$69.38
	Less cash discount	$25.00	
	Insurance	3.00	
	Expenses and postage	2.50	$30.50
	Balance due consignor		$35.12

Note at 60 days; 330 machines unsold.

The X Y Z Company in order to record the transaction in their books would make the following entry

Dr.   CONSIGNMENT OUTWARD ACCOUNT, JAMES & CO.,   Cr.

San Francisco, Cal.

1907			1908		
Oct. 31.	To merchandise ..	$562.50	Jan. 15.	By James & Co. ..	
1908				Account sales ..	$65.62
Jan. 15.	James & Co. ..				
	Expenses ..	30.50			

Dr.	MERCHANDISE, SALES ACCOUNT.		Cr.
	1907		
	Oct. 31.	By consignment .. Account James & Co.	$65.62

Dr.	JAMES & CO., San Francisco, Cal.		Cr.
1908 Jan. 15th. To consignment $65.62	1908		
	Jan. 15.	By expenses	$30.50
	Jan. 15.	By notes receivable	35.12
$65.62			$65.62

Dr.	NOTES RECEIVABLE.	Cr.
1908 Jan. 15. To James & Co. .. $35.12		

The second illustration given below brings out the principle of joint accounts.

Johnson Bros. agree with their friends, Smith & Co., to participate in a consignment to Japan on joint account the following:

Fifty cases of printed cottons, the invoice price of which is $4,200.00, less 2½ per cent. Johnson Bros. pay the packing charges, $22.00; also freight, insurance and other charges, $120.00. They draw on their correspondents in Japan, in advance, $1,500.00 at 90 days, which is discounted at a cost of $20.00 and the proceeds handed to Smith & Co. as part payment. The transaction began March 31, 1907. On November 30, 1907, Johnson Bros. receive the account sales and net proceeds, $2,500.00. They then pay Smith & Co. the balance due to them.

Prepare a joint consignment account, charging interest on the amounts advanced at 6 per cent per annum, in months, closing it by dividing the loss.

Prepare also an account to be rendered by Johnson Bros. to Smith & Co., closed by payment of the balance, and prove that the losses borne by each are equal.

DR. X Y Z, JAPAN, IN ACCOUNT WITH JOHNSON BROS. (JOINT CONS'T WITH SMITH & CO.) **CR.**

1907		Interest Cr. Johnson Bros	Interest Cr. Smith & Co.	Amount
Mch 31	To 50 cases printed cotton........			$4,095.00
Mch 31	To sh, packing charges........	$0.88		22.00
March 31	To sh, freight, insurance, etc....	4.80		120.00
Nov. 30	To int payable to Johnson Bros....			5.68
Nov. 30	To interest payable to Smith & Co......		$163.80	104.60
		$5.68	$163.80	$4,347.28

1907		Interest Dr. Johnson Bros.	Interest Dr. Smith & Co.	Amount
Mch 31	By sh pals of draft at 90 ds of $1,500 less dis-unt of $20.00.			$1,480.00
Nov. 30	By cash, X. Y. Z, as per ac unt sales........		$59.20	2,500.00
Nov. 30	By int per contra.......	$5.68		
Nov. 30	By line, loss: hdn Bros.....		104.60	183.64
	Smith & Co.....			183.64
		$5.68	$163.80	$4,347.28

SMITH & CO., IN ACCOUNT WITH JOHNSON BROS. (JOINT CONS'T TO X Y Z JAPAN)

DR.				CR.
1907			1907	
Mch. 31	To cash............................	$1,480.00	Mch. 31	By twenty cases of printed cottons...... $4,095.00
Nov. 30	Share of loss on venture.............	183.64	Nov. 30	Interest........................... 104.60
Nov. 30	Balance, per check herewith........	2,535.96		
		$4,199.60		$4,199.60

PROOF OF JOHNSON BROS. LOSS.

PAYMENTS:

Packing	$22.00
Freight, etc.	120.00
Interest	5.68
Smith & Co.	2,535.96
	2,683.64

RECEIPTS:

X, Y, Z, Japan	2,500.00
Excess of payments over receipts (loss)	183.64

CHAPTER XIX

REALIZATION, LIQUIDATION AND INSOLVENCY ACCOUNTS

118. *Realization and liquidation accounts.*—In a former chapter the author remarked briefly on the meaning of a realization and liquidation account. At this stage he desires to further elucidate and explain the use of this account. On the dissolution of a partnership the assets will be realized upon and the liabilities liquidated. Rarely, however, if ever at all, will the assets realize the full book value. Consequently there is a loss on the realization of assets. On the other hand it is quite probable that of all the assets of the firm one or two assets will realize more than the book value. It is not desirable to show all such losses or part profits by means of a profit or loss account. The latter as already stated, is a summary of all nominal accounts, showing the results of the operation of a business enterprise. The sale of all the assets of the firm on winding up affairs should not therefore be carried through that summary but through the realization and liquidation account.

Furthermore when a partnership is dissolved the winding up of the affairs may continue for months or even a period of years. Only one or two partners of the firm are likely to remain to realize and liquidate their affairs. These members act then in a dual capacity. They are principals, so far as the outside world is concerned; they are, however, also agents, trustees, representing the interests of the other members of the firm.   In their account keeping these trustees must show their dual capacity, hence the realization and liquidation account.

It will be perceived that this account is for all practical purposes upon the same line as an ordinary profit and loss account. Often, however, the method is adopted of transferring the balance standing upon all the various assets' accounts to the debit of the realization account, as at the date of dissolution.   The asset accounts are thus closed at once, and the cash realized on the disposal of the asset is posted direct to the credit of the realization account.   As the latter method is preferable we conclude as follows:

(1)   The realization and liquidation account is debited with the total book value of the assets as shown in the balance sheet of the firm on the date of the commencement of the liquidation.

(2)   It is credited with the book value of the liabilities to outside creditors as per balance sheet.

(3)   It is thereafter credited with the assets as realized.

(4)   It is thereafter debited with the liabilities as they are liquidated.

(5)   It is also debited with the expenses in connection with the realization and the cost of liquidation.

It will be readily seen that where this method is followed, the first part of the realization and liquidation account will contain on the debit side what we may call "assets to be realized" and on the credit side "assets realized" and the difference would show the loss on the realization proper, exclusive of expenses incurred in that connection thus:

Assets to be realized ...	$500.00	Assets realized	$400.00
		Loss on realization	100.00
	$500.00		$500.00

Whichever method be adopted, however—entering on the realization and liquidation account losses or gains on assets only, or the full accounting of assets and liabilities—the balance of this account will be the same, viz., loss (or profit) on the realization. This balance is then transferred to the capital accounts of the various partners; each partner bearing his share of the loss (or profit) in the proportions that the articles of co-partnership call for.

The following problem will illustrate the treatment of such affairs:

PROBLEM I.

A. Jones, F. Smith and B. Peters are partners: Their respective interests in the profits of the firm are one-half, three-eighths, and one-eighth.

On December 31, 1908, the partnership terminates, the time for its existence having expired, and their balance sheet on that date is as shown on the following page:

On June 30, 1909, when the affairs of the firm have all been liquidated, it is found that the assets have realized $2,000.00 less than the book values, given in the balance sheet, namely; accounts receivable $500.00; leasehold property $750.00; and plant and machinery $750.00.

The expenses of winding up the business amount to $450.00.

In accordance with the provisions of the partnership agreement the partners are entitled to interest at 5 per cent per annum upon their capital that remains in the business.

You are asked to show how to close the ledger on June 30, 1909, the last day of the liquidation of the affairs of the concern, giving each partners' account, with the balance ultimately found to be payable to him.

In solving the problem, it is not necessary to give journal entries for closing, but to show the closing by means of the ledger accounts directly. (Solution on following pages.)

119. *Other uses of a realization and liquidation account.*—We have so far shown an illustration of a realization and liquidation account in the case of a dissolution. Such an account may, however, be desired for other purposes. As already mentioned the dual capacity in which the person (or persons) is placed, who winds up the affairs, is the basic principle of the mechanism of such an account. This does not necessarily mean that in partnership affairs only, we prepare such an account, but that there are other cases as well.

A firm may become financially embarrassed, not necessarily insolvent. It may have all available capital tied up in machinery, plant, materials, or merchandise. The creditors are notified of the state of affairs and are asked to render the firm whatever assistance is possible. If the creditors are willing to do this, and usually they are, they will want some outsider, perhaps a creditor to take charge of the affairs of the firm. This trustee is in the same position as our partner, mentioned before. There is, however, this distinction, that he does not take charge of the concern's affairs for the purpose of discontinuing the business, but for the purpose of continuing operations, realizing on some of the assets that can be converted into cash, and liquidating creditors' claims.

BALANCE SHEET OF THE FIRM JONES, SMITH & PETERS, AS ON DECEMBER 31, 1908

ASSETS:			LIABILITIES:		
Cash..........................			Accounts payable.............		$17,750.00
Bills receivable..............	$1,500.00				
Accounts receivable...........	30,000.00		PROPRIETORSHIP:		
Inventory of merchandise......		31,500.00	A. Jones' capital account......	$17,500.00	
Leasehold property............		5,000.00	F. Smith's capital account.....	7,500.00	
Plant and machinery...........		2,500.00	B. Peters' capital account.....	5,000.00	
		7,500.00			30,000.00
		$47,750.00			$47,750.00

SOLUTION

CASH ACCOUNT

1900				1909			
Jan. 1	To balance............	$1,250.00		June 30	By creditors............	$17,750.00	
June 30	Bills receivable.......	1,500.00		June 30	Liquidation expenses....	450.00	
June 30	Accounts receivable....	29,500.00		June 30	Balance.................	27,550.00	
June 30	Merchandise inventory...	5,000.00					
June 30	Leasehold property.....	1,750.00					
June 30	Plant, etc.............	6,750.00					
		$45,750.00				$45,750.00	
1909							
July 1	To balance.....					$27,550.00	

REALIZATION ACCOUNT

1909				1909		
June 30	To Loss on accounts receivable........		$500.00	June 30	By loss on realization, viz:	
	Loss on leasehold property........		750.00		Jones 50%........	$1,600.00
	Loss on plant........		750.00		Smith 37½........	1,200.00
	Liquidation expenses........		450.00		Peters 12½........	400.00
	Interest on capital:					$3,200.00
	Jones	$437.50				
	Smith	187.50				
	Peters.......	125.00	750.00			
			$3,200.00			$3,200.00

BILLS RECEIVABLE

1909			1909		
Jan. 1	To balance....	$1,500.00	June 30	By cash....	$1,500.00

ACCOUNTS RECEIVABLE

1909			1909		
Jan. 1	To balance....	$30,000.00	June 30	By cash.............	$29,500.00
				Realization account.....	500.00
		$30,000.00			$30,000.00

1909					1909			
Jan. 1	To balance....	$5,000.00			June 30	By cash....		$5,000.00

LEASEHOLD PROPERTY

1909				1909		
Jan. 1	To balance.....	$2,500.00		June 30	By cash....	$1,750.00
					Realization account....	750.00
		$2,500.00				$2,500.00

PLANT AND MACHINERY

1909				1909		
Jan. 1	To balance....	$7,500.00		June 30	By cash....	$6,750 00
					Realization account....	750 00
		$7,500.00				$7,500.00

ACCOUNTS PAYABLE

1909				1909		
June 20	To cash.....	$17,750.00		Jan. 1	By balance....	$17,750.00

A. JOHNS' CAPITAL ACCOUNT

1909				1909		
June 30	To realization account loss....	$16,000.00		Jan. 1	By balance.....	$17,500.00
	Balance.................	16,337.50		June 30	Interest......	437.50
		$17,937.50				$17,937.50
				1909		
				July 1	By balance....	$16,337 50

F. SMITH'S CAPITAL ACCOUNT

1909				1909			
June 30	To realization account—loss......	....	$1,210.00	Jan. 1	By balance......	....	$7,500 00
	Balance..................	....	6,487.50	June 30	Interest...... ....:....	....	187 50
			$7,687.50				$7,687.50
				1909			
				July 1	By balance....	..	$6,487.50

B. PETER'S CAPITAL ACCOUNT

1909				1909			
June 30	To realization accounts—loss.....	....	$400.00	Jan. 1	By balance.....	....	$5,000.00
	Balance.............	.....	4,725.00	June 30	Interest.....	....	125.00
			$5,125.00				$5,125.00
				1909			
				July 1	By balance.....	..	$4,725.00

The realization and liquidation in such case will not only show the loss or gain or realization proper, but furthermore it will show the result of the trustee's own operations. For that purpose a section should be added to the realization and liquidation account headed "Supplementary charges" and "supplementary credits." The former would go on the debit, while the latter on the credit side of the account.

The following problem will illustrate the procedure in such case:

PROBLEM I.

Harvey Bros., became financially embarrassed and a trustee was appointed on January 1, 1908, to take charge of their affairs for the benefit of the creditors.

On that date (January 1, 1908,) their financial condition was as shown by the balance sheet on the next page.

In order to realize advantageously on all assets, the trustee purchased merchandise to the amount of $10,-000.00 and during the year collected $21,350.00 cash for sales. The book debts realized $3,950.00. Of the bills receivable entered in the balance sheet as $18,000.00 there is on hand $8,000.00, the balance of $10,000.00 have been discounted with the bank and are represented on the liability side by the item notes receivable discounted. The $8,000.00 notes on hand are expected to realize the full sum, while of the $10,000.00 discounted with the bank only 70 per cent can be realized; the balance is lost.

The bills payable, taxes and interest on mortgages 5½ per cent were paid in course of settlement. The trustee paid $5,000.00 to the creditors on account.

Current expenses were as follows: Salaries $1,-

BALANCE SHEET OF THE FIRM HARVEY BROS., AS ON JANUARY 1, 1908

ASSETS:

Cash in bank............	$956 50		
Cash in hand............	50 00	$1,006.50	
Bills receivable..........	$18,000 00		
Accounts receivable......	4,500 00	22,500.00	
Merchandise inventory............		4,350.25	$27,856.75
Real estate.....		20,000.00	
Machinery and tools.....		6,000.00	26,000.00
			$53,856.75

LIABILITIES:

Loans payable..............		$1,000.00	
Bills payable..............	$6,000.00		
Accounts payable.........	9,000 00	15,000 00	
Taxes due................		315 00	$16,315.00
Mortgage on real estate............		15,000 00	
Mortgage on machinery and tools.....		5,000 00	20,000.00
Notes receivable discounted............			10,000.00
			$46,315.00

PROPRIETORSHIP:

J. Harvey...........	:	$4,541.75	
S. Harvey...........	:	3,000.00	
			7,541.75
			$53,856.75

REALIZATION AND LIQUIDATION ACCOUNT SUBMITTED BY THE TRUSTEE OF THE FIRM HARVEY BROS.
ON JANUARY 1, 1909

ASSETS TO BE REALIZED

Cash	$1,006.50	
Bills receivable	18,000.00	
Accounts receivable	4,500.00	
Merchandise inventory	4,350.25	
Machinery and tools	6,000.00	
Real estate	20,000.00	$53,856.75

LIABILITIES LIQUIDATED:

Bills payable	$6,000.00	
Accounts payable	5,000.00	
Taxes	315.00	
Contingent liabilities	10,000.00	$21,315.00

LIABILITIES NOT LIQUIDATED:

Loans payable	$1,000.00	
Mortgage on real estate	15,000.00	
Mortgage on machinery, etc	5,000.00	
Accounts payable	4,000.00	$25,000.00

LIABILITIES TO BE LIQUIDATED

Loans payable	$1,000.00	
Bills payable	6,000.00	
Accounts payable	9,000.00	
Taxes due	315.00	
Mortgage on real estate	15,000.00	
Mortgage on machinery, etc	5,000.00	
		$36,315.00
Contingent liability on notes receivable discounted	10,000.00	$46,315.00

ASSETS REALIZED:

Cash	$1,006.50	
Bills receivable	15,000.00	
Accounts receivable	3,950.00	
Merchandise inventory	4,350.00	24,306.75

ASSETS NOT REALIZED:

Real estate	$20,000.00	
Machinery and tools	6,000.00	$26,000.00

SUPPLEMENTARY CHARGES:

Inventory of goods on hand, Jan. 1, 1908	$4,350.25	
Purchases	10,000.00	
Salaries	1,000.00	
Expenses	800.00	
Legal fees	1,200.00	
Trustees' commissions	2,000.00	
Interest on mortgages (5½ on 20,000)	1,100.00	$20,450.25
Net profits		2,949.75
		$123,571.75

SUPPLEMENTARY CREDITS:

Sales	$21,350.00	
Inventory January 1, 1909	5,600.00	$26,950.00
		$123,571.75

TRUSTEE'S CASH ACCOUNT

RECEIPTS:		
To balance on hand January 1, 1908......		$1,006.50
Cash sales......	$21,350.00	
Accounts receivable (old account)....	3,950.00	
Notes receivable......	8,000.00	
		33,300.00
		$34,306.50
To balance.....		$1,891.50

PAYMENTS:		
By purchases of merchandise......	$10,000.00	
Salaries for the year.	1,000.00	
Expenses for the year.....	800.00	
Legal expenses......	1,200.00	
Interest on mortgages......	1,100.00	
Taxes......	315.00	
Trustee's commission......	2,000.00	
Accounts payable......	5,000.00	
Bills payable......	6,000.00	
Withdrawals by the members of the firm......	2,000.00	
Contingent liabilities on discounted notes......	3,000.00	$32,415.00
Balance on hand January 1, 1909....		1,891.50
		$34,306.50

BALANCE SHEET OF HARVEY BROS. AS ON JANUARY 1, 1909

ASSETS:

Cash............................	$1,891.50	
Merchandise Inventory............	5,600.00	$7,491.50
Real estate subject to mortgage......	$20,000.00	
Machinery and tools..............	6,000.00	26,000.00
		$33,491.50

LIABILITIES:

Loan payable....................	$1,000.00	
Accounts payable................	4,000.00	$5,000.00
Mortgage on real estate..........	$15,000.00	
Mortgage on machinery, etc.......	5,000.00	20,000.00
		$25,000.00

PROPRIETORSHIP:

J. Harvey previous capital...	$4,541 75		
One-half of profits..........	1,474 88		
		$6,016 63	
Less withdrawal............		1,000.00	5,016.63
S. Harvey previous capital...	$3,000 00		
One-half of profits..........	1,474 87		
		$4,474 87	
Less withdrawal............		1,000.00	3,474.87
			8,491.50
			$33,491.50

000.00, office expenses $800.00, legal fees $1,200.00, withdrawals for private use by the owners $1,000.00 each, trustee's commissions $2,000.00. On January 1, 1909, the trustee surrendered charge of the estate and paid over the cash balance on hand. There remained on that date merchandise on hand $5,600.00.

Prepare (a) realization and liquidation account, (b) trustee's cash account, and (c) balance sheet of the estate as at termination of trust.

In this solution all the facts in connection with the realization and liquidation are given, but under separate sections. The first section on the debit side, as will be seen, contains the same items as the asset side of the balance sheet under the heading "assets to be realized." It will be noticed that among the other assets the item of cash is included, although this could be left out for the reason that cash is an item which is already realized upon, but in order to have the total of assets to be realized agree with the assets shown on the balance sheet this item was included.

On the credit side we have "liabilities to be liquidated" showing a total of $46,315.00, which equals the total liabilities shown on the balance sheet. It will be noticed that the capital is omitted entirely, and rightly so, as it is not a liability to be liquidated, but on the contrary, after all the liabilities are liquidated what is left belongs to capital.

The second item on the debit side of the realization and liquidation account is "liabilities liquidated." From the wording of the problem we learn that all but four items have been liquidated, namely: the loans payable, the mortgage on real estate, the mortgage on the machinery, and the balance of $4,000.00 due to the creditors of the firm. The total of this section shows

$21,315.00, while on the same side the section "liabilities not liquidated," consisting of the four items mentioned above, amounts to $25,000.00, making up the total of the first section on the credit side.

The second section on the credit side shows "assets realized." The item bills receivable, amounting to $15,000.00 represents the $8,000.00 notes in our possession and 70 per cent of discounted notes, making a total of $15,000.00. The item accounts receivable represents the amount given in the problem. The merchandise inventory is treated as a realized asset because the trustee has utilized the goods and hence the asset is realized. The total of this section amounts to $24,306.75.

The third section, "assets not realized," consists of real estate and machinery. This part of the various sections treats of the realization and liquidation proper. We have not as yet considered the trustee's subsequent operations. If we footed up the items on the debit and credit side of the realization and liquidation account we should find that the total debit side amounts to $100,171.75 while the credit side amounts to $96,621.75, showing a difference of $3,550.00. That difference, so arrived at, indicates the loss on the realization proper. This loss is represented by the following items: $3,000.00 loss on the notes discounted and $550.00 loss on the accounts receivable. However, as the trustee had subsequent operations it is not desirable to show the result of the realization without taking cognizance of his subsequent operations. We arrange then the final sections showing his operation.

On the debit side of this section under the heading of "supplementary charges" are shown all the items that enter into cost of operation. Although the item of legal fees is included there, it is because it cannot very well be arranged in any of the former sections.   The total of this section amounts to $20,450.25.

On the credit side of this section under the heading "supplementary credits" are entered the sales for the period as well as the inventory of goods on hand at the end of the period, making a total of $26,950.00.

If we had footed the former parts of the account separately from the supplementary charges this section would show the profit or loss on the trustee's operation. In this case the cost of operation as mentioned above was $20,450.25, while the returns were $26,950.00, showing a profit on the trustee's operation amounting to $6,499.75.   As we do not show the trustee's operation separately from the realization proper, but combine everything, the loss sustained on the realization is made good out of the profits made on the trustee's operations. That accounts for the net profit shown, amounting to $2,949.75, e.g., the difference between $6,499.75 (profit on the trustee's operation) and $3,550.00 (loss sustained on realization).

The next step in the solution is to show the balance of cash on hand with the trustee.   We arrange for that purpose the trustee's cash account as shown on page 391.

The debit side of this account begins with the balance on hand on January 1, 1908.   To this is added the cash received from the customers, cash sales and also cash collected on the notes which were in our possession, making a total of $34,306.50.

On the credit side we show all the payments made by the trustee including his commission, as well as withdrawals by the members of the firm and the contingent liability on the discounted notes amounting to $3,000.00, making a total of $32,415.00.   That shows the cash balance in the hands of the trustee amounting to $1,-891.50.

Our next step is to show the financial condition of the firm as on the date of the termination of the trust. This is given on page 392. The total assets amount to $33,-491.50. The total liabilities amount to $25.000.00. That leaves a balance of proprietorship amounting to $8,491.50. As the balance sheet (page 392) explains how this sum is arrived at, there is no necessity of giving any explanatory notes on it.

PROBLEM III.

Messrs. Green & Sharp, having given the firm notes to a friendly company as an accommodation, became embarrassed through failure of the payee and appointed a trustee to realize and liquidate. On the following page is a statement of their condition January 1, 1896.

The following is a memorandum of the trustee's transactions for the year: purchases to complete contract orders $70,000.00; sales for year for cash $108,-000.00; uncollected accounts $2,000.00; stock of goods on hand December 31, 1896, $10,000.00; bills receivable collected at a loss of $600.00; book debts receivable, collected $3,600.00; balance lost; received 75 per cent in full settlement of accommodation notes, and paid cash on account of same $48,000.00, giving renewal notes for $10,000.00. The legal fees, interest and petty expenses paid on account of accommodation paper amounted to $2,400.00.

The following payments were also made: mortgage, with interest, and one year's accrued interest to December 31, 1896; taxes, bills payable and book accounts payable; clerk hire, wages and other business expenses, with allowance of $100.00 per month to each of the active partners, one year's interest at 6 per cent to special partner, interest on Green's surplus capital ($6,325.00) one year at 6 per cent and the trustee's fee of $5,000.00 —in all $10,000.00.

The special partner had an interest of 1/10 and the general partners shared alike in the residue of the net profits and losses.

On January 31, 1897, the estate reverted to the firm.

Prepare (a) trustee's realization and liquidation accounts, (b) balance sheet of the estate at termination of trust, (c) partners' accounts.

Comments on solution.—The solution of this problem as shown on pages 398–403 is quite similar to the former one, but with this distinction; instead of showing the realization affairs and the trustee's operation in continuance, the realization proper is shown first with the results of such realization, and the trustee's operations are also shown separately. The recapitulation shows the net results of the affairs.

It will be seen that the ordinary profit resulting from the operation amounts to $5,247.50. The problem tells us that the allowances to the *active* partners were $100.00 per month. Of course we cannot imply that that allowance was also made to the special partner. It also tells us about allowance on interest to the special partner as well as to Green on the surplus capital. The trustee paid these items in cash and we must evidently infer that the partnership agreement provided for such charges prior to the distribution of the net profits. This ordinary net profit is therefore brought down against which the allowance to the partners as well as the interest on capital is charged. The result shows the net profit available for distribution amounting to $1,850.00.

BALANCE SHEET OF MESSRS. GREEN & SHARP AS ON JANUARY 1, 1896

ASSETS:

Cash on hand and in bank	$500 00
Stock of goods	20,000 00
Real estate	25,000 00
Bills receivable	5,000.00
Book debts receivable (including accommodation account of payee, $58,000.00)	62,000.00
	$112,500.00

LIABILITIES:

Mortgage on real estate	$5,000.00
Mortgage interest, accrued to January 1, 1896	250.00
Taxes	375.00
Book debts payable (including accomodation paper of payee, $58,000 00)	61,550.00
Bills payable	1,000 00
Henry Maxwell, special partner	10,000 00
Samuel Green, capital	20,325.00
James Sharp	14,000.00
	$112,500.00

REALIZATION AND LIQUIDATION ACCOUNT SUBMITTED BY THE TRUSTEE OF THE FIRM GREEN & SHARP

DECEMBER 31, 1896.

Assets to be Realized:

Bills receivable............................	$5,000.00	
Accounts receivable (including accommodations)........................	62,000.00	
Merchandise inventory....................	20,000.00	
Real estate (subject to mortgage)......	25,000.00	$112,000.00

Liabilities Liquidated:

Mortgage on real estate..................	$5,000.00	
Mortgage interest to Jan. 1, 1896.....	250.00	
Taxes......................................	375.00	
Bills payable..............................	1,000.00	
Accounts payable (bk accounts)......	$3,550.00	
Accounts payable on account of accommodation..........	48,000 00	51,550.00
		58,175.00

Liabilities Not Liquidated:

Accounts payable (renewed notes)......		10,000.00
		$180,175.00

Liabilities to be Liquidated:

Bills payable...............................	$1,000.00	
Accounts payable (including accommodation)........................	61,550.00	
Taxes......................................	375.00	
Mortgage on real estate..................	5,000.00	
Mortgage interest (accrued to Jan. 1, 1896)................................	250.00	$68,175.00

Assets Realized:

Bills receivable...........................		$4,400.00
Accounts receivable:		
Book Debts.............	$3,600.00	
Accommodation..........	43,500.00	47,100.00
Merchandise inventory...................		10,000 00
		61,500.00

Assets Not Realized:

Merchandise inventory....................	$10,000 00	
Real estate...............................	25,000 00	35,000.00
Loss on Realization proper..............	....	15,500.00
		$180,175.00

TRUSTEE'S OPERATION AND SUBSEQUENT TRANSACTIONS

SUPPLEMENTARY CHARGES:		
Inventory consumed	$10,000.00	
Purchases	70,000.00	
Clerk hire, wages, etc.	1,620.50	
Legal fees and petty expenses	2,400.00	
Interest on mortgage	250.00	
Trustee's commission	5,000.00	$89,270.50
Profit on operation		20,729.50
		$110,000.00

SUPPLEMENTARY CREDITS:		
Cash sales for the year	$108,000.00	
Sales on account	2,000.00	$110,000.00
		$110,000.00

RECAPITULATION

Loss on realization	$15,500.00	
Ordinary profit resulting (carried down)	5,229.50	$20,729.50
Profit on operation		$20,729.50

Green's allowance	$1,200.00	
Sharp's allowance	1,200.00	
Interest on Maxwell's capital	600.00	
Interest on Green's surplus	379.50	
Net profit, available for distribution	1,850.00	$5,229.50
Ordinary profit (brought down)		$5,229.50

TRUSTEE'S CASH ACCOUNT

RECEIPTS:

To balance on hand Jan. 1, 1896		$500.00
Cash sales during the year	$108,000.00	
Accounts receivable (old book accounts)	3,600.00	
Accounts receivable (accommodation)	43,500.00	
Bills receivable	4,400.00	
		159,500.00
		$160,000.00
		$19,175.00

PAYMENTS:

By purchases of merchandise	$70,000.00	
Accounts payable (accommodation)		
Accounts payable (old book accounts)	48,000.00	
Bills payable	3,550.00	
Legal fees and other petty expenses	1,000.00	
Mortgage on real estate	2,400.00	
Interest at 5% (2 years)	5,000.00	
Taxes	500.00	
	375.00	$130,825.00
Clerk hire, wages, etc.	$1,620.50	
Green's allowance	1,200.00	
Sharp's allowance	1,200.00	
Interest on special partners' balance	600.00	
Interest on Green's surplus capital	379.50	
Trustee's commission	5,000.00	
		10,000.00
Balance on hand		19,175.00
		$160,000.00

To balance on hand, Jan. 1, 1897 .... $19,175.00

III—26

401

BALANCE SHEET OF THE FIRM GREEN AND SHARP AS ON DECEMBER 31, 1897

ASSETS:			LIABILITIES:	
Cash................	$19,175.00		Notes payable....	$10,000.00
Accounts receivable............	2,000.00			
Merchandise inventory............	10,000.00	$31,175.00	PROPRIETORSHIP:	
Real estate....		25,000.00	Combined capital as per capital accounts.....	46,175.00
		$56,175.00		$56,175.00

SAMUEL GREEN'S CAPITAL ACCOUNT

To balance December 31, 1896....	By balance January 1, 1896..............	$20,325.00
	One-half of profits (after providing Maxwell's 10%)............	832.50
		$21,157.50
$21,157.50	By balance December 31, 1896....	$21,157.50

JAMES SHARP'S CAPITAL ACCOUNT

To balance December 31, 1896....	By balance January 1, 1896..........	$14,000 00
	One-half of profits (after providing Maxwell's 10%)............	832.50
		$14,832.50
$14,832.50	By balance December 31, 1896....	$14,832.50

HENRY MAXWELL'S CAPITAL ACCOUNT

To balance December 31, 1896....	By balance January 1, 1896....	$10,000.00
	One-tenth of profits........	185.00
		$10,185.00
$10,185.00	By balance December 31, 1896....	$10,185.00

While there is not much difference in following either method, under the latter arrangement the view taken is that the solution showing supplementary charges and credits of the trustee's operation is nothing else but a profit and loss account. It shows the profit made or loss sustained on operation.

Another thing to be noticed is that in the solution of this problem the cash item has been eliminated. This was done in order to give the reader the benefit of the various views that are possible to be taken in the solution of such or similar problems.

The trustee's cash account shows the cash received from various sources as well as the cash payments.

We are told in the problem that the amount paid for clerk hire, wages, partners' allowances, etc., amounts to $10,000.00. The cash payment side shows these payments in itemized form. As the partners' allowance with interest as well as the trustee's commission amount to $8,397.50 the amount paid for clerk hire, wages and petty expenses must have been $1,602.50. That explains this figure shown on the cash payment side and accounts for the balance of cash on hand amounting to $19,175.00.

The balance sheet shows the assets consisting of cash, the outstanding accounts on the trustee's operation ($2,000.00), inventory and real estate amounting in total to $56,175.00. The liabilities consist of notes payable only, amounting to $10,000.00, and represent the renewal on accommodation affairs. That leaves a balance for proprietorship representing the above capital and amounting to $46,175.00.

Although the problem does not call for the partners' accounts they are given separately in order to explain the distribution of profits and therefore the total capital only is shown in the balance sheet.

120. *Insolvency accounts.*—We have so far treated of solvent accounts only. In the case of the realization and liquidation accounts we also had cases of temporary embarrassments, but not insolvencies. At present, however, we wish to treat insolvencies proper. The special points that often arise in connection with accounts relating to the estates of insolvent persons have their origin in the Bankruptcy Law requirements made upon persons administering these trusts.

The trustee in the case of realization affairs treated the business as a going concern. He continued operations not for the purpose of winding up the affairs of the firm, but in order to put it on a more firm basis. He looked mainly to the welfare of the creditors of the firm and when he saw that their claims were fully satisfied or at least reasonably well secured, he surrendered the trust. The estate reverted to the owners under their exclusive control and management as before the appointment of the receiver.

The trustee appointed in the case of insolvent estates is not appointed for the purpose of strengthening the condition of the firm but to wind it up entirely. He is to continue operations, under certain circumstances only, namely, when there are contracts to be completed. He sells all the assets and upon their realization liquidates the liabilities and pays the creditors their pro-rata.

Under normal conditions the object of any system of bookkeeping is to produce, at regular intervals, or whenever required, a statement showing the financial position at that date in the form of a balance sheet, and also an account showing the various sources of income, expenditure, or loss, that have contributed to the change of the position as compared with the previous period. The latter account is frequently divided into several sections, known collectively as the profit and loss or revenue account.

When an estate is found to be insolvent somewhat similar accounts, although different in substance, are prepared. Owing to the special circumstances of the case certain changes of detail in the form of the accounts are necessary for the purpose for which they are required. Thus, in place of the balance sheet showing on one hand the assets and on the other the liabilities—the excess of the former over the latter representing proprietorship—the statement that is required is one that will afford unsecured creditors some idea of the amount of their claims in the aggregate and of the amount of net assets available to meet such liabilities. It is very obvious that the balance sheet form must be so modified that all assets pledged as security for liabilities appear not as assets but as deductions from the claims of secured creditors. If a creditor is fully secured the surplus value of that asset so pledged, after liquidating his claim only, appears as an asset, while if a creditor is partially secured, the unsecured balance of his claim alone appears as a liability against the general assets.

121. *Preferential claims.*—Another thing to be noticed in this class of accounts is that there are certain grades of creditors who are by law entitled to be paid in priority to the general creditors of the firm, known as preferential creditors. The claims of these creditors are stated separately and are deducted from the assets.

Such claims are debts due to the national, state or municipal Government, wages and salaries of employés, —to the extent that the law provides that they shall be paid out of the estate before the general distribution is made—or rent of the premises where the assets of the estate are located.

A prepared statement showing all such facts is known as a "statement of affairs." This statement is divided to show on the one hand the net total of assets which (subject to probable loss on realization and costs) is available for distribution among creditors, and on the other hand the total unsecured liabilities that are expected to rank against the assets for dividends. The excess of the latter figure over the former is the deficiency which the insolvent debtor has to account for. It has already been noted that the statement of affairs is in many instances identical with the balance sheet excepting, of course, the purpose for which it is prepared as well as the result shown.

The deficiency account is similar to the profit and loss account but, of course, contains certain modifications. It must be borne in mind that this account is prepared in order to explain the causes and reasons for the deficiency shown in the statement of affairs. This modified account (deficiency account) differs chiefly from the profit and loss account in that it begins with an opening balance representing the amount of surplus assets of the insolvent firm at some previous period. To this amount are added all sources of profit that have increased the total amount to be accounted for. On the other side of the account are stated all the expenditures of the insolvent firm as well as all losses incurred by it, so that the balance of this account is the same amount of deficiency as shown by the statement of affairs.

With regard to the form of presenting a statement of affairs or deficiency account, the practice varies a great deal. Some would arrange the statement of affairs to show on the left hand side the liabilities, and on the right hand side assets. The deficiency account would be arranged to show on the left hand side the capital and deficiency, and on the right hand side shrinkages and losses. Others arrange the assets on the left hand side of the statement of affairs and the liabilities on the right hand side; the deficiency account would be arranged in the same form as mentioned above. Still others change the deficiency account to show on the left hand side shrinkages and losses and on the right hand side capital and deficiency. The following concrete illustration will show the handling of such accounts.

PROBLEM IV.

Jones and Robinson, merchants, are unable to meet their obligations. From their books and the testimony of the insolvent debtors the following statement of their condition is ascertained:

Cash on hand	$5,500.00
Debtors: $1,000.00 good; $600.00 doubtful, but estimated to produce $200.00; $1000.00 bad	2,600.00
Property, estimated to produce $9,000.00	14,000.00
Bills receivable, good	4,250.00
Other securities: $3,000.00 pledged with partially secured creditors; remainder held by fully secured creditors	28,000.00
Jones, drawings	9,000.00
Robinson, drawings	8,400.00
Sundry losses	13,500.00
Trade expenses	7,400.00
Creditors, unsecured	25,000.00
Creditors, partially secured	23,900.00
Creditors, fully secured	17,000.00
Preferential claims, wages, salaries and taxes	700.00
Jones, capital	10,000.00
Robinson, capital	16,050.00

STATEMENT OF AFFAIRS, DECEMBER 15, 1896, JONES & ROBINSON

Assets:	Nominal Value	Expected to Realize	Liabilities:	Total Liabilities	Expected to Rank
Cash on hand	$5,500.00	$5,500.00	Creditors, unsecured	$25,000.00	$25,000.00
Property	14,000.00	9,000.00	Creditors partly secured $23,900.00	23,900.00	20,900.00
Sundry Debtors:	2,600.00		Securities at estimated value...... 3,000.00		
Good............ $1,000.00			Creditors fully secured, 17,000.00	17,000.00	
Doubtful........ 600.00		1,200.00	Securities at estimated value...... 25,000.00		
Bad............ 1,000.00			Surplus to contra...... $8,000.00		
Bills receivable..	4,250.00	4,250.00			
Other securities in the hands of creditors....	28,000.00		Preferential creditors, for wages, salaries, taxes, etc........ 700.00	700.00	
Partly secured...... $3,000.00			Deduct contra...... 700.00		
Fully secured...... 25,000.00					
Deducted contra...... $28,000.00					
Surplus from securities in the hands of creditors, fully secured per contra.		8,000.00			
		$27,950.00			
Deduct preferential creditors, for wages, salaries, taxes, etc., per contra........		700.00			
		$27,250.00			
Deficiency, as per deficiency account..		18,650.00			
	$54,350.00	$45,900.00		$66,600.00	$45,900.00

DEFICIENCY ACCOUNT JONES & ROBINSON

To capital brought into the business at commencement, and since, viz :			By losses on trading, viz :			
Jones, capital	$10,000.00		Sundry losses	$13,500.00		
Robinson, capital	16,050.00	$26,050.00	Trade expenses	7,400.00		$20,900.00
Deficiency as shown by statement of affairs		18,650.00	Losses and shrinkage in values, as exhibited by statement of affairs,			
			Property	$5,000.00		
			Debtors, doubtful	400.00		
			Debtors, bad	1,000.00		6,400.00
			Drawings from business, viz :			
			Jones, drawings	$9,000.00		
			Robinson, drawings	8,400.00		17,400.00
		$44,700.00				$44,700.00

Prepare a statement of affairs, showing the liabilities and the assets with respect to their realization and liquidation; also a deficiency account showing such of the above stated particulars as would account for the deficiency shown by the statement of affairs.

The statement of affairs shown on page 409 is arranged to disclose the exact status of the firm on the date of December 15. The left hand side of the statement shows in one column the nominal or book value of the assets. The second column shows the amount that we expect these assets to realize. We are not much interested in the book value of the assets, but we are interested to know how much we may expect to realize from these assets. The total of this column after deducting preferential claims is $27,-250.00. On the right hand side of the statement are shown the liabilities. We have there also two columns, the total or book liabilities and the other column showing the amount the liabilities are expected to rank. It will be noticed that the secured creditors are omitted entirely. This is due to the fact that they are not expected to rank to any amount as they are fully secured.

The creditors partially secured are shown in the total liabilities column for the full amount while in the column "expected to rank" only $20,900.00 as the securities in their possession as part pledge are estimated at $3,000.00. Preferential claims are entered only in the total liability column because they have been deducted from the total assets. The total of the column "expected to rank" amounts to $45,900.00. As the assets available for distribution amount to only $27,250.00, we have a deficiency of $18,650.00, which is accounted for and explained in the deficiency account shown on page 410.

This account begins on the debit side with the capital brought into the business at commencement, amounting to $26,050.00. On the credit side are entered the losses on trading as given in the facts, as well as the trading expenses, making the total $20,900.00. The second part on the same side deals with the losses and shrinkages in values as shown by the statement of affairs and which amount to $6,400.00. Finally are entered the withdrawals amounting to $17,400.00, thus showing a total on the credit side amounting to $44,700.00. We have against this only the capital, amounting to $26,050.00, hence there is a deficiency amounting to $18,650.00, which is the exact sum shown on the statement of affairs.

PROBLEM V.

Parker and Riley, being unable to meet their obligations, have made an assignment. You are asked to prepare a statement of their affairs for presentation at a meeting of their creditors. Some of the creditors are entirely or partially secured, the security being a part of the assets. It is desired to ascertain the true condition of the assets with reference to realization and the extent of the deficiency with respect to liquidation. Prepare also in connection with the statement of affairs a deficiency account, explaining the deficiency shown in the statement of affairs. Following is a trial balance of their ledger at the date of the assignment:

Cash on hand and in bank	$1,200.00
Stock and material (inventory from prior period) ..	12,000.00
Reliance Trust Co. stock, 20 shares at cost	2,200.00
Accounts receivable	10,550.00
Notes receivable	2,000.00
Mortgage receivable (second) on 194 Front St.	1,000.00
Real estate (store building and lot)	14,000.00
Fixtures	1,700.00
Horses, trucks and harness (property account)	1,400.00
Accounts payable	$28,000.00

Loans payable		7,000.00
Mortgage payable (on store building and lot)		5,000.00
Purchases	30,000.00	
Sales		36,000.00
Rents		1,200.00
Salaries	3,500.00	
Interest and discount	960.00	
Taxes, insurance and building repairs	1,240.00	
General expenses	2,650.00	
Parker's capital		8,000.00
Riley's capital		4,000.00
Withdrawals, Parker	3,000.00	
Withdrawals, Riley	1,800.00	
	$89,200.00	$89,200.00

The accounts receivable are divided as good, $8,000.00, doubtful, $1,500.00 (estimated to produce $1,000.00), worthless, $1,050.00. Notes receivable are estimated to realize $1,800.00; the second mortgage is estimated to produce $800.00; the trust company shares $1,800.00; the horses, trucks and harness $900.00; fixtures $1,000.00; store building and lot $12,500.00.

Of the amount due creditors (accounts payable) $20,000.00 is unsecured and $8,000.00 is secured by the second mortgage and trust company stock. The loans payable are secured by the equity in the store, building and lot.

The inventory of merchandise on hand, which foots $5,000.00, is expected to realize $3,000.00. Other liabilities are employés' wages, $550.00, and accrued interest on mortgage, $125.00.

SOLUTION.

We have so far shown only the statement of affairs and the deficiency account, without accompanying it by any exhibits or schedules. The usual practice, however, is to accompany such statements by exhibits. In the following problem the statement of affairs is arranged in somewhat different form from the first one; so is also the deficiency account, in order to give the reader the benefit of some other possible view. The solution of this problem is also accompanied with schedules to which reference is made in the statement of affairs. As the working of such statement and the respective deficiency account has been fully explained the comments on the solution of the problem are rather brief.

Our first step in this solution is to show the result of operation up to the date of the assignment. We therefore prepare the profit and loss account shown on the following page.

It will be noticed that this account is not prepared strictly according to the principles advocated before. It is not subdivided nor classified. If we bear in mind that it is prepared only in order to show the loss sustained, and that the affairs are closed out, it will be quite obvious why that arrangement is followed.

The balance sheet on page 416 shows the financial condition of the firm. Riley has withdrawn $1,800.00 and as his share of the losses was $4,075.00, that makes a total of $5,875.00. His capital in the firm was $4,000.00, hence he has overdrawn $1,875.00. As Parker's account shows a credit of $925.00, there remains a debit balance of only $950.00.

PROFIT AND LOSS ACCOUNT OF THE FIRM PARKER & RILEY, COVERING THE PERIOD UP TO DATE

OF THE ASSIGNMENT

Inventory prior period..........	$12,000.00	Inventory goods on hand......	$5,000.00
Purchases..........................	30,000.00	Sales.............................	36,000.00
Salaries...........................	3,500.00	Rents.............................	1,200.00
Interest and discount.............	960.00	Loss excluding depreciation or other reserves.....	8,150.00
Taxes, etc.........................	1,240.00		
General expenses..................	2,650.00		
	$50,350.00		$50,350.00

415

BALANCE SHEET OF THE FIRM PARKER & RILEY, ON DATE OF ASSIGNMENT

ASSETS:

Cash on hand and in bank............		$1,200.00	
Reliance Trust Company stock (20 shares)	$2,000.00		
Notes receivable.........	$2,000.00		$2,200.00
Accounts receivable...........	10,550.00	12,550.00	
Inventory of merchandise............	5,000.00	18,750.00	
			$20,950.00
Real estate...........	$14,000.00		
Mortgage receivable...........	1,000.00		
Fixtures............	1,700.00		
Horses, trucks, etc...........	1,400.00	18,100.00	
			$39,050.00
Riley's excess withdrawals............			950.00
			$40,000.00

LIABILITIES:

Loans payable............		$7,000.00	
Accounts payable............		28,000.00	$35,000.00
Mortgage payable............			5,000.00
			$40,000.00

PROPRIETORSHIP:

Parker's previous capital..		$8,000.00	
Deduct:			
One-half of losses. $4,075			
Withdrawals...... 3,000	7,075.00		$925.00
Riley's previous balance.............		4,000.00	
Deduct:			
One-half of losses. $4,075			
Withdrawals...... 1,800	$5,875.00		
Debit excess..........$1,875.00			
Deduct Parker's credit balance............	925.00		
Contra............			$950.00

STATEMENT OF AFFAIRS PARKER AND RILEY

Nominal Value	Assets		Estimated to Produce	Total	Liabilities:		Expected to Rank
$1,200.00	Cash		$1,200.00	$20,000.00	Creditors unsecured as per schedule D		$20,000.00
8,100.00	Property as per schedule A		4,900.00	8,000.00	Creditors partly secured, as per schedule E	$8,000.00	
10,550.00	Accounts receivable, as per schedule B				Deduct security	2,600.00	5,400.00
	Good	$8,000.00	8,000.00	12,125.00	Creditors fully secured, as per schedule F	12,125.00	
	Doubtful	1,500.00	1,000.00		Store and lot	12,500.00	
	Bad	1,050.00			Surplus to contra	375.00	
2,000.00	Notes receivable		1,800.00	550.00	Preferred creditors. Wages due, deducted contra	550.00	
17,200.00	Other assets in hands of creditors, as per schedule C						
	Surplus in hands of fully secured creditors, schedule F		375.00				
	TOTAL ASSETS		$17,275.00				
	Deduct preferred claims as per contra		550.00				
			$16,725.00				
	Deficiency as per deficiency account		8,675.00				
$39,050.00			$25,400.00	$40,675.00			$25,400.00

DEFICIENCY ACCOUNT, PARKER AND RILEY

Dr.			Cr.		
CAPITAL:			Trading losses, as per profit and loss account..............		$8,150.00
Parker....	$8,000.00		Sundry losses, interest due.....	$125.00	
Riley......	4,000.00	$12,000.00	wages due.....	550.00	675.00
			Shrinkage in value of assets.....		7,050.00
DEFICIENCY AS PER STATEMENT OF AFFAIRS..		8,675.00	WITHDRAWALS:		
			Parker..........	3,000.00	
			Riley.........	1,800.00	4,800.00
		$20,675.00			$20,675.00

SCHEDULE A

PROPERTY

	Nominal Value	Estimated to Produce	Shrinkage
Stock and materials	$5,000.00	$3,000.00	$2,000.00
Horses, trucks, etc.	1,400.00	900.00	500.00
Fixtures	1,700.00	1,000 00	700.00
	$8,100.00	$4,900.00	$3,200.00

SCHEDULE B

CUSTOMERS' ACCOUNTS

(Omitted in this case)

Good	$8,000.00	
Doubtful	1,500.00	
Bad	1,050.00	
		$10,550.00

SCHEDULE C

OTHER ASSETS

Store and lot	$12,500.00	
Second mortgage	800.00	
Trust company stock	1,800.00	
	$15,100.00	
Shrinkage in value	2,100.00	
		$17,200.00

SCHEDULE D

Unsecured Creditors

Sundry creditors.. $20,000.00

SCHEDULE E

Partly Secured Creditors

Sundry creditors..........................	$800.00	
Second mortgages expected to realize......	1,800.00	
Trust company stock.......................		$8,000.00
		2,600.00
		$5,400.00

SCHEDULE F

Creditors Fully Secured

Loans payable.............................	$7,000.00	
Mortgage payable..........................	5,000.00	
Interest payable..........................	125.00	
		$12,125.00
Security:		
Store and lot.............................		12,500.00
Equity....................................		$375.00

420

PART V: ACCOUNTANCY PROB-
LEMS AND SOLUTIONS

CHAPTER XX

QUESTIONS AND ANSWERS IN THEORY OF ACCOUNTS

Question 1.—Is it necessary to journalize your cash receipts and payments in order to be able to balance your books by double entry? Give reasons for your reply.

It is not necessary. The cash book should be regarded as a ledger account. The mere posting of the entries therein to the opposite side of the ledger account completes the double entry in respect to all cash items. In the early days of accounting practice it used to be considered necessary when books were kept by double entry to pass every single transaction through the journal so that the total debit entries in the ledger might agree with the total of the debit column in the journal and the total of the credit entries in the ledger with the credit column in the journal. But this system is no longer employed.

Question 2.—Give a definition of the term "depreciation" and state briefly your views on the chief consideration which should determine this amount.

Depreciation is the deterioration in the value of an asset—wear and tear arising in the ordinary course of events through use, either from lapse of time or from progress of invention. In as much as the possession of these assets has contributed towards the earning of revenue, depreciation is a charge against such revenue.

It is not always absolutely necessary that the assets should be written down each year to their actual value, and the depreciation styled depreciation, but at the time the assets have become valuelsss for the purposes for which they are intended, the difference between the original cost and the residual value (if any) must be charged against revenue. It is, however, usual to provide for depreciation by a fixed percentage on the annual balance or by some other method. Where the life of an asset is known, it is always best to divide the cost of the asset by the number of years that the asset is expected to exist, assuming, of course, that there is no residual value.

Question 3.—Give forms for "notes payable" book and "notes receivable" book respectively, and make an entry in each. (For answer see pages 423–424.)

Question 4.—State as briefly as you can the method of producing cost accounts.

By dissecting and analyzing all direct expenditures in the various departments of production and apportioning standing charges ratably.

Question 5.—What systems of bookkeeping are in general use? Describe the books peculiar to each and state how the profit or loss is ascertained by the different methods.

There are two principal systems of bookkeeping in general use, namely, single entry and double entry. The books peculiar to each are practically identical, varying only according to the nature of the transactions to be recorded. Under the double entry systems, the profit or loss is ascertained first by the profit and loss account, which is a summary of all the nominal or economic accounts, and afterwards checked and verified by the

NOTES RECEIVABLE BOOK, JANUARY,, 1908

No. of Note	When Received	From Whom Received	Maker or Drawer	Acceptor	Where Payable	Date of Note or Draft	Time	When Due													Folio	Amount of Paper	Remarks
								Jan.	Feb.	Mar.	Apr.	May	June	July	Aug.	Sept.	Oct.	Nov.	Dec.			
1	1908 Jan. 5	John Brown	J. Brown		1st N. B.	1908 Jan. 4	2 mos.			5										1	500.00	

423

NOTES PAYABLE BOOK—JANUARY, 1908

No. of Note	When Accepted (In case of acceptance)	Drawer (In case of draft)	To Whom Payable	On Whose Account	Date of Instrument	Time	When Due — Jan.	Feb.	Mar.	Apr.	May	June	July	Aug.	Sept.	Oct.	Nov.	Dec.	Folio	Amount of Paper	Remarks
1	1908 Jan. 5	John Smith.	James & Co.		1908 Jan. 5	3 mos.				5									1	1,500.00	
2			F. Jones...	John Smith	Jan. 4	2 mos.			5										2	500.00	Payable at our bank.

424

agreement of the totals of the balance sheet. Under the single entry system the profit or loss is arrived at by ascertaining the surplus of assets over liabilities and comparing that surplus with the surplus at the beginning of the period, after taking into consideration aceretions to and diminutions of capital. Thus by the single entry method there is no check whatever on the clerical accuracy of the profits arrived at.

Question 6.—Explain fully the difference between a manufacturing or trading, and a profit and loss account. What does the result of each show and how are the balances of each treated on closing the books?

Opinions rather differ as to the precise distinction between a manufacturing or trading account and a profit and loss account. It may, however, be said that the manufacturing or trading account shows the gross profit after all the expenses incurred necessary to acquire or produce the goods, and to bring them into a saleable condition, have been charged up. A profit and loss account begins with the gross profit carried down from the former accounts and adds thereto other sources of income not directly arising from trade, and deducts therefrom all administrative, financial and general expenses, the final balance being the net profit.

Question 7.—What class of expenditures should be treated as assets at the closing of a fiscal period?

That class of expenditures made through a current fiscal period which is not utilized or consumed during the period under review is an asset at the close of a fiscal period until its consummation. To illustrate:

Suppose a merchant pays his rent quarterly, say $500.00 per quarter, and that his fiscal year ends May 1. When he pays on April 1 $500.00, he pays rental up to and including June 30. Therefore, there are two months' rental, May and June, paid for but not consumed, and that expenditure is, at the close of the fiscal period, May 1, an asset amounting to $333.33. The same applies to unexpired insurance premium or unconsumed advertising outlay.

Question 8.—Into what general classes should ledger accounts be divided? State the distinctive feature of each class. Mention three accounts belonging to each class.

The ledger accounts are generally divided, as already mentioned, into personal and impersonal accounts. The latter are subdivided into real or specific and nominal or economic accounts.

The distinctive feature of the real accounts is that they represent specific value and the distinct feature of the nominal accounts is that they treat of revenue, income and expenditures.

Three accounts that belong to the nominal accounts are as follows: interest, salaries, general expenses, etc.

Three accounts that belong to the real or specific class are: cash, notes receivable, plant and machinery, etc.

Question 9.—Describe the profit and loss account, show how this account is made up and also what accounts it is made up from.

What does the balance of the profit and loss account represent and how should such balances be finally treated?

The profit and loss account as an account proper is the intermediate account intervening between the economic and proprietary accounts. This account is made up from the nominal or economic accounts containing on the debit side all the balances of the operating accounts and on the credit side the sources of income. The balance shows either the profit made or loss sustained according to whether it be a credit or a debit balance. This final balance of the profit and loss account in the case of a sole owner is transferred either to the debit or credit side of his account, as the case may be; if it is a profit, to the credit side, if a loss, to the debit side of his account. In the case of partnerships it would be distributed to the partners' accounts according to the partnership agreement. In the case of a corporation it would be carried to the surplus account.

Question 10.—What is the value and use of a journal?

The chief use of a journal is to provide a medium record of transactions as they occur which cannot be entered in any of the other books of original entry. Generally we find in such a book opening or closing entries, adjustment entries, whenever required, and also a record of notes received or issued. The latter is only true where a notes receivable and notes payable book is not used as a medium of posting.

Question 11.—A firm is in the habit of discounting all notes received by it; state how you would arrange to show the contingent liabilities on the notes discounted at the bank and which are not yet due.

The best way to provide for such contingent liabilities is by opening a notes receivable discounted account, which account is to be credited for all notes discounted by the firm instead of crediting such notes discounted to the notes receivable account. By this method we have an asset and liability of the same amounts, thus showing the contingent liability. When the note is paid for the contingent liability is wiped out; notes receivable discounted would then be debited and notes receivable account would be credited. When the note is dishonored and we have to refund to the bank the cash received, we would still debit notes receivable discounted as we settled the contingent liability and would credit cash, the notes receivable account showing that asset in our possession.

Question 12.—What is an income and expenditure account and wherein does it differ from an account of receipts and payments?

An income and expenditure account is nothing but a summary of the nominal accounts, which is synonymous with the profit and loss account. The balance of this account is the net income or excess expenditure for the period under review. The income is placed on the credit side and the expenditure on the debit side of the account. It differs from an account of receipts and payments in so much that the latter is a summary of the cash account only. The income or expenditure account takes cognizance of outstanding accounts showing income or expenditure and shows as a balance net income or expenditure, while the account of receipts and payments deals *only* with cash items, omitting entirely accounts due to us or by us, and which deal with income or expenditure, respectively and shows as a balance the excess of receipts over payments. The term "income and expenditure" is generally used by non-trading concerns, while "profit and loss" is spoken of in cases of trading firms.

Question 13.—Describe the different methods of determining the loss or gain of a business. How is the loss or gain of a business determined from books kept by single entry? What is the usual method of procedure when the books are kept by double entry?

There are in general two methods used for determining the loss or gain of a business. One is known as 'the loss and gain method, the other is known as the resource and liability method.

The usual method of procedure in determining the profit or loss of a business when the books have been kept by single entry is to compare the state of affairs of one period with that of another period. The different results shown will disclose a loss or a gain. This is known as the resource and liability method. We have no other means, where this system is used, to determine the profit or loss but by a comparison of the assets and liabilities of one period with those of another period. Lisle in his "Accounting in Theory and Practice" gives the following rule for determining the profit or loss in a set of books kept by single entry, assuming that complete capital accounts for proprietorship have been kept:

Prepare a statement of affairs as at the close of the period and so ascertain the capital at the end of the period. Prepare a capital account or capital accounts, if the business is a partnership, for the period. From the capital brought out by the statement deduct the capital shown by the capital account, or the capital accounts prepared. The difference is the net profit for the period. If the capital shown by the capital accounts is greater than the capital shown by the statement, the result of the period's transactions is a loss.

Where the books have been kept by double entry the profit or loss is determined by the profit and loss method. The gross profit or loss is determined first by the manufacturing or trading account. This account is debited for costs and credited for returns and inventories. The difference shows the gross profit or gross loss. The balance so ascertained is then transferred to the profit and loss account. This profit and loss account is credited or debited, according as the case may be, for the balance carried through the manufacturing or trading account. It is charged with all debit balances of the remaining nominal accounts and is credited with all credit balances of the remaining nominal accounts. Depreciation and reserves are also charged against one of the sections of this account; the final balance will show a loss or a gain; a loss if a debit, a gain if a credit balance.

Question 14.—What is meant by: (a) Fixed assets; (b) floating assets; (c) wasting asets. Give an example of each.

(a) Fixed assets are assets permanently held by a concern for the purpose of enabling it to carry on its business and to earn revenue.

(b) Floating assets are assets kept with the object of converting them conveniently into cash.

(c) Wasting assets are such assets as in the ordinary course decrease in value, such decrease being caused either by wear and tear, by lapse of time or by the progress of invention.

Machinery is an example of a fixed asset, when used in an ordinary manufacturing company. If it be made for purposes of selling it becomes a floating asset in the accounts of such a concern.

Notes receivable is an example of floating assets, being easily converted into cash.

All classes of machinery that become wasted by reason of wear and tear are illustrations of wasting assets. A patent is another good example of a wasting asset. The waste may arise either from lapse of time or by some new invention taking the place of the old patented article.

Question 15.—What is the meaning of premiums on stock? How do they arise and how should they be dealt with in a company's account?

Premiums on stock are entered as a separate item on

the liability side of the balance sheet. This item represents the amount received by the company from stockholders in excess of the amount credited as being paid up on the stock. It is not advisable that such premiums be carried in the profit and loss account of the corporation. Extraordinary charges, however, may be carried against this account. For a full discussion of this topic refer to pages 298–302.

Question 16.—State briefly what you consider to be the principal points to be observed in devising a system of bookkeeping for a manufacturing concern.

The principal points to be considered are that the books should be so designed as to offer readily all information that will enable those responsible for its management to have detailed data as to the actual results that they have achieved and how they have been brought about. In a well-conducted manufacturing business, proper cost accounts are usually kept and it is quite important that these should be independent of the financial books in order that they may, to some extent, at least, be a check upon their accuracy.

Question 17.—In compiling a profit and loss account and a balance sheet of a passenger steamship company, to what points should a bookkeeper direct special attention?

The main points to be considered are as follows:

First, return passages paid in advance should be carried forward as a liability, at least until such time as is shown that they may be safely written off.

Second, the proportion of insurance up to date should be included in the account.

Third, no credit should be taken for estimated profits upon uncompleted voyages.

Fourth, careful inquiry must be made with a view to

ascertaining that all outstanding liabilities are included.

Fifth, due provision must be made for depreciation.

Question 18.—Give your opinion as to the best method of keeping a petty cash account.

The petty cash account should be kept by the columnar system, e.g., a separate column should be kept for each class of expenses. There should be a column showing the cash received for petty disbursements. There should be, furthermore, one column in which all the payments are entered and then each payment should be extended in the proper distribution column.

At the end of the month a summary should be made and such summary posted to the respective ledger accounts. It is advisable that vouchers should be obtained for all payments.

A much better method is that known as the "Imprest System." The use of this system has already been explained in another part of the text.

Question 19.—Prepare a form of cashbook with columus covering the following:

Receipts from customers.	Purchase ledger accounts
Discounts allowed.	Discounts deducted.
Cash sales.	Petty cash.
Private ledger accounts.	Private ledger accounts.

(For answer refer to next page.)

Question 20.—What general principles should be observed in differentiating between capital and revenue expenditures?

By the term "Capital Expenditures" is meant, expenses incurred for the sake of acquiring, or completing the plant and equipment of an enterprise, with a view to placing it on a revenue-earning basis, whereas, by the term "Revenue Expenditures" is meant all those expenses incurred in connection with the earning of rev-

Dr.

Date	L.F.	Account to be Credited and Explanation	Receipts from Customers	Discounts Allowed	Cash Sales	Private Ledger Accounts	Total
1909							
Jan. 5	1	To A. B........	$23.75	$1.25			
Jan. 10		To cash sales...			$100.00		
Jan. 10	9	To old materials........				$150.00	$273.75
			$23.75	$1.25	$100.00	$150.00	$273.75
1900 Feb. 1		To balance....					$179.75

Cr.

Date	L.F.	Account to be Debited and Explanation	Purchase Ledger Accounts	Discounts Deducted	Petty Cash	Private Ledger Accounts	Total
1909							
Jan. 10	6	By C. D......	$49.00	$1.00			
Jan. 10	7	By petty cash......			$20.00		
Jan. 10		By drawings				$25.00	$94.00
Jan. 31		By balance.					179.75
			$49.00	$1.00	$20.00	$25.00	$273.75

enue. In differentiating between capital and revenue expenditures we must bear in mind what the outlay is for. If it is such that it will improve the equipment and thereby increase the earning capacity of the firm, then it is a proper charge to capital and is a capital expenditure; otherwise it is a revenue expenditure.

Question 21.—A wholesale fruit concern transacts both a commission and a general business. They sell their own and consigned goods in the same invoice. Give the form of sales book making provision for the separation of such sales—consigned and general.

Date	Name	Particulars	No. of Consignment	L. F.	Consignment Sales	Sales	Total
1908 March 1	John S. Smith	100 bbls. apples @ $5.00 50 bbls. @ $4.00	1		$500.00	$200.00	$700.00

Question 22.—Under what circumstances and for what purpose is a statement of affairs required? What facts should be made clear in such a statement? What conclusion is shown in the final balance?

The only circumstances under which a statement of affairs is prepared are as follows:

First, where the books are kept by single entry and it is desired to find out the profit made or loss sustained during a given period, a statement of affairs is prepared. Such a statement usually contains the assets and liabilities, and by a comparison of such a statement with that of the former period we find the result.

Second, in the case of an insolvent concern. The statement, under such circumstances, contains all the assets as per book values and separately, the amount that such assets are expected to realize. It contains the book value of the liabilities and the amounts that they are expected to rank. All preferred claims are deducted from the assets and the deficiency shown.

This statement is usually accompanied by a deficiency account, the latter accounting for the deficiency.

Question 23.—What is meant by the term "goodwill"? What kind of property is goodwill?

Goodwill is that intangible quality of patronage that attaches to an established business and is presumed to attach to it regardless of change of ownership. It is a legitimate asset; its value depending on many circumstances, such as location, duration of lease, annual profits, etc.

Guthrie, in discussing goodwill, says:

The measure of value in pecuniary terms of this intangible thing is the difference between the value of the normal results of the working of any business or profession which may be established by, and as worked by, any person in any place, and the results of working any individual business of a similar character. Thus, given a business, the goodwill of which is for disposal, there would be no valuable goodwill if anyone could do just as well by establishing a business anew. To start a business has its risks, which may often be described as very serious risks, but apart from the mere perilous risks of failing to take proper root, there is the often weary time—sometimes a long term of years — during which a sufficient connection is being got together to bring the business up to a standard paying basis which will give it a goodwill value, or bring a goodwill value into sight. To be spared this period of what I may call perilous probation is something worth paying for, even though its maintenance from this point needs the continued energy and industry by which it was built up by the original proprietor. Time, money and anxiety saved is money made. This is what is worth paying for and in this degree a goodwill value attaches to an established business.

Goodwill should be classed as a fixed asset in as much

as the valuation is fixed for a period of years even though it be written off annually.

Question 24.—A merchant who has been in business for twenty years decided to put a valuation on the goodwill of his business and carry same as an asset on his ledger, the entry being to charge goodwill and credit surplus. Another merchant five years later buys the entire business including the goodwill and after making a careful inventory finds that the annual net resources, exclusive of goodwill, amount to $5,000.00 less than the sum he paid for it. Discuss the subject of goodwill in respect to the above cases and state the correct manner of dealing with same.

Whether goodwill can be valued in the yearly statements, as some merchants think, finds a good illustration in an English case of Steuart v. Gladstone in 1879, which relates to the making out of the annual accounts. A clause in their articles of co-partnership stated that the annual accounts were to comprise "all particulars that might be susceptible of valuation." The contention of one of the partners was that it included goodwill also. The presiding justice ridiculed the absurdity of such a claim and decided that the clause mentioned above does not comprise goodwill. He stated that this intangible asset has a value only when the business is sold, and not otherwise.

With regard to the other case—the purchaser of the business who overpaid for the goodwill—this sum which he overpaid should be written off. This may be done in one sum or distributed over a period of two or three years.

Question 25.—What would be the proper classification of revenue, operation and maintenance, fixed charges and construction of a telephone company?

REVENUE OR INCOME.

(a) Rentals; (b) tolls (calls) ; (c) excess calls; (d) miscellaneous.

(a) To include receipts from all rentals, either for the use of circuits or long distance lines.

(b) To include the receipts for all tolls for telephoning outside the circuit, either on the company's or other lines.

(c) To include the receipts for all calls in excess of the contract limitation.

(d) To include receipts from all sources not otherwise enumerated

OPERATION AND MAINTENANCE.

(e) Expenses; (f) salaries and wages; (g) repairs, renewals and maintenance; (h) fuel.

(e) To include all charges for rent and care of offices, insurance of real estate and other property against fire, steam boiler, accident and liability insurance; legal expenses including therein damages to persons or other property and office supplies.

(f) To include salaries of operators, collectors, general office force and executive offices.

(g) To include all charges for repairs, renewals and maintenance of instruments, booths, wires, exchanges, manholes, real estate and buildings and their appurtenances, together with the cost of all supplies necessary, including freight and cartage.

(h) To include all charges for coal, wood or other fuel, including in it the handling of same, and freight and cartage thereon.

FIXED CHARGES.

(i) Fixed charges; (j) taxes; (k) leased lines.

(i) To include interest on bonds and other interest-bearing securities, also interest and discount on notes and open accounts. Interest and discount on notes, the proceeds of which are applied to construction items. Such interest should go under the account headed interest and discount, on floating debt or miscellaneous interest.

(j) To include all taxes of whatever nature, assessed against the property.

(k) To include all charges for rental of leased lines and exchanges.

CONSTRUCTION.

(l) Instruments; (m) extensions; (n) tools; (o) exchanges; (p) manholes; (q) miscellaneous.

(l) To include the cost of all instruments of whatever nature, such as telephones, switchboards, etc., with freight and cartage thereon and cost of labor in installation, including supervision.

(m) To include cost of all poles, wires, cross-arms, standwires, freight and cartage thereon, to the point of use, together with the cost of all labor in erecting same, including supervision.

(n) To include the cost of all tools and other appliances, with freight and cartage thereon.

(o) To include the cost of all buildings used as exchanges and any improvements thereon, including the equipment therein, such as wiring, switchboards, telephones, etc.

(p) To include the cost of all manholes, together with the cables laid therein, with freight and cartage on the supplies necessary thereon to point of use; also to include all labor in the construction and supervision thereon.

(q) To include the cost of all other construction not previously included.[1]

Question 26.—What is understood by the term "net profit"? State the final disposition of the net profit in the books of a partnership; of a corporation.

By the term "net profit" is meant the net increase of the original investment, after all current and fixed charges have been deducted, including therein provisions for reserves. In the case of a partnership the net profit is disposed of by being credited to the respective partner's accounts. In the case of a corporation it is credited to an account headed surplus. When the dividends are declared this account is debited and the dividend account credited.

Question 27.—Give a form of a stock ledger, showing at least three entries, covering in such entries the following facts: (a) Original issue; (b) acquisition of stock on transfers; (c) transfer of stock to other parties.

The answer to this question is given in Part III, page 263.

Question 28.—What are the various theories advocated with regard to treating "Treasury Stock" on the books of a corporation? What is and what is not "Treasury Stock"? How is "Treasury Stock" created on the books of a company?

The various theories advocated, result from the various definitions given of treasury stock.

Some define treasury stock to be the unsubscribed stock of a corporation or the amount remaining after the stockholders have received their stock.

[1] Mulhall on Quasi-public Corporations.

Some designate unpaid subscribed stock treasury stock.

Some define it to be the amount of stock that is reserved to be sold at some future time and hence they advocate to treat all these various forms on the books, under the heading "treasury stock," as assets.

None of the above definitions of "treasury stock" are correct. Treasury stock, properly speaking, is that portion of the paid-up stock of a corporation which reverts to the treasury and thereby reduces the corporation's liabilities, without any impairment to the assets, and, therefore stock donated to the company that has once been issued and fully paid for, or stock that has been forfeited should be called "treasury stock."

It is created on the books of a company by debiting treasury stock and crediting a reserve account with a proper heading indicating the purpose for which this treasury stock has been donated.

Question 29.—Wherein do "secret reserves" differ from "ordinary reserves"? How are "secret" or "hidden reserves" created? What purpose or purposes do they serve?

A "secret reserve" does not differ materially from any other reserve except that it is not shown on the books and consequently does not appear on the balance ,sheet. There are various ways of creating secret reserves. First, by excessive charges for depreciation, although conditions do not warrant it, or by providing a large reserve for bad debts, although conditions do not justify it. Some concerns eliminate entire assets from the balance sheet or greatly understate them by over- estimating the liabilities.

The bonafide use of a secret reserve is that it tends to prevent the fluctuations of stock, thus enabling the corporation to equalize the dividends at a regular rate, even at such times when there are no profits. On the other hand a secret reserve deprives one class of stockholders of profits earned during the period, and enables future stockholders to reap that benefit. It also opens a loophole for fraud.

Question 30.—Explain the object of a "reserve" in connection with the business of a manufacturing firm. How would it appear on the books of the firm? In what way would it be dealt with should the firm dissolve partnership?

The object of a "reserve" is to provide an account against which unexpected or expected losses may be written off, without in any way disturbing the profits of the year in which the losses occur. It would appear on the books by means of a journal entry. The profit and loss account would be debited and the reserve account credited.

Such an account represents a portion of the ordinary profits reserved instead of being divided among the partners. In the event of a dissolution such a reserve would be divisible among the partners in the same proportion as profits, deducting from it actual decreases in the value of the assets for which the reserve was provided.

Question 31.—Describe the chief distinctive principles of bookkeeping by double entry.

The chief distinctive principles of bookkeeping by double entry are as follows:

First, every debit requires a credit.

Second, the total is equal to its component parts.

The application of these principles is to give full facts of each transaction, e.g., to record the exchange, as a passing of money, or its equivalent, from one account to another. To make this possible, the business is regarded as something impersonal which holds property and makes profit on behalf of its owners, who become its creditors for capital and profits, and debtors for losses and withdrawals. Thus the assets and liabilities of a business are always exactly equal.

Each new transaction affects both sides of the account equally, thus leaving the balance undisturbed. Some transactions or exchanges may indicate a change of assets or liabilities and result in neither profits nor losses. Summarizing we may say that in every case:

If assets are increased either other assets are decreased or liabilities are increased.

If assets are decreased either other assets are increased or liabilities are decreased.

If liabilities are increased either other liabilities are decreased or assets are increased.

If liabilities are decreased either other liabilities are increased or assets are decreased.

In double entry therefore each transaction—no matter what its nature—is recorded once upon each side of the ledger. It is debited to the account of an asset increased or a liability decreased and credited to the account of a liability increased or an asset decreased.

Question 32.—What do you understand by a deficiency account? In the case of a trader who had been in business for five years and did not keep proper accounts, by what process would the first item of a deficiency be ascertained?

A deficiency account is an account which usually accompanies a statement of affairs of an insolvent firm, the object of which is to explain how the deficiency, shown on the statement of affairs, has arisen. It usually commences with the surplus of assets over liabilities when the business commences or at some more recent date before the time when the statement of affairs is prepared, and shows what income has been earned as well as expenses and losses incurred, winding up with a balance known as a deficit, which balance must agree with the balance shown on the statement of affairs.

As the first item of a deficiency account is the surplus of the assets over liabilities at the commencement or of some more recent date, it is obvious that if no proper accounts have been kept, that it is impossible to ascertain this item and the deficiency account could therefore not be prepared.

Question 33.—A business has increased until the transactions assume large proportions and the entries disclosed through the books are so numerous that the agreement of a trial balance in the ordinary way becomes very difficult. Suggest a means by which this may be rendered more easy.

Every ledger should be so arranged as to contain all the materials for taking a trial balance. That is to say, each departmental ledger should contain a general ledger adjustment account while the general ledger should contain a controlling account for each of the departmental ledgers, thus becoming self-balancing. By this means each ledger can at any time be balanced with the least amount of labor and absolutely irrespective of the other ledgers. Dicksee in his "Bookkeeping for Accounting Students," in this connection, states the following:

Let us now turn to the Bought (Purchase) Ledger. The Bought Ledger will be of the usual type, the various items being posted to the credit of the merchandise (sales) in the ordinary way. The double entry of the Bought (Purchase) book is completed by posting the total of each month's purchases to the debit of the general ledger account in the Bought (Purchase)

Ledger. The Bought Ledger payments (from cash book) are posted to the debit to the various creditors, the double entry being completed by posting the monthly total of the Bought Ledger payments to the credit of the general ledger account in the Bought Ledger. We thus see that the Bought Ledger possesses a complete system of double entry of its own, and, consequently, that it is self-balancing—i. e., a list of all these balances constitutes a complete trial balance.

Question 34.—Prepare an imaginary deficiency account for a wholesale trader, who commenced business four years ago with a capital of $12,500.00 and made a profit of $500.00 during the first two years, his present liability being $88,000.00 and assets estimated to realize $51,500.00. The imaginary items of the account must not exceed twelve in number, and should be representative of items usually found in such accounts.

(Answer given on next page.)

Question 35.—What important principle ought to be the guide in a proper stock taking and would you make this a special point of inquiry and examination in connection with any business in which you were professionally interested?

Where a concern employs a manager whose remuneration is wholly or partly dependent upon profits, it is quite important that the stock should be taken by a distinterested person. The stock should be valued either at cost or, if the market price be lower than cost, at market price. Calculations and prices should be thoroughly checked and a general examination be made of stock sheets when completed. Care must be taken lest undelivered sales and purchases for which no invoices are at hand be taken into stock.

Question 36.—In an old established business where the rule had been to charge as against the profits inter-

DEFICIENCY ACCOUNT.

Net loss arising from carrying on business from .... to date, ...		$20,000.00
Bad debts as per schedule		2,500.00
Expenses incurred since ...., other than usual trade expenses		10,000.00
Other losses and expenses—specula-tions	$15,000.00	
Law costs in an action against ..	1,250.00	
Defalcations of	1,000.00	17,250.00
Surplus as per statement of affairs (if any) ..		
Total amount to be accounted for		$49,750.00

Excess of assets over liabilities on the		$12,500.00
Net profit arising from carrying on business from .... to ...., after deducting usual trade expenses		500.00
Income or profit from other sources since		250.00
Deficiency as per statement of affairs		36,500.00
Total amount accounted for		$49,750.00

445

est upon the capital of the respective partners, and where the parties were arranging to dispose of their business upon the basis of profits over a period of years, what would be your course of action were you called in to prepare a statement of their affairs on their behalf?

Interest upon partners' capital and cash loans should be excluded from a statement of profits prepared for this purpose. But it would be desirable to call attention to the fact that such a change had been made in the accounts as they appear in the firm's books. It would be well to emphasize the fact if the insufficiency of working capital had caused the firm to lose cash discounts upon purchase. It would not however be within the accountant's province to make an estimate of the discounts actually lost from this cause.

Question 37.—Differentiate between an executor, a trustee, and an administrator, and state also under what circumstances and in what manner the latter is appointed.

An executor is a personal representative appointed by the will of the deceased person. A trustee is one entrusted with property for the benefit of another. An administrator is a personal representative appointed by the court when there is no provision in the will or where a person dies without leaving a will.

Question 38.—The firm of Smith & Co. consists of John Smith, whose capital is $9,000.00, and James Brown, whose capital is $6,000.00. They agree to receive as a third partner Frederick Jones with $6,000.00, of which one-fourth is to be considered as payment for goodwill and to be added to the capital of John Smith and James Brown in proportion to the amounts thereon. In what proportions would you divide the profits so that each should receive a due share in proportion to the capital of each?

In the absence of expressed provision to the contrary, profits would be divided equally. In this case, however, it is expressly stipulated that they should be divided in proportion to the respective capital of the partners.

As the relative shares of the partners are:

John Smith's capital	$9,000.00	
Plus his share of goodwill	900.00	$9,900.00
James Brown's capital	6,000.00	
Plus his share of goodwill	600.00	6,600.00

that makes Frederick Jones's capital in the business to be $4,500.00. The respective profits would be:

John Smith $33/_{70}$
James Brown $22/_{70}$
F. Jones $15/_{70}$

Question 39.—What is meant by the term "hire agreement"? Is there any difference between a "hire agreement" and a "hire and purchase agreement"?

While the two terms are synonymous, there is a distinction with regard to the legal point of the different agreements.

Dicksee makes no distinction whatever between a "hire" and "hire and purchase agreement." In fact, throughout all of his books he calls it "hire and purchase agreement," defining it as follows:

The general nature of a contract of this description is that if the hirer makes the necessary periodical payments regularly, the manufacturer agrees to hand over the ownership (give title) of the articles in question to him at the end of the prescribed term upon the payment of a further nominal sum.

As a matter of accounting this definition is very cor-

rect and no further explanation is necessary. From a
legal point of view there is quite a difference. Dawson
in his "Accountant's Compendium" differentiates between the two terms as follows:

> Under a hiring agreement (simply) no property in the goods
> so hired passes to the hirer, but under a "hire and purchase"
> agreement a distinction must be drawn between those which in-
> volve an agreement to buy, and those which do not. There is
> an agreement to buy, if the hirer is bound to pay the whole of
> the agreed sums for hire, whether he returns the subject-matter
> before the expiration of the agreed priod or not.

Question 40.—A corporation has an issue of preferred
stock entitled to cumulative dividends at 7 per cent a
year. The dividend payments are in arrears. Should
the arrears of dividend appear on the balance sheet?
If so, how should they be stated?

It is improper to include arrears on dividends among
the ordinary liabilities of the balance sheet. As a corporation's liabilities for dividends on preferred cumulative stock is contingent on the earnings, it is not a
liability against the assets of the company.

It is advisable, however, that the attention of the
reader be called to a foot-note in the balance sheet
stating the fact that the dividends on the preferred
stock are in arrears. This procedure is important in
order to protect a prospective common stock purchaser
who, by the suppression of such facts, may find himself
at a disadvantage.

Question 41.—Explain briefly the various methods
by which depreciation on buildings, leases, machinery
and plant may be provided for and give your comments
on the working of the various methods.

There are four methods of providing depreciation.

First, a fixed percentage of the original cost being

written off each year, the percentage being based with a view to writing off the whole of the asset at the time it becomes valueless. This system is suitable for patents or short-term leases.

Second, a fixed percentage upon the reducing amount at which the assets appear in the books at the commencement of each period, a part of the percentage being based upon the same lines as under the preceding method. By means of this system the installments charged against revenue are heavier in the early years and are gradually and automatically reduced. When no separate provision is made for equalizing the charges in respect of repairs it is a very convenient method to adopt in connection with machinery and plant, provided, of course, that the rate of percentage selected is sufficiently high.

Third, the annuity system. Under this system a fixed amount is written off the asset each year calculated so that if the amount of such asset be invested at a fixed rate per cent, the depreciation installments will suffice to reduce it to the zero at the end of the prescribed period.

This is a very good method to adopt with regard to leaseholds that run for a long period of years.

Fourth, the sinking fund method. This system is similar to the first named except that as each installment is set aside, interest on it being deducted from the book value of the asset, it is credited to the sinking fund and simultaneously an investment of the same amount of cash is made. These investments are accumulated at compound interest so as to provide an actual fund, available in cash, for the replacement of the asset at the time it has become valueless. As these installments earn interest, the periodical payments charged against

III—29

INCOME AND EXPENDITURE ACCOUNT
INCOME:

Subscriptions and donations:—

Annual subscriptions, as per list	$2,885.00	
Donations, as per list	1,615.00	
Boxes, as per list....................	125.00	$4,625.00

Patients' payments:—

In-patients	636.00	636.00

Invested property:—

Interest on deposit accounts	12.00	
Rents	50.00	62.00

Other receipts:—

Hospital Sunday fund	305.00		
Entertainments	120.00		
Local hospital Saturday collection ...	510.00		
Trade and Friendly Society collection	422.00		
Trade and Friendly Society balance ..	18.00	$1,375.00	$6,698.00

Petty cash on hand, January 1, 1905 ...		14.17
Balance in bank, January 1, 1905		1,156.00

$7,868.17

EXPENDITURE:

MAINTENANCE:—

Provisions:—

Meat	$528.50	
Fish, poultry, etc.	365.50	
Butter, cheese, etc.	257.89	
Eggs	112.11	
Milk	375.00	
Bread, flour, etc.	135.46	
Grocery	374.34	
Vegetables	124.20	$2,273.00

Surgery and dispensary:—

Drugs, chemicals, disinfectants, etc. ..	265.00	
Dressings, bandages, etc.	198.75	
Instruments and appliances	101.25	
Ice and mineral waters	35.00	
Wine and spirits	175.00	
Sundries	45.00	820.00

Domestic:—

Renewal of furniture	175.00	
Bedding and linen	130.00	
Hardware, crockery, brushes, etc.	95.00	
Washing	436.00	
Cleaning and chandlery	47.00	
Water	32.00	
Fuel and lighting	500.00	
Sundries	150.00	1,565.00

Establishment charges:—

Insurance	24.00	
Garden	114.00	
Repairs (ordinary)	254.00	392.00

Salaries, wages, etc.:—

Nursing	750.00	
Other salaries and wages	380.00	1,130.00

Miscellaneous expenses:—

Printing, stationery, postage, etc.	75.00	
Sundries	43.00	118.00

ADMINISTRATION:—

Official printing and stationery	90.00		
Official postage, telegrams, etc.	45.00		
Official advertisements	5.50		
Sundries	27.50	168.00	$6,466.00

EXTRAORDINARY EXPENDITURE:—

Repairs	940.00
Balance at bank December 31, 1905 ...	450.00
Petty cash in hand December 31, 1905 .	12.17
	$7,868.17

revenue are not so much as under the first system. This method is partly advisable in cases where it will be necessary to replace the worn-out asset by another, and the amount is of sufficient importance to make it expedient to make the necessary provisions by installments.

Question 42.—X, Y and Z enter into partnership. X invests $4,000.00, Y $2,000.00 and Z $1,000.00. In making up their accounts at the end of the first year of the existence of the partnership you ascertain that the profit divisible is $2,100.00. On asking for the articles of co-partnership you are informed that there is no agreement of any description, and the partners agree that they shall each have the profit they are legally entitled to and place the matter absolutely in your hands. Apportion the profits.

As already remarked in answer to some other similar question, in the absence of any specific provision profits are divided, share and share alike, and therefore the apportionment would be:

X 1/3 of profits	$700.00
Y 1/3 of profits	700.00
Z 1/3 of profits	700.00

Question 43.—Give a form of an income and expenditure account of a hospital, properly classified:

(Answer given on pages 450–451.)

Question 44.—What is a trial balance and in what way does it differ from a balance sheet?

A trial balance is a list of all the accounts, with their respective balances, appearing in a ledger at any particular date.

A balance sheet is a summary of the assets and liabilities as well as proprietorship of an undertaking on the date named. It differs from a trial balance because of the following:

(a) It is not taken out until after all the nominal accounts showing losses or gains, have been closed.

(b) After the nominal accounts have been closed it represents a trial balance of the accounts still open in the ledger, these accounts being summarized in a form for inspection and subsequent reference instead of being taken out in the order of the ledger folios.

Question 45.—Explain what is meant by a suspense account and give an example of a debit and credit on a balance sheet.

A suspense account is an account raised for the purpose of posting small outstanding assets and liabilities in the books on the date of balancing or for the purpose of providing for a liability which is debited and which it would therefore be inexpedient to credit to an account standing in the name of the claimant. All items appearing on the debit side of a balance sheet are as follows:

Disputed claims, prepaid rent, prepaid wages, etc.

Examples of items appearing on the credit side of a balance sheet are as follows:

Rents, taxes, etc., which, at the time of preparation of the balance sheet, are doubtful.

Question 46.—What is the object of charging depreciation in the Profit and Loss Account?

As the depreciation is the loss arising from the shrinkage in value of an asset, owing to use or to lapse of time, the object of debiting the Profit and Loss Account with the allowance for depreciation is to make the profits of the current period bear their share of the loss which is accruing or which will eventually accrue, in connection with those assets which are being used for the purpose of earning such profit.

Question 47.—Explain the difference between "gross

profit" and "net profit"; between "sales" and "consignments."

Gross profit is the difference between the price at which goods are sold and the price of making them or of placing them in a salable condition—assuming the former to be a greater sum. Net profit is properly profit—the sum which has been earned by trade through any given time, after all charges have been deducted.

A sale is the exchange of commodities for money or its equivalent. A consignment is the placing of goods by a trader in some place other than his own to be sold by such other person on his account.

Question 48.—Mention some of the points which a bookkeeper should specially look into before he closes his books for balancing purposes. What is meant by "closing entries"?

Before closing the books the bookkeeper should ascertain that all transactions up to date have been posted and allowance made for all assets or liabilities accrued. The "closing entries" are those generally made after the trial balance has been taken and show the transfers from nominal accounts to revenue, provision for bad debts, depreciation, discount for bad debts, etc.

Question 49.—State briefly what you consider the advantages and disadvantages of the Continental system of posting all entries through the journal.

The advantages of the Continental system may be summarized as follows:

First, that a summarized record of the transactions is recorded in the journal from time to time and is therefore available without the necessity of balancing the books.

Second, irregular entries, such as direct transfers

from one ledger to another may be readily deducted. If the books do not balance it is readily possible to ascertain upon which side of the ledger the mistake has occurred, thus limiting the investigation greatly.

The disadvantages are as follows:

First; work is entailed which often quite outweighs the advantage.

Second; the compulsion to record all transactions through the journal leads to the temptation of omitting necessary details from the ledger.

Third; the compulsion to record every transaction through the journal often renders it difficult to introduce labor saving devices.

Question 50.—Corporation **X** makes a practice of charging to expense and carry to depreciation reserve account every half year, a certain percentage of the book value of its plant and machinery. What, in your opinion is the correct method of dealing in this case with repairs and renewals, i.e., should the latter be charged to profit and loss or should they properly be charged to depreciation reserve account? Give reasons for your answer.

Repairs and renewals should be charged to profit and loss and not against the reserve account. Dicksee, in his "Advanced Accounting," defines depreciation as follows:

It is necessary, in addition to charging actual expenditure upon repairs, and replacements to revenue, to charge against the revenue account of each year a further sum, with a view to (as far as possible) averaging the expenditure on revenue account over a term of years, and that provision which it is so necessary to charge is usually called by the name of depreciation.

This definition makes it quite clear that ordinary repairs, necessary to maintain the property in good condition in order to earn revenue, should be charged to profit and loss because, if they are charged against the depreciation reserve account, the reserve is depleted and the wear·and tear of the property remains unprotected.

CHAPTER XXI

PROBLEMS AND SOLUTIONS IN PRACTICAL AC-COUNTING

PROBLEM I.

X, a trader, commences business October 1, 1902, with a capital consisting of cash $100,000.00; land and buildings worth $80,000.00, subject to a mortgage of $30,000.00.

An abstract of his books October 1, 1903, discloses the following accounts: purchases, $75,000.00; sales, $90,000.00; cash expenses, $15,000.00; cash drawings, $8,000.00; profit and loss debit, $5,000.00; sinking fund, $5,000.00; goods returned to creditors, $4,000.00; returned sales, $3,000.00; contingent fund, $2,000.00; reserve for bad debts, $5,500.00; due sundry creditors, $61,000.00; sundry customers, $34,480.00; discounts allowed customers on accounts paid, $520.00; no goods sold to creditors nor purchased from customers.

The inventory on October 1, 1903, amounts to $7,000.00. Interest on mortgage is 6 per cent. Supply the missing items and furnish a profit and loss account and a balance sheet.

SOLUTION.

Our first step in connection with the solution of this problem is to arrange the accounts in trial balance form and then seek the missing items. We therefore prepare the following partial trial balance:

Purchases	$75,000.00	
Sales		$90,000.00
Cash expenses	15,000.00	
Cash drawings	8,000.00	

Profit and loss	5,000.00	
Sinking fund	5,000.00	
Goods returned to creditors		4,000.00
Returned sales	3,000.00	
Contingent funds	2,000.00	
Reserve for bad debts		5,500.00
Creditors		61,000.00
Customers	34,480.00	
Discounts allowed	520.00	
Land and buildings	80,000.00	
Mortgage payable		30,000.00
X capital account		150,000.00

The footing of this trial balance indicates a total debit of only $228,000.00 against a total credit of $340,-500.00, or a difference of $112,500.00. We are asked in the problem to supply the missing items. It is therefore quite obvious that there must be two or more missing items to make up for the difference of $112,500.00.

As a general rule, if items are missing in a trial balance, they will always be of such a nature that can be supplied by an indirect procedure. The first item that we note particularly being absent in the trial balance is the item of cash.

In the first part of the problem we are told that X commences business with a cash capital of $100,000.00. As the cash payments shown in the problem are less by far than the amount received there must evidently be a cash balance. Our next step therefore is to find out how much is the cash balance, which will surely be one of the missing items. In order to find this out we prepare the following cash account:

Dr.		CASH ACCOUNT.		Cr.
To investment	$100,000.00	By creditors' accounts..	$10,000.00	
customers' accounts..	52,000.00	drawings	8,000.00	
		sinking fund	5,000.00	
		contingent fund	2,000.00	
		expenses	15,000.00	
		balance	112,000.00	
	$152,000.00		$152,000.00	
To balance	$112,000.00			

This cash account requires a little analysis. It will be noticed that the debit side contains an item—customers' accounts $52,000.00, which of course, is not shown directly in the problem. This figure is arrived at in the following way: We are told that our sales amounted to $90,000.00 and that there were returned sales amounting to $3,000.00, leaving a net balance of $87,000.00. We are further told that at the present the outstanding accounts due from customers amount to $34,480.00 and that in settling their payments, the customers have deducted $520.00 in discounts. The last two items make a total of $35,000.00, which deducted from $87,000.00 leaves a balance of $52,000.00 to be accounted for. We therefore must assume that this amount must have been paid by the customers in cash.

We follow the same analysis with regard to the item of creditors appearing on the credit side of the cash book. Our purchases were $75,000.00 from which we returned $4,000.00 leaving the net purchases $71,000.00. As the problem tells us that we still owe the creditors $61,000.00 it is quite evident that we must have paid to these creditors only $10,000.00.

With regard to the items of sinking fund and contingent fund appearing on the debit side of the trial balance, it will be recalled that in a previous chapter the author stated that in the absence of any other information the term "fund" is to be taken as indicating an asset. Following this assumption the two items, sinking fund, $5,000.00 and contingent fund, $2,000.00, respectively, must be taken to represent cash investments, an exchange of one form of assets for another. It is therefore quite clear how we have arrived at the cash balance of $112,000.00. That does not, however, account as yet for the full amount of the difference, as that sum is $112,500.00. We have, therefore to seek yet another item amounting to $500.00.

A glance at the trial balance will reveal that while the profit and loss account shows a debit balance of $5,000.00, the reserve for bad debts, which as is already known to the reader, is created by a debit to profit and loss and a credit to the reserve, is credited for $5,500.00. Evidently the person who made the entry, or who posted such entry, transferred the wrong figure to the profit and loss account, e.g., instead of debiting that account with $5,500.00, and crediting the reserve for bad debts for the same amount, the former account was debited for $5,000.00 only, while the latter was credited for the right sum $5,500.00. That gives us the second missing item, namely, an additional $500.00, to the profit and loss account. We are now in a position to prepare the corrected trial balance.

As the problem calls for a profit and loss account and a balance sheet it is quite advisable to arrange the trial balance in systematic order so as to facilitate the preparation of subsequent statements. The trial balance would appear then as follows:

Cash	$112,000.00	
Sinking fund (investment)	5,000.00	
Contingent fund (investment)	2,000.00	
Accounts receivable	34,480.00	
Land and buildings	80,000.00	
Mortgage payable		$30,000.00
Accounts payable		61,000.00
Purchases	75,000.00	
Expenses	15,000.00	
Returned purchases		4,000.00
Discounts allowed	520.00	
Sales		90,000.00
Returned sales	3,000.00	
Profit and loss	5,500.00	
Reserve for bad debts		5,500.00
X drawing account	8,000.00	
X capital account		150,000.00
	$340,500.00	$340,500.00

PROFIT AND LOSS ACCOUNT OF THE FIRM OF X FOR THE PERIOD EXPIRING OCTOBER 1, 1903

To purchases........		$75,000.00	By sales........	$90,000.00	
Deduct:			Less returns.......	3,000.00	$87,000.00
Inventory....	$7,000.00				
Returns........	4,000.00	11,000.00	$64,000.00		
Gross profits.....			23,000.00		
			$87,000.00		$87,000.00

By expenses.........		$15,000.00	To gross profit....		$23,000.00
Reserve for bad debts......		5,500.00			
Ordinary business profit....		2,500.00			
		$23,000.00			$23,000.00

To interest on mortgage.........		$1,800.00	By ordinary business profit.....		$2,500.00
Discount on customers' accounts (settled).......		520.00			
Net profit.........		180.00			
		$2,500.00			$2,500.00

461

BALANCE SHEET OF THE FIRM OF X AS ON OCTOBER 1, 1903

ASSETS:

Cash..................			$112,000.00
Investments:			
Sinking fund....	$5,000 00		
Contingent fund.	2,000.00		7,000.00
Accounts receivable.....	$34,480 00		
Less reserve for bad debts	5,500 00		28,980.00
Merchandise inventory....		7,000.00	$154,980.00
Land and buildings........			80,000.00
			$234,980.00

LIABILITIES:

Accounts payable.....		$61,000.00	
Mortgage payable.....		30,000.00	$91,000.00
Interest on mortgage accrued...........			1,800.00
PROPRIETORSHIP:			
X original investment..	$150,000 00		
Net profits...........	180 00		
	$150,180 00		
Less withdrawals......	8,000.00		142,180.00
			$234,980.00

Having prepared the corrected trial balance our next step would be to prepare the profit and loss account as required in the problem. This is shown on page 461.

We do not need to analyze the profit and loss account because the reader is already familiar with such statements. One fact, however, is to be noted, that while the problem does not say anything about providing for interest, the simple statement "Interest on Mortgage 6 per cent" is of sufficient implication to provide for such interest charge in the profit and loss account.

The next step in the solution is to prepare the balance sheet. This is the most important step in a problem of this kind for the reason that not only have we to verify and prove results shown in the profit and loss account but we must also verify the cash balance of $112,000.00. We therefore prepare the balance sheet shown on page 462.

This balance sheet is self-explanatory, for every item is clearly indicated. This completes the solution of the problem.

PROBLEM II.

On January 1 the Fairview Real Estate Association was incorporated, the capital subscribed and paid in being $30,000.00, divided into 30 shares. The Association purchased improved property for speculative purposes, paying cash $30,000.00 and giving a first mortgage for $60,000.00 at 6 per cent.

The Association organizes and incorporates on the same day the Fairview Club with 30 proprietary members (being the stockholders of Real Estate Association) and 30 associate members, who have no proprietary interest, but who enjoy all the privileges without incurring liabilities. The annual fees are $100.00 a year, paid by all in advance.

The Association leases to the club the property afore-said, the consideration being, in lieu of rent, the payment by the club of all sums for taxes, betterments, interest, fixtures, furniture, etc.

The proprietary members are assessed $300.00 each, and by a subsequent resolution of the Association are to receive credit therefor with interest at 6 per cent. Five members fail to pay the assessment.

The Association having executed a contract for the sale of the property for $110,000.00, the club disbands at the end of the year.

The club expenditures for the year were as follows: Taxes, $1,800.00; interest on mortgage, $3,600.00; repairs, $1,000.00; improvements, $3,000.00; furniture and fixtures, $2,000.00; general expense, $500.00; help (sundry employés) $1,600.00.

There were house charges against the members, $500.00, which were subsequently collected; and there were payable book debts of $4,000.00. A second assessment of $100.00, called for to pay off the club debts, was paid by the proprietary members of the Association.

Frame journal entries, raise and close accounts on the Association and the Club books, and prepare balance sheet and revenue account for each.

SOLUTION

In connection with this problem we are asked to frame the journal entries, raise and close the accounts on the books of the Association as well as on the books of the Club and to prepare final balance sheet and revenue ac-

THE FAIRVIEW REAL ESTATE ASSOCIATION,

A CORPORATION ORGANIZED JANUARY 1, 1897, UNDER THE LAWS OF THE STATE OF ——, WITH A CAPITAL SUBSCRIBED AND PAID IN OF

$30,000.00,

DIVIDED INTO 30 SHARES, EACH $1,000 PAR.

Subscribers $30,000.00
  For their shares of subscribed stock of The Fairview Real Estate Association.

  To capital stock $30,000.00
    Issued to the subscribers, as per their subscriptions.

Cash 30,000.00
  Payments of subscribers for their subscription.

  To subscribers 30,000.00
    Being settlement for capital stock issued.

Real estate 90,000.00
  Purchased this day for speculative purposes.

  To cash 30,000.00
    Part payment for improved property bought this day.

  First mortgage $60,000.00
    For balance of purchase price of property bought with 6% interest.
The association organizes and incorporates the Fairview Club with 30 proprietary members (stockholders of the Real Estate Association) and 30 associate members, who have no proprietary interest, but enjoy all privileges without incurring any liabilities. Annual dues to be $100.00.

The association leases to the club their property, for the payment by the club of all taxes, betterments, interest, fixtures, etc.

Cash $110,000.00
  Selling price realized on the sale of the property of the association.

  To real estate $110,000.00

  Sale of the improved property.

First mortgage 60,000.00
  Settlement of mortgage issued at the time of purchase of real estate.

  To cash 60,000.00
    The property being sold, the mortgage is now settled.

III—30   465

LEDGER

FAIRVIEW REAL ESTATE ASSOCIATION.

Subscribers.

To capital stock	$30,000.00	By cash	$30,000.00

CAPITAL STOCK.

		By subscribers	$30,000.00

CASH.

To subscribers	$30,000.00	By real estate..........	$30,000.00
Real estate	110,000.00	First mortgage	60,000.00
		Balance	50,000.00
	$140,000.00		
			$140,000.00
To balance	$50,000.00		

REAL ESTATE.

To sundries	$90,000.00	By cash	$110,000.00
Income	20,000.00		
	$110,000.00		$110,000.00

FIRST MORTGAGE.

To cash	$60,000.00	By real estate	$60,000.00

INCOME AND REVENUE ACCOUNT.

To surplus	$20,000.00	By real estate..........	$20,000.00

SURPLUS.

		By income and revenue account	$20,000.00

BALANCE SHEET.

To cash	$50,000.00	By capital	$30,000.00
		Surplus	20,000.00
	$50,000.00		$50,000.00

THE FAIRVIEW CLUB

ORGANIZED BY THE FAIRVIEW REAL ESTATE ASSOCIATION WITH 30 PROPRIETARY
MEMBERS, AND 30 ASSOCIATE MEMBERS. ANNUAL DUES, $100.

Cash	$6,000.00	
Dues received from the 60 members of the club.		
To dues		$6,000.00
Collected from the proprietary and associate members, each $100.00.		
The club agrees to lease the property of the Real Estate Association and in consideration of rent to pay all taxes, interest charges, repairs and improvements of the association.		
Members (indiv.)	9,000.00	
For assessment of $300.00 each proprietary member.		
To assessment		9,000.00
Assessing the 30 proprietary members.		
Cash	7,500.00	
Collected of 25 members the assessment levied.		
To members (indiv.)		7,500.00
For cash assessment of $300.00 each, paid by the 25 proprietary members.		
Assessments	7,500.00	
According to a subsequent resolution of the association the responded assessment is credited to the members individually.		
To members		$7,500.00
Crediting each member individually with the responded assessment.		
Cash	$3,000.00	
Collected another assessment, levied upon the proprietary members.		
To assessment		3,000.00
Proprietary member responded to a second assessment of $100.00 each.		
Assessment	1,500.00	
To members (ind.)		1,500.00
This entry to close the accounts of the five members who failed to respond with the first assessment of $300.00 each.		
Expenses	13,500.00	
Taxes.................................$1,800.00		
Interest on mortgage.................... 3,600.00		
Repairs 1,000.00		
Improvements 3,000.00		
Furniture and fixtures.................... 2,000.00		
General expense 500,00		
Help (employment) 1,600.00		
To cash		$13,500.00

LEDGER

OF THE

FAIRVIEW CLUB.

Dues.

To income	$6,000.00	By cash	$6,000.00

CASH.

To dues	$6,000.00	By expense	$13,500.00
Members	7,500.00	Balance	3,000.00
Assessment	3,000.00		
	$16,500.00		$16,500.00
To balance	$3,000.00		

MEMBERS.

To assessment	$9,000.00	By assessment	$7,500.00
Balance	7,500.00	Cash	7,500.00
		Assessment	1,500.00
	$16,500.00		$16,500.00
		By members	$7,500.00

ASSESSMENT.

To members	$7,500.00	By members	$9,000.00
To members	1,500.00	Cash	3,000.00
Income	3,000.00		
	$12,000.00		$12,000.00

EXPENSE.

To sundries	$13,500.00	By revenue	$13,500.00

INCOME AND REVENUE ACCOUNT.

To expense	$13,500.00	By dues	$6,000.00
		Assessment	3,000.00
		Loss	4,500.00
	$13,500.00		$13,500.00

DEFICIENCY ACCOUNT.

To income account......	$4,500.00		

BALANCE SHEET.

To cash	$3,000.00	By members	$7,500.00
Deficiency	4,500.00		
	$7,500.00		$7,500.00

468

count for each. On page 465. journal entries in respect to the affairs of the association are given which are self-explanatory. The organization and incorporation of the Fairview Club is only shown as a memorandum entry because, so far as the association is concerned, no actual business transaction took place. As we are, however, interested to show all the facts pertaining to the association, we make the memorandum as shown on page 465.

On page 466 are shown all the ledger accounts pertaining to the association which are self-explanatory.

The credit side of the surplus account shows a balance of $20,000.00 which is verified by the balance sheet shown on the same page, having a credit to capital $30,-000.00 and a debit to cash of $50,000.00, hence accounting for the difference—the surplus of $20,000.00.

On page 467 are given the journal entries of the Fairview Club and on page 468 are given the ledger accounts of the Fairview Club.

In the case of the Fairview Club the deficiency account shows a debit balance of $4,500.00 which is also verified by the balance sheet. As we owe the members $7,500.00 and there is only cash amounting to $3,000.00 to offset this, there is consequently a deficiency of $4,-500.00.

PROBLEM IV.

A B, a commission merchant, doing business on a 5 per cent basis, hands you the following abstract from his ledger, showing his transactions for the year. Furnish A B's capital account showing his original investment, a balance sheet and a detailed cash account.

Sales	$45,000.00	$60,000.00
Freight	2,100.00	1,400.00
Claims and allowances on settled a/c only	600.00	1,500.00
Expense	900.00	

Customers' accounts	60,000.00	45,000.00
Creditors' accounts	37,950.00	39,850.00
Cash	59,000.00	40,950.00
Discount lost	400.00	

SOLUTION.

Our first step in this case will be to get the accounts in equilibrium. For this purpose we have to arrange a trial balance. If we foot up the abstract given in the problem we find the total debit to be $205,950.00, while the total credit is $188,700.00. The first account that we notice missing is the capital account. The second account missing, which is quite obvious, is the commission account. The problem tells us that the sales were $60,000.00. We therefore must be entitled to a 5 per cent commission on those sales. As we have not accounted for all the sales because the debit side of the sales account shows only $45,000.00, we are therefore entitled to a discount of 5 per cent on such $45,000.00 accounted for, or $2,250.00. As the commission is earned, it should appear on the credit side. Adding the $2,250.00 to the credit side of the trial balance ($188,-700.00) we find that the debit side is $15,000.00 in excess of the credit side. We therefore conclude that this difference represents the capital of A B, and so we prepare the complete trial balance shown below:

TRIAL BALANCE.

Cash	$59,000.00	$40,950.00
Accounts receivable	60,000.00	45,000.00
Accounts payable	37,950.00	39,850.00
Sales	45,000.00	60,000.00
Freight	2,100.00	1,400.00
Claims and allowances on settling accounts only	600.00	1,500.00
Expenses	900.00	
Discount lost	400.00	
Commission		2,250.00
A B capital account		15,000.00
	$205,950.00	$205,950.00

Our next step is to prepare a detailed cash account, as follows:

Dr.	CASH ACCOUNT.		Cr.
To A B's investment ...	$15,000.00	By creditors	$37,950.00
To customers	44,000.00	By freight	2,100.00
		By expenses	900.00
		By balance	18,050.00
	$59,000.00		$59,000.00
To balance	$18,050.00		

The amount shown to the customers' account appearing on the debit side of the cash book is arrived at in the following way: The abstract of the ledger shows that customers were credited for $45,000.00. It also discloses that the claims and allowances on the accounts settled were $600.00 and that the discount lost was $400.00, making a total deduction of $1,000.00. Therefore, the difference must have been received in cash. The item "creditors" appearing on the cash credit side represents the payments made to creditors as shown by the abstract of the ledger.

In order to show A's capital account we have to prepare the following profit and loss account:

PROFIT AND LOSS ACCOUNT.

To discount	$ 400.00	By commission earned .	$2,250.00
Expenses	900.00	Commission accrued	750.00
Net profit	2,600.00	Claims and allow-	
		anees	900.00
	$3,900.00		$3,900.00

The discount and expense items appearing on the debit side are self-explanatory. The two commission items represent the commission earned, the first account which has already been deducted; the second one which has accrued but undeducted as yet. The claims and allowances show an excess debit balance of $900.00 because $600.00 are claims and allowances actually deducted. That shows us a net profit to A B of $2,600.00. We arrange then A B's capital account as follows:

A B'S CAPITAL ACCOUNT.

Present capital	$17,600.00	Investment	$15,000.00
		Net profit	2,600.00
	$17,600.00		$17,600.00
		By balance	$17,600.00

We verify the condition shown as follows:

BALANCE SHEET.

Cash	$18,500.00	Creditors	$1,900.00
Customers	15,000.00	Account sales	13,550.00
		Capital	17,600.00
	$33,050.00		$33,050.00

The item of $13,500.00 appearing on the credit side of the balance sheet under the heading of account sales requires a little explanation.

We have so far accounted for part of the goods sold, namely, $45,000.00 as follows:

Sales		$45,000.00
Less the following charges:		
Freight	$1,400.00	
Claims and allowances	1,500.00	
Commission	2,250.00	5,150.00
Leaving net proceeds		$39,850.00

This is the exact sum credited to the creditors' or consignors' account. Now we have to account as yet for the balance of the goods sold; the pro-forma account sales would be as follows:

| Total sales .... | | $60,000.00 | |
| Less accounted for .... | | 45,000.00 | $15,000.00 |

Charges to be deducted:			
Freight	$700.00		
Commission 5%.................	750.00		$1,450.00
Net proceeds			$13,550.00

PROBLEM V.

Show the rulings and headings which you would adopt for the cash book of a charitable institution having income from subscriptions, legacies, capital, donations and payments from inmates, and expenditures on buildings, maintenance and usual expenses. Also insert five transactions on each side.

(Solution given on pages 474 and 475.)

PROBLEM VI.

Give a short example of an account of receipts and payments, also an account on income and expenditure and explain the difference between these two accounts.

SOLUTION.

The statements are given on pages 476–477, and, as will be seen, the former deals with cash receipts and payments while the latter deals with all income and expenditure.

As has already been remarked, the account of receipts and payments is merely a record of moneys received and moneys paid during the period covered by such account. Such an account may be either in respect of capital or of revenue and the balance of the account will be the cash on hand or cash overdrawn as the case may be.

An account of income and expenditure, on the other hand, is the account—showing upon the credit side—in-

Dr.

CASH BOOK—JANUARY, 1909

Date	Particulars	Voucher No.	Ledger Folio	Subscriptions	Legacies	Donations	Total
1st	To balance......	900	1				$565.00
1st	A. B..........	5		$25.00			
1st	C. D..........	10	15	100.00			
5th	Executors of E. F.	950	110		$1,000.00	$200.00	1,325.00
8th	G. H..........						
				$125.00	$1,000.00	$200.00	$1,890.00
February 1st	To balance......						$890.00

CASH BOOK—JANUARY, 1909

Date	Particulars	Voucher Number	Ledger Folio	Buildings	Maintenance	General Expense	Total
1st	To J. F.....	90	50	$500 00			
1st	Salaries........	2	50			$150.00	
1st	Medical staff...	5	50		$100.00		
5th	Rent.........	11	50			200.00	$1,000.00
6th	Petty cash.......	12	50		50.00		890.00
	Balance........			$500.00	$150.00	$350.00	$1,890.00

ACCOUNT OF RECEIPTS AND PAYMENTS DURING THE YEAR ENDED DECEMBER 31, 1908

To balance in bank, January 1, 1908.		$3,000.00	By goods purchased...........	$50,000.00	
Proceeds from bond issue......	$25,000.00		Wages......................	60,000.00	
Cash received from customers...	125,000.00		General expenses...........	6,000.00	
Sundry small receipts..........	3,000.00	153,000.00	Land and building purchased...	15,000.00	
			Investment in stocks and bonds.	10,000.00	$141,000.00
			Balance at bank, December 31...		15,000.00
		$156,000.00			$156,000.00
To balance.....		$15,000.00			

476

Dr.   ACCOUNT OF INCOME AND EXPENDITURE FOR THE YEAR ENDING DECEMBER 31, 1908   **Cr.**

To rent...............	$2,500.00		By sundry subscriptions......	.....	$35,000.00
Salaries..............	21,000 00		Sundry small receipts.....	.....	2,500.00
General expense......	10,000 00				—————
		$33,500.00			$37,500.00
Balance being surplus for the year		4,000.00			
		$37,500.00			$37,500.00

come earned during the period referred to, regardless of whether such income was actually received in cash or not; the debit side of this account shows the expense incurred in earning such income and otherwise properly chargeable to the period under review, whether such expenditure was actually paid or not. The balance of such an account will therefore be the surplus of income over expenditures for the period, e.g., net profit.

PROBLEM VII.

A firm manufacturing but one grade of cloaks, insured against burglary, claims to have been robbed on the night of September 10.

The proof of the loss filed by the assured, contained two items for 600 cloaks, $12,000.00; silk 1,000 yards, $1,500.00.

An inventory of stock on hand consisting of cloaks, cloth and silk had been taken January 1 amounting to $118,500, the particulars of which have been lost or destroyed.

An analysis of the firm's books produced the following information:

Purchases of cloth 37,500 yards at	$1.00	
Purchases of silk 10,000 yards at	2.00	
6000 cloaks manufactured, consuming		
cloth 40,000 yards at	$1.00	
silk 10,000 yards at	2.00	
9000 cloaks sold between Jan. 1 and Sept. 10, ...		
Cost of sales, per cloak, for material		$10.00
Cost of sales, per cloak, for labor and sundries		7.00
		$17.00
Inventory Sept. 11 2,500 cloaks at	$17.00	
12,500 yards cloth at	1.00	
5,000 yards silk at	2.00	

Prepare a report proving or disproving the claim.

SOLUTION.

Sales 9,000 suits (at cost) $17.00 .... $153,000.00
Inventory 2,500 suits $17.00 .... 42,500.00

Total 11,500 suits to be accounted for $195,500.00
Manufactured 6,000 suits during the period 102,000.00

5,500 suits in inventory January 1 .... $93,500.00

Inventory January 1 .... $118,500.00
Deduct 5,500 suits at $17.00 .... 93,500.00

Cloth and silk January 1 .... $25,000.00

Cloth purchased 37,500 yards at cost $1.00 .... $37,500.00
Deduct inventory Sept. 11, 12,500 yards at cost $1.00 .... 12,500.00

Cloth consumed from purchases 25,000 yards at cost $25,000.00
Total cloth consumed 40,000 yards at cost 40,000.00
Cloth in inventory January 1 .... $15,000.00

Inventory cloth and silk, Jan. 1 .... $25,000.00
Cloth in inventory Jan. 1 .... 15,000.00

Silk in inventory Jan. 1 .... 10,000.00
Inventory Jan. 1 .... $118,500.00

Suits to be accounted for in inventory Jan. 1 .... $5,500.00
Suits manufactured during period 6,000.00 $11,500.00

Suits in inventory Sept. 11, 2,500 ....
Suits sold during period, 9,000 .... $11,500.00

479

NO LOSS.

The solution begins with the sales of 9,000 suits at cost, to which is added the inventory of September 11, also at cost, making a total of $195,500.00.

The inventory of suits on January 1 was 5,500 from which we deduct the cost of such suits at $17.00 or $93,-500.00. That leaves a balance of cloth and silk on January 1 amounting to $25,000.00.

If we add to the cost of the suits the inventory of cloth on hand on January 1—$15,000.00 and the inventory of silk on hand at that date—$10,000.00, that will account for the total inventory on January 1 of $118,500.00.

We have therefore to account for 5,500 suits as per inventory on January 1, to which we add the suits manufactured during the period—6,000, making a total of 11,500 suits.

The suits sold during the period as given were 9,000. The inventory on September 11 was 2,500 and that also equals $11,500.00. There could not therefore have been any loss at all and the claim of the assured is disproved.

PROBLEM VIII.

The following balances appearing on the books of John Smith, broker, represent the condition of the business for the six months ending June 30, 1908. Prepare from these: Trial Balance, Profit and Loss Account and Balance Sheet.

Cash in hand	$50.32 [1]
Cash in bank	2,382.57
Bills receivable	3,082.46
Furniture and fixtures	405.66
Drawings	2,000.00
Expenses: New York office	1,881.09
Expenses: Branch office	220.55
Expenses: General office	276.76
Bills payable	650.95
Discounts received	4,412.11
Discounts allowed	2,620.26

Purchases 127,821.21
Sales 133,361.70
Debtors 10,451.94
Creditors 3,131.56
Reserve for bad debts 725.98
Capital account January 1, 1902 .... 8,910.52

Our first step in solving this problem is to prepare a trial balance. As already explained where a set of facts is given and such facts are not arranged in systematic order, it is advisable that in preparing the trial balance the accounts be put in some systematic order so as to facilitate the preparation of further statements. We therefore prepare the following trial balance:

TRIAL BALANCE JUNE 30, 1908.

Cash	$2,432.89	
Bills receivable	3,082.46	
Accounts receivable	10,451.94	
Furniture and fixtures	405.66	
Bills payable		$650.95
Accounts payable		3,131.56
Purchases	127,821.21	
Discounts on purchases		4,412.11
Expenses	2,378.40	
Sales		133,361.70
Discounts on sales	2,620.26	
John Smith, capital account		8,910.52
John Smith, drawing account	2,000.00	
Reserve for bad debts		725.98
	$151,192.82	$151,192.82

Having prepared the trial balance our next step will be to prepare a profit and loss account. The profit and loss account in this case is rather simple and there is only one important principle to be noted and that is that the item of furniture and fixtures amounting to $405.66 which appears on the trial balance is not treated in this case as an asset as is the usual case in trade concerns, but is treated as an expense. This is due to the fact that the brokers, as a rule, consider the first outlay for furniture and fixtures as an expenditure and treat it as

PROFIT AND LOSS ACCOUNT OF THE FIRM JOHN SMITH FOR A PERIOD OF SIX MONTHS, ENDING JUNE 30, 1908

To purchase..................	$127,821.21			By sales...................	$133,361.70	
Less discounts received........	4,412.11	$123,409.10		Less discounts allowed..........	2,620.26	$130,741.44
Gross profit........		7,332.34				
		$130,741.44				$130,741.44
To expenses..............	$2,378.40			By gross profit.....		$7,332.34
Furniture and fixtures (charged off as an expense)........	405.66					
Reserve for bad debts (3% on accounts receivable).....	313.65					
Net profit, carried to Smith's account............	4,234.63					
	$7,332.34					$7,332.34

BALANCE SHEET OF THE FIRM OF JOHN SMITH AS ON JUNE 30, 1908

ASSETS:			
Cash............................			$2,432.89
Bills receivable...............		$3,082.46	
Accounts receivable......	$10,451.94		
Less reserve...........	313.65	10,138.29	13,220.75
			$15,653.64

LIABILITIES:			
Bills payable...............		$650.95	
Accounts payable..........		3,131.56	$3,782.51
PROPRIETORSHIP:			
John Smith original investment......		$8,910.52	
Net profit................		4,234.63	
		$13,145.15	
Less withdrawals.........		2,000 00	11,145.15
Reserve for bad debts....		...	725.98
			$15,653.64

such. While this is not absolutely in accordance with proper accounting principles, nevertheless accountants cannot overlook the fact that they do not live in a sphere of their own, but must follow business customs and practice. The profit and loss account will appear as shown on the following page:

The balance sheet verifying the condition of the profit and loss account is shown on page 483. As already mentioned, on the balance sheet, the item of furniture and fixtures is naturally omitted, and rightly so, as we have charged it off as a loss.

While the problem does not mention anything about a reserve for bad debts, however as there is a reserve for bad debts created at some former time, it is quite safe to imply that a reserve for bad debts is desirable and hence the provision for such bad debts. The reserve was provided at the rate of 3 per cent because as the sales were $133,000.00 and the present outstanding accounts are only $10,000.00, 3 per cent is quite an adequate provision.

PROBLEM IX.

The Cash Book of a firm showed at a given date a balance available by their bankers amounting to $10,-000.00. Their bank pass book, however, showed a balance of $10,010.00 at credit. The firm had deposited in checks $3,264.00 which had not been collected by the bank and for which no credit had been given. They had also issued various checks which had not been presented for payment, viz., in favor of John Smith, $200.00; Edward Roberts, $400.00; Peter Simpson, $750.00; Alfred Styles, $586.00; J. Thompson, $182.00; Thomas Stevens, $241.00; Charles Milbourne,

$346.00; Richard Higgins, $150.00; T. Phillips, $125.00; J. Edgers, $294.00. Prepare a statement reconciling the cash book and the pass book.

SOLUTION.

RECONCILIATION ACCOUNT .... 190..

Balance as per pass book		$10,010.00
Add checks not credited		3,264.00
		$13,274.00
Less checks outstanding, viz.:		
John Smith	$200.00	
Edward Roberts	400.00	
Peter Simpson	750.00	
Alfred Styles	586.00	
J. Thompson	182.00	
Thomas Stevens	241.00	
Charles Milbourne	346.00	
Richard Higgins	150.00	
T. Phillips	125.00	
J. Edgers	294.00	3,274.00
Balance as per cash book		$10,000.00

This Reconciliation Account, as will be noticed, accounts for the difference in the balance. There are $3,264.00 checks which we have deposited and for which the bankers have not given us any credit, until such checks have been collected. On the other hand there are $3,274.00 outstanding checks which we have issued but which have not been charged as yet against our account. That gives a difference of $10.00. Our cash book shows a balance of $10,000.00 while the bank pass book shows a credit balance of $10,010.00, also a difference of $10.00 and that difference is accounted for by the Reconciliation Account.

If we take for illustration a case where the cash book shows an overdraft at the bank and the pass book the reverse we would then reconcile the facts as follows:

```
Balance to Dr. of Bank, as per pass book ....................    $520.00
Add checks not collected .................................      30.00
Deduct checks not presented:
    A ...........................................   $442.00
    B ...........................................    110.00
    C ...........................................    243.00
                                                   ─────────
                                                    $775.00
    Less ......................................     550.00   to Cr. of
                                                   ─────────  Bank, as
    Balance of ..............................       $225.00   per cash
                                                   ─────────  book.
```

PROBLEM X.

"The Society for the Support and Reformation of Discharged Felons" makes up its accounts yearly to March 31st and on the 1st of April, 1894, there was invested in bonds and stocks the sum of $25,400.00 in buildings $100,000.00; and there was a balance in the hands of the First National Bank on revenue account of $450.00. All the liabilities had been discharged. There was received during the current year (1894-1895) in subscriptions and donations, $6,480.00; in legacies, $2,225.00, and in interest on bonds, $762.00. There had been paid for housekeeping, $2,182.00; clothing and general expenses, $946.00; salaries and wages, $2,-303.00; rates, taxes, and insurance, $315.00; gas lighting, and coals, $465.00; medical officer and chaplain, $513.00; and for printing, stationery, and advertising, postages, etc., $769.00; and there had been expended in the erection of a new swimming bath the sum of $2,-165.00. The balance in the hands of the First National Bank on March 31, 1895, amounted to $259.00. There were no outstanding labilities.

Prepare the necessary journal entries, and make out a Capital and Revenue Account for presentation to the subscribers at the annual meeting.

SOLUTION.

While the problem calls for journal entries there are not, properly speaking, any journal entries. The only necessary journal entries that could be made would be the closing entries which are as follows:

JOURNAL 1894.

March 31, 1895.

Subscriptions and donations	$6,480.00	
Interest on investments	762.00	
To revenue account		$7,242.00
Being income for the year ended this date.		
Revenue account	7,493.00	
To housekeeping		2,182.00
Clothing and general expenses		946.00
Salaries and wages		2,303.00
Rates, taxes and insurance		315.00
Gas, lighting and coals		465.00
Medical officer and chaplain		513.00
Printing, stationery and advertising		769.00
Being expenditure for the year ended this date.		

The next step would be to prepare the revenue and capital account as required in the problem. These are shown on the next pages.

It will be seen that the revenue account is debited for all the expenditures in connection with the maintenance, and is credited for the subscriptions and donations received through the year's sales for the interest on the investments and the balance from last year's account. The excess of the income over the expenditures up to date is $199.00. As will be noticed, if not for the balance from last year there would have been a deficit for this year, as the expenditure for the year proper amounts to $7,493.00 while the income for the year proper amounts to $7,242.00 or a deficit of $251.00. This deficit has been made good by applying against it the balance from last year's revenue amounting to

THE SOCIETY FOR THE SUPPORT AND REFORMATION OF DISCHARGED FELONS

REVENUE ACCOUNT FOR THE YEAR ENDED MARCH 31, 1894

Dr.		Cr.	
To housekeeping..............................	$2,182.00	By balance last year's account............	$450.00
Clothing and general expenses.......	946.00	Subscriptions and donations......	6,480.00
Salaries and wages expenses..........	2,303.00	Interest on investments........	762.00
Rates, taxes and insurance............	315.00		
Gas, lighting and coal..................	465.00		
Medical officer and chaplain........	513.00		
Printing, stationery and advertising	769.00		
	$7,493.00		
Balance, being excess of income over expenditure to date........	199.00		
	$7,692.00		$7,692.00

CAPITAL ACCOUNT FOR THE YEAR ENDED MARCH 31, 1894

Dr.		Cr.	
To balance carried forward to next year's account.................	$127,625.00	By balance from last year's account	$125,400.00
		Legacies.................	2,225.00
	$127,625.00		$127,625.00
		By Balance.....	$127,625.00

488

BALANCE SHEET, MARCH 31, 1894

ASSETS:

Cash at bankers:
On capital account.......... $60.00
On revenue account......... 199.00 $259.00

Investment on capital account:
Bonds................. $25,400 00
Buildings.............. 100,000.00
Swimming baths (expenditures
to date)............. 2,165 00 $127,565.00

$127,824.00

LIABILITIES:

To capital account............. $127,625.00
Revenue account............... 199.00

$127,824.00

$450.00, thus resulting finally in a balance of income amounting to $199.00.

The capital account is credited for the balance from last year's account amounting to $125,400.00, made up of the amount invested in buildings and the amount invested in bonds to which is added the amount of $2,225.00 received by us, as remittance, making a total to be carried forward to next year's account amounting to $127,625.00.

While the question does not specifically ask for a balance sheet, nevertheless, such a statement is appended on page 489, so as to verify the result of the revenue account and also to give the subscriber all the possible information.[1]

PROBLEM XI.

On January 15, 1896, A of New York sent to B of London, account sales showing net proceeds due February 15, 1896, $17,500.00, and remitted—sixty-day sight exchange—at $4.82 for balance of account.

A had, on November 15, 1895, invested $5,000.00 in a demand draft, exchange at $4.85, which he remitted to B, and on December 15, 1895, he had further remitted to B a thirty-day date draft for £1759, 16s. 8d., exchange at $4.83, drawn on C of London, who owed A $9,000.00 on open account.   Interest to be calculated at 6 per cent (360 day basis), London date twelve days subsequent to New York date.

Prepare account current as rendered by A to B; also the accounts of B and C as they appear in A's ledger.

---

[1] See " Accountants' Manual."

(A's LEDGER)

CONSIGNMENT.........EX. S/S.........FOR ACCOUNT "B," LONDON

Dr.						Cr.
1895					............By Sundry sales (gross)...........	....
Nov. 15	To sundry charges, petties and discounts				Net proceeds........	.... $17,500.00
	To cash, demand draft, £1,030 18/7 @ $4.85........	C	$5,000.00			
Dec. 15	To C, London, 30 days date draft, £1,759 16/8 @ $4.83........	J	8,500.00			
1896						
Jan. 15	To interest per account rendered	J	185.17			
	To cash 60 days' sight draft to balance, £791 9/2 @ $4.82........	C	3,814 83			
			$17,500.00			$17,500.00

(A's LEDGER)

"C" OF LONDON

Dr.				Cr.
1895				1895
	To balance, £	@........ $9,000.00		Dec. 15—By consignment account B, London. Draft 30 days date @ 4.83, £1,759 16/8........ $8,500.00

491

Dr. "B" OF LONDON IN ACCOUNT CURRENT WITH "A" OF NEW YORK Cr.

1895		Amount	Date of Value	Days	Int.
Nov. 15	To remittance demand draft, £1,030 18/7 @ $4.85....	$5,000.00	Nov. 15	61	$50.83
Dec. 15	To remittance 30 days date draft £1,759 16/8 @ $4.83..	8,500.00	Dec. 15	31	43.92
1896 Jan. 15	To interest, as per balance......	185.00	Contra		90.42
Jan. 15	To remittance 60 days sight £791 9/2 @ $4.82......	3,814.00	Jan. 15		
		$17,500.00			$185.17
£3,582 4/5					

1895		Amount	Date of Value	Days	Int.
	By net proceeds, per account sales rendered.........	$17,500.00	Feb. 15	31	$90.42
	" Balance of interest......				94.75
		$17,500.00			$185.17

SOLUTION.

In this problem we are asked for an account current. By an account current is meant an account showing the interchange between two merchants representing the outlay and receipts of moneys at various intervals on which the interest is to be adjusted.

Accounts current are usual in commission business where a consignee would render an account current in connection with his account sales to the consignor in order to account for the various charges of interest on the advances made by the former as well as for the interest on expenditures.

The account current in this case shows a final balance of $3,814.83 as the balance due. As this is remitted the account is closed, but of course, no charge of interest is made for that remittance.

A's consignment account will naturally balance as he accounts for his sales and remits proceeds to the consignor.

C's account will show a debit balance of $500.00 due to A. C originally owed $9,000.00 to A but repaid $8,500.00 by the thirty days draft drawn upon him by A, in favor of B, hence a balance of $500.00.

QUIZ QUESTIONS

(The numbers refer to the numbered sections in the text.)

CHAPTER I

1. Give a technical definition of the term "bookkeeping." What important facts must be borne in mind in recording business transactions? How may the exchanges be classified? In how many ways are exchanges recorded in the books of a firm?

2. In what respects does double entry bookkeeping differ from single entry?

3. Define the term "account." Into how many classes are assets divided? Name two items of each class. What is meant by the term "journalizing?" What is meant by the term "value," in reference to an exchange?

4. Into how many classes are accounts usually divided? Name them. Mention at least three accounts of each class.

5. Name some of the universal principles of debit or credit.

CHAPTER II

6. Into how many classes are mercantile books divided? Name them? Name some of the books belonging to each class. Wherein do books of original entry differ from books of subsequent entry? What are the requisites of books of original entry?

7. What kind of transactions are usually recorded in the journal? What are the functions of the purchase book? Is it of any advantage to columnarize this book? What is meant by the "Imprest" system?

8. What is meant by the term posting? Are there any other forms of ledger ruling in addition to the ordinary form?

9. What are memoranda books? Name some of them.

CHAPTER III

10. What is the reason for omitting from the books of account the transaction pertaining to the opening of the bank account? What is the reason for omitting the entry of the withdrawal from the bank of $100 for petty cash?

11. Why is the purchase book, cash book and petty cash book columnarized in this system? Wherein does the entry in the journal on the second of January differ from the entry in the same book on the 4th of January? Why? Of what advantage are the ledger figures given underneath each column representing the purchases in the purchase book? How is the purchase book posted? How is the sales book posted?

12. Is the posting of the cash book done in the same way as the posting of the purchase or sales book? Why are cash sales not posted individually from the sales book? Where is the corresponding debit of the cash sale transaction recorded?

13. How is the cash book usually closed? What does the summary made in the cash book show?

14. What is meant by the term trial balance? How is it usually prepared?

15. How is Foster Brothers' account closed after we compromise with them? Where do we get the interest lost under the transaction of the 13th of February?

16. How do we arrive at the summary given in the petty cash book?

CHAPTER IV

17. Wherein does a trial balance differ from a balance sheet? Should a trial balance be prepared in a systematic order or not? In grouping the accounts what order would you follow?

18. What is meant by the trial balance book? What errors will not be revealed by a trial balance? What errors will be revealed by a trial balance?

19. What is the relation of the trial balance to the business statements? Are there any adjustment entries to be made after the trial balance of the ledger accounts is taken?

20. What are the facts that should be shown in a profit and loss account? Are there items that should be taken into consideration although they do not appear on the books? What are they?

21. Is a statement of assets and liabilities the same as a balance sheet or not? Wherein do they differ?

22. Is the arrangement of the items in a balance sheet of any importance? What method of arrangement would you follow? Do English accountants arrange a balance sheet in the same form as American accountants do?

23. In arranging the profit and loss account why are

III—32

such items as exchange, interest, etc., classed separately from the other items? How is the item of office salaries accrued taken care of in the balance sheet.

24. How is the gross profit or turnover determined?

25. Is the net profit shown in the first profit and loss statement the actual net profit made or have there any items been omitted? Does the balance sheet verify any result of the profit and loss account? If so, which result does it verify? Why is the proprietorship separated from the liabilities?

26. What is meant by closing entries? What are the objects in closing a ledger? What does the process consist of? What account shows the net profit?

27. What items does the trading account contain? How is this account closed?

28. Wherein does the statement of profit and loss differ from the closing entries? What facts are brought out by this statement that are covered by the closing entries?

29. What kind of an asset is the item headed "advances."

CHAPTER V

30. What are the advantages of double entry over single entry? Can a single entry system be so arranged as to show all the facts of a business?

31. What is meant by the term "proprietorship." If the result of the year's operation is a loss how is the proprietorship affected by that?

32. How are the profits or losses of a business determined under the single entry system? Can the result shown be verified?

33. What is the procedure in connection with a change from single entry to double entry bookkeeping?

34. In making a journal entry for the purpose of converting a single entry ledger to that of double entry how are we to deal with the accounts that appear in the ledger? What additional accounts would be introduced?

CHAPTER VI

35. Why are manufacturing accounts necessary?

36. What are the manufacturers' functions? What information would a manufacturer require in order to determine the price at which he can afford to sell an article?

37. How may the goods manufactured be treated on the books of a concern? What items should a manufacturing account contain?

38. What does the balance of the manufacturing account represent?

39. Which is the first item on the trading account and what does it represent? Why is it important to take into consideration the item of depreciation? When should depreciation be charged in the manufacturing section?

40. What does the operating account represent? What relation does it bear to the other accounts? How are overhead charges usually treated? When and why are the amounts, in such accounts as Factory, General Expense and Management Expense, although expended during one period treated as assets?

CHAPTER VII

41. Should a partnership agreement provide only for the present status of a firm or should it take into consideration possible futurities?

42. Is the financial responsibility of a partner to be taken into consideration in forming a partnership. Why?

43. Must all agreements of a co-partnership be in writing? Is the intention of the parties entering into agreement to be taken into consideration when interpreting partnership clauses? What are the essential elements necessary to form a legal partnership?

44. Is a verbal agreement as binding as a written one?

45. Into how many main classes are partnerships divided? Name them. What is meant by a limited partnership?

46. How many kind of partners are there? What is meant by a dormant partner?

47. Name a few of the distinctive characteristics of partnerships.

48. What important provisions does the English Partnership Act of 1890 contain?

49. Wherein does a business man's ideas of partnership differ from the legal view?

50. Is the ownership of partnership property a joint tenancy? What are the essential elements to enable an outsider to hold a partner liable for partnership debts?

51. What are the usual clauses contained in co-partnership articles? Name some of the accounting clauses that should be embodied in partnership agreements.

52. Is goodwill an item to be considered in partnership affairs? How should it be dealt with?

53. What is meant by a partnership settlement? Is it proper accounting to consider a rise or fall in the value of fixed capital or real estate belonging to a partnership as profit or loss of the partnership?

54. What are the reasons why business men often misunderstand financial and business statements?

55. What are the advantages of a fixed rate of interest on capital? What is the effect of an omission to charge interest on capital?

56. Is the treatment of partnership accounts different from the treatment of an individual's account in a business?

57. Where the profits or losses in a partnership are to be divided in proportion to capital invested what method is to be followed? Would you apply the same method if the profits or losses were to be divided in proportion to the capital invested and also the time that such capital was employed?

58. In preparing partnership accounts at the end of a fiscal period of what advantage is the profit and loss appropriation account? Why is interest on capital charged in this latter account instead of in the ordinary profit and loss account?

59. Why is a reserve for discount provided? What would be the effect if no such provision was made?

CHAPTER VIII

60. Mention some of the causes by reason of which partnerships would be dissolved. Does the insolvency of one partner dissolve the partnership firm?

61. How should partnership assets be applied at a dissolution? In the absence of an agreement for sharing profits or losses how would they usually be divided?

62. Why is it important to show the amount due from B to A in respect of goodwill from time to time? Why can Phillips not claim a share of the profits as per clause 4?

63. Why have we to make adjustment entries in some cases?

64. Why is the trade discount shown as a deduction in the manufacturing section while the cash discount gained is shown in the last section on the credit side?

65. After making the adjustment entries what accounts are debited or credited respectively? Where do we get the item of goodwill which appears in the balance sheet?

66. Why is the special reserve for merchandise entered on the credit side of the balance sheet?

CHAPTER X

67. What is meant by the term limited partnership?

68. Into how many classes are corporations divided? What is meant by a stock corporation? Wherein are joint stock companies similar to corporations?

69. What are the books incidental to corporations? Describe the stock ledger. Show some entries in an installment ledger.

CHAPTER XI

70. Is the use of the term capital in accounting identical with its use in economics? Are increases and decreases of proprietorship shown in the same way as under partnerships.

71. How can the capital stock be increased or decreased? What are the essentials in a procedure of this kind?

72. Of what use is a surplus and deficiency account? Are there any other names used instead of surplus?

73. Wherein does a reserve fund differ from a reserve account? Define the term reserve fund.

74. What does a sinking fund denote?

75. Define redemption fund. Define contingent fund. Wherein do they differ. What is meant by the term dividend account? Define treasury stock.

CHAPTER XII

76. What is the ordinary form to show the opening entry after the organization of a corporation?

77. Is the procedure different when a partnership is converted into a corporation? If the same set of books is used what is to be done at such procedure with the old accounts?

78. How is an increase of capital stock usually recorded? How is a decrease of capital stock usually recorded? When is capital stock usually decreased?

CHAPTER XIII

79. How should stock sold at a premium be treated on the books of a corporation? Is the procedure any different when the stock is sold at a discount?

80. What is the procedure in the case of bonds being sold at a discount?

81. In purchasing bonds at a premium do we follow the same method as in purchasing them at a discount?

82. Is the procedure the same in the case of the purchase of such securities as stocks?

CHAPTER XV

83. Describe the waiver of notice. When is it used?

84. What is meant by the term Proxy? When is a Proxy generally used?

85. What is the usual form of the waiver of notice of directors' meetings?

86. What is the form of the notice of the annual meeting?

87. When is the certificate as to paid up stock prepared? What is the form in such case?

88. What is the form of the treasurer's report? Have you any criticism to suggest in connection with it?

CHAPTER XVI

89. What is meant by the term capital receipts? Wherein do they differ from revenue receipts? What is meant by the term capital expenditure?

90. Are revenue receipts the same as cash receipts or not?

91. Are there cases where capital and revenue expenditures are intentionally confused?

92. Can there be a case of showing a surplus by means of wrong classification?

93. What rule should generally be followed in determining whether an expenditure represents the acquisition of assets and hence to be classed as capital expenditure and when as revenue expenditure?

94. How should replacements be charged?

95. Are there cases when renewals can be capitalized? Wherein do acquisitions differ from mere renewals?

96. Can there be a case of capital assets decreasing in value without effecting revenue by such decrease?

CHAPTER XVII

97. What is meant by the term "depreciation?" Can the correct net profit of a business be shown without taking into consideration depreciation?

98. Is depreciation an item to be considered in determining the cost of production? Why?

99. Can depreciation of some assets be offset by appreciation of other assets?

100. Is an appreciation of assets as actually effecting as the depreciation of them?

101. Does depreciation apply to fixed assets only or also to current assets?

102. In how many ways may depreciation be provided? Describe the various methods.

103. Wherein does the second method differ from the fourth?

104. What should be the minimum rate of depreciation to be charged on engines? What on boilers?

105. How should out of date machinery be treated?

106. At what rate should boilers which are a part of the plant be depreciated?

107. Should goodwill be depreciated? If so, how?

108. Define the term reserve. How is a reserve usually provided?

109. How should a reserve which applies to special assets be shown? Does the same rule hold good when a reserve applies to general assets?

110. What is meant by the term secret reserve? Wherein does it differ from ordinary reserve?

111. Discuss the proprietory or improprietory of secret reserves?

112. Is the method of charging sinking fund provisions against revenue general or not?

113. Is the theory of charging sinking fund provisions at variance with the practice? Wherein is the difference?

114. How should the sinking fun be shown on the books of the company? Why is this method pursued?

CHAPTER XVIII

115. Wherein do consignments inward differ from outward consignments?

116. What is the usual procedure in the case of consignments received to be sold in behalf of another person?

117. Are joint transactions treated in the same way or not?

CHAPTER XIX

118. What is meant by realization and liquidation accounts? What are the usual sections contained in such account? What results do they show?

119. To what other uses is a realization and liquidation account usually adopted? Should such an account be accompanied by any other statements? What are they?

120. What is meant by insolvency accounts? Wherein does a statement of affairs differ from a

realization and liquidation account? What is the usual form adopted for such class of accounts? What information does it render? What is the chief feature of a deficiency account? What does it usually prove? Is it absolutely essential that such an account accompany a statement of affairs?

121. How should preferentials be treated? How are they shown on the liability side? What items constitute preferred claims?

INDEX

A

Account, definition of, 5.
Accounts, classification of, 7.
Accounts payable, definition of, 7.
Accounts receivable, definition of, 7.
Administrator, definition of, 446.
Appreciation, treatment of, 358.
Assets, division of, 5.
Assets and liabilities, statement of, 94.
Athenian system of accounting, xiv.
Auxiliary books, definition of, 13.

B

Balance sheet, American practice, 95.
Balance sheet, arrangement of, 94, 102.
Definition of, 94.
English practice, 95.
Preparation of, 102.
Bills payable, see "Notes Payable."
Bills receivable, see "Notes Receivable."
Bonds, bought at a discount, 302.
Bought at a premium, 302.
Sold at a discount, 299.
Sold at a premium, 301.
Bookkeeping, definition of, 1.
Leading principles of, 2.
Books of account, definition of, 13.
Books of account, illustrated, 26–31.
Books incidental to corporations, definition of, 256.
Books of original entry, 13.
Books required by New York State laws for corporations, 258.
Books of subsequent entry, definition of, 13.

C

Capital, definition of, 266.
Expenditures, definition of, 352.
Receipts, definition of, 352.
Stock, procedure in decrease of, 267.
Stock, procedure in increase of, 267.
Cash book, closing of, 40.
For February transactions, 59–60.
For January transactions, 30–31.
Uses of, 15.
Certificate upon payment of capital stock, form of, 347.
Classification of exchanges, 2.
Classification of revenue, etc., for a telephone company, 436–439.
Closing entries, definition of, 103.
Illustration of, 104–105.
Consignments, definition of, 371.
Treatment of, 371–372.
Contingent funds, definition of, 271.
Contingent liabilities, definition of, 6.
Corporation forms, 342–351.
Corporations,
Classification of, 254.
Annual meeting notice, form of, 345.
Credit, definition of, 4.
Current assets, definition of, 5.
Current liabilities, definition of, 6.

D

Debit, definition of, 4.
Deferred assets, definition of, 6.
Deferred liabilities, definition of, 6.
Deficiency account, form of, 410.
Definition of, 268.

509

Depreciation,
  And appreciation, distinction be-
    tween, 358.
  Definition of, 357.
  Of goodwill, 363.
  Methods for providing, 360.
  How to provide, 359.
  Rates, 362.
Dividend,
  Account, definition of, 272.
  Arrears, treatment of, 448.
  Book, 258.
Double entry bookkeeping, defini-
  tion of, 4.

E

Entries, at the organization of a
  corporation, 274–277.
  Special, in corporation books, 295–
    297.
Executor, definition of, 446.

F

Fixed assets, definition of, 6.
Fixed liabilities, definition of, 6.
Floating assets, see "Current."
  Liabilities, see "Current."
Fundamental methods for recording
  exchanges, 3.

G

Goodwill, definition of, 443.
  Treatment of, 435–436.
Great Britain, system of accounting,
  xiv.

H

Higher agreement, definition of, 447.
Higher and purchase agreement,
  definition of, 447.

–

Impersonal accounts, subdivision of,
  8.

Income and expenditure account,
  Definition of, 428.
  Form of, 450–451.
Insolvency accounts,
  Definition of, 405.
  Statement for, 409–410.
Installment book, definition of, 257.
Installment ledger, form of, 263.
Installment script book, definition
  of, 257.
Investment fund, definition of, 271.

J

Joint adventure, problem in, 240–
  242.
Joint stock companies, 255.
Joint transactions, treatment of,
  372–373.
Journal,
  For February transactions, 55.
  For January transactions, 26.
  Uses of, 14.
Journalizing, definition of, 7.

L

Ledger,
  Explanation of, 16.
  For February transactions, 66–76.
  For January transactions, 41–49.
Liabilities, division of, 6.
Limited partnerships, 253.
Loan capital, definition of, 272.

M

Manufacturing account, contents of,
  127–128.
Manufacturing accounts,
  Analysis of, 130.
  Definition of, 125.
  For a contractor, 136.
  Illustrated, 129–130.
  Treatment of, 127.
Manufacturing concerns, purpose of,
  126.
Memorandum books, definition of,
  13.

Mercantile books,
Classification of, 13.
Explanation of, 12.
Methods for determining profit or loss, 428.
Minute book, description of, 256.
Mixed corporations, definition of, 255.
Municipal corporations, definition of, 254.

N

Net profit, definition of, 439.
Nominal accounts, definition of, 8.
Non-stock corporations, definition of, 254.
Notes payable book, form of, 424.
Notes payable, definition of, 7.
Notes receivable book, form of, 423.
Notes receivable, definition of, 6.
Notes receivable discounted, explanation of, 36.

P

Partnership,
Accounting clauses in, 164.
Accounts adjusted, 154.
Accounts, preparation of, 176–181.
Advantages of a fixed rate of interest of capital in, 171.
Application of assets in a, after a dissolution, 186.
Business men's ideas of, 161.
Characteristics of a, 157.
Classes of, 155.
Dissolution of, 185.
Division of profits in a, 173–175.
English act of, 160.
Essential elements in connection with legality of, 154.
Goodwill in, 166–167.
Illustration of adjustments in a, 187–192, 195–214.
Illustration of dissolution, with special provisions, 214–221.
Importance of agreement, 147.
Kinds of partners in a, 156.

Legal provisions in agreement of, 150.
Legal view of, 162.
Problems in, accounts, 226–252.
Qualifications of partners entering into, 149.
Reasons for dissolution of a, 185.
Settlement of, 168.
Statutory provisions in connection with, 151.
Petty cash book,
For February transactions, 61.
Uses of, 16.
Posting, definition of, 7.
Of January transactions, 38–39.
Preferential claims, definition of, 406.
Principles of Debit and Credit, 8–11.
Problems,
In corporation accounting, 303–341.
In partnership accounts, 226–252.
Problems and solutions in practical accounting, 457–493.
Procedure,
In change from single to double entry, 120.
In conversion of a partnership to a corporation, 277–287.
Profit and Loss account,
Arrangement of, 93.
Contents of, 92–93.
Illustration of, 98–99.
Preparation of, 92.
Profit and Loss account and Balance sheet, distinction between, 95.
Profits determined under single entry, 116.
Proprietorship, definition of, 116.
Proxy for incorporators, form of, 343.
Public accountant, definition of, xvi.
Purchase book,
For February transactions, 56.
For January transactions, 27.
Uses of, 15.

Q

Questions and answers in theory of accounts, 421–456.

R

Real accounts, definition of, 8.
Realization and liquidation accounts;
Form of, 380.
Problems in, 381–404.
Purpose of, 379.
Redemption fund, definition of, 271.
Requisites of books of original entry, 13.
Replacements, how to charge, 355.
Reserve accounts, definition of, 269.
Reserve funds, definition of, 269.
Reserves, definition of, 269.
Revenue receipts, definition of, 352.
Roman system of accounting, B.

S

Sales books,
For February transactions, 57–58.
For January transactions, 28–29.
Uses of, 222.
Sale of a business, 222.
Final adjustment of a, 223.
Secret reserves, definition of, 364.
Propriety of, 365.
Shrinkage, accounting of, 356.
Single entry bookkeeping, definition of, 4.
Single entry changed to double entry, 122.
Single entry and double entry, distinction between, 114.
Sinking fund,
Definition of, 270.
Place of, in company's books, 367–368.
Sinking funds, theory of, 367.
Solutions in practical accounting, 457–493.

Statement of affairs, form of, 409.
Statement of assets and liabilities, definition of, 94.
Statement of assets and liabilities, form of, 118–119.
Stocks,
Bought at a discount, 302.
Bought at a premium, 302.
Stock,
Certificate book, definition of, 257.
Corporations, definition of, 254.
Ledger, definition of, 257.
Ledger, form of, 261.
Transfer book, definition of, 258.
Transfer book, form of, 259.
Subscriptions, definition of, 256.
Surplus account, definition of, 268.

T

Tally system of accounting, xiv.
Treasurer's report, form of, 348–351.
Treasury stock, definition of, 272.
Trial Balance book, 101.
Explanation of, 90.
Trial Balance,
Definition of, 89.
Errors not revealed by, 91.
Error revealed by, 91.
Form of, 50.
For February, 86.
Relation of, to business statements, 91.
Various methods of arrangement of, 89–90.
Trustee, definition of, 446.

U

Uses of books of account, 14.

V

Value, meaning of term, 7.
Venetian system of accounting, xv.
Ventures, definition of, 371.

W

Waiver of notice for directors, form of, 344.

Waiver of notice for incorporators, form of, 342.

Wrong classification, purpose of, 354.

Lightning Source UK Ltd.
Milton Keynes UK
UKHW02n0141110818
327082UK00003B/24/P